The Communist Party
in post-Soviet Russia

MANCHESTER
UNIVERSITY PRESS

The Communist Party in post-Soviet Russia

LUKE MARCH

MANCHESTER UNIVERSITY PRESS

Manchester and New York

distributed exclusively in the USA by Palgrave

Copyright © Luke March 2002

The right of Luke March to be identified as the author of this work has been
asserted by him in accordance with the Copyright, Designs and Patents Act 1988.

Published by Manchester University Press
Oxford Road, Manchester M13 9NR, UK

Distributed exclusively in the USA by
Palgrave, 175 Fifth Avenue, New York
NY 10010

Distributed exclusively in Canada by
UBC Press, University of British Columbia, 2029 West Mall,
Vancouver, BC, Canada V6T 1Z2

British Cataloguing-in-Publication Data
A catalogue record for this book is available from the British Library

Library of Congress Cataloging-in-Publication Data applied for

ISBN 0 7190 6043 5 *hardback*
0 7190 6044 3 *paperback*

First published 2002

10 09 08 07 06 05 04 03 02   10 9 8 7 6 5 4 3 2 1

Typeset in Palatino with Frutiger
by Servis Filmsetting Ltd, Manchester, UK
Printed in Great Britain by
Biddles Ltd, Guildford and King's Lynn

To my family, and all my close friends

Contents

Figures and tables

Figures

Tables

Preface

Studying Russian politics in the post-Soviet era has often been like chasing a moving train, such has been the rapidity of political change, the rise and fall of predicted next presidents, of prime ministers, above all of political parties. The reader needs only to look at the glossary in this volume to see the profusion of movements that have arisen to fill the vacuum created by the fall of the Soviet Union's ruling communist party, many of which have differed only by the time they have taken to dissolve.

One (relative) constant in the post-Soviet aftermath was the Communist Party of the Russian Federation (CPRF), which maintained an influential role whilst many of its challengers faded from the scene. It is this party which is the subject of this book – its successes, failures, its ideas and its overall role in Russian politics. This party has tended to polarise analysis within Russia, while even in the West (particularly in media sources) the prevailing view has tended to be profoundly negative and at times openly impatient for the party to take its due exit, stage left, without much applause.

This author takes a different view. Neither communist, nor anti-communist, I believe that the communists should be seen as an integral part of Russia's transformation and not just as 'full of obvious hatred for reform and change' as Boris Yeltsin would have it. Indeed their activity has shaped, and will likely continue to shape, the Russian polity, and not always in a profoundly negative way. I have sought to provide a comprehensive and objective account of the party's development to date. This is not to deny that many of the communists' ideas are both obscure and extremely distasteful to Western minds, particularly the neo-Stalinist tones of many members. However, there are many contradictory signals, and hence the communists' ideas are explored in depth in this work. Indeed one of my

motivations was to investigate a force which is in many ways profoundly alien to the Western liberal democratic experience, as a way
of investigating just what it is about Russia that makes it repeatedly
confound our expectations. One commonly held expectation that I
sought to analyse throughout was the possibility of a democratic left
emerging from the space still monopolised by the communists. As we
shall see, such expectations can be extremely problematic but, like the
equally problematic expectation that Russia can become a functioning
representative democracy, that is not to say that they cannot ultimately be realised.

Finally, a note on methodology and sources: the main primary
source used for this study was the Russian press. The pro-communist
and patriotic press (papers such as *Sovetskaya Rossiya*, *Pravda* and
Pravda Rossii, and various party journals and Internet publications)
provide the best sources for internal party affairs, although they are
not always comprehensive or unbiased. The non-communist press
usually provides a diametrically opposed and equally partisan
approach. Between them, some sense of balance can be found. In
addition to these, Russian and English secondary sources were used
for analyses of Russian party politics and politics in general.

Media sources were backed up by a number of long interviews
conducted by the author between 1995 and 2000 with senior figures
in the CPRF. Although this study has by no means exhausted the
scope for interviewing CPRF members, particularly at lower and
regional level, emphasis was put on conducting detailed interviews
with the most relevant political figures such as Central Committee
secretaries for ideology (Kravets and Bindyukov). Documents provided by party members supplemented written documentation more
widely available.

The transliteration scheme used throughout this work is based on
the British Standard scheme without diacritical marks. Soft sign
marks are thus ignored (for example, Lukyanov not Luk'yanov).
Moreover, some common names preserve their popular form (for
example, Yeltsin, not El'tsin).

Acknowledgements

The completion of this book would have been all but impossible without significant financial and personal support. A grant from the Economic and Social Research Council provided the original impetus, and funding for research trips in 1997 and 1998 to collect written material and conduct interviews. The British Academy (award number SG-31133), University of Edinburgh Faculty of Social Sciences Initiatives Fund and University of Edinburgh Development Trust Small Projects Grant provided the funding for return trips in 2000, for which I am most grateful.

I owe heartfelt thanks to innumerable people, among whom I can mention but a few: first to staff and students at the Centre for Russian and East European Studies (CREES), Birmingham, England, where it was a privilege to spend several years and embark upon the work which has eventually become this book. Particular thanks are due to the staff at the CREES Baykov library, for assisting in my endless search of back copies of *Sovetskaya Rossiya* and other communist gems, and to Marea and Tricia in the CREES office for fielding innumerable enquiries. Thanks to Anona Lyons for cartography, Ewan Harrison and Fiona Mackay at Edinburgh for keeping my caffeine levels high.

My warm thanks to those who have given me logistical support, research assistance or friendship on my visits to Russia, including Oksana Zdorenko, Marat Bashimov, Sasha Livshin, Sarah Davies, Anya Tarasevich, Sveta Dementeva and Valerii Solovei. Special thanks must go to Anya Latynina, to Ali Willis at BBC Bureau Moscow, and to my interlocutors, most of whom are cited in the endnotes in the text.

Several people have read earlier versions of this work, either in full or draft, and have provided constructive and penetrating analysis, so my thanks in abundance to Julian Cooper, Arfon Rees, Richard

Sakwa and Joan Barth Urban, and in particular to Edwin T. Bacon for his exhaustive and repeated reading of its various stages.

Above all, the patience and kindness of my close friends, particularly Mel and Lucy, sustained me throughout this study, while my family have been more supportive than I could ever have wished for. It is to them that I dedicate this book.

Abbreviations and key terms

ACPB	All-Union Communist Party of Bolsheviks
aktiv	Communist Party activists
apparat	Communist Party administrative apparatus
APR	Agrarian Party of Russia
CC	Central Committee
CIM	Communist Initiative Movement
CIS	Commonwealth of Independent States
CPBM	Communist Party of Bohemia and Moravia
CPRF	Communist Party of the Russian Federation
CPSU	Communist Party of the Soviet Union
CPUn	Communist Party of the Union of Belarus and Russia
CRC	Congress of Russian Communities
CREES	Centre for Russian and East European Studies
DLA	Democratic Left Alliance
FAR	Fatherland-All Russia
FITUR	Federation of Independent Trade Unions of Russia
GDR	German Democratic Republic
gorkom	city/town committee (of CPRF)
HSP	Hungarian Socialist Party
IMF	International Monetary Fund
KGB	Committee for State Security
Komsomol	Communist Youth League
krai	territory
kraikom	territory committee (of CPRF)
LDPR	Liberal Democratic Party of Russia
MIA	Ministry of Internal Affairs
MIC	Military Industrial Complex
MSA	Movement in Support of the Army, the Defence

	Industry and Military Science
narodniki	nineteenth-century peasant revolutionaries
NATO	North Atlantic Treaty Organization
NEP	New Economic Policy
nomenklatura	communist office-holding class
NPUR	National-Patriotic Union of Russia
NSF	National Salvation Front
NTV	Independent Television
obkom	regional committee (of CPRF)
oblast	region
okrug	(autonomous) region, (electoral) district
okruzhkom	autonomous region committee (of CPRF)
OHIR	Our Home Is Russia
ORT	Russian Public Television
PCB	Communist Party of Belgium
PCE	Communist Party of Spain
PCF	Communist Party of France
PCI	Communist Party of Italy
PCP	Communist Party of Portugal
PCRM	Party of Communists of the Republic of Moldova
PDS	Party of Democratic Socialism
PPO	Primary Party Organisation
raion	district, borough
raikom	district committee (of CPRF)
RAPU	Russian All-Peoples' Union
RCP	Russian Communist Party (Communist Party of the Russian Soviet Federated Socialist Republic)
RCP-CPSU	Russian Communist Party–Communist Party of the Soviet Union
RCUY	Russian Communist Union of Youth
RCUY (b)	Revolutionary Communist Union of Youth (Bolsheviks)
RCWP	Russian Communist Workers' Party
reskomy	republican committees (of CPRF)
RNC	Russian National Council
RNU	Russian National Unity
RPC	Russian Party of Communists
RSFSR	Russian Soviet Federated Socialist Republic
RSSO	Russian Scholars of Socialist Orientation
RUY	Russian Union of Youth

SDRP	Social Democracy of the Republic of Poland
SMD	single mandate district
SPU	Socialist Party of Ukraine
SPW	Socialist Party of Workers
START	Strategic Arms Reduction Treaty
UC	Union of Communists
UCP-CPSU	Union of Communist Parties–Communist Party of the Soviet Union
UCY	Union of Communist Youth
UFW	United Front of Workers
UN	United Nations
URF	Union of Right Forces
USSR	Union of Soviet Socialist Republics
VLCUY	Vladimir Lenin Communist Union of Youth
VTsIOM	Russian Center for Public Opinion and Market Research
WR	Working Russia movement

Glossary of key political organisations

Accord for Russia: National-patriotic umbrella organisation founded in March 1994 by CPRF leader Zyuganov and several nationalists. Foundered by mid-1994 over presidential ambitions of its key players.

Agrarian Party of Russia: Party of regional farm directors and former CPSU members formed in 1993 as an agricultural lobby group. A close ally of CPRF until 1999 when it split into pro- and anti-CPRF wings.

All-Union Communist Party of Bolsheviks: Extreme neo-Stalinist organisation founded in November 1991 and led by Nina Andreeva. Utterly marginal to post-Soviet development and split in 1996.

Communist Initiative Movement: Neo-Leninist movement founded in early 1990 in Leningrad and prime mover in foundation of RCP.

Communist Party of Bohemia and Moravia: Neo-communist successor to former Czech ruling party formed in March 1990. Largely marginalised in Czech politics, but popularity improved in 1999 because of unpopularity of ruling social democrats. Led by Miroslav Grebenicek.

Communist Party of the Russian Federation: Main subject of this book. Main successor to CPSU and headed since refoundation in February 1993 by Gennadii Zyuganov.

Communist Party of the Soviet Union: Former Soviet ruling party from 1917 until suspension by Boris Yeltsin in August 1991 and ban in November 1991.

Communist Party of Ukraine: Main neo-communist successor. Banned 1991–93. The Ukraine's largest political party, although excluded from government. Led by Petro Symonenko.

Communist Party of the Union of Belarus and Russia: Stillborn party formed by UCP-CPSU head Oleg Shenin in July 2000.

Congress of Russian Communities: Nationalist organisation formed March 1993, and headed in 1995 elections by Yurii Skokov and Aleksandr Lebed. Thereafter marginal.

Democratic Left Alliance: Polish social democratic party, formed as election coalition of successor party Social Democracy of the Republic of Poland (SDRP) and Confederation of Polish Trade Unions to contest elections from 1991. Formed government 1993–97, and its representative Aleksander Kwasniewski was president from 1995. Formally a party from 1999, when SdRP was disbanded. Headed by Leszek Miller.

Democratic Russia: Umbrella democratic group founded January 1990 and playing major role in Yeltsin's rise to power, but split in November 1991.

Derzhava: Nationalist movement formed to support former Russian vice-president, Aleksandr Rutskoi, in 1994. An ally of the communists in 1996–98, but thereafter insignificant.

Edinstvo: Also called 'Unity' – and often known as *Medved* (Bear). A centrist patriotic electoral coalition headed by Russian emergencies minister, Sergei Shoigu, in support of Vladimir Putin in September 1999. Held second place in parliamentary elections and parliament from 1999.

Fatherland-All Russia: A centrist patriotic coalition formed mid-1999 by Moscow mayor, Yurii Luzhkov, and ex-prime minister, Yevgenii Primakov. After poor electoral performance, it increasingly gravitated towards Edinstvo, with a formal alliance proposed in mid-2001.

For Victory!: Notional bloc formed by Communist Party of Russian Federation to contest 1999 and 2000 elections.

Hungarian Socialist Party: Hungarian democratic left successor party founded October 1989 and forming government from 1994 until 1998. Leader Laszlo Kovacs.

Liberal Democratic Party of Russia: Ultra-nationalist, later increasingly opportunistic party founded in 1989 and headed by Vladimir Zhirinovskii. An influential (and generally pro-government) parliamentary force from 1993 to 1999, thereafter more marginal.

Movement in Support of the Army, the Defence Industry and Military Science: Military lobby group created in 1997 by popular general Lev Rokhlin. Headed after Rokhlin's death (in July 1998) by Viktor Ilyukhin and Albert Makashov, under whom it marched into obscurity.

National Bolshevik Party: Neo-fascist organisation formed 1993 by writer Eduard Limonov and inspired by Mussolini. Remained on the fringes.

National-Patriotic Union of Russia: National-patriotic coalition set up by CPRF in August 1996 to contest regional elections. Headed by Gennadii Zyuganov, and a debilitated force, although a revival was undertaken from June 2000.

National Salvation Front: Radical nationalist umbrella opposition coalition founded in October 1992, but banned by Yeltsin in October 1993 and thereafter marginal.

Our Home Is Russia: Pro-government bloc set up to support prime minister, Viktor Chernomyrdin, in 1995. Disintegrated after his removal in March 1998.

Party of Communists of the Republic of Moldova: Neo-communist successor party, the victor in parliamentary elections in February 2001, and able to install its leader, Vladimir Voronin, as Moldovan president.

Party of Democratic Socialism: Eastern German left-wing successor party, founded January 1990, and achieving relative success as an Eastern German regional force. Headed by Lothar Bisky and Gregor Gysi (after October 2000 by Gabi Zimmer).

Power to the People!: Coalition of communists (led by ex-Soviet prime minister Nikolai Ryzhkov) and nationalists (led by Sergei Baburin). Participated in 1995 elections and formed parliamentary bloc 'Popular Power' allied to communists.

Revolutionary Communist Union of Youth (Bolsheviks): Militant and marginal offshoot of Russian Communist Union of Youth.

Rifondazione Comunista: Neo-communist offshoot of Italian PCI.

Rossiya: Centre-left movement 'Russia' formed May 2000 and headed by Duma chair and CPRF member, Gennadii Seleznev.

Russia's Choice: Later Russia's Democratic Choice. Neo-liberal bloc former by former Russian prime minister, Egor Gaidar, in 1993. Later became part of Union of Right Forces.

Russian All-Peoples' Union: National-patriotic group set up by parliamentarian Sergei Baburin in December 1991. Still extant, but marginal.

Russian Communist Party: Conservative communist organisation representing the Russian Republic set up as constituent part of CPSU in June 1990, and the predecessor of the CPRF.

Russian Communist Party–Communist Party of the Soviet Union:

Neo-Leninist organisation set up in early 1995 by Aleksei Prigarin to re-found the CPSU. It failed, and faded into obscurity.

Russian Communist Union of Youth: The main communist youth organisation until 1997, when it split from the CPRF.

Russian Communist Workers' Party: Militantly neo-Leninist party formed from Communist Initiative Movement and United Front of Workers by Viktor Tyulkin and Viktor Anpilov. Split in 1996, though still a force in Saint Petersburg. Formed 'Communists–Workers of Russia–For the Soviet Union' bloc with RCP-CPSU and RPC, but got 2.2 per cent of the vote in 1999.

Russian National Council: Russian nationalist organisation formed by KGB General Aleksandr Sterligov and communist Zyuganov in February 1992. Insignificant after 1993.

Russian Party of Communists: The smallest neo-Leninist successor party, headed by Anatolii Kryuchkov.

Russian Scholars of Socialist Orientation: A Marxist theoretical society founded in October 1994, which pressurises the CPRF from the left.

Socialist Party of Ukraine: Moderate Marxist offshoot of Ukrainian ruling party, formed October 1991 and headed by former parliamentary chair Oleksandr Moroz. Polled 8.5 per cent of parliamentary vote in 1998.

Socialist Party of Workers: Moderate Marxist successor party set up in October 1991 by Roy Medvedev and others, but marginalised by CPRF.

Union of Communist Parties–Communist Party of the Soviet Union: Formed February 1993 by ex-CPSU members as an umbrella communist organisation. Headed by Oleg Shenin and since 2001 by Gennadii Zyuganov.

Union of Communists: Prigarin's earlier attempt to re-found the CPSU; a traditionalist successor party founded in 1991 and superseded by the RCP-CPSU.

Union of Communist Youth: The CPRF's youth wing, formed 20 February 1999.

Union of Right Forces: Liberal bloc formed for 1999 parliamentary elections and including liberal luminaries such as Gaidar and ex-deputy prime minister, Boris Nemtsov.

United Front of Workers: Radical neo-communist mass movement formed in 1989 to mobilise anti-reform workers. Faded after 1990 but was launch pad for careers of many radical communists (including Tyulkin and Anpilov).

Vladimir Lenin Communist Union of Youth: Marginal communist youth organisation affiliated to UCP-CPSU.

Working Russia movement: Anpilov's radical successor to the United Front of Workers, formed in autumn 1991. Split from Russian Communist Workers' Party in 1996 and formed nucleus of unsuccessful Stalinist bloc at 1999 elections.

Introduction

The Communist Party of the Soviet Union (CPSU) was once one of the most powerful organisations of the entire twentieth century. According to the 1977 Soviet constitution, the CPSU was the 'leading and guiding force' of the political system, moulding Russia and its satellite states in its own image. At the apex of a so-called 'totalitarian' regime, the party long had an apparently unshakeable grip over its domain. Yet this appearance proved hard to reconcile with the events of the late 1980s, when the CPSU perished with inglorious irrelevance, its membership in precipitate fall and its press circulation in steep decline. It was widely perceived to be unreformable and powerless in the face of change. The abortive 'communist' coup of August 1991 when the Soviet leaders temporarily took power from Mikhail Gorbachev was in fact anything but – the party was largely bypassed. Worse was to follow. After the CPSU leadership had made unconvincing condemnations of the putsch many of them had earlier welcomed, the party and its republican organisations were disowned by their own General Secretary Gorbachev, suspended and later banned on Russian territory by the party's chief antagonist Boris Yeltsin. The coup thus completed the CPSU's humiliation and 'was the mechanism for the destruction of the party's remaining standing in Soviet society'.[1]

In the ensuing months it seemed credible to proclaim an end to the clash of ideologies, and the death of communism, as did, famously, Francis Fukuyama.[2] Communists themselves did not disappear in Russia, but their initiatives seemed either ineffectual or near farcical, such as the resurrection of the defunct Union of Soviet Socialist Republics (USSR) parliament (the Congress of Peoples' Deputies) in a candlelit hall in 1992.[3] Such initiatives seemed no more than the last twitches of the communist corpse, and in 1993 few would have disagreed that as a political force communism was dead, 'part of an exhausted tradition nursed only by the old generation'.[4]

Yet a communist party it was, the CPRF, which emerged to become the most disciplined, nationally organised and, after the 1995 election, the most popular political party in the Russian Federation. Although it lost the 1996 presidential elections, the CPRF actually increased its share of the vote in the Russian parliamentary elections of December 1999 and challenged again in the presidential elections of March 2000. Despite repeated predictions of its imminent demise, it would seem that the CPRF has played no small role in the 'post-communist' Russian political system.

It is the resurrection of the communists as a serious political force and the role they have played in the Russian political system that form the focus of this book. It studies the political, organisational and ideological development of the CPRF from 1990 until the aftermath of Vladimir Putin's victory in the presidential elections of March 2000. Studying the CPRF in detail is highly important as there is still no consensus as to what the party actually represents. Reflecting its prominence, there have been few Russian political forces written about more in recent years, yet although at times insightful, coverage of the CPRF is often partisan or impressionistic. A Western view of the CPRF as a 'dreary has-been' is certainly of little help in explaining its durability.[5] There is a distinct lack of consensus over the party's major features such as its ideological profile. Some see it as an 'unreconstructed' communist or 'Stalinist' organisation, others as a nationalist or even quasi-fascist party, others still as showing definite tendencies towards moderation and even Western-style social democracy.[6] Understanding how best to characterise Russia's largest party is of obvious use in understanding Russian politics as a whole.

The only book-length study of the CPRF to date, Joan Barth Urban and Valerii Solovei's excellent 1997 study, *Russia's Communists at the Crossroads*, filled the gap to a degree, focusing upon developments in the CPRF and the communist movement in Russia as a whole until 1996.[7] Yet much has happened since then, and the study's central conclusion, that the CPRF's development was motivated by the interaction between three clearly demarcated ideological tendencies, is open to qualification in the light of more recent developments. Also, that study's focus on the internecine programmatic conflicts between the communist parties tended to take priority over analysis of the CPRF's role in the Russian polity, which has become more and more problematic in recent years. When an ex-Committee for State Security (KGB) man (Putin is a former colonel in the Soviet-era security services) and a communist compete for the presidency on Russian patriotic platforms, it is clear that the common stereotypical demarcation between 'reformers' and 'anti-reformers' in the Russian transformation needs modifying.

So this book will also deal with the larger and broader issues of the party's relationship with the Russian polity and post-communist politics as a whole. The electoral success in the early and mid-1990s of several ex-communist 'successor parties' which evolved from the former ruling communist parties in East-Central Europe (such as the Polish Democratic Left Alliance, the Hungarian Socialist Party, and the Lithuanian Democratic Labour Party) has produced a burgeoning literature on the role of these successor parties in post-communist development.[8] While space precludes a full comparative analysis of these parties in addition to a detailed study of the CPRF, this literature is highly relevant: Richard Sakwa's contention that the CPRF 'for historical, geopolitical and political reasons . . . is . . . reconstituted in a quite different historical matrix and out of quite different elements to successor parties elsewhere' is overstated.[9] Although increasingly divergent in their trajectories, the successor parties share elements of the communist political and organisational history which allows meaningful insights to be gleaned both from comparison between them and from literature on Western European communist parties. Therefore, some areas of enquiry suggested by this literature which will be explored in this book are these:

- To what degree is the CPRF the 'successor' party of the CPSU; how and in what way has it changed organisationally from the former party?
- To what extent is there still a distinct 'communist' ideology in Russia today? What is the nature of such an ideology?
- What tactics and strategy has the CPRF used to adapt to post-communist conditions?
- What explains the 'success' of the CPRF in Russian politics and what is the degree of this success?
- Is the CPRF a long-term feature of the post-communist political scene?
- What role has the CPRF played in hindering or furthering democratisation in Russia?

Theoretical approach

This study draws upon 'transition' and 'democratisation' approaches towards post-communist politics, although with qualifications. The drawbacks of such approaches, which focus on the processes of a 'transition to democracy' in post-communist states and derive from work concerned with the successful transition of authoritarian countries in Southern Europe and South America to democracy in the 1970s, are now well-known. Certainly, they can be seen as *ethnocentric* – importing Western constructs wholesale into the study of completely individual societies, with distorting results.[10] In addition, they can be seen as *normative* – a liberal democratic replication of the historicist and teleological assumptions of Marxism itself.[11] According to Bill Lomax, this suggests a unilinear process moving through clearly delineated phases (such as 'transition', 'consolidation' and 'founding elections') to an expected and desired end, such as from 'socialism to capitalism', 'dictatorship to democracy', 'totalitarianism to authoritarianism'.[12]

The process of transition itself, defined by O' Donnell and Schmitter as the 'interval between one political regime and another'[13] may overstate the differences between the pre-transition and post-transition regimes, thus making the 'questionable . . . assumption that the changes involved are characterised by the abandonment of one system and its replacement by another'.[14] Clearly, countries such as Russia, Belarus and the ex-Soviet republics of Central Asia show much more structural continuity with the past than was envisaged at the collapse of the USSR. In Russia, the continuing roles for a bloated bureaucratic state, for the security services (as personified by Putin) and indeed for the communist party are a case in point. Moreover, the idea of any transition 'forwards' in Russia, where the last decade has seen socio-economic collapse on a scale unseen in twentieth-century peacetime politics has been disparaged by Stephen Cohen, who sees 'collapse', 'regression' and 'demodernisation' as more appropriate terms.[15]

Nevertheless, there are still good reasons for drawing upon the transition approach. In particular, the notion of transition is dynamic, and does seem to capture an important element of empirical reality. It is abundantly clear that the post-Soviet polities have been in 'transition', in a process of profound systemic change following the breakdown of the Soviet state.[16] In the period between the breakdown of one regime and the emergence of another, the main characteristic is that the rules of politics are ill-defined and in flux, as the institutions and norms of an old regime are broken down and remoulded and new institutions, rules and norms struggle to emerge.[17] This weak institutional framework allows political actors unprecedented freedom of action, and 'fierce battles are fought for the institution of new rules'.[18] The effect of politicians' political choices, elite agreements and institution-crafting in such fluid circumstances may affect the shape of the polity for years to come, and so transition theorists' concern with the role of political elites as vital to the eventual outcome of transition would appear to be well placed.[19]

Moreover, contrary to critics like Lomax, a democratic outcome is *not* integral to transition theory. Because the rules of the political game are contested the outcome is unpredictable, and the process may break down.[20] 'Transition' does allow for a different array of outcomes, including 'the installation of some form of democracy, the return of some form of authoritarian rule, or the emergence of a revolutionary alternative'.[21] Yet critics are surely right in their assertion that the concept of transition has a propensity to overplay the discontinuity between one regime and another. Also, as Bunce argues, preoccupation with the 'green shoots of democracy' shown by transitologists can lead to an obsessive focus on the obstacles and prospects of democracy.[22] Similarly, the focus on the influence of elites, and the balance of forces between proponents and opponents of democracy in transition may lead to underestimation of the constraints facing actors, such as entrenched institutional, social, historical and political cultural factors that may account for significant differences of outcome between countries.[23]

Notions of 'transition', 'democratisation' and 'consolidation' should thus be used with care, noting that the transition from communism is not the same as the transition to democracy – a variety of 'hybrid' post-communist outcomes are possible, and liberal democracy is by no means inevitable.[24] Supplementing transition with awareness of national specifics, cultural and institutional factors is thus vital: in this way theories and inferences derived from Western political science can be tested. After all, the aim of using such sources is not to apply generalisations mechanically to transitions in East-Central Europe and Russia, rather, they are often more useful in locating and explaining differences between countries than in searching for homogeneity.[25] However, contrary to Cohen, what is occurring in

Russia is not simply 'regression' or demodernisation' – these are concepts with a unilinear sense equal to 'transition'. Rather, as Stephen White has noted, there has hardly been a single 'transition', rather a complex series of changes, non-changes and reversals.[26] This book takes such an approach. The study of individual political parties' structural, organisational and ideological 'transition' has been so far rare in comparison with the analyses of post-communist party systems,[27] but in this author's view the study of a communist party in particular offers a perfect opportunity to study the interaction of an entrenched 'communist' ideology and organisation with the challenges of finding a 'post-communist' ideology, identity and viability.

So throughout this book the concept 'transition' is used in the sense it is used by O' Donnell and Schmitter – the interval between one regime and another, ended by the exit from abnormality and the establishment of broad ground rules for the polity. 'Consolidation' is used to refer to the stabilisation and routinisation of the post-transitional regime, whether democratic or something else. 'Democratisation' will be used only as a comparative yardstick for measuring how political events might further or hinder the establishment of democracy. It will not be assumed beforehand that the general processes occurring in Russia and most of the post-Soviet space since 1991 equate to 'democratisation', which indiscriminate use of this rather loaded word often implies. For the general changes and political processes occurring since 1991, the more open-ended word 'transformation' will be used. Thus in the ensuing chapters as we examine the CPRF's role in the Russian transformation, we will see that in important respects the political 'transition' in Russia ended with the defeat of the communist challenge to the Yeltsin regime in the 1996 elections. This, though, was hardly the establishment of democracy, and the Russian polity 'appeared to have entered a post-transition stage without having achieved the gains suggested by classic transition theory', including stable and functioning democratic institutions and party system.[28]

Plan of chapters

This book has two main foci: First, it concentrates on the CPRF's ideological and organisational development in the post-Soviet era. It does not deal in detail with the myriad other groups that comprised the communist 'movement' in Russia. Developments up to 1995 were comprehensively covered by Urban and Solovei, and since then such a 'movement' was conspicuous by its absence. The CPRF increasingly dominated the 'left-wing' opposition, and faced more formidable challenges to its authority than the increasingly marginal splinter parties. The second focus is upon the broader issues of the CPRF's significance and viability in contemporary Russian politics, and its contribution (or lack of) to democratisation and transformation in Russia.

Chapter 1 outlines the CPRF's origins in the late Gorbachev era and its early incarnation as the Communist Party of the Russian Soviet Federated Socialist Republic (CP RSFSR, usually called the Russian Communist Party or RCP), established in 1990. It looks at the reasons for the CPRF's emergence as the dominant political movement in Russia by 1993. The emergence of a communist party as the successor to the CPSU, rather than a social democratic or nationalist party as in many countries in East-Central Europe is a further subject of analysis. The chapter sees the emergence of the CPRF as a product of the strong cultural and historical legitimacy of communism in Russia, and the structural entrenchment of the Soviet system which proved problematic to overcome and left the party's competitors weak. The CPRF leadership was able to exploit its competitors' weakness to gain control of the Russian Communist Party on its refoundation in 1993. They then attempted to turn it into a more pragmatic conservative opposition party committed to adapting to the post-communist situation.

The next three chapters concentrate on the CPRF's complex ideological development since 1993. Chapter 2 introduces the major party actors and their worldview, while Chapter 3 concentrates on the major programmatic developments and issues of debate within the party. Chapter 4 looks at the implications of party ideological development outlined in the previous chapter, and looks at explanations for communist ideology, which is often extremely perplexing to the Western mind. It asks whether the CPRF was a 'nationalist' or 'fascist' party, whether it was still appropriate to describe the party as 'communist' and whether the party might develop into a social democratic party. Moreover, it looks at how successful the CPRF was in staking out a cohesive post-communist identity accepted by its supporters, and what implications this had for the development of the Russian polity. The CPRF is seen not as an 'unreconstructed' communist party, but as a 'conservative communist' party which contains a mix of revolutionary and conservative elements. It was thus increasingly difficult to speak of any comprehensive ideology which is shared by *all* party members. Consequently, the party faced a potential 'crisis of communist identity'. However this was not likely to lead to social democracy in the near future.

Chapter 5 turns to the organisational development of the party, concentrating on its membership and electorate, its internal dynamics and relationship between leaders and rank and file, financing and structural development. It also looks at the CPRF's relationship with other important social groups and organisations, such as youth, the trade unions, the army and the Church, as well as the Russian political elite and business groups. It asks to what extent the CPRF retained continuities with the CPSU and to what extent it was a genuine political party. While the CPRF adapted to post-Soviet political conditions more than generally realised, the party remained attached to constituencies and organisational forms which might have no long-term viability in post-Soviet conditions. This problem was partially offset by the willingness of the party leadership to become integrated into the Russian political system. In doing, so the party replicated many 'statist' tendencies from the former CPSU, such as clientelistic politics in the party's upper echelons.

Chapter 6 concerns itself with the CPRF's electoral performance from 1993 to 1996, asking why success for the CPRF in parliamentary elections did not translate into victory for the CPRF's candidate, Gennadii Zyuganov, in the presidential contest. The power and prerogatives of the Russian presidency, the structure of the Russian electoral system and the partial nature of the CPRF's adaptation to electoral politics will be seen as factors contributing significantly towards this outcome. Chapter 7 then analyses regional elections and the party's performance in the election round of 1999–2000 as it faced fundamentally different electoral circumstances, querying the generally held view of the CPRF's electoral decline. As in earlier contests, the party was able to translate considerable organisational strength into good performances in regional and parliamentary contests. In 1999 the party did better than expected, but largely because it was helped by media attacks on its key opponents and because it won voters from its former allies. The problems the party faced in the 1996 presidential election were largely replicated in 2000. However, although this period marked a decline in influence of the CPRF, the party preserved a stronger national and regional influence than is generally realised.

Chapter 8 further analyses the theme of the CPRF's adaptability by looking at its interaction with the post-communist regime, contribution to democratisation and performance in parliament. The CPRF is seen as becoming increasingly integrated in the Russian political system by engagement in parliamentary politics and the cautious inclinations of its leaders. In many ways the party furthered the stability and democratisation of Russia's political system. However, the extent of its adaptation to the system was limited by the CPRF's own ideological and organisational heritage.

The central arguments of this study are that the CPRF's strategy in the post-Soviet period has been largely defined by the interaction between the moderates and radicals in its ranks. The ambiguities of this process meant that the CPRF's 'conservative communist' ideology became increasingly incoherent, and it developed a number of conflicting political faces. This incoherence increasingly threatened the CPRF's identity as a communist political organisation, its capacity for ideological innovation and its strategy of political opposition. It also hampered its ability to respond electorally. These problems amounted to a crisis seriously affecting the party's long-term future.

The CPRF remained the only genuine political party in Russia, with a programmatic identity, relatively strong attachment to a clearly defined electorate and a well-developed regional and national structure. This was the main source of its continued viability. However, the party preserved strong 'statist' (quasi-authoritarian) continuities with the Communist Party of the Soviet Union, which it shared with much of the Russian political elite. These tendencies were in tension with the party's incorporation in the parliamentary process. Its internal development into a truly democratic party was prevented by its party structure, its ideological heritage and the lack of democratisation of the Russian political system as a whole.

Finally, the party's contribution to Russian transformation was far more complex than the common perception of an anti-democratic party. The CPRF actually greatly contributed towards the development of the parliamentary and electoral process and the overall stability of the political system in Russia, which it nominally opposed. In its ideology and rhetoric the party approved of such issues as pluralism, constitutionalism and the welfare state which would be conducive to further democratic development of both party and polity. Differences between the regime and communist opposition constantly narrowed. However, simultaneously, the CPRF acted to strengthen many tendencies of the Russian political system that are strong continuities from the Soviet period. This process should be seen in context: the CPRF's continuing reluctance to embrace social democracy reflected the ambivalence over liberal democracy and lack of a true democratic revolution in Russia as a whole, and its future is clearly contingent on the development of that revolution.

Notes

1 G. Gill, *The Collapse of a Single-Party System: The Disintegration of the Communist Party of the Soviet Union* (Cambridge, Cambridge University Press, 1994), pp. 174–5.
2 F. Fukuyama, *The End of History and the Last Man* (New York, Free Press, 1992).
3 O. Latsis, *Izvestiya (Iz)*, 18 March 1992.
4 R. Sakwa, *Russian Politics and Society* (London, Routledge, 1993), pp. 137, 143.
5 A typical view from *The Economist*, 26 March 1998, at www.economist.com.
6 For analysis of some of the standard views of the CPRF's ideological position, see Chapter 4 of this study.
7 J. Barth Urban and V. Solovei, *Russia's Communists at the Crossroads* (Boulder, CO, Westview, 1997).
8 These sources will be used throughout, but among the most useful are A. Mahr and J. Nagle, 'Resurrection of the successor parties and democratization in East-Central Europe', *Communist and Post-Communist Studies*, 28:4 (1995), 393–409; M. Waller, 'Adaptation of the former communist parties of East-Central Europe: a case of social-democratization?', *Party Politics*, 1:4 (1995), 473–90; J. T. Ishiyama, 'Communist parties in transition: structures, leaders, and processes of democratization in Eastern Europe', *Comparative Politics*, 27:2 (1995), 147–66; J. T. Ishiyama, 'The sickle or the rose? Previous regime types and the evolution of the ex-communist parties in post-communist politics', *Comparative Political Studies*, 30:3 (1997), 299–330.
9 R. Sakwa, *The Communist Party of the Russian Federation and the Electoral Process* (Glasgow, University of Strathclyde Centre for the Study of Public Policy, Studies in Public Policy 265, 1996), p. 27.
10 V. Bunce, 'Should transitologists be grounded?', *Slavic Review*, 54:1 (1995), 124.
11 Sakwa, *Russian Politics*, p. 408.
12 As Lomax parodies it: 'Where Latin America and Southern Europe have already set foot, there East-Central Europe will invariably follow'. See B. Lomax, 'Impediments to democratization in post-communist East-Central Europe', in G. Wightman (ed.), *Party Formation in East-Central Europe: Post-Communist Politics in Czechoslovakia, Hungary, Poland and Bulgaria* (Aldershot, Edward Elgar, 1995), p.195; Sakwa, *Russian Politics*, p. 408.
13 G. O'Donnell and P. C. Schmitter, *Transitions from Authoritarian Rule: Tentative Conclusions about Uncertain Democracies* (London, Johns Hopkins University Press, 1986), p. 6.
14 Lomax, 'Impediments to democratization in post-communist East-Central Europe', p. 189.
15 S. F. Cohen, 'Russian studies without Russia', *Post-Soviet Affairs*, 15:1 (1999), 37–55.
16 Sakwa, *Russian Politics*, p. 408.
17 O'Donnell and Schmitter *Transitions*, p. 6, and J. Löwenhardt, *The*

Reincarnation of Russia: Struggling with the Legacy of Communism, 1990–1994 (Harlow, Longman, 1995), p. 18.

18 Löwenhardt, *Reincarnation of Russia*, p. 15.

19 O'Donnell and Schmitter, *Transitions*; G. Gill, 'Democratic consolidation in Russia?, *Acta Politica*, 32:3 (1997), 282–3.

20 O'Donnell and Schmitter, *Transitions*, p. 72.

21 *Ibid.*, p. 6.

22 Bunce, 'Should transitologists be grounded?', p. 124.

23 T. F. Remington, 'Regime transition in communist systems: the Soviet case', in F. J. Fleron, Jr and E. Hoffman (eds), *Post-Communist Studies and Political Science* (Boulder, CO, Westview, 1993), p. 286.

24 B. Parrott, 'Perspectives on postcommunist democratization', in K. Dawisha and B. Parrott (eds), *Democratic Changes and Authoritarian Reactions in Russia, Ukraine, Belarus and Moldova* (Cambridge, Cambridge University Press, 1997), p. 5.

25 Löwenhardt, *Reincarnation of Russia*, p. 17, R. Bova, 'Political dynamics of the post-communist transition: a comparative perspective', in F. J. Fleron, Jr and E. Hoffman (eds), *Post-Communist Studies and Political Science* (Boulder, CO, Westview, 1993), p. 241.

26 S. White, 'Rethinking the transition: 1991 and beyond', in M. Cox (ed.), *Rethinking the Soviet Collapse* (London, Pinter, 1998), p. 136.

27 A. Ágh, 'Partial consolidation of the East-Central European Parties: the case of the Hungarian Socialist Party', *Party Politics*, 1:4 (1995), 491.

28 R. Sakwa, 'The Crisis of the Russian State', unpublished paper presented at the CREES Annual Conference, 18–20 June 1999, p. 1.

1

The CPRF's emergence as the dominant successor party

A political party's organisational origins are highly significant, often maintaining an influence on party organisation and practice long after the party founders have ceased to.[1] Whereas Richard Sakwa sees the creation of the fundamentalist anti-reform Russian Communist Party (RCP) in 1990 as the founding moment of the CPRF, the reality is somewhat more complex.[2] Consideration of the founding processes of the CPRF needs to take fuller account of the relationships between the many groups claiming the mantle of 'successor party' in the years 1991–93 and the process of refoundation of the CPRF itself in 1993. So this chapter focuses upon the process of reconstitution of the CPRF during 1991–93 and its immediate prehistory in the late Gorbachev period. It looks at why the party became so influential in Russian party politics just two years after communism's apparent demise in August 1991, and at why it was a communist party which became the dominant 'successor party' instead of a social democratic or national-ist successor party as in many countries in East-Central Europe.

The main influences on successor party adaptation

As Herbert Kitschelt notes '[b]oth historical legacies and actors' strategic choices matter in the path-dependent process of creating new polities and economies'.[3] Following Kitschelt, John Ishiyama has focused on the interaction between legacies and political actions in the evolution of post-communist 'successor parties'.[4] The interaction between *structural* factors (the communist regime's institutional and cultural legacies that structure the post-communist political environment), and *political* factors (the key actions of major political actors in the struggle for power both outside and within communist parties during transitions) are major factors in successor party development.

So Kitschelt and Ishiyama's work provides a useful framework for understanding successor parties. However, as Ziblatt notes, comparative frameworks only take us so far: these parties' evolution is complex, and they increasingly exhibit differences which outnumber the similarities of their 'ex-communist party' heritage. So in order to explain an individual party's further evolution we need a greater concentration on both the national specifics and the party's internal dynamic.[5] It is such an approach that is taken in this chapter to analyse in greater detail the interaction between institutional and cultural legacy and political agency on the origins of the CPRF in Russia.

Among the structural factors outlined above, it is previous regime type which has the most influence on transition process and post-communist outcomes.[6] This effect is indirect, but it is significant, affecting both the competitive conditions which ex-communists have had to face and the organisational ability of the ex-communists to adapt. Kitschelt has outlined a threefold typology of communist regimes, based on their historical and institutional legacy:

- *Patrimonial communism* (countries such as Serbia, Romania, Bulgaria, and much of the ex-USSR including Ukraine, Belarus and Russia). These were communist regimes built in historically underdeveloped agricultural countries, with hierarchical traditions and, with the exception of an inchoate and generally conservative peasantry, weak social classes who might oppose the communist takeover. They became repressive systems characterised by the perpetuation of pre-communist forms of governance including extensive patronage and clientelism, and hierarchical social structure (involving rule by a small clique, low levels of popular interest articulation and low levels of rational-bureaucratic institutionalisation). Such systems emphasised the hierarchical dependence of leaders and led. The extensive dominance of the party-state system in patrimonial communist regimes means that forces emerging from the party-state such as successor parties benefit from a 'lop-sided power balance'. Their opponents lack sufficient skills and organisation to compete on a level field. Moreover, the persistence of clientelist traditions and survivors from the previous regime, combined with the weakness of non-communist intellectual traditions dilutes the influence of programmatic parties and leaves all political parties (including

the successor parties) relatively disorganised and weak compared with the other models surveyed.[7]

- *Bureaucratic authoritarian communism* (for example, the German
  Democratic Republic and Czechoslovakia). These were relatively
  developed countries on the communist takeover, with experience of liberal-democratic politics, comparatively advanced
  industrialisation and class-based politics. The ruling communist
  parties, strong through a base in an organised working class and
  pre-existing professional state bureaucracy, ruled repressively
  and were able largely to resist clientelistic politics. However,
  owing to the more developed pre-communist experience, they
  always faced stronger competition from domestic social forces,
  which though muted, formed potentially more powerful opponents to the successor parties than in the patrimonial communist
  regimes, while the successor parties preserved strong hardline
  tendencies.

- *National consensus communism* (Poland, Hungary, Slovenia,
  Croatia, the Baltic states). These were countries with semi-demo-
  cratic pre-communist polities, with strong political mobilisation
  but weaker class-based politics. The communist regime had a
  weaker working-class power base than in bureaucratic authoritarian regimes, with incomplete domination of civil society. They
  therefore sought to rule by 'national consensus', with co-optation
  rather than repression, and allowed a medium level of contestation and interest articulation alongside strong professional
  bureaucratic organisations. Successor parties emerging from
  these systems tended to have strong pragmatic/reformist
  impulses owing to the lack of legitimacy of the communist regime
  and faced stronger competitors able to organise because of the
  less repressive nature of the preceding regime.

The relative *electoral* success of different successor parties is itself
dependent on a number of variables such as issue opportunities
(exploitable ethnic cleavages such as in Romania and Serbia, and the
socio-economic distress of transitions) and political space (the relative
effects of political institutions such as proportional representation
versus majoritarian systems, parliamentary systems versus presidential). The effect of such factors on the electoral behaviour of the CPRF
will be analysed in later chapters. However, whether the party is able
to exploit the issues it faces in the post-Soviet era in the first place is

heavily affected by the difference in communist regime type. Regime type affects the internal balance of forces in the party during transition. This in turn affects the party's behaviour in the post-communist era: 'the degree to which the intra-party struggle was resolved (or not resolved) in favour of the democratic reformists during the transition period, around the time of the first elections, had a major impact on the ability of the party to adapt successfully later'.[8] By way of illustration, let us look briefly at how the interaction between regime type and transition affected the political trajectory of other successor parties in East-Central Europe, before focusing in detail upon the interaction between communist regime type, historical legacy and the political matrix of transition on the CPRF.

Hungary and Poland – the reformist impulse uppermost

The successor parties in Hungary (the Hungarian Socialist Party or HSP) and Poland (the Democratic Left Alliance or DLA) were considered to have adapted the most successfully of all the ex-communist parties, and both formed national governments in the 1990s.[9] They changed their names, renounced communism and accepted the legitimacy of democratic politics, capitalism and the market economy, thus taking on a social democratic hue.[10] Much of this can be explained by historical legacy. Marxism-Leninism in these countries was an alien import imposed by Stalin after the Second World War. Communist parties therefore had to reform themselves to reflect national conditions and gain sufficient legitimacy to guarantee their own survival. The Polish and Hungarian 'national consensus' regimes were unable to penetrate society as effectively as their Soviet counterpart the CPSU and instead they allowed a degree of compromise with existing social institutions. Such compromises include Kadar's market socialist 'goulash communism' in Hungary, and Poland's tolerance of private farming and achievement of a modus vivendi with the Catholic Church. Increasing economic failure finally discredited the orthodox Marxist wings of these parties, and allowed the pragmatic reformist wing to gain a mass base and be in the ascendant during transition.[11] The dominance of pragmatic modernisers in each party endowed them with the necessary skilled personnel to manage the organisational transition of the party, modernise their ideological foundations with little internal opposition and, above all, to negotiate and compromise with political opponents over the shape of the new polity.[12]

The 'hardline' wing in the ascendant

Like the regimes in Hungary and Poland, 'bureaucratic authoritarian' regimes suffered from the lack of mass legitimacy of imposed communism. However, in contrast to the evolutionary strategies of the former countries, the political regime in countries like the German Democratic Republic (GDR) and Czechoslovakia did not liberalise or compromise, which ultimately allowed mass movements to rise up against the party and sideline it during transition. The parties remained under the control of the hardline wing during transition and into the post-communist era. This condemned these parties to a niche position in the new regime and prevented them from benefiting electorally from its problems to the same extent as the 'reformed' parties of Poland and Hungary. In both the Czech Republic and eastern Germany, the successor parties remained relatively unreconstructed and marginal. Votes for the orthodox Czech Communist Party of Bohemia and Moravia (CPBM) hovered in the 10–14 per cent mark after 1990. The more reformed but still conservative Party of Democratic Socialism (PDS) became the third-strongest political party in eastern Germany but faced little prospect of participating in national government.[13]

Structural factors in the Russian transformation

In contrast to the above examples, the Russian transformation contained a number of features creating a more amenable nursery for the emergence of a 'hardline' variant of communism and simultaneously for the weakness of democratic and social democratic alternatives. These factors helped the CPRF move from a niche position (unlike the parties evolving from 'bureaucratic authoritarian' regimes, where 'hardline' parties faced fewer exploitable issues and stronger competitors) while remaining relatively 'hardline' or 'unreformed', unlike the parties evolving from national consensus regimes.

Communism in Russia possessed a far greater residual legitimacy than elsewhere, because it was indigenous – this was where the first communist government was created in 1917. The Communist Party's long tenure of power meant that the CPSU and communism itself were identified with the state and intertwined with the concept of nation. The Soviet system elevated the Russians' status while undermining their previous traditions.[14] Indeed, it was under communism that the Russian state achieved its zenith, with the achievements of industrialisation, the victory over Nazi Germany, superpower parity with the USA and the Sputnik flight into space. Consequently, all these might be seen as achievements of the Communist Party *and* the nation *and* the state. The notions were moulded into a strong alloy in the minds of many brought up in the USSR, and it was this association that could prove a potent weapon for Russian communists to exploit.

Moreover, with the collapse of the Soviet state in 1991, Russia lost much of the territory, status and prestige it acquired from its exalted position. Although in a sense Russia lost the Cold War and an empire, its peculiar self-destruction from within meant it lacked the 'psychology of total ruin' that helped countries like Germany and Japan rebuild as nation-states after war and tame their imperialistic reflexes.[15] As Russia possessed a strong tradition of Messianic imperialism, such historical reflexes became a major barrier to the forming of a more modest identity and remained a pool of discontent for exploitation by nationalists and communists alike. This helped the emergence of a vociferous communist-nationalist so-called 'red-brown' camp in the late Soviet era, exploiting this residual statist identity.

Since the CPSU was a native creation of long duration, it managed to a large extent to engineer society in its own image. Party domination of society and the economy in Russia lasted longer and reached deeper than in East-Central Europe. As Sakwa notes, in much of East-Central Europe there was a pre-Soviet experience to appeal to in creating liberal democratic polities and thus transformation involved an element of *re*democratisation, *re*privatisation and *re*liberalisation.[16] In contrast, Russia's tradition of pluralist politics before communism was confined to partial political representation and limited capitalism under late Tsarism. So there was little 're' about the Russian transformation – the socio-economic and political infrastructure of democracy had to be constructed from scratch. The extent of the penetration of the Soviet state into every aspect of civil society in the former USSR bequeathed a baleful inheritance. Autonomous 'meso-institutions' such as trade unions, an independent middle class and a risk-taking farming sector that might act as harbingers of a pluralist, capitalist and democratic society merely atrophied.[17]

Moreover, the USSR was the patrimonial communist state par excellence – where 'reliance upon personal contacts and upon mutual obligations constituted the essential currency that made the system . . . work'.[18] This clientelistic system with the lion's share of political resources in the hands of the elite contributed to a situation where, in contrast to much of East-Central Europe, mass mobilisation and the formation of counter-elites against the communist regime were stifled.[19] Indeed, the movement for political change came from *within* the party, from above and not below. This explained the exaggerated role of the Soviet elite in the Russian transformation, whereby several high-ranking CPSU officials such as Yeltsin (ex-CPSU Politburo candidate) and Viktor Chernomyrdin (prime minister from 1992 to 1998, and an ex-member of the CPSU's Central Committee) occupied powerful posts in the new polity. Much of this elite was educated and trained in the communist milieu, and bore the imprint of communist political culture to a much greater extent than the 'counter-elites' headed by figures such as Lech Walesa and Vaclav Havel, who came from outside the ruling communist regime and could act far more as the bearers of values that were antithetical to it.

The Soviet domination of state over civil society carried over to its Russian successor. The hierarchical structure of the CPSU was reflected in 'administrative-command behaviour', evinced in elite aversion to mass initiative, the concentration of politics in the state (statism), and clientelist politics. As we shall see, this approach continued to mark not just the communists, but many nominally 'democratic' political actors, making their behavioural differences somewhat less than their ideological differences would suggest. Similarly, social norms remained marred by the 'Soviet syndrome' – the Soviet negation of politics that produced a political culture biased against parties and their divisiveness, a stress on political unity and aversion to the concept of opposition as disloyal, a lack of trust in institutions and a personalisation of politics.[20] Another problematic for a Russian transition to democracy was the seismic shift of political power involved in moving from a 'totalitarian state' with politics concentrated in the political elite, to a pluralist society with multiple centres of power. As Claus Offe notes, this would mean Russia undergoing a 'triple transition': *political*, from one party-state to party politics, and from social atomisation to civil society; *economic*, from command economy to market; and *national*, from supra-national empire to nation-state.[21]

None of this precluded eventual democratic consolidation in Russia, but it meant that the learning of new democratic political rules and values was problematic from the outset, and disadvantaged forces which sought to do so. In Russia the above factors conspired to give Soviet norms more generally and communism in particular a much stronger milieu than elsewhere where it was not associated with state and empire and the Soviet state did not penetrate society so deeply, giving much 'residual loyalty' for communists to exploit when the post-communist regime ran into difficulties in socio-economic, political and national rebuilding. If it could exploit such issues, as Jeremy Lester argues, a communist party in Russia 'was always going to be a key political player'.[22]

Political factors and the Russian transformation

While the problems outlined above provide the framework for the political processes during transition, the key actions of major political actors in the struggle for power during transition impacted on the origins of the Russian Communist Party, the forerunner of today's CPRF. Although the emergence of a 'hardline' Russian communist party was always a probability, this was much aided by the actions of Gorbachev, Yeltsin, and the process of the intra-party struggle itself.

In contrast to many other transitions to democracy, which have involved roundtables, pacts, interim agreements or negotiated settlements between *ancien régime* and new order, Russia's transition was neither negotiated not pacted.[23] Dahl argues that consensus over the 'rules of the game' is the cornerstone of democratic politics. Pacts aim to foster such consensus and to bring opposing political forces into the political process, marking the recognition of 'contingent consent' and the end to zero-sum 'winner takes all' politics.[24] In East-Central Europe consensus was stimulated by the economic and political bankruptcy of the Soviet-imposed regimes, which lost their *raison d'être* with Gorbachev's renunciation of support during 1987–88. This served both to critically weaken 'hardliners', who were forced to compromise or be marginalised, and to bolster the positions of opponents of the regime.

However, as McFaul has long argued, in the Russian transformation, in contrast to Poland and Hungary, consensus over the fundamentals such as capitalism and liberal democracy, let alone the character of the future state, has been almost entirely lacking.[25] Such political polarisation was a consequence of the process of extracting the entrenched patrimonial communist regime, which affected so many institutional and ideological interests that it imbued politics with the Manichaean qualities of an Olympian battle.[26] With economic failure and state collapse, views crystallised into two clearly defined camps, 'empire-savers' and 'nation-builders', who held antithetical conceptions of the state, polity and economy, with little room for compromise as they 'squared off in stalemate' until one side won.[27] This stalemate forced a 'split in the elite' as positions hardened. Gill argues convincingly that those who 'sought to remain broadly in step with the flow of events were driven away from the tenets of party orthodoxy, while those who opposed this trend were forced back even more heavily on to the positions of the past'.[28] Whereas in many transitional countries defeated communists either negotiated or caved in, in Russia they never consented to the parameters of the new polity and continued to argue that the collapse of the USSR was artificial and illegitimate. Their acceptance of the post-Soviet order could be gained only gradually if at all, and the gradual and grudging nature of the CPRF's acceptance will be evident throughout this book.

It is at least arguable that if Gorbachev had tried to split the CPSU at around the time of the Twenty-Eighth Party Congress in 1990, as his colleague Aleksandr Yakovlev had long argued, he could have placed himself at the head of a reformed social democratic successor party and marginalised the nationally unpopular hardliners, perhaps indefinitely.[29] But the risk of an internecine battle within the state over the CPSU's organisational resources was huge indeed and Gorbachev made only a hesitant social democrat, placing himself firmly in the 'empire-saving' camp by the end of 1990. The small window of opportunity for socialism to retain its popular legitimacy closed, and many deserted the 'unreformable' CPSU and the socialist idea itself in the following months. The party continued to hamper the emergence of multiparty politics by inertia (through such means as renouncing its constitutionally guaranteed leading role only after republican elections in March 1990 and legalising political parties only in October 1990 when it was virtually on its deathbed). But politics in its upper echelons stayed deadlocked, and the more pragmatic second echelon of the former party elite headed by Yeltsin increasingly seized the initiative from the 'hardline' wing of the CPSU. The USSR's fifteen republican governments increasingly challenged the Party's right to organise in and possess state property, culminating in Yeltsin's decree of 20 July 1991 banning the CPSU's cells (Primary Party Organisations or PPOs) from state enterprises. By the time this second echelon had come to power after the failed coup in August 1991, some of the defining parameters of Russian politics were already clear. The reform wing of the CPSU had essentially seized power by divesting itself of socialist ideology and making a commitment to 'democracy' and 'reform', at least rhetorically. But the paralysis of state institutions, the lack of elite agreement on the way forward, and the limited involvement of the general populace in fundamental state decisions were to test this commitment to the utmost.

The consequence of this for the evolution of the successor party was profound. The reformist wing privatised the property of the state after August 1991 and appropriated the majority of the CPSU's organisational resources, but did so under the banner of democracy. The socialist banner was increasingly held by a 'hardline' rump who in 1990 founded the RCP. So in contrast to Hungary and Poland, the 'hardline' wing was dominant in the early stages of the founding of the successor party and has remained dominant in the evolution of the Russian left to date.

Such 'hardliners' were actually politically diverse, as the RCP united those who were 'anti-reform' for a variety of motives, rather than those who were *for* any particular political position. Four main groupings were observable at the outset:

- an orthodox Marxist-Leninist grouping, typical members of whom were the RCP's first secretary Ivan Polozkov and RCP Central Committee members Viktor Tyulkin, Anatolii Kryuchkov and Aleksei Prigarin;
- a group inclining towards Russian nationalism, such as the RCP's ideology secretary Gennadii Zyuganov and the Afghan veteran Aleksandr Rutskoi, vice-chair of the national-socialist group *Otechestvo*, and later to be Yeltsin's vice-president;
- more moderate Marxist leftists such as Valentin Kuptsov, a member of the CPSU's Central Committee (CC) department for mass organisations and beaten by Polozkov for the party leadership in June 1990;
- those members of the CPSU's social democratic Democratic Platform such as Vasilii Lipitskii (an academic at the CPSU CC's Institute of Marxism-Leninism) who had not yet left the party and were trying to prevent it falling into the hands of the 'hardliners'.

An important incipient cleavage from the outset was between moderate communists from the risk-averse and conservative Soviet oligarchy (*nomenklatura*), best represented by Kuptsov and other functionaries 'who initially backed wide-ranging political and economic reform but who drew the line at systemic transformation', and the lower ranks, who tended to be more ideologically inflexible and radical.[30] Those like Viktor Tyulkin (secretary of a CPSU PPO in Leningrad) were incensed by Gorbachev's insistence that in order to stimulate civil initiative the party should refrain from interfering in economic and social affairs, and staunchly defended its constitutionally guaranteed 'leading and guiding' role. Such radicals were and remain deeply suspicious of the intentions of their comrades in the *nomenklatura*.[31] Gorbachev's attempt to pre-empt a hardline Russian Communist Party through a largely consultative Russian Bureau in December 1989 did not placate them. It was Tyulkin's Communist Initiative Movement (described below) with grass-roots activists and orthodox theoreticians in the Leningrad-based radical communist United Front of Workers (UFW) who dictated the timing and ideological nature of the Russian Communist Party because of the CPSU leadership's inertia. At the founding Congress of the RCP on 19–23 June 1990, Krasnodar Party leader Ivan Polozkov was elected as RCP first secretary. Notorious for his staunch opposition to the 'malignant tumour' of non-state co-operatives, Polozkov precisely expressed the militant Marxist-Leninist mood of much of the Party's lower echelons.[32]

The RCP was deeply ideologically split from the outset, paralysing its effective operation. As for the CPSU, *perestroika* and partial pluralism forced the party's direct administrative role in Soviet society, its ideology, and organisation to be publicly challenged, and the multiplicity of new demands and solutions proved too much for the bureaucratic party to cope with.[33] Even after several attempts, no RCP programme emerged, and leading positions in the party organs were only fitfully and belatedly filled.[34] The party failed to find an identity and purpose that would satisfy the majority of its rank and file right up to the August coup.[35] In the view of party ideologist Gennadii Zyuganov the RCP 'failed to cope even with its basic responsibilities'.[36] Intra-party fighting was compounded by Gorbachev's vacillation and tacking, which only temporarily placated the radicals. During Gorbachev's 'swing to the right' in the winter of 1990–91, when he increasingly took conservative positions, the party seemed to enjoy a brief Indian summer of influence and vociferousness, but when he tacked back to the democrats in April 1991, the RCP entered a period of crisis and drift. The leadership did little except bewail the CPSU's adoption of a social democratic programme draft 'Towards a

Humane Democratic Socialism' or Yeltsin's ban on PPOs in July 1991.[37]

The essential problem for both the RCP and the CPSU was that those from the *nomenklatura* continued to prefer bureaucratic to mass and electoral politics, remaining dependent on party structures and awaiting their cues from the General Secretary, which allowed the party to be outflanked by new pluralist organisations, and to completely fail to seek a popular mandate. As Gill puts it, many party leaders were in a state of 'virtual psychological shock . . . and quite unable to lose the habit of the former methods of leadership of the yea or nay kind'.[38] This problem also crippled the national-communist alliance as a whole in the Gorbachev era. Only belatedly did an incipient national-patriotic alliance emerge and go to the people in the elections of 1990, and in the process suffered a crushing defeat.[39] The RCP thus had little room for manoeuvre, lacking any popular legitimacy and relying on the CPSU which was leaking power by the day. With Gorbachev's power base increasingly in the Soviet Presidency and not the Party, the RCP became almost completely bypassed by the main decision-makers, and its ability to influence events was minimal. Simultaneously, many radicals like Tyulkin, who had adapted to pluralist politics through new left-wing mass organisations such as the UFW and the Communist Initiative Movement (CIM), grew deeply dissatisfied with Polozkov's leadership.[40]

Meanwhile, many social democrats and moderates simply left the party, the defection of the 'Communists for Democracy' faction in the Russian Supreme Soviet headed by Lipitskii and Rutskoi being most fateful for the influence of the RCP. This faction split the communist vote in the Third Russian Congress of People's Deputies in March–April 1991, and prevented them from ousting Yeltsin as chair of the Russian Supreme Soviet. At the same time, the mass exodus of more moderate members of the party concerned at its conservative leanings bled the party of manpower and money. Nearly 1.3 million of the Russian party's nine million members had left by March 1991.[41] The perceived weaknesses of the party leadership led to the replacement of Polozkov by Valentin Kuptsov with Gorbachev's approval in August 1991. The election of the more conciliatory Kuptsov marked a victory for the RCP's moderate wing over the radicals.[42] The complete ascendance of the moderates in the RCP was however forestalled by the coup on 19 August.[43] Gorbachev's failure to split the party earlier was thus a clear factor in its failure to build a clear identity before the coup, although it arguably prevented the party falling into the hands of the real hardliners.

The failure to consolidate democracy in the post-Soviet era

In the early years of post-Soviet transformation, both structural and political factors continued to grant hardliners an advantageous starting position vis-à-vis other political forces. Of the 'triple transitions' it was the national transition which proved the most problematic for Russia. In most East-Central European countries, the end of communist rule had been a process of national liberation, which united the democratic and national revolutions in the search for a new identity as democratic, capitalist and European states. In Russia, however the pluralist revolution took place before the national revolution.[44] Indeed, Russia had no history as a nation-state independent of empire. Its national consciousness was formed at the same time as Russian colonial expansion into adjacent countries and so was tangled with both imperialism and the might of the state.[45] When the very integrity of this state was threatened, the establishment of a new national self-identity was essential.

So Russian definition of the territorial, cultural and historical integrity of this nation-state really began only after the fall of the USSR in December 1991. Defining the nation at the same time as the polity proved immensely problematic. This was a major factor in undermining a nascent party system, forcing parties to find a new synthesis of the national idea and democratic principles, and challenging the fragile alliances between new social groups and parties. The regional and centrifugal tendencies of the Russian polity itself further challenged attempts to form mass national political parties, and the many social cleavages revealed in such a vast multiethnic space have proved problematic in party building.[46] The definition of a non-communist national identity, by its nature directed against a system which had 'made Russia great', proved difficult, and unsurprisingly many patriots gravitated towards the communist camp. Together, the revived 'red-browns' could trade on their 'residual identity' and exploit new causes such as the rights of compatriots in the former Soviet republics and perceived national humiliation. The economic woes of transformation proved to be another issue from which the anti-reform camp could benefit, more by exploiting the weaknesses of their opponents than by formulating their own viable alternatives.

Whereas, as we shall see further in ensuing chapters, the communists exploited their residual political capital by resurrecting a party structure modelled on the CPSU, many of their democratic and social democratic opponents rejected this legacy of patrimonial communism to such an extent that they negated strategies which could have been a basis for level competition with the CPRF.[47] Lack of organisational nous was indeed largely responsible for the liberals' poor showing at the 1995 parliamentary elections.

Most important to the eventual rise of the CPRF as the dominant left-wing force was the absence of a viable social democratic competitor. Such non-communist left alternatives were weak in the majority of East-Central European countries, the Czech Republic excepted, and this very weakness was a precondition for the revival of the ex-communist left in East-Central Europe. New social democratic parties' positions were complicated, because in effect, they arrived on the scene too early. In the first post-communist years, 'socialist' politics in general were anathema to the majority of the electorate. Moreover, social democrats struggled to define an ideological platform, having the acute problem of simultaneously defending redistributive policies and the interests of workers and supporting a capitalist revolution in the economy.[48] Thus, by the time the post-communist electorate swung back 'leftwards' after marketisation had caused unemployment, inflation and social insecurity, new social democratic parties were often marginal and far less well placed than the ex-communist successor parties to exploit this.[49] The ex-communists in countries like Hungary and Poland used their superior organisational resources to supplant potential rivals in the social democratic political niche and to steal their ideological clothes when the first shock of the transition to market relations had been felt. In Russia, the historical weakness of social democracy in an indigenous communist system has been compounded by the continuing polarisation of the electorate and economic depression. The non-communist left remains a plethora of fragmented micro-parties, in the main because social democracy is both too socialist for the democratic pro-reform camp and too democratic for the socialists in the anti-reform camp.

The cultural and organisational problems involved in completing the democratic transition in Russia were themselves compounded by a failure of political leadership by the post-Soviet era. Whereas some of the newer parties run by academics or inexperienced politicians might be forgiven a lack of organisational skill, the Yeltsin regime, headed by an ex-communist and heir to much of the property of the CPSU, dwarfed the communists in residual advantages. However, as has been well documented, the regime squandered its resources. It did not use them to build a strong reformist party in Russia during 1991–92 and instead of completing the democratic revolution, preferred to concentrate on economic revolution. It left many hardliners in place in the regions and soviets, most importantly in the Soviet-era parliament, the Congress of People's Deputies. The failure to call elections before 1993 allowed hardline interests to continue to have a disproportionate influence on politics. Thus the 'red-brown' National Salvation Front's (NSF's) zenith in late 1992 to mid-1993 derived mainly from its representation in the Congress, where its 'Russian Unity' bloc had accumulated one third of the seats by 1993. It had only weak links with extra-parliamentary support, which was deeply divided between communists and non-communist patriots, and this weakness meant that the NSF only garnered the qualified support of half of regional soviets in the crisis of October 1993. Its extremism alienated important interests like the media, armed forces and public, yet its vociferous criticism of the regime's pro-Western foreign and economic policy had a very real effect on the general political climate.[50]

All in all, the diminished pressure of circumstance in the years 1991–93 was vital to the resurrection of the opposition. These years allowed radical parties such as the NSF and the communist groups mentioned below to thrive, idealising the *status quo ante* and making vastly inflated claims of support. It was only with the eventual convocation of elections that these claims were put to the test and the anti-reform group was forced to adapt to post-Soviet politics. By the time electoral politics started in Russia in 1993, a crucial window of opportunity for new democratic forces to level the playing field with such rejectionist forces had been lost.

The intra-party struggle for unity

The coup had seemed to sound the deathknell for the CPSU. On 23 August 1991, Yeltsin suspended the RCP, and two days later nationalised its property, heralding the sealing of party buildings and dissolution of Party bodies. One day before the 7 November Revolution anniversary, he banned it completely.[51] Yet numerous communist parties quickly regained ground, and the CPRF itself was re-founded with remarkable speed after its ban was lifted in 1992. What explains the speed of the reconstitution of the communist movement, and more specifically how the CPRF came out on top?

One reason for the rapidity was that party splinter groups had been organising already. The Twenty-Eighth CPSU Congress in 1990 had shown the party to be deeply split into at least eight ideological trends from liberal and social democratic to Stalinist and nationalist, and as party unity began to disintegrate some of these began to take more defined ideological and organisational form outside party fora.[52] Once the coup came they were thus able to emerge rapidly on the basis of platforms and contacts already made. The most influential of the left-wing groups were the ultra-orthodox Communist Initiative Movement and United Front of Workers (which became the Russian Communist Workers' Party) the Stalinist Bolshevik Platform (one offshoot of which became the All-Union Communist Party of Bolsheviks) and the ideologically diverse Marxist Platform (which split to become the Russian Party of Communists and the Union of Communists).

As Urban and Solovei rightly note, Yeltsin's ban was a major impetus for the rapid realignment of the communist movement.[53] Whereas the fall of the Soviet state and Communist Party destroyed the unity of the nascent democratic movement as their chief opponents disappeared, the ban at once ended the paralysis and drift into which communists had fallen. Not only did they have the advantage over the democrats of the commitment to a cult of unity and 'communist' community (see Chapter 2), but the ban gave them a grievance, and a sense of 'hang together or hang separately' which prevented splits as catastrophic as those which befell Democratic Russia in winter 1991.[54] Although divisions over the heritage of the CPSU remained acute, the need for unity against a common enemy which was perceived to have organised an illegal putsch provided a new impetus for common efforts. The ban thinned out the ranks of communists still further, from 6.8 million in the RCP at the time of the coup to little over six hundred thousand in the communist movement two years later.[55] From the communists' point of view many of these were 'unwanted baggage', uncommitted 'careerists' whose presence had hamstrung the party during *perestroika*. This left a more streamlined and committed group of socialist 'true believers', while many of the more moderate party members (such as Gorbachev himself) left the communist movement permanently. Significant also for future development of the communist movement was an exacerbated split between mass and elite, as the party was decapitated and vertical links broken. The communist *nomenklatura* sought to maintain its activity largely through the state, in the Supreme Soviet and via the contestation of the ban in the Constitutional Court, while a number of communist successor parties operated relatively independently at street level.

Although the communists retained a common front during this period in aversion to the regime, the ideological spectrum among them broadened. Gradually the following distinct movements emerged to stake their claim to the CPSU's heritage. They are listed in order of founding:

The Socialist Party of Workers (SPW)

Significantly more moderate than any of the other splinter groups was the 'democratic socialist' SPW headed by Lyudmilla Vartazarova and founded in October 1991 by moderate leftist intellectuals such as the historian and CC CPSU member, Roi Medvedev, and CC CPSU member, Anatolii Denisov, deputies from the Russian parliamentary fraction 'Communists of Russia', a number of deputies from local soviets and many middle-level and younger-generation CPSU functionaries.[56] The high profile of its leadership, and its connections with the Russian parliament and CPSU hierarchy helped its membership to rise rapidly to some eighty to one hundred thousand by early 1993, with a widespread structure in virtually every Russian region. This group's aim was the creation of a democratic left party based upon the structures and heritage of the CPSU, but dissociating itself from the organisation's worst excesses.[57] It concentrated on parliamentary activity, critical of the government, but making moderation, constitutionalism and legality its watchwords. This moderation proved anathema to many other would-be communist leaders, prompting them to set up their own communist organisations in response.

The All-Union Communist Party of Bolsheviks (ACPB)

The remainder of the splinter groups were significantly more 'leftist' than the SPW, all supporting the speedy reconstitution of the USSR and having a vehement opposition to private property and preference for non-parliamentary methods of struggle such as political strikes. The most extreme and least influential of all tendencies was formed in November 1991 and headed by 'the iron lady of Stalinism', Nina Andreeva, famous for her anti-*perestroika* manifesto 'I cannot forego my principles' published in 1988. Unsurpassed in its sectarianism and arch-Stalinism, the ACPB was extremely critical of all other communist parties bar the RCWP (below) for their lack of principles, taking the view that 'all true Leninists are with us, and if you are not with us, then you are not a true Leninist'. This 'true Leninism' was extremely exclusive, since the group rejected all changes to communism since the death of Stalin.[58] The group played only a limited, 'hands off' role in alliances with the other radical communist parties mentioned here, usually only as an observer. Unlike them, the ACPB remained hostile towards the re-creation of the CPSU, seen as an 'appeasing' and 'opportunist' organisation under Khrushchev and Gorbachev.[59]

The Union of Communists (UC)

This group and the Russian Party of Communists mentioned below were offshoots of the umbrella Marxist Platform in the CPSU, which took a moderately orthodox communist ideological position based on a return to Leninism. Aleksei Prigarin's UC, founded in November 1991, was the more doctrinaire. Its chief distinguishing feature was its support for the immediate restoration of the USSR and CPSU as the most vital demand of the time, and consequently it was the main instigator behind efforts to re-create the CPSU during 1992–93.[60] Its political programme was motivated by the aim of maintaining continuity with the communist system of the past, on to which the UC grafted elements of trade union co-operative socialism.[61]

The Russian Party of Communists (RPC)

Anatolii Kryuchkov's Russian Party of Communists occupied its own semi-isolated niche, and was distinguished from the SPW on its 'right' and the other more radical communist parties on its 'left' by the attention it devoted to elaborating socialist theory and several unique, almost Eurocommunist ideological positions that result from this, including fierce anti-Stalinism combined with a strong anti-bourgeois stance. The party looked to the late Leninism of New Economic Policy (NEP) as its model and thus condoned private property, though only in the services, consumer sector and individual labour activity, and only in a 'transitional period' leading up to the building of socialism.[62]

The Russian Communist Workers' Party (RCWP)

This group and the Working Russia Movement below arose from the ultra-orthodox Communist Initiative Movement and its affiliate the

UFW in November 1991, under the leadership of CIM head, Viktor Tyulkin. His relations with Viktor Anpilov, the 'anarchist Stalinist'[63] secretary of the Moscow branch, remained beset by rivalry and ideological differences (Anpilov taking a more nationalist slant) until Anpilov was dismissed in 1996. Apart from its sheer size (at its peak it claimed some one hundred thousand people), the party was distinguished from the other radical groups by its militant Leninism. Less dogmatically Stalinist than the ACPB, the group was much more aggressive and declared it would incite conflict and take on the regime face to face wherever possible. The party saw itself as a classical vanguard party adhering to strict Leninist unity (democratic centralism), and actively espoused the 'dictatorship of the proletariat' and the arrival of socialism through a political strike leading to revolution. Also distinctive was its militant working class activism and explicit 'class character' imposing quotas on its membership.[64]

The Working Russia movement (WR)

The WR, headed by Anpilov, acted as a front organisation for the RCWP aiming to replace the Democratic Russia movement as a street agitator, to whip up class-consciousness among the urban population and provoke the masses into a revolutionary mass political strike. Compared with the RCWP, it placed greater emphasis on sloganeering and organisational questions than ideological aims, and sought to incorporate members from all communist parties in a loose and flexible organisation able to emerge and melt away rapidly to resist repression.[65] Having rapidly created structures in more than eighty regions during 1991–92, it became a major force in co-ordinating and heading some two dozen street demonstrations in the years 1991–93, such as celebrations of the October Revolution anniversary, and the siege of the Ostankino television centre (which it called the 'Empire of Lies') in June 1992. Some of these demonstrations, particularly the 'People's Assembly' on Moscow's Manezh square on 17 March 1993, and the Victory Day march on 9 May 1993 mustered as much as two to three hundred thousand people.

    Although these groups were the most visible evidence of communist activity during 1991–93, even at their peak their claims to hegemony over the communist movement were far weaker than they appeared. Only the SPW and RCWP/WR could claim to be anything more than the 'divan parties' common at the time – groups with small memberships created from above with no connection to a mass membership or social constituency, and based around ex-party workers or intellectuals. The RCWP had the strongest claim to a mass membership and indeed aimed for it; even in 1999 it retained regional organisations in sixty-nine regions and around fifty thousand members.[66] Yet even this party remained strongly based on pensioners, the ex-CPSU party *aktiv* and impoverished workers. The extreme radicalism of the leaders and their abstract and reactionary slogans alienated many workers and communists, and in general 'did much to discredit the idea of a serious alternative to shock therapy' (the neo-liberal economic course attempted by Yeltsin and his prime minister, Egor Gaidar, in early 1992).[67] None of the communist divan parties seriously threatened to become the basis for a reconstituted party. Personal disagreements and ideological disputes prevented any such unity being achieved among the leadership, while many communists remained wary of their sectarianism.

However, these groups did much to stimulate the re-emergence of joint communist activity on street level, which itself did much to prompt the speedy reconstitution of the CPRF once it was unbanned.[68] At the same time, despite the fact that 'the party structure in large parts of the country effectively melted away following the coup',[69] several regional and local sections of the CPSU continued their activity, most notably in Lvov (Ukraine) and Tatarstan. Such activity was often inchoate and partial, relying on grass-roots initiative in the absence of directives from the leadership, but helped to maintain morale, cohesion and contacts among communists.[70] All the while, the impulse for unity in a proper 'successor party' remained strong, with many communists maintaining an ideological commitment to a larger communist community, and knowing little of the substantive differences between these new groups. Indeed, many groups overlapped at local level, and it being common to have dual or triple membership. The renewal of communist activity and the enduring strength of the communist aspiration to unity above all else was thus the precondition for the rapid revival of a unified communist party.

How the CPRF became the main successor party

The eventual CPRF leadership were to emerge as the beneficiaries of the unification process ahead of the splinter groups as a result of the pragmatism, caution and manipulation of the party moderates which contrasted with the extreme sectarianism of some of their competitors.

The first such instance was the RCP leaders' attitude to the coup. Unlike members of the CPSU leadership like Anatolii Lukyanov, Yurii Prokofev and Oleg Shenin, who openly helped the plotters, the RCP leadership sat on the fence.[71] This caution cost the party dear in the short term, but the long-term consequences proved more positive. Yeltsin's decrees suspending and banning the party were based on highly dubious legal grounds, which might never have been publicly questioned in the fraught climate after the coup's failure had RCP leaders actually been sitting on the coup's Emergency Committee.[72]

Second, the party carried on with significant underground sub-legal work aimed at rebuilding its channels of communication. It was suggested that the communist hierarchy had long had plans to operate clandestinely in conditions of oppression, with secret meeting points, safe houses and financial reserves.[73] Plausibly it was such fore-planning which helped the RCP Politburo to work every single day after the coup (in the garden of Moscow's Hotel Rossiya and the base-ment of the Lenin Museum, among other places), preparing a legal defence for the party in the constitutional court and providing fora for meetings with all the communist groups, which immediately stimu-lated the growth of regional organisations calling on the reactivating of the party from below. Meanwhile on 25 October 1991, RCP leader Kuptsov met Yeltsin to repeal the suspension of the party, but the hos-tility of the encounter only made the ban more likely.[74]

The decision to contest the ban in the courts was also a pragmatic concession to reality which proved beneficial. It consolidated the leadership group which was later to play a leading role in the CPRF. Those such as Kuptsov and Zyuganov restored their prestige in the communist movement which they might have lost with the debacle of the RCP.[75] Given the highly charged atmosphere in the country at the time, widespread public belief that the Communist Party should be put on trial and the threat that such a trial would turn into a new Nuremberg, as well as the inexperience of the new Constitutional Court itself, success for the communists was against the odds to say the least.[76] Their eventual success was helped by the determination of the Constitutional Court chair, Valerii Zorkin, to concentrate on legal issues and avoid turning the hearings into a 'political tribunal', thereby limiting the potential for a 'trial of communism' itself. He limited the purview of the case to the party's activity since March 1990, and so prevented the presidential side from focusing on the CPSU's 'reign of terror' since 1917. The communists were then able to focus directly on the president's legal arguments, which were 'tenuous at best and did more to damage Yeltsin's credibility than to provide legal grounds for his actions'.[77] Cleverly, and not for the last time, the communists used the arguments of democracy and consti-tutionality against Yeltsin. Was it not grossly undemocratic to ban a whole political party for the alleged actions of a few of its leaders? And how could the party be deemed unconstitutional in trying to pre-serve its constitutionally guaranteed leading and guiding role?

The court's final decision of 30 November 1992 attempted a deli-cate compromise, yet nevertheless marked a clear moral victory for the communists against what the presidential side had regarded as a fait accompli. Although the communists did not win back the CPSU's former property, the ban on the local structures of the party was declared unconstitutional, in effect re-legalising the Russian party. The question of lustration, implemented in Czechoslovakia and raised repeatedly in Poland, could not now be raised and, so, commu-nist sympathisers remained in the state apparatus at all levels.

Although the court case was the main activity of the former RCP leadership during 1991–92, the leadership did not neglect contact with the rank and file. Indeed, they helped create the communist splinter parties and delegated a significant number of their own acti-vists to them, allowing them both to continue legitimate political functioning and also a measure of control over these groups' activity. The RCP insisted from the outset that should a united party be created, these parties should return to it.[78] The Socialist Party of Workers was used by the RCP leadership as a structure in which to preserve their continued political activity if the Communist Party remained banned.[79] Moreover, the communists used the Communists of Russia fraction in the Russian Supreme Soviet to rebuild their links with their own members and allies.[80]

Similarly, ideology secretary Gennadii Zyuganov was delegated to work in the national-patriotic movement, building up contacts he had initiated before the coup, helping to set up a number of 'red-brown' groups such as the Russian National Council and the National Salvation Front, which became a haven for grassroots communist activity. Such organisations differed in details but their aims were the same – to provide some organisational and ideological platform upon which the communists and national-patriots might unite and rehabil-itate themselves in the public eye.[81] An astute organiser and propa-gandist with a long background in the CPSU's ideology department,

Zyuganov served in the leadership of the majority of these groups and as a consultant to the Russian Unity Fraction in the Supreme Soviet, thereby maintaining a political role while he had no deputy's seat.[82] At this time he emerged as the foremost proponent of the ideological unity of nationalists and communists, and managed to appear as a vehement combatant of the regime through his coverage in the opposition press and presence at mass demonstrations. All of this stood him in good stead in terms of the leadership of the CPRF when it was re-founded.

The vitriolic process of communist reunification after the repeal of the ban from November 1992 until the revival Congress of the CPRF in February 1993 showed a similar pragmatism on behalf of the leaders of the RCP. Although the arguments were complex, most positions crystallised around whether to restore the Russian Party independent of the CPSU (the position of the RCP leadership) or as a constituent part of it as before the coup (the position of most remaining radical groups).[83] The RCWP and ACPB for their part insisted that the CPSU should not be reformed, but a new party be founded on the basis of their own organisations and programmatic positions. The position of the RCP leadership was self-serving, but at least motivated by recognition of the reality that the USSR and CPSU no longer existed. The positions of their opponents were more doctrinaire, motivated both by ideological considerations and leadership ambitions.

This relative pragmatism enabled the RCP leadership to outflank their opponents in the revival process. Although Kuptsov's position as first secretary was barely established before the coup, the very tenure of the leading position in a traditionally hierarchical organisation gave him significantly greater moral authority than radical competitors such as Tyulkin, Kryuchkov and Prigarin, who had only been RCP Central Committee members. The RCP leaders played on this in the revival process by stressing unity above ideological purity. They staked out a moderate political position leaving the final ideological and organisational profile of the party open and to be decided at the Congress itself. It stressed the need for unity of all wings of the communist movement above all else.[84] At the same time the RCP hierarchy blocked or interfered with all competing initiatives to re-found the Communist Party.[85]

A similar mixture of pragmatism, inclusivity and manipulation marked the Second 'Revival-Unification' Congress of the CPRF, as the RCP was now called, in February 1993. At the Congress, Kuptsov outlined a rather vague moderate leftist platform and also spoke of the need to allow platforms within the CPRF. Places in the new party's leadership were to be reserved for the other communist parties.[86] In the event, Congress delegates forced a more hardline programmatic statement to be adopted by the Congress, caused the party leadership to water down its tolerance of fractions and forced many of the more moderate members of the SPW out of the leadership.[87] However, it was alleged that the published programmatic statement was 'doctored' and amended to re-emphasise its more moderate and inclusive credentials in the search for allies, specifically among the 'national bourgeoisie'.[88]

The most significant compromise at the Congress was the election of former RCP ideology secretary Zyuganov as the new party leader (now 'chair') instead of the incumbent Valentin Kuptsov. This appeared to be a deal designed to prevent splits and promote inclusivity. Kuptsov's moderate position and past association with Gorbachev was unpopular in the party and had come under increasing criticism.[89] Zyuganov's image as a strong statist patriot, good alliance builder and fighter against the regime appealed to the more orthodox members of the party, while simultaneously, as time was to show, he was far more moderate than his rhetoric suggested. He was thus able to bridge most ideological and attitudinal tendencies within the party. Despite rumours of rivalry, Kuptsov and Zyuganov thereafter worked in relative harmony. Kuptsov, the unambitious but skilled organiser, concentrated on internal party affairs and explained Zyuganov's public position to the party ranks. Zyuganov became the public face of the party, developing its image and seeking allies, confident that through Kuptsov his hold on the party was still secure.[90]

The RCP leadership's stake on unity above all else was successful. The CPRF Congress achieved the de facto unity of the majority of active communists in Russia (some four hundred and fifty thousand) and immediately made it the biggest political force in Russia, dwarfing its other communist rivals. The radical groups' sectarianism had pushed them into self-isolation. While they attacked the CPRF for ideological heresies, they proved unable to unite with each other or induce the rank and file to join their parties. Many such communists defied the wishes of their leaders and migrated to the CPRF en masse during and after the Second Congress, a blow from which none recovered. This most affected the SPW, which lost 90 per cent of its membership after the Congress, and its prominent leaders Mikhail Lapshin (future leader of Russia's Agrarian Party) and Ivan Rybkin (the future chair of Russia's Duma from 1993 to 1995). Refusing to approve of the election of Zyuganov, it soon split off from the communist movement as a whole, thereby ending the immediate prospects for a genuine democratic left party in Russia. In the final analysis, many members of these groups proved to be 'free-riders', who were simply waiting on the Constitutional Court's decisions, and did not necessarily share their leadership's opinions.[91]

The CPRF also faced down the challenge from the RCWP, which tried to form its own Russian Communist Party on the same day. It also managed to pre-empt the formation of yet another successor to the CPSU, the Union of Communist Parties–Communist Party of the Soviet Union (UCP-CPSU) which was eventually founded in March 1993 by elements of the old CPSU Central Committee and Prigarin's Union of Communists and headed by former CPSU CC secretary Oleg Shenin.[92] This organisation took a markedly more orthodox Marxist-Leninist stance than the CPRF in its attitude to private ownership and parliamentary politics, and indeed one of its leaders summed up the majority view when he suggested that there were 'more enemies within the party than without', the main being 'social democrats and nationalists' within the CPRF. The UCP-CPSU's main distinguishing point was its claim to be a temporary stage towards the full re-creation of the CPSU and USSR, envisaged within fifteen years at the latest.[93]

The Second Congress of the CPRF saw the further consolidation of the moderate group in the leadership over radical challengers. Indeed, none of the radical splinter parties' leaders chose to take up their positions within the CPRF, an event aided by the party leadership's canny use of quotas.[94] Had they done so, they could have crucially weakened the CPRF's ability to adapt to its new circumstances and plagued it with disputes. With many of the overtly social democratic SPW leaders not making it into the leadership either, the leadership emerged more united and less ideologically diverse. This was to prove highly significant, as such moderates as Zyuganov and Kuptsov were to prove committed to forcing the party to adapt to the new rules of the game, while not abandoning altogether its communist heritage. Despite an evident softening of position towards the mixed economy and political pluralism, there was no suggestion of renaming the party, of a complete renunciation of Marxist socialism or of a move towards social democracy even among the moderates.

At the same time the Congress revealed that the CPRF was still very divided. There was a clear division between more radical members from the rank and file and the moderates in the leadership, and the pressure of radicals could be significant (such as in the election of Zyuganov). Members of the radical influx such as Richard Kosolapov and Albert Makashov were to be a thorn in the leaders' sides in ensuing years.[95] Above all, the CPRF had achieved the physical unity of the majority of communist movement but had not at all defined its ideology and strategy – as one delegate said, 'working out a new model of socialism still awaits the party'.[96] The ideological spectrum within the CPRF was still broad, as shall be explored in the next chapter.

The CPRF was now dealing with its radical communist competitors from a position of strength. Most notably, after Yeltsin's April 1993 referendum had shown majority support for his political and socio-economic policies, the CPRF appeared to decide that the Yeltsin regime was too strong to bring down through a spontaneous insurrection, which could provoke a crackdown, and made a definite shift towards preparing for eventual elections and more peaceful methods of seeking power. This tactical shift only increased the incipient rift with the radicals in the communist movement and the NSF.[97] Whereas most radical groups were on the barricades at the Russian parliament after Yeltsin forcibly dissolved it in September 1993 and during the bloody climax of the resulting stand-off on 3–4 October 1993, the CPRF was highly ambivalent. Zyuganov himself apparently left the parliament every evening and publicly appealed for compromise at the eleventh hour.[98] The lack of co-ordination and spontaneous radicalism of leaders like Anpilov and Makashov, who led the crowds in a doomed attempt to storm Moscow's Ostankino television centre, contrasted with the extreme caution of the CPRF, which was able to re-emerge from the October debacle after a brief period of suspension and contest the December 1993 elections.

Those radical parties which participated directly in the October 1993 events were either banned during the 1993 elections or boycotted them. This deprived them of much of their remaining influence. In contrast, participation in Russia's political processes strengthened the position of the CPRF still further, as will be described in later chapters. Despite initial membership fluidity, the CPRF's successes created a bandwagon effect as more members left the radical parties to join it. An attempt by Aleksei Prigarin to split the CPRF in 1994 accompanied

by a concerted campaign against the party's ideological position did
not succeed. His new 'united' communist party, the Russian
Communist Party–Communist Party of the Soviet Union' (RCP-
CPSU) created in 1995 had only some five thousand members at most,
and the membership of all the other radical parties also declined pre-
cipitately.

The CPRF was able to deal with its main rival for hegemony in
the communist camp, the UCP-CPSU from a position of similar
strength. The UCP-CPSU found itself in the position of being a 'party
without a country',[99] and much as the Union state had found earlier,
could not dictate to a resurgent Russian party. So the CPRF, which
only joined the UCP-CPSU as a full member in July 1994, was increasingly able to force it to adopt a more compliant stance.[100] The organisation continued to exist as an umbrella forum for consultation and
co-ordination between twenty-two communist parties from fourteen
former union republics including most of the Russian groups, but its
increasingly strident calls for a unified CPSU were entirely unsuccessful. In the view of the CPRF leadership this was putting the 'cart
before the horse' and would not be achieved before a union state itself
was reconstituted, and most communists in the post-Soviet republics
agreed that any premature attempts at cross-border unity only
brought the risk of a further ban from the republican authorities.[101]
The UCP-CPSU's attempts to slip the CPRF's leash and declare a
united Communist Party of the Union of Belarus and Russia (CPUn)
in July 2000 led to an apparently fatal split in an already ephemeral
organisation, and the replacement of Shenin by Zyuganov.[102]

The CPRF increasingly took the attitude that it did not need to
deal with such groups as equals, having absorbed all of the more
useful members, and seeing their influence as destructive.[103]
However, the party still occasionally reckoned with them publicly.
The increasing moderation of the leadership's position left open a
political space for the hard left. The appeal to communist unity still
held a strong symbolic resonance for the CPRF's more radical
members and the fear of being outflanked meant that the party continued to pay lip-service to such symbols and to co-operate with the
radical groups when necessary. To date, a strong hardline successor
party has not emerged, as the radical groups' splits brought ever-
diminishing returns. Most notably, the RCWP and WR split after the
1996 election between pro-Tyulkin and pro-Anpilov wings.[104]
Numerous attempts to unite the radical parties into one united

organisation came to little, with the radical left split into fragments
by the December 1999 elections.[105]

Conclusion

This chapter has seen the re-emergence of the CPRF in 1993 as the
interaction of historical legacy and the political processes both of
transformation in general and of the ongoing intra-party struggle.
Certain structural factors always made it likely that there would be a
role for a communist successor party in Russia – the legacy of statism
and nationalism, the relative legitimacy of communism and the sheer
number of obstacles required in building a democratic order from
scratch from a patrimonial communist system where many of the key
resources were in the hands of the elite and there were few chances
offered to new forces. However, political decisions, although themselves affected by structural constraints, also impacted on the development of the CPRF. Had Gorbachev split the party in 1990, the
conservative wing of the party might have been marginalised. Had
Yeltsin not banned the party or not banned it for so long, it might have
stayed paralysed by internal division and not been able to adapt to the
changes of circumstances which confronted it in the post-Soviet era.
Had the first post-Soviet elections been held sooner, the Communists
might have faced an immediate choice of adapting quickly or remaining marginalised, and may well have faced stronger democratic competitors in the short and longer term.

   As it was, Yeltsin's ban allowed the communists' paralysis to end
and the factions to bring their struggle into the open. The moderates'
eventual victory in the intra-party struggles of 1991–93 was itself partially a product of the patrimonial communist legacy, whereby the
elite groups possessed the lion's share of organisational and ideological resources and could rely on hierarchical dependence between
leaders and led. Thus the RCP leadership managed to control the
revival process through a combination of greater political acumen,
tactical awareness, manipulation and above all greater loyalty than
their ideologically more doctrinaire competitors, whose political
naïveté and inexperience the CPRF leadership exploited well.

   So what of the long-term implications of the founding process
for the CPRF? By 1993 the leadership of the main successor party was
in the hands of pragmatic moderates who did not want to divorce
the party from its past, but were sufficiently adaptable to attempt to

reorientate the CPRF towards its new political circumstances. This period also showed a decisive split between the CPRF and the radical groups outside it: the party increasingly sought to demarcate itself from 'radical' nationalist and communist groups and move towards a more moderate strategy, while being very concerned to defend its opposition credentials from the radicals. However, the emergence of the CPRF during 1991–93 clearly demonstrated its 'residual' nature. It was reconstituted out of the commitment to a community, organisation and ideology derived from Soviet times. Above all, the commitment to party unity helped the party reunite in a way that democratic competitors did not. Yet from the outset its organisational coherence was greater than its ideological coherence and the party had not resolved its ideological profile, so remaining potentially highly divided and united mainly by its aversion to its opponents. Yet while the moderate elite dominated the party's organisational resources they remained in uneasy symbiosis with the radical rank and file. So the extent of CPRF's true adaptation to post-communist conditions remained problematic. Whereas the successor parties in countries like Poland and Hungary faced more organised competitors and less domestic residual legitimacy from the outset, and so had much further to travel in order to adapt successfully to post-communist conditions, the CPRF, as will be seen, managed to achieve much by exploiting the mistakes and weaknesses of its competitors. Once the party became incorporated in the post-Soviet regime, and its aversion to it began to break down, the CPRF's ideological coherence and unity came into serious question.

Notes

1 A. Panebianco, *Political Parties: Organization and Power* (Cambridge: Cambridge University Press, 1988), p. 50.
2 R. Sakwa, 'Left or right? The CPRF and the problem of democratic consolidation in Russia', *The Journal of Communist Studies and Transition Politics*, 14:1&2 (1998), 129.
3 H. Kitschelt, Z. Mansfeldova, R. Markowski and G. Tóka, *Postcommunist Party-Systems: Competition, Representation and Inter-Party Co-operation* (Cambridge: Cambridge University Press, 1999, p. 19.
4 J. T. Ishiyama, 'Communist parties in transition: structures, leaders, and processes of democratization in Eastern Europe', *Comparative Politics*, 27:2 (1995), 147–66, and J. T. Ishiyama, 'The sickle or the rose? Previous regime types and the evolution of the ex-communist parties in post-communist politics', *Comparative Political Studies*, 30:3 (1997), 299–330.
5 D. F. Ziblatt, 'The adaptation of ex-communist parties to post-communist East

   Central Europe: a comparative study of the East German and Hungarian ex-communist parties', *Communist and Post-Communist Studies*, 31:2 (1998), 122.

6 Ishiyama, 'The sickle or the rose?', 301–3.

7 This model and the others described are taken from Kitschelt *et al.*, *Postcommunist Party-Systems*, pp. 19–76.

8 Ishiyama, 'Communist parties in transition', 159.

9 The Polish successor party, the Social Democracy of the Republic of Poland (SDRP), dissolved itself into its umbrella organisation the DLA in 1999.

10 See A. Mahr and J. Nagle, 'Resurrection of the successor parties and democratization in East-Central Europe', *Communist and Post-Communist Studies*, 28:4 (1995), 405–7.

11 V. Zubek, 'The Reassertion of the Left in Post-Communist Poland', *Europe-Asia Studies*, 46:5 (1994), 805, 814; A. Ágh, 'Partial consolidation of the East-Central European Parties: the case of the Hungarian Socialist Party', *Party Politics*, 1:4 (1995), 493.

12 Zubek, 'Reassertion'.

13 For the CPBM, see S. Hanley, 'From "subcultural party" to neo-communist force? The Communist Party of Bohemia and Moravia 1990–2000', *Journal of Communist Studies and Transition Politics* (forthcoming). For the PDS see J. Olsen, 'Germany's PDS and varieties of "Post-Communist" socialism', *Problems of Post-Communism*, 45:6 (1998), 42–52.

14 R. Sakwa, *The Communist Party of the Russian Federation and the Electoral Process* (Glasgow, University of Strathclyde centre for the Study of Public Policy, Studies in Public Policy 265, 1996), p. 27.

15 J. Löwenhardt, *The Reincarnation of Russia: Struggling with the Legacy of Communism, 1990–1994* (Harlow, Longman, 1995), p. 6.

16 R. Sakwa, *Russian Politics and Society* (London, Routledge, 1993), pp. 407–8.

17 G. Evans and S. Whitefield, 'Identifying the bases of party competition in Eastern Europe', *British Journal of Political Science*, 23:4 (1993), 528, 544.

18 G. Gill and R. Markwick, *Russia's Stillborn Democracy? From Gorbachev to Yeltsin* (Oxford, Oxford University Press, 2000), p. 10.

19 M. McFaul, *Post-Communist Politics: Democratic Prospects in Russia and Eastern Europe* (Washington, DC, Center for Strategic and International Studies, 1993), p 32.

20 Löwenhardt, *Reincarnation of Russia*, p. 6.

21 C. Offe, 'Capitalism by democratic design? Democratic theory and the triple transition in East Central Europe', *Social Research*, 58:4 (1991), 865–92.

22 J. Lester, 'Overdosing on Nationalism: Gennadii Zyuganov and the Communist Party of the Russian Federation', *New Left Review*, 221 (1997), 36.

23 M. McFaul, 'Russia's 1996 presidential elections', *Post-Soviet Affairs*, 12:4 (1996), 321.

24 R. A. Dahl, *A Preface to Democratic Theory* (Chicago, University of Chicago Press, 1956), pp. 132–3. 'Contingent consent' between opposing groups is when one group is allowed to temporarily dictate to another on condition that the other group may come to power through election, and exercise its own authority in turn (Löwenhardt, *Reincarnation of Russia*, pp. 33–5).

25 McFaul, *Post-Communist Politics*, p. 19.

26 M. Urban, *The Rebirth of Politics in Russia* (Cambridge, Cambridge University Press, 1997), p. 245.

27 McFaul, 'Russia's 1996 presidential elections', 321.

28 G. Gill, *The Collapse of a Single-Party System: The Disintegration of the Communist Party of the Soviet Union* (Cambridge, Cambridge University Press, 1994), p. 172.

29 A. Brown, *The Gorbachev Factor* (Oxford, Oxford University Press, 1996), p. 272; and Sakwa, 'Left or right?', 131.

30 J. Barth Urban and V. Solovei, *Russia's Communists at the Crossroads* (Boulder, CO, Westview, 1997), p. 43.

31 For the concerns of the radicals, accusing the CPSU leadership of diluting the power of the Politburo and Secretariat, failing to provide the rank and file with theoretical guidance, and making the party's dominant position highly fragile, see *Sovetskaya Rossiya (SR)*, 20 June 1990.

32 For the weakness of the CPSU Central Committee's Russian Bureau, see R. W. Orttung, 'The Russia right and the dilemmas of party organisation', *Soviet Studies*, 44:3 (1992), 459. For Polozkov, see J. Harris, *Adrift in Turbulent Seas: The Political and Ideological Struggles of Ivan Kuz'mich Polozkov* (Pittsburgh, University of Pittsburgh, 1993).

33 For the debates surrounding the CPSU's leading role, see S. White. 'Background to the XXVIII Congress' in E. A. Rees (ed.), *The Soviet Communist Party in Disarray* (London, Macmillan, 1992), pp. 6–28.

34 *Iz*, 22 June 1990, I. Osadchii, 'Pravda o nepravde', *Dialog*, 3:96, 68.

35 G. Gill, *The Collapse*, p. 150.

36 *SR*, 7 May 1991.

37 Harris, *Adrift in Turbulent Seas*, pp. 25–6. The RCP's nadir came when it could not field a popular candidate in the 1991 presidential elections, instead supporting the heavily defeated Nikolai Ryzhkov. Since it had no programme it could not register and enter a candidate.

38 Gill, *The Collapse*, p. 104.

39 Orttung, 'The Russian right', 445–78.

40 *Moskovskie novosti (MN)*, 16 September 1991.

41 Gill, *The Collapse*, p. 154.

42 The radicals supported ideology secretary Zyuganov, but he withdrew from the race, while the radicals also failed to have the Second Congress of the RCP brought forward before the Twenty-Ninth CPSU Congress scheduled for December 1991, and thereby influence the new party programme (*Nezavisimaya gazeta (NG)*, 8 September 1991; and A. Salutskii, *Pravda 5 (P-5)*, 17–24 May 1996).

43 Kuptsov had not held a single Politburo session by the time of the coup (*Pravda Rossii (PR)*, 3–10 December 1997).

44 Sakwa, *Russian Politics*, p. 42.

45 Löwenhardt, *Reincarnation of Russia*, p. 48.

46 McFaul, *Post-Communist Politics*, p. 91.

47 Ishiyama, 'The sickle or the rose?', 317.

48 Sakwa, *Russian Politics*, p. 145.

49 Waller, 'Adaptation', 479.

50 For an excellent description of the NSF, see J. Lester, *Modern Tsars and Princes: The Struggle for Hegemony in Russia* (London, Verso, 1995), pp. 157–9.

51 The immediate consequences were catastrophic. For example, by November 1991 a special commission had disbanded the All-Army Party Committee, and had stopped the activity of one million communists in the army and navy, appropriating party money for the welfare of military servicemen and their families (*SR*, 27 November 1991).

52 J. Wishnevsky and E. Teague, '"Democratic Platform" created in CPSU',
    Report on the USSR (2 February 1990), 8.
53 Urban and Solovei, *Russia's Communists*, pp. 10–11.
54 Democratic Russia, the umbrella movement of twenty-seven democratic
    blocs formed in March 1990, split in November 1991 over the issue of preserv-
    ing a union state.
55 *PR*, 11–17 February 1998.
56 For more detail on the splinter groups than space permits here see Urban and
    Solovei, *Russia's Communists*; B. I. Koval, *Partii i politicheskie bloki v Rossii*,
    vypusk pervyi (Moscow, Nipek, 1993); J. Barth Urban and V. Solovei,
    Kommunisticheskoe dvizhenie v postsovetskoi Rossii', *Svobodnaya mysl*, 3
    (1997), 14–28, V. Oleshchuk, V. Pavlenko, *Politicheskaya Rossiya: partii, bloki,
    lidery. god 1997* (Moscow, 'Ves Mir', 1997). Unless otherwise stated, informa-
    tion on the groupuscules comes from these.
57 See *Pravda (P)*, 17 December 1991.
58 In total the group claimed ten thousand members, who were largely teachers,
    former Marxist-Leninist instructors, and pensioners.
59 Of the other communist groups mentioned here, it was closest to the RCWP
    and was a member of WR. It never registered, and boycotted all elections and
    any contact with the bourgeois authorities, reserving special hatred for the
    CPRF and its 'bourgeois' politics.
60 *SR*, 28 November 1991.
61 Lester, *Modern Tsars and Princes*, p. 223.
62 *Mysl* (special edition, 1997).
63 The phrase is Richard Sakwa's. Anpilov was a fiery but monomaniac orator
    who was repeatedly accused by rivals of *vozhdizm* (leaderism) and attempts
    to subvert other communist parties in his own name.
64 Its rules emphasised that at least 51 per cent of its membership, and especially
    its leading bodies, be made up of manual workers.
65 The movement had no fixed membership, but sought to incorporate 'all sup-
    porters of socialism and the red flag' who wished to demonstrate. It was based
    around the organisations of the RCWP and the UFW, and small 'red' groups
    such as Women of Siberia, and the Congress of Soviet Women (*P*, 3 February
    1996).
66 S. Chernyakovskii, 'Kommunisticheskie obedineniya', in M. McFaul, N.
    Petrov and A. Ryabov, *Rossiya nakanune dumskikh vyborov 1999 goda* (Moscow,
    Moscow Carnegie Center, 1999).
67 P. Funder Larsen and D. Mandel, 'The Left in Russia', in R. Miliband and L.
    Panitch (eds), *The Socialist Register 1994: Between Globalism and Nationalism*
    (London, Merlin Press, 1994), p. 285.
68 See Ia. Ermakov, T. Shavshukova and V. Yakunechkin, 'The communist move-
    ment in Russia during the period of prohibition: From the CPSU to the
    Communist Party of the Russian Federation', *Russian Politics and Law*, 32:4
    (1994), 53; *SR*, 7 July 1992).
69 Gill, *The Collapse*, p. 176.
70 In Moscow for instance, fifteen CPSU members worked 'practically under-
    ground' exchanging contacts and financial support with other party organisa-
    tions, the new left parties, and helping PPOs to renew activity immediately
    after the ban was repealed (*SR*, 4 February 1993).
71 The RCP first secretary Kuptsov later claimed that the RCP was not prepared

for the coup at any level. While Zyuganov absented himself from Moscow (fortuitous or forewarned?), Kuptsov rejected approaches from both sides. He refused to support Yeltsin in a phone call on 20 August 1991, but did not sign any documents supporting the coup, realising it would have spelt the end of the party (*PR*, 3–10 December 1997; *P-5*, 17–24 May 1996).

72 The president could only ban a party if a state of emergency had been declared, which was not the case. Otherwise only the courts had this right. See Carla Thorson, 'Has the Communist Party been legally suspended?', *Report on the USSR* (4 October 1991), 4–8.

73 E. Teague and V. Tolz, 'CPSU R.I.P', *Report on the USSR* (22 November 1991), 8.

74 For Kuptsov's role in co-ordinating the first attempts to challenge Yeltsin's decrees, see *PR*, 3–10 December 1997; I. Osadchii, 'Gody borba i trevoga', *Dialog*, 12 (1996), 50–9. For the stimulation of communist activity, see *SR*, 20 September 1991, 5 October 1991.

75 Other figures who made their name in the Court case included Ivan Rybkin, Viktor Zorkaltsev and Oleg Mironov (Osadchii, 'Gody borba i trevoga', 56–7).

76 A poll published in March 1992 showed 46 per cent of respondents against 32 per cent believing the party should be banned, and 51 per cent against 29 per cent believing it should be put on trial (Gill, *The Collapse*, p. 177).

77 Carla Thorson, 'The fate of the Communist Party in Russia', *RFE/RL Research Report* (18 September 1992), 1–6. As well as picking up on the legal flaws in Yeltsin's original ban, the communists stressed the achievements of the Soviet Union under communist rule and refuted allegations of complicity in the coup, arguing that the party was in the process of reforming itself when it was halted by the coup. See *KPSS vne zakona?! Konstitutsionnyi sud v Moskve* (Moscow, Baikalskaya akademiya, 1992).

78 Kuptsov, *PR*, 11–17 February 1998.

79 Indeed, Kuptsov himself was rumoured to be a member of the SPW, although he took a background role (Teague and Tolz, 'CPSU R.I.P', 8).

80 Ivan Rybkin, co-leader of the 'Communists of Russia' parliamentary fraction, played a key role as an intermediary between the fraction and activists in the regions during the revival of a united party. (See Urban and Solovei, *Russia's Communists*, p. 47.)

81 Zyuganov's political alliances were prolific. In December 1991 he entered the leadership of the Russian All-People's Union (RAPU) founded by Russian parliamentarian Sergei Baburin. In January 1992 he became chair of the Co-ordinating Council of National-Patriotic Forces of Russia. In June 1992 he joined (as co-chairman) ex-KGB General Aleksandr Sterligov's Russian National Council. Finally in October 1992 he became co-chair of the NSF.

82 For a succinct summary of Zyuganov's background, see Urban and Solovei, *Russia's Communists*, pp. 43–4.

83 For more on the precise arguments, see Urban and Solovei, 'Kommunis-ticheskoe dvizhenie', p. 18.

84 *SR*, 3 December 1992.

85 For example, Aleksei Prigarin of the Union of Communists convoked a sparsely attended CPSU CC Plenum in June 1992, and a twentieth CPSU Conference in October 1992. RCP leaders Kuptsov and Zorkaltsev believed that the Constitutional Court would not allow the revival of both the Russian and Soviet parties, refused to work in the CPSU organising committee, and

dissuaded regional communists from attending (N. Garifullina, *Tot, kto ne predal. Oleg Shenin: stranitsy zhizni i borby* (Moscow, Vneshtorgoizdat, 1995), pp. 197–202).

86 For the Congress reports see *SR*, 16 February 1993, and Urban and Solovei, *Russia's Communists*, p. 52.

87 See B. Kurashvili, *Kuda idet Rossiya: otsenka Sovetskoi istorii* (Moscow, 'Prometei', 1993), p. 43.

88 Garifullina, *Tot, kto ne predal*, pp. 202–7.

89 Kuptsov was attacked before and during the Congress by RCWP member Albert Makashov for alleged collaboration with Yeltsin, 'Gorbachevism' and failure to protect the party from the ban. Makashov instead supported Zyuganov as a radical patriotic leader. Kuptsov had already become a favourite target for the radicals, at a time when it was felt that they might still be incorporated within the CPRF (*PR* 3–10 December 1997; *Den*, 14–20 February 1993; *P-5*, 17–24 May 1996).

90 *P-5*, 17–24 May 1996.

91 The SPW then experimented with various tactical and ideological approaches but continually lost support, numbering no more than four thousand members. See Lester, *Modern Tsars and Princes*, pp. 221–2, and for the effects on the other parties see Urban and Solovei, *Russia's Communists*, p. 28.

92 *NG*, 2 February 1993; *SR*, 13 March 1993.

93 *P*, 26 March 1993; *Glasnost*, 9 (1993), 13 (1993).

94 During the pre-Congress elections at regional party conferences, places were reserved for those who had worked in the Constitutional Court case, and for deputies from the Russian Congress of Peoples' Deputies (*SR*, 29 January 1993).

95 Kosolapov took his Leninist Platform from the RCWP to work within the CPRF, while Makashov accused former RCWP colleagues of leader-worship and dictatorial tendencies (*SR*, 13 March 1993).

96 *P*, 16 February 1993.

97 *SR*, 1 June 1993.

98 The CPRF leadership did nothing to provoke radical action or national strikes and held no meetings in Moscow. Apart from Makashov and Goryacheva, CPRF leaders took a relatively low profile among the inhabitants of the White House. On 1 October Zyuganov appeared on Russian television calling for non-violence (Urban and Solovei, *Russia's Communists*, p. 86).

99 *Ibid.*, p. 113.

100 The UCP-CPSU remained a debilitated organisation, legally registered in neither Russia nor any of the former republics, with a secretariat restricted to the editorial staff of its newspaper *Glasnost*. For the proceedings of the UCP-CPSU Thirtieth Congress of 1995, which made concessions to the CPRF, apparently under pressure, see *Glasnost*, 15 (1995).

101 Author's interviews with deputy head of CPRF Central Committee department for international affairs, A. Filippov, on 6 December 1997, and CPRF Central Committee secretary for connections with foreign parties and movements, N. Bindyukov, on 18 December 1997.

102 Shenin was denounced by some UCP-CPSU leaders and Valentin Chykin, leader of the Communist Party of Belarus, for undertaking the action without consultation, and then expelled from the Central Committee of the CPRF. For differing interpretations of the formation of the CPUn, see *Glasnost*, 6 (2000); *SR* (web version: www.sr.park.ru) 14 July 2000.

103 Author's interview with CPRF Central Committee secretary for ideological work, A. Kravets, on 22 November 1997.
104 The long-term infighting came to a head when supporters of Tyulkin used Anpilov's support for Zyuganov in the presidential elections to expel him and his supporters from the leadership, thereby precipitating a split between Anpilov's supporters (based largely in Moscow) and the rest of the party.
105 Anpilov's 'Stalinist Bloc' and the 'Communists–Workers of Russia–For the Soviet Union' bloc formed from the RCWP, RCP-CPSU and RPC got 2.8 per cent of the vote combined.

2

A broad church:
the CPRF's ideological currents

We now analyse the beliefs of the main communist protagonists, before in future chapters looking at the CPRF's programmatic evolution and evaluating its ideological position. First, we will outline some common preconceptions which unite the communists, before looking at the nuances of their diverse ideological currents.

Communism and the importance of ideology

Much literature on post-Soviet democratisation appears to downplay the role of ideological challenges to liberal democracy after the 'crisis' of communism. This tendency is particularly apparent in approaches to communist successor parties, which are often seen as 'dinosaurs' – an irrelevance whose constituencies and ideas are obsolete.[1] The frequent but loaded term 'losers' of transition adds to the impression that they are a transient force. Such views do capture important elements of the problems confronting contemporary communists. The term 'crisis' is hardly overused to describe the chronic weakness that the world communist movement entered from the 1980s. The transition to post-industrial socio-economic growth in the West placed a serious challenge before the communist model to which it proved unable to respond, making the future of communism as a world-view very precarious. The disadvantaged constituencies of parties like the CPRF, such as the former party bureaucracy and the agro-industrial complex, would *a priori* seem likely to play a diminished 'loser' role in a freer market and more open democracy.

However, evidence for the emergence of liberal democracy in Russia should be sought and not assumed, as do the more teleological transition approaches. In particular, Schmitter and Karl's view that we should focus on generic and structural, rather than particular, cultural or ideational properties in transition helps little in understanding many of the facets of post-communist transformation.[2] The stubborn persistence of 'Soviet-era' parties like the CPRF cannot be adequately understood without reference to historical legacy, political culture and, particularly, ideology. This is apparent when we look at the CPRF's prehistory and current development. Recent research has tended to reaffirm the centrality of ideology both to the Soviet system and to Gorbachev's project of *perestroika* in particular.[3] No unambiguous definition of ideology has been reached, but the definition used here is a neutral one: a framework of thought through which individuals and groups construct an understanding of the political and social world, and a guide to practical political and social conduct.[4] In communist one-party states this was taken to extremes. Marxism historically placed a high premium both on the role of ideologies, seen as the political consciousness of competing classes, and on socialist ideology as the scientific reflection of the interests of the proletariat.[5] So in the USSR, control of ideas and propaganda was all-important in maintaining power. The ideological apparatus was institutionalised at the apex of the political system, and thus ideology became an agent of social and political control.[6]

The importance of ideologies persisted after the collapse of one-party systems. As Jeremy Lester notes, the *potential* for post-Soviet ideologies (even if not realised) remained great. The issue space created by the ideological crisis of the preceding power bloc, allied with the weakness of civil society, provided a great opportunity for ideologies to mobilise in the new political terrain.[7] They had opportunities to motivate collective action, to decipher the world and provide a 'conceptual road map' for inchoate social groups in times of social turbulence.[8]

However, whether communist successor parties could take these opportunities was problematic, and the problem was their ideology. The precise definition of 'communism' will always be hotly disputed, since Marx declined to define except in general terms a society which he believed would be produced by specific historical processes from a future stage of capitalism. Yet the central Marxist notion that communism would be a coherent and superior alternative to and repudiation of capitalism was developed fully by Lenin. Soviet Marxism-Leninism was inherently flexible over tactics but was always consistent in its 'philosophy of certainty' and 'militant separatism' – the conviction it was an alternative system of thought that would sweep all other competing capitalist and socialist ideologies away.[9] Furthermore at its core was a denial of liberal democracy per se, and as Lenin said openly 'less politics is the best politics'. Pluralism, negotiation and disagreement (and institutions which legitimated these, such as parliaments with a division of powers) were dangerous 'bourgeois' tendencies seen by Lenin as undermining the essential process of class struggle, where individual motivations were based on economic class interests, and not values or opinions.[10] This denial of politics explains why communism has historically shown itself to be structurally resistant to reform beyond narrow limits.[11] As Neil Harding has argued, Leninism's rejection of all eclecticism and eccentricity, and all competing ideologies meant that its space for theoretical innovation was extremely narrow and it defined itself in 'ever narrower concentric circles'.[12] When its apparently unchallenge-able postulates such as the superiority of state economic planning and the inevitability of building communism were undermined by the decline in the Soviet socio-economic model in the post-Stalin period and by Gorbachev's *perestroika* the sense of coherent explanatory alter-native could, unsurprisingly, no longer be maintained.

Moreover, the purity of this 'philosophy of certainty' was easier to maintain when stipulated by a communist regime in a closed society where ideology acted as a 'state religion demanding universal obeisance'.[13] Non-coercive and pluralistic polities demand a different role for ideology where persuasion and securing the consent of would-be supporters and social groups becomes all-important.[14] The demands of electoral politics place a premium on tactical flexibility and compromise that may feed into strategic changes. However, such tactical compromises raise acute ideological difficulties for commu-nist ideology, and challenge it to renounce some of these characteris-tics of its 'philosophy of certainty' without destroying itself altogether. Marxism-Leninism's denial of politics has historically meant that in has entered a crisis when it has encountered 'cultures and institutions that legitimise difference'.[15] It is the dialectic between absorption in and denial of the pluralist politics of the post-Soviet political order that has so marked the conduct of the CPRF since 1991, and will be seen as a constant thread throughout this book.

The contemporary communist world-view

Urban and Solovei's view of the Russian communists as a 'true believ-ers', motivated more by ideological commitment than by careerist, cynical or opportunistic motives is persuasive, and the CPRF itself claimed to be 'the party of the communist idea'.[16] A strict dichotomy between believers and careerists is always somewhat artificial, as humans have complex motives that lie between complete commitment to every tenet of an ideology and cynical manipulation of it. Nevertheless, the polarisation of *perestroika* indeed forced an artificial dichotomy, leaving the CPRF with a much more ideologically committed community.

The effects of this will become clear. The fact that there was a residual organisational and ideological mythology to aspire to was a major factor facilitating the quick resurrection of the CPRF, and its long-term durability compared with potential competitors, such as many forms of Russian nationalism whose appeal was grounded in an abstract concept of nation for which there was no contemporary model, or liberalism and social democracy, which had weak grounding in Russian traditions. Contrary to the above view of communists as merely 'losers', ideological commitment might not evaporate even in more propitious economic circumstances. However, the nature of this 'communist idea' was itself contentious. Like other ideologies in Russian society, Russian communism was very much an ideology in transition, combining an array of potentially contradictory tendencies and potentials.

Many communist values were shared by the national-patriotic camp as a whole, and formed a distinctive version of Russian conservatism. What drew the national-patriotic and communist movements together in the Gorbachev era has been described as a radical form of 'fundamentalist rejectionism' of key features of modernity by the appeal to traditionalism and national exceptionalism.[17] The Soviet Union in the late 1980s found itself in the position of a relatively backward and traditionalist regime, which preserved many 'pre-modern' elements, particularly in isolated rural areas, and had only comparatively recent exposure to encroachment from the global forces of modernisation and capitalism. Just as in Europe in the nineteenth and early twentieth centuries the destructive side effects of capitalist modernisation such as social atomisation and differentiation threatened older communal solidarities of class and nation', and provided fertile ground for the potential of the 'nationalisation of socialism' against a common enemy, so too the joint protest of communists, fascists and nationalists in the post-Soviet era had precedent and logic.[18]

Yet, these rejectionists were always united more by what they opposed than any future vision, which became more apparent in plu-ralist conditions: although they were rightly called conservative (in the sense of trying to conserve elements of the Soviet state), they quite clearly differed in their attitude towards the post-Soviet present, and not all were fundamentalists. The 'radicals' we have alluded to (Tyulkin, Anpilov, Andreeva and their ilk) espoused a near total rejec-tion of the present, while many moderates tended to have a more ambiguous view of the present. We will return to this below. We can now isolate the key assumptions to which the majority of communists (and indeed pro-communist nationalists) would subscribe:

The viability of the Soviet system

The prelude to the evolution of an avowedly revolutionary and class-based doctrine into an apparently conservative communism is the Soviet period's 'indigenisation of socialism', and its indelible link with notions of state, nation and empire. This began with the retreat from internationalism into national self-reliance in the period of 'socialism in one country' from the mid-1920s onwards. The Bolsheviks had to rec-oncile themselves to the improbability of world revolution and defend the USSR as the homeland of socialism. This tendency was strength-ened through Stalin's use of nationalism in the 'Great Patriotic War' to forge an emotional bond with the Soviet state. Not for nothing did many Russian nationalists see Stalin as 'the greatest anti-communist of the twentieth century'.[19] Moreover, Soviet communism and a form of Russian nationalism known as national bolshevism developed an 'elec-tive affinity'. National bolshevism was a 'red', statist form of Russian nationalism developed by ex-émigré servants of the Tsarist regime after the 1917 revolution. Reflecting a historical schism in Russian national-ism, 'white' nationalists who emphasised Russia's cultural and relig-ious traditions abhorred the Soviet regime for its atheism and materialism, while many nationalists who emphasised Russia's authoritarian and imperialist traditions supported Marxism and inter-nationalism as a façade which facilitated the restoration and expansion of the Russian state as never before.[20] The Soviet regime, while never entirely renouncing Marxism-Leninism, relied heavily in its latter years on national bolshevism as a state-sponsored 'official nationalism', par-ticularly in the armed forces. This legitimised the institutions of the Soviet state from a national-imperialist point of view and grounded them in an emotional and patriotic sentiment absent from Marxist-Leninist discourse.

Consequently, many forms of conservative rejectionism were akin to Western conservatism in their nostalgic, sentimental reverence for past institutions as the guarantors of order and stability. The viability of the Soviet state was justified less by reference to any higher future ideal than through time, tradition and past utility. Its structures are seen as proving their fundamental soundness through tempering in the cauldron of war and beating the Nazi war machine, and by the feats of turning a backward agricultural country into an urban, educated superpower able to create one of the most comprehensive social security systems in the world. Since such achievements had cost the blood of millions it was impermissible to renege on them.[21] Arguably, crucial differences between such conservatism and Western conservatism related only to what was considered traditional – in Western cultures it has tended to be a liberal economy, private property, individualism and a weak state, whereas the Russian conservatives would defend collectivism and a strong state.[22] Both types of conservatism emphasised social and national unity cemented by a reverence for institutions, customs, morality and even religion and spirituality (for many Russian nationalists and some communists). The Russian 'moderates', espoused a view akin to the British conservative Robert Peel, not opposing change per se, but seeking to 'reform in order to protect' their traditions.[23] This position was echoed repeatedly by CPRF leaders, who insisted that their aim was to preserve continuity with the best of Soviet tradition while eliminating its worst features.[24]

Conspiracy theories

When the belief in the soundness of the Soviet system was combined with its apparently spontaneous internal combustion, what emerged was what Sakwa calls the 'Versailles syndrome' – the idea that the destruction was entirely artificial, if not premeditated.[25] How could the USSR have collapsed so quickly without outside aggression? It could only be that it had been engineered from within. Gorbachev's inability to explain his reform project to the rank and file and his constant tactical manoeuvres were compounded by the fact that many conservatives supported his reform plans initially. When the outcome became clear, the feeling that they had been duped by people with ulterior motives was only too natural.[26] The mutual contempt between those discarding communist ideology and those still clinging to it was exacerbated by their common past in a Stalinist tradition, which sought outside enemies to explain domestic mishaps. The communist and national-patriotic movement were united in their incomprehension and scorn for those 'traitors' among their former comrades, such as Gorbachev, Shevardnadze and Yeltsin, who seized power 'illegitimately' in August 1991 and then dismantled the Soviet state and economy, apparently in the interests of Western expansionism. Some would not hesitate to locate the instigators of this so-called 'fifth column' among the shadowy phantoms of Jewish and Masonic conspirators, a tendency that is a leitmotif of the more radical forms of Russian nationalism.

Outcry at 'the blackening of history'

The control of historical interpretation and memory was crucial to communist power, and a reinterpretation of history was a core component of *perestroika*. Once communist parties lost control of the past, they lost control of the present.[27] However the uncovering of 'blank spots of history' led to widespread denunciations of Stalinism and the rewriting of Soviet history, sometimes as ideologised as the orthodoxy they sought to destroy. As the conservatives saw it: 'our state they have branded criminal, our achievement criminal, our history criminal'.[28] Nowhere was the conservatism of the rejectionists more apparent. For the typical conservative, the past is essential as 'a treasure house of inspiration for the present',[29] without which there is no reference point, just disorganisation and chaos. Soviet conservatives insisted on 'balanced' and not negative or nihilistic portrayals of the Soviet past, in effect diluting the thrust of *perestroika*'s historical iconoclasm.[30] Gorbachev's 'pan-human values' which stressed the universality of world civilisation were seen as 'the denial of national experience'.[31] A 'Russophile' conservative cultural orientation, defending national cultural values such as language and religion against Western (particularly American) mass culture was common even to more internationalist communists.[32] Some expressed a traditionally conservative view of humankind as organically and spiritually linked to national tradition, while the 'liberal' view of universal human rights and norms was seen as culturally impoverished and rootless.[33]

Residual Marxism-Leninism

What distinguished the communists most from other 'statist' nationalists was their continued commitment to various elements of the Marxist-Leninist heritage. First, those teachings about the exploitative and divisive nature of capitalism or the colonial aspirations of impe-rialist powers were considered especially relevant to post-Soviet Russia.[34] Second, there was a continuing commitment to socialism and communism as superior systemic alternatives to capitalism, however nebulous the nature of these terms (itself an inherent feature of post-Marx communism). In an attitudinal sense, the CPRF was barely a revolutionary party. The revolutionary fervour of early Leninism has gradually been replaced with a more sober realism among many communists, which since 1991 has verged on 'post-traumatic shock' and ideological self-doubt.[35] Valentin Kuptsov even noted a general 'loss of historical optimism' afflicting the party.[36] Yet, publicly at least, the defiant assertion that Russia would be socialist once more, and the search for systemic social amelioration encapsu-lated in the slogan of 'social justice' were still the prime motivating factors. Third, the party remained 'communist' in many more senses than generally realised. The CPRF's party programme, as will become clear below, was Marxist-Leninist in its strategic aims and guiding philosophy. Internal party discourse remained strongly tinged by Marxist-Leninist theory, as the CPRF's party propagandists made clear.[37]

Fourth, vital in uniting the CPRF was the adherence to commu-nism as an *ideology of organisation*. Organisation and structure has been described as the *raison d'être* of post-Leninist communism.[38] Allied to this was the self-perception of communism as a 'moral community' of believers, a subculture imposing both high activism and loyalty.[39] This sense of 'communist subculture' was evident in the CPRF's rev-erence for marches and rallies, in the premium still placed on selfless-ness for the cause, and the internationalist sentiment which remained, though diluted by its patriotic slant. For this reason the CPRF made great efforts to restore connections with other communist parties such as the Chinese, Greek and French Communist Parties, and to exchange guests at party Congresses.[40] Moreover, the cult of disci-pline and unity in communist parties was traditionally not just a formal aspect of party organisation, but a key principle internalised as a code of ethics.[41] Such an aspiration to unity and the abhorrence of dissent combined made schism a real danger, but nevertheless, a less fanatical 'unity in diversity', as Urban and Solovei felicitously name it, was the overriding principle uniting the CPRF and avoiding sectar-ian excesses.[42] Within the party the maintenance of discipline, the respect for higher authority and unwillingness to risk unsanctioned activity, together with the aspiration for consensus and conflict-avoidance remained paramount, and this was regarded as one of the most important principles the CPRF salvaged from the CPSU.[43]

Intra-party ideological tendencies

The RCP was founded originally as the 'historical repudiation' of Gorbachev's universalist reform communism.[44] However, the nature of the *CPRF's* rejectionism was ambiguous. As noted in the last chapter, many radicals ended up outside the refounded CPRF. The CPRF's ideological range was narrower and more moderate than the movement as a whole, relying heavily on those who valued unity above the fundamentalism of the radical communist groups, but it was nevertheless a broad church.

Radical party member Richard Kosolapov considered the chief party cleavage to be between a radical 'left' and a moderate 'right', which united all CPRF leaders who supported parliamentary politics.[45] Within the CPRF this division reflected a hierarchical sociocultural cleavage in the Soviet system between the party-state apparatus and society.[46] The moderates, who predominated in the party's upper echelons, tended to be those with significant administrative experience before 1991, possessing a bureaucratic and pragmatic attitude characteristic of the *nomenklatura*. Typical were CC members Yurii Maslyukov, former head of Gosplan (the USSR's economic planning organisation), and Anatolii Lukyanov, former chairman of the USSR Supreme Soviet.[47] The radicals, who predominated in the party's base, tended to originate from the CPSU's lower echelons (those most vilified during *perestroika* and now among the real 'losers' of transition), or those who had joined the radical opposition during 1991–93 and gained the status of martyrs and heroes within the party (such as CC members General Albert Makashov and Viktor Ilyukhin).[48]

Urban and Solovei's three-fold delineation of the CPRF's ideological tendencies remains a persuasive broad categorisation, confirmed by party sources and the author's own research, although like the moderate–radical division, these categories were mutable and amorphous.[49] After resolution of divisive programmatic debates during 1993–95, these tendencies became less obvious and were crosscut by the moderate–radical division. On ideological questions there was a tendency for the moderates to equate to the 'Marxist reformer' and 'statist-patriotic communist' groups outlined below, and the radicals to equate to the 'Marxist-Leninist modernisers', but this was not always the case. Moreover, the party was divided over many functional cleavages over influence and resources, between Kuptsov's party apparatus, the CC and the parliamentary fraction, regional and central leaders. Yet these ideological proto-groups remained a key determinant of the party's programmatic development.

Most prominent but probably numerically smallest was the so-called 'nationalist' group, whom I follow Sakwa in dubbing 'statist-patriotic communists' for their ambivalent Soviet/Russocentric nationalism and latent commitment to supra-ethnic principles.[50] This trend was espoused by CPRF chair, Gennadii Zyuganov, and his close colleague, Yurii Belov, a member of the party's governing Presidium and prolific publicist. What distinguished this tendency was an updated national bolshevism which identified communism with the interests of the Russian state rather than Marxist purity. Other members of this tendency included Aleksandr Shabanov, deputy chair of the CPRF from 1995 to 1997, and Svetlana Goryacheva, Presidium member and vice-speaker of the Russian State Duma from 1995 to 1999, although she latterly drifted towards social democracy. A positive attitude towards Russian Orthodoxy was distinctive of this tendency. By way of illustration (Zyuganov's views are explored in the next chapter), Petr Romanov, director of the 'Yenisei' chemical plant in Krasnoyarsk and Duma vice-speaker from 1999 was a representative of this tendency, having been previously a member of national-patriotic groups and possessing close ties to the Church, while almost completely reneging on internationalism. Their economic preference was nationally orientated state capitalism with state ownership of the 'commanding heights' of the economy (the military and agro-industrial sectors).[51]

The 'Marxist reformer' group included many prominent party leaders, such as party deputy leader Valentin Kuptsov, and other leaders such as Ivan Melnikov, Viktor Peshkov and Aleksandr Kravets, many of whom were once members of the left-democratic SPW. The Duma speaker from December 1995, Gennadii Seleznev demonstrated this group's social democratic tinge, publicly praising the welfare achievements of Swedish social democracy.[52] They advocated a more left-wing, purely Marxist, internationalist and class-based approach reminiscent of early Gorbachevism or even the Prague Spring of 1968. However, they lacked Gorbachev's emphasis on universal human values, remained suspicious of bourgeois and imperialist forces, and were collectivist rather than individualist.[53]

Compared with the statist-patriotic communists they tended to support greater social pluralism and intra-party democracy, had less reverence for a strong state, were atheists or at best neutral to the Church. They also supported a mixed economy, but with a greater emphasis upon defending the social welfare of workers within it, and cultivating ties with other left-wing movements and trade unions, rather than purely patriotic non-communist groups as Zyuganov advocated.[54]

Urban and Solovei's 'Marxist-Leninist moderniser' tendency is a rather 'catch-all' tendency encompassing several trends on the 'left' wing of the party and much of the rank and file, and needs substantiation. This trend professed more caution towards theoretical change, less emphasis on anti-bureaucratism and pluralism than the 'Marxist reformers', and a more positive view towards the radical communist parties and extra-parliamentary politics than the other tendencies. Among them were moderates, such as Lukyanov, co-conspirator in the August 1991 coup and regularly branded a reactionary, who was indeed a fierce critic of Western cultural influences, and a supporter of the sharpening of the class struggle. Yet he strongly supported Zyuganov's themes of Russian spirituality and collaboration with the national-patriotic movement and rarely dissented from the leadership position.[55]

Prominent among the modernisers was a stratum of theoreticians. Nikolai Bindyukov, CC secretary since 1995, outlined the main concerns of this group – the need for the primacy of theoretical work, an ideological battle against the 'Mafioso-predatory bourgeoisie' and the inculcation of class-consciousness in the activation of the class struggle.[56] More radical were the other orthodox party intellectuals who were prolific writers in the party press. Many, most prominently *Pravda Rossii* writer Viktor Trushkov, used this platform to be critical of Zyuganov's statist-patriotic 'mythology' from a relatively orthodox Marxist-Leninist perspective, concerned to preserve the Marxist-Leninist class approach, oppose the leadership's acceptance of private property and any renunciation of internationalism.[57] One of the most inveterate critics of the leadership was Richard Kosolapov, leader of the informal 'Leninist platform' within the CPRF.[58]

Also important were those espousing a less theoretically complex and consistent, yet more traditionalist viewpoint that might be dubbed 'red patriotism'. The spectrum of 'red patriotism' ranged from conservative communists of the Brezhnev sort to neo-Stalinists, representing both the more internationalist trend of early Stalinism and the more national bolshevik period of Stalinism during and after the Second World War. Most prominent of this latter group was Viktor Ilyukhin, a political hawk, a fierce public opponent of corruption, obsessed by Zionist conspiracy theories but not a noted ideologue.[59] Other prominent figures in this group included CC members Albert Makashov and Teimuraz Avaliani. This tendency (particularly the rank and file) shared a traditionalist and nostalgic commitment to the 'sacred' institutions, traditions and symbols of late Soviet power such as proletarian internationalism, the union state and welfare guarantees, and above all the *vozhdi* (great leaders) Lenin and Stalin.[60] For them, the CPRF was heir to the CPSU, and must not relinquish the CPSU's most revered traditions.[61] As one said to this author in 2000, 'I'm a member of the CPSU – I never betrayed it'.[62]

The relative balance of these positions within the party was difficult to judge, since party leaders sought to present a united front. According to ex-party member Boris Slavin, 10 per cent were inclined towards social democracy (the 'Marxist reformer' group), 15 per cent supported basically Stalinist positions, whereas the remaining 75 per cent broadly supported Zyuganov's ideological position.[63] This wide consensus over Zyuganov's position indicates that the extent of the party's discontent with him was often overrated. Several factors explain this. The radicals were from the more impoverished strata of society, many were former members of the radical communist groups, little different from them in ideological orientation, and they often co-operated with them at street level. But even most of these 'radicals' were conservatives by age and inclination, and were not broadly supportive of the activities of the radicals like Anpilov and Tyulkin.[64] Conservative mentality and organisational loyalty cemented by the cult of unity hindered the articulation of coherent ideological alternatives, kept an otherwise quite divided organisation together and prevented dissent from evolving into defection on a large scale.

Moreover, there was consensus among the moderates that Marxism-Leninism in isolation was no longer sufficient to understand the world, and had to be supplemented by other approaches. This viewpoint was shared by moderates of all party trends.[65] Consequently, there was agreement that 'civilisational analysis' (Zyuganov's 'cultural-historical' or 'state-patriotic' approach, described in detail in the next chapter) was necessary when drawing on people's creative and spiritual energies.[66] His strategy could be supported by other ideological tendencies as a tactical matter of necessity in specific post-communist conditions, despite the fact that committed converts to Zyuganov's ideological line appeared relatively few.[67] So the 'state-patriotic' approach could be supported by other communists who recognised the drawbacks of a strong state and on these grounds atheist communists (the vast majority) could co-operate with the Church.[68] As Urban and Solovei point out, even the most traditionalist communists could 'only be flattered' by Zyuganov's equation of communism with such themes as the historical greatness of Russia, and thus broadly accepted Zyuganov's linking of communism with national historical, cultural and spiritual values.[69] Even the Marxist-Leninist moderniser Kosolapov acknowledged that *dukhovnost* (religious spirituality) was an essential part of the Russian idea.[70] Similarly, 'Marxist reformers' Gennadii Seleznev and Viktor Zorkaltsev were closely linked to the religious and national-patriotic movement.[71] So, overall, there was much more mingling and blurring between tendencies than allowed for by Urban and Solovei. However, the CPRF's programmatic evolution was to reveal that deep disagreement over the problems of post-communism was still prevalent. The precise ideological problems posed by post-Soviet events and the solutions attempted will now be analysed.

Notes

1 J. D. Nagle and A. Mahr, *Democracy and Democratization* (London, Sage, 1999), p. 180; M. Orenstein, 'A genealogy of communist successor parties in East-Central Europe and the determinants of their success', *East European Politics and Societies*, 12:3 (1998), 488–9.

2 P. Schmitter with T. Lynn Karl, 'The conceptual travels of transitologists and consolidologists: how far East should they attempt to go?', *Slavic Review*, 53:1 (1994), 179.

3 For example, N. Robinson, *Ideology and the Collapse of the Soviet System: A Critical History of Soviet Ideological Discourse* (Aldershot, Edward Elgar, 1995); M. Sandle, 'Gorbachev's ideological platform: a case study of ideology in the USSR' (PhD thesis, University of Birmingham, 1993).

4 This definition is based upon M. Freeden, *Ideologies and Political Theory: A Conceptual Approach* (Oxford, Clarendon Press, 1996), pp. 3, 6; and J. Donald and S. Hall, *Politics and Ideology* (Milton Keynes, Open University Press, 1986), pp. ix–x.

5 For the Marxist definition of ideology see T. Bottomore, *A Dictionary of Marxist Thought*, 2nd edn (Oxford, Blackwell, 1991), p. 251.

6 M. Sandle, 'Gorbachev's ideological platform'.

7 J. Lester, *Modern Tsars and Princes: The Struggle for Hegemony in Russia* (London, Verso, 1995), 'Introduction', particularly pp. 12–21.

8 S. E. Hanson, *Ideology, Uncertainty, and the Rise of Anti-System Parties in Post*

Communist Russia (Glasgow, University of Strathclyde Centre for the Study of Public Policy, Studies in Public Policy 289, 1997), p. 10.

9 N. Harding, *Leninism* (Basingstoke, Macmillan, 1996), pp. 13, 53.
10 A. Polan, *Lenin and the End of Politics* (London, Methuen, 1984).
11 R. Sakwa, *Gorbachev and his Reforms 1985–1990* (Englewood Cliffs, NJ, Philip Allan, 1991), pp. 34, 39.
12 Harding, *Leninism*, pp. 267–80.
13 Sakwa, *Gorbachev*, p. 124.
14 J. Lester, *Modern Tsars and Princes*, pp. 1–21.
15 Polan, *Lenin and the End of Politics*, p. 174.
16 Author's interview with CPRF CC secretary for connections with foreign parties and movements, N. Bindyukov, on 18 December 1997.
17 R. Sakwa, 'Left or right? The CPRF and the problem of democratic consolidation in Russia', *Journal of Communist Studies and Transition Politics*, 14:1&2 (1998), 129, 145.
18 V. Vujacic, 'Gennadiy Zyuganov and the "third road"', *Post-Soviet Affairs*, 12:2 (1996), 121.
19 *Den*, 15–21 August 1993.
20 For a full treatment of national bolshevism's origins in the ideas of the émigré, Nikolai Ustryalov, and the collection *Smena Vekh*, published in 1921 see M. Agursky, *The Third Rome: National Bolshevism in the USSR* (Boulder, CO, Westview, 1987), p. 248.
21 Zyuganov, *SR*, 30 July 1992.
22 M. A. Molchanov, 'Russian neo-communism: autocracy, orthodoxy, nationality', *Harriman Review*, 9:3 (1996), 72.
23 P. Suvanto, *Conservatism from the French Revolution to the 1990s* (Basingstoke, Macmillan, 1997), p. 32.
24 Author's interview with Bindyukov on 18 December 1997.
25 Sakwa, 'Left or right?', 146.
26 E. Ligachev, in D. Remnick, 'Gorbachev's last hurrah', *The New Yorker*, 11 March 1996, p. 71.
27 Sakwa, *Gorbachev*, p. 44.
28 Nationalist Eduard Limonov, *SR*, 23 May 1992.
29 F. O'Gorman, *British Conservatism: Conservative Thought from Burke to Thatcher* (London, Longman, 1986), p. 20.
30 E. Ligachev, *Uchitelskaya gazeta*, 27 August 1987, 1.
31 E. Volodin, *SR*, 2 July 1992, 1.
32 Author's interview with deputy head of CPRF CC department for international affairs, A. Filippov, 31 January 1998.
33 *SR*, 2 July 1992. For a Western conservative's view see R. Scruton, *The Meaning of Conservatism* (Basingstoke, Macmillan, 1990), p. 19.
34 J. Barth Urban and V. Solovei, *Russia's Communists at the Crossroads* (Boulder, CO, Westview, 1997), p. 2.
35 In Valerii Solovei's apt phrase, conversation with the author, 18 September 2000.
36 *P*, 13–17 February 1998.
37 Author's interviews with Bindyukov, 18 December 1997, and with CPRF CC Secretary for Ideological Work, Aleksandr Kravets, on 20 November 1997.
38 N. McInnes, *The Communist Parties of Western Europe* (London, Oxford University Press, 1975), p. 97.

A broad church

61

39 C. Shore, *Italian Communism: The Escape from Leninism* (London, Pluto Press, 1990), p. 142.

40 Author's interview with Filippov on 6 December 1997.

41 Shore, *Italian Communism*, pp. 17, 143.

42 Urban and Solovei, *Russia's Communists*, p. 186.

43 Author's interview with Dmitri Gorovtsov, parliamentary aide to Duma deputy Oleg Mironov on 25 November 1997. J. Barth Urban and V. Solovei, 'Kommunisticheskoe dvizhenie v postsovetskoi Rossii', *Svobodnaya mysl*, 3 (1997), 28.

44 Sakwa, 'Left or right?', 129.

45 Author's interview with Richard Kosolapov on 10 February 1998.

46 M. Steven Fish, *Democracy from Scratch: Opposition and Regime in the New Russian Revolution* (Princeton, NJ, Princeton University Press, 1994), p. 21.

47 Other prominent moderates were Duma deputies Vladimir Semago, Oleg Mironov, Viktor Zorkaltsev, Aleksandr Shabanov, Viktor Peshkov (chair of CC election campaigns commission), Sergei Potapov (chair of the CC organisational work committee), Gennadii Seleznev and Svetlana Goryacheva. This information is based on (although I disagree with a number of their evaluations) S. Chugaev, *Iz*, 21 March 1996; G. Cherkasov, *Segodnya* (*S*), 23 April 1996.

48 Ilyukhin, a former KGB prosecutor, was Duma security affairs committee chair until 1999, a member of Anpilov's 'Working Russia', and the NSF, Makashov a member of the RNC and RCWP. Other chief intra-party radicals were CC members Richard Kosolapov, Leonid Petrovskii and the Duma deputies Teimuraz Avaliani, Valentin Varennikov, Igor Bratishchev, Viktor Shevelukha, Tatyana Astrakhankina, Aleksandr Kuvaev, Vasilii Shandybin, and Aleksandr Mikhailov.

49 See Urban and Solovei, *Russia's Communists*, pp. 55–64. N. Bindyukov and P. Lopata, 'Put vybran, neobkhodimo uspeshno ego prioiti', *Dialog*, 10 (1997), 43, and the author's interview with Boris Slavin on 29 November 1997 confirmed these views.

50 R. Sakwa, 'Left or right?', 139.

51 *P*, 17–24 October 1997.

52 *NG*, 19 January 1996.

53 Kuptsov, *P*, 13 January 1995.

54 *P*, 24 December 1993; *Glasnost*, 28–9 (1994).

55 Sakwa, 'Left or right?', 139; *Zavtra*, 21 (1996).

56 *PR*, 30 March 1995.

57 Trushkov, *P*, 21–27 January 1998.

58 Kosolapov was considered hardline even in 1986, when Gorbachev removed him as editor of the CPSU's theoretical journal, *Kommunist*. For his views see R. Kosolapov, *Idei razuma i serdtsa* (Moscow, 1996).

59 For his views see V. Ilyukhin, *Na trone porazit porok* (Moscow, 'Federatsiya', 1997).

60 Urban and Solovei, 'Kommunisticheskoe dvizhenie', 25.

61 *Za SSSR*, 3 (16) (1996).

62 Author's interview with Moscow rank-and-file communist, Vladimir Sukhadeev, 20 September 2000.

63 Information from B. Slavin in J. Lester, 'Overdosing on nationalism: Gennadii Zyuganov and the Communist Party of the Russian Federation', *New Left Review*, 221 (1997), 35.

64 See L. Byzov, 'What about the voters?', in M. McFaul, N. Petrov, A. Ryabov and E. Reisch (eds), *Primer on Russia's 1999 Duma Elections* (Washington, DC, Carnegie Endowment, 1999), p. 20.

65 Author's interviews with Bindyukov on 18 December 1997, Filippov on 6 December 1997.

66 Bindyukov and Lopata, 'Put vybran, neobkhodimo uspeshno ego prioiti', 46; *PR*, 30 March 1995.

67 Marxist-Leninist moderniser R. Gabidullin asserted that state patriotism was supported by only three or four party leaders (R. Gabidullin, 'O klassovom podkhode i gosudarstvennom patriotizm', *Dialog*, 10 (1997), 10).

68 Author's interview with Kravets on 20 November 1997, and Bindyukov on 18 December 1997.

69 Urban and Solovei, *Russia's Communists*, p. 101.

70 *P*, 15 August 1992.

71 Seleznev held a place on the central council of the national-patriotic 'Spiritual Heritage' organisation, while Zorkaltsev was chair of the State Duma committee for social and religious organisations.

3

Programmatic evolution

With the key party tendencies within the CPRF now outlined, we can look at how these tendencies have interacted in the evolution of party policy positions. The CPRF's programmatic evolution has been convoluted, but the overriding leadership aim of forging a new role for the party in post-Soviet conditions is apparent. The CPRF was not therefore a 'hardline' or 'unreconstructed' communist party as is often portrayed, but was engaged in a complex and often contradictory effort to 'conserve' communism. The leaders were driven by an awareness of the crisis of communism, but attempted to salvage as much as possible from core values and the communist identity. In turn, this conservatism influenced the choice of 'state patriotism' as the motivating principle of the external public face of the party, a face which existed in a state of unresolved tension with the party's internal ideological trends.

Responding to the crisis of communism

The choices facing communist parties in 'post-communist' conditions have been extremely problematic, as they have been forced to respond to the widely perceived crisis of communism and the left in general. For communists after 1989 the basic dilemma was whether to abandon their attempt to construct a coherent alternative to capitalist modernity, along with their principles, names and heritage, or if not, how to keep these principles intact and remain politically relevant.[1]

Three broad responses to this dilemma formed:

1   The favoured alternative for many was to reject communism itself, the precise trajectory taken depending on the inclinations of the leadership and the issues they could exploit. One choice

involved transformation into a non-communist party of the left, allowing parties to become vehicles for a combination of social democracy and technocratic modernisation. The successor parties in Poland and Hungary are the main examples, having renounced the Marxist heritage and joined the Socialist International. The alternative is the choice of nationalist particularism and clientelist patronage politics espoused by many successor parties in the Balkans, principally Slobodan Milosevic's Socialist Party of Serbia, and the Bulgarian Socialist Party.

2   An alternative was remaining unchanged, rejecting the need for adaptation outright and any modification being in the direction of a more orthodox or 'hardline' model of socialism. This was the choice of several communist parties in Western Europe such as in Portugal (the Communist Party of Portugal, or PCP), France (the Communist Party of France, or PCF) and Belgium (the Communist Party of Belgium, or PCB) in the immediate post-communist aftermath. The majority of the radical communist parties in Russia would also fall into this category, as would the main Ukrainian successor party, the Communist Party of Ukraine.

3   The final option was becoming a 'renewed communist party', simultaneously maintaining and rejuvenating a communist identity. A favoured strategy was the rejection of Stalinism and a return to unsullied Marxism. In East-Central Europe, this path was chosen by the Czech CPBM, and the Russian Party of Communists most clearly represents this tendency in Russia itself. In Western Europe the Spanish and Greek Communist parties and the Italian Rifondazione comunista are among those pursuing this strategy.

As the example of Eastern Germany's PDS shows, there may be adherents of all three positions within one party. This party rejected the communist name but united a broad spectrum of social democratic, Marxist-Leninist and nationalist socialisms.[2] The CPRF will be seen as aiming for the third path, but oscillating between all three, but because of the 'elective affinity' of Russian communism and national bolshevism it found the choice of nationalist particularism attractive. All post-communist leftists faced the challenge of defining a new and popular left identity when the general political dynamic involved movement from Marxist-Leninist socialism, and increased exposure to liberal democracy and market economics, backed by Western governments and their financial institutions such as the International Monetary Fund (IMF). A common desire appeared to be for a 'nationally authentic' left, neither a complete capitulation to Western models nor a full return to Leninist politics.[3] This was most clearly shown with the Hungarian and Polish successor parties, who sought to combine enthusiasm for Westernising reform with preservation of the traditional socialist value culture of those most harmed by reform.

Particularly problematic, however were the choices of defending or renewing a communist identity. Behind the crisis of communism in Western Europe was the emergence of a post-industrial European political culture from the 1960s onwards which challenged traditional collectivist and industrial working-class identities that had formed the bedrock of communist party support. Such long-term processes have been condensed into a few years in post-Soviet countries like Russia, where the decimated industrial 'proletariat' now comprises only 13 per cent of the workforce.[4] Even without such problems, as we have already alluded, renewing communism in pluralist conditions threw a direct challenge to its notion of distinctiveness. Trying to carve out an identity which was distinguishable from both 'bourgeois' parties and orthodox communist parties involved borrowing from both traditions, an ambiguity which aroused deep suspicion among many communists.[5]

Public ideology

Herbert Kitschelt describes two competing but not incompatible logics which electoral parties may follow. First, a logic of *constituency representation* in which party strategy is derived from the ideology of their core support groups in society or, second, a logic of electoral competition in which parties change their political stances to appeal to their marginal sympathisers, in order to maximise electoral support.[6] Western communist parties operating in pluralist electoral systems generally preferred the former, putting class considerations and the concerns of their ideologically narrow constituency before electoral politics.[7] The role of ideology is again at the root. 'Programmatic' political parties are those which espouse a strong commitment to a 'pure ideology' (the fundamental principles which distinguish the main ideological families such as 'socialism' or 'conservatism'). These parties tend to conduct their everyday electoral politics using a more pragmatic 'practical' ideology which governs tactics and may change significantly from one election manifesto to the next, eventually perhaps altering some features of the 'pure' ideology.[8] But the inflexibility of the 'pure' ideology of communism imposes limits on how far communist parties in democratic systems may adopt practical ideology. A degree of aloofness from the taint of 'bourgeois' multiparty politics helps preserve the integrity of their 'pure' ideology. In view of the challenges of post-communism it was unsurprising that many post-Soviet communists preferred to confine themselves to an ideological niche at the possible expense of electoral marginalisation – such were the strategies of the radical communist groups in Russia and parties such as the Czech CPBM.

Historically, when communist parties sought to engage in electoral politics they did so through the use of fronts and blocs, which potentially allowed them to extend their electorate without tainting their 'pure' ideology.[9] As will be seen, the CPRF's strategy was similar. The party tried to balance both logics. Its more realistic moderates sought to move beyond a niche position to recapture at least a part of its former hegemony, and thus increasingly adopted a 'logic of electoral competition'. Simultaneously the CPRF sought not to abandon completely either its core constituency or its ideological heritage. The key strategy adopted by the CPRF in balancing these potentially contradictory logics was a revival of the 'national front strategy', with which, as a lifelong party propagandist, Zyuganov was clearly familiar. In both form and language this derived from the anti-fascist fronts used from 1942 onwards by the Comintern, the national communist ideology of the Great Patriotic War, and the electoral front strategies of the Western European communist parties after the war. The common thread linking these earlier models was the attempt to downplay ideological differences to unite disparate class forces against a common enemy.[10] The crucial difference in the CPRF's adaptation of this strategy was the extent to which it developed a separate practical 'public' ideology to cement the national patriotic front, which contrasted and conflicted with its pure 'party' ideology designed for internal party purposes, and resulted in two contradictory, intertwined, though analytically distinct, ideologies side by side.

The distinction between these 'public' and 'party' ideologies is hard to overstate. It is missed by many commentators, and yet is one maintained by party members themselves. Of the two ideologies, it is that expressed in the party programme which is considered the basis of the party's activity and a statement of its main strategic tasks.[11] It is not considered an electoral document, but an objective long-term evaluation of the political situation. The public ideology in contrast was designed explicitly to reinvent the communist idea for public consumption and the non-communist electorate. This is the ideology which appeared in Gennadii Zyuganov's writings, the electoral platforms of the various national-patriotic blocs from the National Salvation Front of 1992 to the National-Patriotic Union of Russia (NPUR) of 1996 and the CPRF's electoral platforms. As its chief proponent Zyuganov was fulfilling a specific task, delegated by the CPRF leadership to seek new allies and broaden alliances in the public sphere, particularly among the nationalist electorate.[12] This agreed division of labour explained why even when Zyuganov publicly expressed opinions which conflicted with the party programme, party members would consider them tactically expedient if they strengthened party authority. However, this division of labour was still contentious and the marked tendency of the public ideology to take priority over and interfere with the party ideology as the CPRF participated in electoral politics will become apparent.

Developing a new ideology of statehood

What were the chief features of this public ideology? The most commentated upon factor in was the move away from class as the main subject of politics towards 'civilisation', encompassing both state and nation (though not solely nation, as we shall see). There were two main factors behind this move from Marxist-Leninist orthodoxy towards a form of national bolshevism. First, as it often was in the Soviet era, national bolshevism could be used to justify many of the same de facto goals as communism, such as state power, anti-liberalism and collectivism, but from a different *nationalist* perspective, thereby maximising alternative sources of support while minimising ideological compromise. Hence the continued ideological contortions made by the CPRF to court nationalists rather than democrats or democratic socialists. The change was thus not a vast leap and followed the pattern of ideological change in times of ideological crisis. In order to salvage something from the ideological wreckage, formerly subordinate elements of ideology come to the fore to replace what was previously considered central.[13]

Second, the communists' ideological defensiveness aided the shift. Many of the moderates accepted that the pre-1985 system was in need of reform, and were fully aware of the crisis in ideology there-after.[14] Orthodox Marxist-Leninists such as Ivan Polozkov and Egor Ligachev, who had affirmed the need to remain 'profoundly faithful to Party ideology', and stressed the vitality of the class struggle and internationalism in the late 1980s found no answer to state and party collapse.[15] The universalist, supra-national and futuristic elements of Marxism-Leninism offered few solutions to national crisis, and were increasingly deemed insufficient by figures in the Soviet hierarchy who tacitly sidelined and replaced the increasingly discredited communist ideology with a new Russian nationalism to re-legitimise their own rule. Nationalists like Aleksandr Prokhanov and Sergei Kurginyan advocated harnessing the spiritual potential of the Orthodox Church and turning communism into a 'meta-religion', the latter proposing a draft CPSU programme which essentially rejected Marxism.[16] The Russian national-patriots themselves found a voice and rediscovered their tradition in the *perestroika* years. Just as in the Great Patriotic War, it is unsurprising that the discourse of emotional patriotism, tradition, reverence for the state and national defence against hostile surrounding forces was deemed to have a more potent mobilising and unifying effect than orthodox Marxism-Leninism.[17]

In the aftermath of the Soviet Union's collapse such trends could only continue. Communist ideas were fighting for legal survival in the Constitutional Court. National separatism and final state collapse were real threats. In these circumstances, most of the ideological mileage was made by the national-patriots, and even for more ortho-dox communists, it was a case of ignoring nationalism at their peril. Extreme ideological defensiveness was apparent early on. In late 1991, Zyuganov and his close colleague, Yurii Belov, were the first high-ranking RCP members to admit publicly the need to radically rejuvenate communism by ample doses of patriotism.[18] They argued that communists had made major mistakes and were under an obli-gation to 'morally rehabilitate themselves' before society, to cede ideo-logical ground to the national patriots because of the discrediting of their own ideology, and to form a new union of democracy, the Russian idea and socialism.[19]

From the outset, the Communists did not have a monopoly on this public ideology and sometimes played a junior role. Although Zyuganov was undoubtedly its most high-profile proponent, the cross-fertilisation of ideas between him and his closest colleagues in the national-patriotic front was extensive. The production of the 'public ideology' was a collegiate process during which Zyuganov admitted he was on a learning curve, his association with patriots opening his eyes to many lacunae in traditional Marxism-Leninism, such as its omission of patriotism.[20] Prokhanov and the editorial team of the national-patriotic newspaper, *Den* (later *Zavtra*), played a prominent role in this process, befriending Zyuganov in the aftermath of the August 1991 coup and appearing to co-write some of Zyuganov's earlier work such as his 1994 book *Derzhava*.[21]

While Prokhanov was a major organisational and ideological link between the communists and patriots, finding a place in the leadership of most of the influential national-patriotic groups in which the communists took part, more influential still was the role of Aleksei Podberezkin, head of the national-patriotic analytical group Spiritual Heritage and a close confidant of Zyuganov until 1999. Podberezkin, contrary to many accounts, was *not* a CPRF ideologist. He was not even a party member, having left in 1990, and claimed not to 'make any pretence at forming the CPRF's policy'.[22] Rather his brief was entirely with the production of the 'public ideology', and the aim of 'Spiritual Heritage' (set up with Zyuganov during 1994–95) was to further the CPRF's contacts with the patriotic movement, and explicitly to persuade the non-communist electorate that Zyuganov was a genuine patriot.[23] His co-operation with Zyuganov dated from immediately after the August coup, when he helped organise Zyuganov's entry into national-patriotic groups. He was included on the CPRF party list for the parliamentary elections of 1995 to appeal to the national-patriotic electorate. In return for support given by the CPRF, Spiritual Heritage helped the CPRF in analysis and organisation.[24] Podberezkin's influence extended to speech-writing for Zyuganov and being a major organiser of the 1996 NPUR.

This close relationship between Zyuganov and Podberezkin caused many problems. Like previous experiences of communist 'entrism' into 'fronts', one of the key tensions caused by the CPRF's public ideology was between the needs of the party and those of the wider bloc.[25] While Zyuganov was always keen to stress the compatibility of his public views with the communist outlook, Podberezkin was much less careful of party feelings. He described himself as a 'democratic patriot', and denied he was a communist, saying he subscribed to little of the CPRF party programme or rules.[26] Unlike Zyuganov, Podberezkin saw the future as belonging neither to capitalism nor communism, and saw communism as merely one (and not the defining one) of the components of a new synthesis of democracy and authoritarianism, capitalism and socialism, national uniqueness and even pan-human values.[27] He (once more unlike Zyuganov) declared himself a Russian Orthodox believer, and insisted on the primacy of spiritual values over material.[28]

Yet there was much mutual exchange of ideas between Podberezkin and Zyuganov, which resulted in Podberezkin's poor relationship with most CPRF leaders, who saw him as a meddler with dubious intentions towards their party and its ideology, even casting a spell over the leader.[29] Many of the radicals saw him as an obvious *éminence grise* acting in the interests of the Yeltsin regime.[30] However, Podberezkin's role should not be overstated – he was as used by Zyuganov as he used him. Podberezkin was useful not just as an ideological ally, but as a non-party figure who could deflect much criticism that would otherwise be aimed at Zyuganov, and who was to take much of the blame for reversals in policy during 1996–98.

Nevertheless, evidence for the allegation that the allies of the party rather than the party itself set the agenda of the public ideology was not hard to find. During their 'learning process', Zyuganov and Belov, the other major propagandist of public ideology, increasingly departed from traditional Marxist-Leninist theories, arguing that class could not encompass all of the features of contemporary society, and must be supplemented by awareness of the role of national specifics in politics (the so-called 'cultural-historical' approach).[31] But in the party's view such a strategy had to remain instrumental. New approaches could supplement but not simply replace Marxism-Leninism. That Zyuganov stressed the 'cultural-historical approach' over Marxism now was not to preclude him returning to Marxism to deal with a different historical situation in future.[32] The tensions caused by maintaining this delicate balance were to infuse much of the party's behaviour.

Refilling the ideological gap

The ideology of the national-patriotic front encapsulated a hegemonic project in the Gramscian sense. It was a battle of ideas and values attempting to gain power through a 'war of position' against liberal ideology through a mixture of cultural indoctrination, persuasion and consent.[33] The ultimate (though often denied) aspiration was to refill the 'ideological vacuum' vacated by state socialism. In Zyuganov's view, the state could not live without an ideology as the essential orientation for its citizens.[34] Zyuganov seemed fully aware of the need to fill the vacuum fast before Russia's choice of Westernisation and liberal democracy became final.[35] Throughout, this showed itself to be a conservative ideological project. Zyuganov sought to conserve past traditions but, aware of some of the flaws in these traditions, he sought a 'new' ideology that simultaneously preserved historical continuity.[36]

The search for new allies was paramount. This arose originally out of sheer necessity in the face of state collapse. Attention focused initially in healing the rifts solely among the anti-democratic anti-Western opposition which had perennially hampered alliance against a common enemy in the Gorbachev era, and the cause of national-patriotic unity to overcome the historical schism of 'reds' and anti-communist 'whites' was taken up by many of the national-patriots in 1991. Propounded by Zyuganov most vociferously of all, this theme became one of the central tenets of the myriad new nationalist groups during 1992–93, including the self-professed 'United Opposition' of March 1992 and its successor the NSF. Yet also implicit from an early stage were Zyuganov's hegemonic ambitions – to 'reideologise' society *as a whole* and to collect under the wing of this new ideology 'all Russian people who believe Russia their motherland'.[37] This was only feasible when elections in 1993 made it possible for patriotic ideas to be propounded to new audiences, after which the national-patriotic front increasingly became an electoral strategy as well as an ideological one.

In attempting to provide a platform for national unity and reach out to new constituencies, the communists had to achieve three tasks simultaneously: to provide consensus over the new values and ideas around which people might unite, to reinvent communism in popular perception and thus 'morally rehabilitate' it, and to discredit the liberal democratic challenge. The first aim of national interclass consensus was repeatedly emphasised not just by the stress on overcoming historical schisms between reds and whites, but also by Zyuganov's declaration that 'Russia has had enough revolutionary upheavals'.[38] This was coupled with a declared preference for constitutional methods of reaching power and the calling for a 'government of national trust' based on common national goals. The major concept offered by Zyuganov and Belov to achieve this consensus was the concept of 'state patriotism' at whose core was the idea that state interests take precedence over all individual, ideological, class, religious and ethnic interests in the face of national crisis. In a radical departure from classical Marxism, the state was seen not as an instrument of class supremacy, but as the cradle of Russian civilisation throughout history, the 'machine of survival' without which it could not survive.[39] State patriotism had a dual focus. For the benefit of traditional communist supporters it was implicitly identified as a new version of Soviet patriotism which 'recognises the Soviet form of statehood as answering Russian traditions'.[40] Yet it was simultaneously defined as *Russian* patriotism, whose aim was to provide non-communists and even anticommunists, particularly among management and national entrepreneurs, the security of living within a strong peaceful state. In this sense it was a neutral supra-class concept able to unify a wide variety of social groups.[41] National organic unity and interclass accord were further stressed by the invocation of *Rodina* (Motherland) and *dukhovnost* (spirituality) as the emotional responses linking individuals indelibly to the state.[42] Finally, the replacement of the class approach by the 'cultural-historical approach' was justified on the grounds of national unification, although class analysis was still considered relevant for examining socio-economic questions and for its critique of capitalism.[43]

One important corollary of 'state patriotism' was the reinterpretation of Russian and Soviet history to incorporate the so-called 'continuity thesis', asserting that the 1917 revolution brought no break in Russia's thousand-year history of statehood and harmonious empire which reached its apogee through communism.[44] Equally heretically for Leninists, communism was only the most perfect expression of Russia's national and cultural traditions of community and national solidarity.[45] Communism thus became statehood, not some Bolshevik 'experiment' that could be derided as a historical aberration.[46]

The moral rehabilitation of communism was achieved in several ways. Much was made of the way the Communist Party had changed. It had accepted pluralism, multipartism and private property. It supported 'national capital', was no longer a ruling party and publicly promised not regime change or revenge but, rather stability and an end to corruption.[47] Most notable of all was Zyuganov's attitude to religion. He repeatedly stressed that the CPRF had repudiated militant atheism and repression, and was open for believers to enter without restriction.[48] To some degree this was merely exploitation of the religious vote for electoral gain, and designed as symbolism that, by tolerating those it formerly persecuted, the communists had

repented of former mistakes. Indeed, Zyuganov's defence of the
Church against the 'corrosive influence' of foreign sects, and promises
that the state would protect the 'traditional religions' were blatant
attempts to reassure the concerns of believers and reflect the current
fears of the Church.[49] Zyuganov's use of spiritual and religious
themes indeed reached its apogee in the 1996 election campaign.

However, a more extensive reinvention of communist ideology
itself was also under way, inspired by Prokhanov and Kurginyan's
ideas of a 'meta-religion'. For Zyuganov, too, communism was no
longer a materialistic but a religious and spiritual phenomenon. The
fantastic lengths to which Zyuganov went to accommodate Orthodoxy as an essential component of the Russian Idea looked at times
like the 'theologisation' of socialism.[50] Such an ideological synthesis
of Orthodoxy and communism derived directly from Zyuganov's
attempts to unite 'red' and 'white' and merge the statist and cultural
traditions in Russophile thought. Accordingly the key components of
Zyuganov's modern Russian Idea were on the one hand the values of
gosudarstvennost and *derzhavnost* (both of which can roughly be translated as 'state-ness' and imply Great Power status under a powerful
state apparatus), and on the other the spiritual-religious values of *dukhovnost* and *sobornost* (conciliarism) derived from the nineteenth-
century cultural nationalist thinkers such as the Slavophiles, which
define man as a collectivist being able to live in 'symphonic' unity
with the state, and which idolise harmony and vilify division.[51] Like
the Slavophiles, Zyuganov made Orthodoxy central to Russian identity and the embodiment of the values that distinguished it from the
West, along with the other 'traditional religions', Buddhism and
Islam. These religions, he said, embodied spiritual and collectivist
values rather than the consumerist and individualist values promoted
by Western religions.[52] This was little more than lip-service to the
other religions, for it was clear that Orthodoxy expressed Russia's
motivating idea throughout history, and would be the key value of a
revived USSR based upon the core 'religious unity' of the three Slavic
nations.[53] As such it could mobilise and unify Slavs beyond their new
national borders.

However, Zyuganov used Orthodoxy in a very instrumental
way. Not accidentally, he cited the slogan of the nineteenth-century
arch-conservative Count Uvarov of 'Orthodoxy, Autocracy and
Nationality' as the 'invariant' of Russian state development.[54] This
demonstrated that Zyuganov supported Orthodoxy not because it

reflected national identity per se, but because it had historically strengthened statehood, empire, unity and order.[55] Similarly he used another favoured historical slogan, that of Moscow as the 'Third Rome', implying the interdependence of Russian statehood and Orthodoxy and that the Church had been instrumental in stabilising the state and bestowing unity upon the empire.[56] Like Uvarov, Zyuganov recognised that religious morality, altruism and traditions could foster impulses both towards internal spiritual strength and the national unity necessary for healing a fractured nation. This supplemented 'state patriotism', by bestowing upon the state quasi-religious qualities as the supra-individual entity which was the ultimate repository of the nation.

But Zyuganov went much further. He asserted openly that, having compared the Bible and communist moral code, Christianity and the socialist ethic fully coincided because of their innate collectivism, altruism and concern with morality and social justice. He even declared that Christ was the first communist.[57] Communism was 'secular Christianity' and Zyuganov confessed that he respected figures such as Mohammed and Buddha as much as he did Lenin.[58] There was a purpose to such contortions. Ultimately, the reconciliation with religion was to reinforce the communism = state = nation = tradition matrix at every turn. It aimed to bridge the gap with 'white' anticommunist nationalists and to use religious emotional and spiritual community to rekindle national solidarity against perceived crisis and humiliation, even from among its former enemies. In the process, the conservative revolution was complete. Communism was offered not as the harbinger of a brighter future through the materialist interpretation of history, but because it was in every way a national tradition.

Discrediting liberalism was neatly done through the 'two parties–two countries' thesis. This described the history of the CPSU as the interaction between a party of 'true patriots' believing in 'our country' (the workers, peasants, military, national capitalists and intelligentsia, and Soviet heroes such as Marshal Zhukov and Yurii Gagarin) and a party of 'national betrayal' who allegedly saw Russia only as 'that country' and served outside enemies. To this party the usual suspects (Gorbachev, Yeltsin, the 'comprador' capitalists and pro-Western intelligentsia) were demoted, along with villains such as Trotsky and Beria.[59] In Zyuganov's thinking, the 'that country' party had been organising a plot against Russia in cahoots with the West since at least Khrushchev's time. The use of such conspiracy theories had its logic, conveniently transferring the blame for any crimes and failures committed under communism from the 'true patriots' and the USSR's own institutional weaknesses to visible and controversial figures, thus purporting to explain the apparently inexplicable collapse, and recalling Stalinist conspiratorial thinking. Similarly, Belov's equation of bourgeois liberalism with Trotskyism, and Zyuganov's constant attacks on the 'anti-national regime', 'comprador Mafia-capital' and 'genocide' of the current regime tapped the same vein of Manichaean language.[60]

Zyuganov's multitudinous determinist geopolitical tracts further played on the feelings of national insecurity of a people surrounded by hostile enemies. These name-checked a mix of sources whose main aim was to demonstrate Zyuganov as a profound thinker. So use of the Eurasianist Lev Gumilev's term 'ethnos' or the pan-Slavist Nikolai Danilevskii's term 'cultural-historical type' to describe Russia legitimised the replacement of class as a motor of history. The inherently antagonistic nature of international relations was described by references to Samuel Huntington's 'clash of civilisations.' Western culture, religion and values were thereby seen as an independent organism, the eternal enemy to Russia since the religious schism between Orthodoxy and Catholicism in 1054.[61] Now they were seen as reaching a new stage of global dictatorship through the 'New World Order' whose aim was to achieve global Western hegemony and foist its values on a weakened Russia through a 'fifth column' of 'agents of influence'. References to the geopolitics of Oswald Spengler, Arnold Toynbee and Halford Mackinder further reinforced the antithesis of Russian culture and history to that of the West.[62] Civilisations were seen to have their own 'sphere of influence' and avoidance of global conflict might only be kept by a 'balance of interests' which left Russia to a self-sufficient role as hegemony in the Eurasian landmass, free from Western and especially American interference.[63] Russia's position as the 'heartland' of Eurasia doomed it to have a central role as 'geopolitical pivot' of a region with whose culture and history it had most in common.[64]

In sum, all of these eclectic sources and concepts are mutually reinforcing, and their combined thrust is clear: the differences between 'cultural-historical types' such as the 'Western' and 'Orthodox-Slavic' are not minor, but 'civilisational'. Zyuganov followed the nineteenth-century *narodniki* (peasant revolutionaries) in seeing the Russian people as bearers of their own unique qualities – a folkish nationalism (*narodnost*), religious *sobornost*, devotion to the state (*derzhavnost*) and predisposition to socialist justice.[65] In contrast Western individualism, rationalism, culture, institutions and economics were deeply alien to Russian collective traditions, and their imposition could only cause 'genocide'. In Zyuganov's thinking, it was the Western cultural heritage, not communism that was the unhistorical 'experiment'.[66] Much could be made of the essential incoherence of an eclectic programme which draws on such an immense array of sources.[67] For example, where are Lenin and Stalin in the 'two-party' scheme?[68] Moreover, if as Zyuganov argued, the structures of the Soviet state were so viable and organically rooted in popular consciousness, how could even a well-planned conspiracy manage to dismantle them? This incoherence was not necessarily a disadvantage. Like the most effective mobilising ideologies, this spoke in eschatological absolutes which had the virtue of their very simplicity, and appealed to 'ideals, dreams and the heart's impulses' rather than 'reason . . . or sober calculation'.[69] The West was effectively demonised by reference to all of the phantoms of nationalist paranoia, and its values denied a foothold on Russian soil. In contrast, Russia already had the strength to repel them and real, national communist traditions with which to replace them.

The CPRF's party ideology

Programmatic development, 1993–95

It was one thing for Zyuganov to propound these ideas in public and as part of the national-patriotic front (as he did more concretely in articles and books from 1992 onwards), another to sell them to his party.[70] The period 1993–95 marked the formative phase of the CPRF in which internal party debates were extremely controversial. The Second Congress of February 1993 had achieved little more than the physical unity of the party, and defining the organisation's political profile was left open. The 1993 Congress had resulted in moderate statist-patriotic communists and Marxist reformers dominating the leadership, while it adopted an eclectic and all-inclusive interim programme aimed at maximising communist unity. Plan and market, patriotism and internationalism were linked, and the party voiced its commitment to freedom, humanism and the rights of human beings, while voicing its adherence to Marxist-Leninist dialectic.[71] In line with historical tradition, a full theoretical analysis of the prevailing political situation was thought essential to orientate the party, and its the absence was seen as a serious deficit.

The intricate developments of the evolution of party doctrinal debates in this period are most persuasively described by Urban and Solovei, although they underplay the moderate–radical split and their concentration on the theoretical arguments of 1993–95 masks deeper disputes about the CPRF's relation to its heritage and to the prevailing political system.[72] However, they are surely right (contrary to Devlin, who sees little difference between Zyuganov's views and the final party programme) to note that the main development in this period was an attempted theoretical renewal of the party launched by the statist-patriotic communists (principally Zyuganov and Belov, who became party ideological secretary after the Second Congress), culminating in the new party programme at the party's Third Congress in January 1995.[73] In the process, Marxist-Leninist modernisers reasserted their position and Zyuganov's ideas underwent continued dilution.

A parallel process was that by which the moderates sought to consolidate their control over the party and reorientate it towards the new political system with an explicitly electoral aim. After the April 1993 referendum and violence in the May Day 1993 demonstrations the leadership began to embrace constitutionalism and non-violence as means in themselves. Simultaneously, they started to acknowledge their weakness among their traditional working-class constituency – workers were inactive, divided and eroding as their social base. Thus the need to attract new strata was stressed repeatedly by many leaders.[74] Given that some successes for the communists in regional elections in 1993 had shown that free elections (unlike in the late Gorbachev period) were not to be feared, ideological renewal was closely linked to becoming electorally competitive. Leaders argued that the current political rules, even if 'foisted from without', had to be turned to the communists' advantage, and that simultaneous parliamentary and presidential elections could even offer a path out of the executive-legislative gridlock which convulsed the country.[75]

Accordingly, the policy taking shape in both electoral platforms and the discussion of the new programme was based on state patriotism to attract non-communists (patriots, national capitalists, the middle class and even democrats).[76] Zyuganov stressed the inability of Marxism-Leninism to answer the problems of the day, and advocated new contributions to socialist theory.[77] The national-patriotic front was now to become an electoral bloc aimed at 'all citizens' with the CPRF at its core.[78] After electoral victory the bloc would form a power-sharing 'government of national trust' as the first step in the return of socialism. The aim of power-sharing in a bloc of sympathetic national-patriotic forces because of the communists' own electoral weakness became the enduring theme of the CPRF's electoral strategy. Power was to be sought peacefully and constitutionally, and the CPRF's near-term aims were to be modest, with a mixed economy preferred to the Soviet command economy, which communists admitted had been 'super-centralised' and bureaucratic.[79]

The most controversial attempts at theoretical renewal involved Zyuganov's insistence on Russia's cultural-historical continuity and uniqueness, and his elaboration of the concept of ecologically balanced 'sustainable development'. This concept was presented as a major innovation but was clearly inspired by a United Nations (UN) environment conference in Rio de Janeiro in 1992, which argued that environmental concerns were a necessity for the economic prosperity of all.[80] Zyuganov gave this concept a distinct anti-capitalist twist. He argued that the practices of advanced industrial economies were not just environmentally damaging but both enslaved the 'golden billion' (rich Westerners) in the first world to the ideals of consumerism and created a wider geopolitical chasm between this 'golden billion' and the exploited world periphery who were being coerced into capitalist development. This concept was intended to reinforce Zyuganov's concept of a necessary world 'balance of interests' between national and global development. Yet this direct appropriation of a 'bourgeois' concept and its description of exploitation as a geopolitical and not socio-economic phenomenon proved too contentious for many in the party.[81]

Indeed, the leadership was forced to backtrack in the face of increased dissent from the party base right up to the party programmatic commission, where the theoreticians Richard Kosolapov and Boris Slavin provided coherent rebuttals of state patriotism from a Marxist perspective, rebuttals echoed by many party critics since. They argued that in Marxist terms the state could not be a neutral supra-class phenomenon and always implied the dictatorial ambitions of the ruling class.[82] The priority of cultural-historical factors over an internationalist social-class perspective implied the loss of critical and theoretical distance from a bourgeois state for whom social-class oppression was the most significant policy, and thereby the acceptance of capitalism by the back door![83] Slavin's criticism of Zyuganov was all the more significant since he was no dogmatist, but an anti-Stalinist, anti-bureaucratic democratic socialist, who produced a well-publicised open letter against Zyuganov and repeatedly clashed with him and Belov in private.[84] Radicals in the party and outside weighed in, accusing the party of theoretical heresy, of drifting towards parliamentary politics and losing its role as the 'vanguard' of class consciousness.[85]

The CPRF responded by quoting ideologically correct precedents for its tactics, such as Lenin's New Economic Policy and Stalin's policies in the Great Patriotic War.[86] But they were forced to appease criticism, not just because the deteriorating socio-economic situation in Russia and imminent parliamentary election campaign of 1995 demanded a more militant opposition riposte, but because of peculiarities in the CPRF's internal structure and culture which proved of longer significance. As a response both to the RCP's origins as a rank-and-file reaction against the *nomenklatura*, and to the enforced loss of leadership control over the rank and file during 1991–93, the CPRF insisted that it was an internally democratic party, rejecting the schism between leaders and led that was the experience of *perestroika*.[87] The deference to the rank and file was reinforced by an attachment to the Marxist notion of ideology as a reflection of objective social tendencies not dependent on individual ideologists themselves. So 'there [was] no official party ideologist', and Zyuganov was merely 'first among equals'.[88] Indeed, all party members had the right to contribute proposals to the leadership, whose ability to reach the party programme depended only on whether they accurately reflected the concrete socio-economic situation.[89] Party members were thus the 'collective ideologist', contributing proposals for the programme through constant consultation and debate and regular formal 'report and election' campaigns where the party base's concerns were put to the leadership. Although the party leadership maintained a role in co-ordinating the ideological process (and sought to strengthen this over time), this 'hyper-democratic centralism' led to a long-term reversal of the past balance of forces within the party to favour the membership in the ideological process.

In the evolution of the 1995 programme, the pressure the party rank and file put on the leadership to take a more purist Marxist-Leninist line during mutual consultations was intensified by the fact that the leadership was consulting its membership en masse for the first time since before 1991. The leaders found that the membership wanted them to 'make up the theoretical deficit', strengthen the 'class content of communist ideology' and avoid 'social democratism' in evaluating such questions as the role of revolution and religion.[90] This was compounded by the apparently autonomous formation of the leftist society, Russian Scholars of Socialist Orientation (RSSO), in October 1994, with the express aim of developing modern scholarly work on socialism. This society comprised the Marxist tendencies within and outside the party, predominately but not exclusively Marxist-Leninist modernisers (such as its leaders Ivan Osadchii and Richard Kosolapov).[91] Hence it amplified the propagandist and organisational role of the left-wing theoreticians in programmatic debates, directly pressurising the leadership to take these into account in the programmes of 1995 and 1997.

So, the party debates of 1993–95 had already signposted difficulties the CPRF was to have in adapting to its new political situation. In addition to the divisions between ideological tendencies within the party was a split over the very role of ideology. What the moderate leaders were doing implied a controversial movement away from pure to practical ideology. They recognised that external constraints and opportunities forced them increasingly towards a 'logic of electoral competition' (vote maximisation) and the search for non-communist allies. This was evidence of a pragmatic acceptance of the status quo which postponed socialist restoration, while pro-Soviet 'state patriotism' was designed to legitimise this choice to their core supporters. Yet Zyuganov's simultaneous insistence on putting state patriotism into the party's internal documents meant that practical and pure ideology, public ideology and party ideology were becoming intertwined. Tactical and ideological change were intrinsically interlinked. Radical critics alleged that by orientating the party towards parliamentary politics, and allying with nationalists (the 'national bourgeoisie') even on a temporary basis, Zyuganov implied that 'the most pressing tasks of party are bourgeois democratic' and not socialist.[92] They preferred doctrinal purity to tactical flexibility and a 'logic of constituency representation' aimed at the party's historic class constituency, even at the risk of losing long-term influence.

And what of the 1995 programme? It was, admittedly a 'compromise',[93] and was markedly more 'orthodox' than the earlier drafts. Zyuganov and Belov's ideas suffered significant reverses. For instance, the notion of the party being the 'party of state patriotism', and the phrase 'state patriotism' itself did not appear, rather 'developing Marxism Leninism' and 'dialectical materialism' were reaffirmed as its guiding stars.[94] The equation of the Soviet Union with Great Russia was one of the key sections scrubbed from the final draft. Crucially, Zyuganov's thesis of 'an end to revolutions' was rebutted by the assertion that revolutions were the 'locomotive of history'. The 'leftward' tilt was further reaffirmed by continual stress on the socialist content of patriotism. At the same time, the ideas of the Marxist reformers (the trend most prone to allegations of 'Gorbachevism' or social democratism', although prevalent in the upper echelons) suffered most attrition – references to humanism and multipartism present in earlier drafts were absent, there was no mention of NEP and criticisms of Stalinism were removed, though commitments to rights and freedoms were retained.[95]

Overall the influence of orthodox ideas was clearest in the socio-economic sphere. The conflict between capitalism and socialism as a geopolitical phenomenon was toned down and buttressed by a reaffirmation of the economic injustices of capitalism and its exploitative nature. Support for a mixed economy was barely registered except in the first stage of a three-stage transition to socialism, to which stage collaboration with national-patriots and the 'government of national trust' was confined. The final stage was now explicitly defined with direct reference to Lenin as a 'classless society' free of exploitation and scientifically planned. The predominance of orthodox ideas was not absolute, showing the programme's somewhat eclectic nature. There was no mention of class struggle, and many of Zyuganov's ideas did make the grade. These were diluted but, along with a theoretical examination of the contemporary socio-economic situation, couched in a theoretical perspective and language more palatable to the orthodox. Thus Russocentric values were identified with more Soviet terminology. For instance, *derzhavnost* was described vaguely as 'the connection of individual, society and state', and *sobornost* was explicitly identified with collectivism. While patriotism and internationalism were espoused, the statist-patriotic line achieved its vindication with statements that the USSR was geopolitical heir to the Russian empire (implying the continuity thesis), and that socialism and the Russian idea were indelibly linked.

The main feature of the new programme was its militant and wide-ranging attack on all things capitalist. Starting with a searing attack on the Yeltsin regime for returning Russia to primitive barbaric capitalism, provoking military conflicts and reducing its population, it accused the regime of turning the country into a 'raw materials appendage', and leading the proletarianisation of the country. There followed a renunciation of capitalist development in its entirety, declaring that the conflict between capitalism and socialism was far from over. The exploitative nature of capitalism was reaffirmed with its aspiration to 'turn everything into a good' and consumer society was accused of deforming the personality. Finally, the global nature of capitalist destruction was detailed with a reference to 'sustainable development' as the only choice available to the world if it was to avoid division into the 'golden billion' and exploited periphery. Concomitant with this was a eulogy to Soviet achievements such as industrialisation and collectivisation. Even compared with earlier drafts, the admissions of past mistakes were few, with the deformations of state socialism attributed mainly to the 'petit-bourgeois' and 'careerists'. Zyuganov's 'two parties – two countries' thesis took pride of place, with Gorbachev *et al.* branded as traitors with personal responsibility for breaking up the country.

Rejection of the post-1991 order was further reinforced when it came to concrete proposals. The 'party of national treachery' was to be removed by a 'national liberation struggle' using both parliamentary and non-parliamentary methods. Whereas most of the document concerned itself with theoretical and strategic tasks, the 'programme minimum' set out broad general parameters of what the party would do if it won an election. These included denunciation of the Belovezha accords by which Yeltsin and the leaders of Belarus and Ukraine had finally announced the end of the USSR in December 1991, and the replacement of the 'anti-popular constitution' of 1993 and its presidential form of government with a Soviet-style constitution introducing a parliamentary republic, a system of soviets and 'popular power'. In the economic field, the promises were clearer, even if the means were not: state regulation of the 'commanding heights' of the economy after nationalisation of the banks, with the predominance of social forms of ownership – private ownership of land was expressly forbidden, with the ultimate aim social ownership and the collectivisation of labour led by the working class. Other proposals showed the pre-eminence of politics over economics. All welfare guarantees were to be kept, while people were to be compensated for losses in the liberation of prices undertaken by the Gaidar government in 1992.

All in all, what this amounted to was an eclectic mix of the least contentious elements of the various party positions which allowed adherents of most diverse positions to find at least something in it. For Zyuganov the result was equivocal – his ideas were not so much defeated as qualified and compromise was found. Boris Slavin claimed 30 per cent of party support for his position but in the event 95 per cent of the leaders' positions were supported at the Congress.[96] The programme had the further benefit of rebutting the radical communist accusations of social democratisation and presenting a united, aggressive façade.[97] Moreover, it was sufficiently declaratory, long term and vague to allow the leadership some leeway in defining tactics. Yet, according to Slavin, it was party unity not ideological conviction which lay behind such support for the leadership.[98] So major disagreements were blurred rather than resolved, and no coherent vision shared by all party members appeared. Significantly, the balance of elements in the programme proved that Zyuganov was unable to convince party members unambiguously to endorse the main thrust of his new line, that the vital current conflict was not between classes but between the 'compradors' – ruling regimes relying on a narrow stratum of bureaucracy and foreign capital – and the rest of the population. So the rationale of the national-patriotic bloc and compromise with bourgeois nationalists and capitalists remained contentious. The programme thus represented a delicate balance of different positions, while unresolved ideological questions remained potential running sores which might flare up if ideological debate was renewed.

Ideological stasis, 1995–99

From 1995 to 1999 many of these big questions appeared to have been 'frozen' rather than resolved, and debate focused largely on tactical questions. The Fifth Congress of May 1998 concentrated on strengthening party unity and the Sixth Congress (held in two stages in September 1999 and January 2000) concerned itself with the ongoing election campaigns. Neither dealt with doctrinal issues. Such a shift from doctrinal to tactical debate was enforced by the CPRF's gradual engagement in parliamentary and electoral politics, which increased its incentive to operate according to 'practical ideology'. The party increasingly sought to keep its tactics and ideological approach more flexible, and disengage ideology from its every action. The wide-ranging ideological debate of 1993–95 became a luxury it could no longer afford.

However, balancing the strategic and ideological aims of the programme and the tactical aims of party platforms proved extremely
problematic. From 1995 onwards the party increasingly said totally
different things to its core membership and wider electorate, and tensions between party and public ideology became ever more apparent,
giving increasing incoherence to the party's public profile, and initiating an internal ideological crisis. For example, the platform for the parliamentary election in 1995 made no reference at all to socialism or
Marxism-Leninism, and only referred to the existence of a separate
and recently adopted party programme in passing.[99] The platform's
goals, such as a government of national trust and the mixed economy
were relatively moderate compared with the party programme. Yet all
of these goals were contained within the initial 'bourgeois-democratic'
phase of the three-stage transition to socialism contained in that programme. The programme and platform would thus signify utterly different things to a committed party member (hoping for an eventual
resurrection of communism) and a non-communist voter who might
identify with the conservative nostalgia of the platform but little else.

Later electoral platforms of the national-patriotic bloc diverged
from the party programme still more markedly, with populist patriotism dominating and no mention of programmatic aims such as socialism, restoration of the USSR or nationalisation. For example,
Zyuganov's 1996 presidential election platform made much of his
adherence to patriotic notions such as *sobornost*, yet failed to mention
the existence of the CPRF at all.[100] The platform of the NPUR, the
national-patriotic coalition formed around the CPRF in August 1996,
emphasised a centrist conservative patriotism, with moderate goals
such as 'welfarism' and 'collectivist values' replacing any mention of
socialism.[101]

The potential for discrepancy between public and party faces
might always be present in a programmatic party, but was intensified
in the CPRF's case, with a separate party programme endorsed by full
membership participation and electoral platforms (which were sometimes, but not always put to party discussion) fully endorsed by so
few.[102] The increasing tendency for the leaders to prioritise public
ideology became especially marked after the communists' electoral
defeat of 1996, when the CPRF leadership spoke of updating the party
both programmatically and ideologically. Party documents at this time
largely confined themselves to seeking a more constructive position
towards the government and, since this was controversial enough, did

not explicitly mention ideological change. Yet this aim remained. Zyuganov published a new book, *Rossiya – rodina moya* (Russia – My Motherland), in which he indulged further in revisionism, admitting the obsolescence of standard tenets of Marxism such as the theories of dictatorship of the proletariat and proletarian revolution, and sought to draw on patriotic and social democratic thought.[103] His rhetoric became much more forward orientated than hitherto, and he started to demand, albeit obliquely, that the CPRF re-examine its ideological heritage.[104] Kuptsov, with a more marked left-democratic orientation, talked of the CPRF becoming a 'modern party of socialist orientation'.[105] Both main party leaders several times called for a comprehensive review of party documents in reaction to the defeat in 1996.[106] However muted, the public emphasis on social democracy was new and followed directly from the 1996 campaign, where Zyuganov used social democratic themes patchily in an attempt to dispel the prevailing climate of anti-communism. However opportunistic, this showed the party leaders trying to change party policy in line with electoral fortune like a genuine electoral party.

However, such a process was not lost on the party, and resulted in a gradual backlash from those who sought a more restrictive 'scientific' ideology. Chief of these was RSSO, which sought to arrogate to itself the position occupied by the ideological apparatus in Soviet times at the summit of party power, inextricably linked to all political decisions and activity, irrespective of tactical prudence. In the 1996 election campaign it proposed a number of doctrinaire legislative laws 'on nationalising industry' and 'on self-regulated national industries', which were manna from heaven for a liberal press looking for evidence of the communists' revanchist tendencies.[107] The RSSO leader Osadchii continued to demand that more of the CPRF's ideological work be overseen by its members. Other RSSO members demanded that communist politicians should more actively put Marxism-Leninism 'into practice', and avoid being drawn too much into the legislative process.[108] Many directly accused the leadership of encouraging a split between theory and practice, ignoring the party programme and trying to use 'state patriotism' as the ideology of the opposition without recourse to Marxist-Leninist theory.[109] Richard Kosolapov openly condemned Zyuganov for deconstructing Marxism-Leninism as a world-view – 'supporting pluralism in the methodology of cognition and equality of different ideological teachings and doctrines'.[110]

Such a backlash effectively thwarted the leadership's efforts at ideological renewal. Despite Zyuganov's criticism of many of the changes proposed by party members, the Fourth Congress in April 1997 produced only cosmetic and minor additions to the Third Congress programme, which hardly accorded with Zyuganov's exhortations to base a new programme on election documents.[111] The most notable change at the Congress was a tactical one – the description of the CPRF as a 'responsible and irreconcilable opposition' which significantly was included only in the resolutions and not the programme itself.[112] Moreover, the only two significant ideological changes marked a further more radical 'leftward' shift. First, there was a return to the notion of class conflict lacking in the 1995 version; entailing the growing conflict between labour and capital. Second, it was now stated unambiguously that the 'national-liberation struggle' was to be inextricably linked with the 'social-class' struggle. This was an obvious retreat from Zyuganov's earlier public position. As during 1994–95, pressure from radical communists in the party ranks was largely responsible for what the radical communist paper *Glasnost* called a 'long-awaited step to the left'.[113] Again it seemed that the party's internal balance of forces inhibited the CPRF's ability to renew its programme except in an even more radical and traditionalist direction, a process that would only intensify the contradiction between its electoral and party imperatives.

Ideology in the post-Yeltsin era: new tasks, new answers?

A radical change in the political environment confronting the CPRF was brought about by the resignation of Russia's self-styled 'First President' Boris Yeltsin on New Year's Eve 1999 and his eventual succession by Vladimir Putin in the presidential elections of March 2000. Simultaneously, the party suffered ambiguous electoral results: it managed first place in the parliamentary elections of 1999, yet Zyuganov came a distant second in the ensuing presidential elections, not even forcing a second-round run-off as he had in 1996. As described in ensuing chapters, this began to show that long-term complexities within the party had become a full-blown crisis, the ideological elements of which concern us now. The period after the 1999–2000 election round sparked the reopening of ideological infighting within the party as it sought to readjust to its environment, and the party leaders fought a rearguard action to defend their ideological changes from vociferous party criticism.

The first evidence of serious party discontent manifested itself in the run-up to the party Plenum on 20 May 2000 devoted to analysis of the preceding electoral period and explicitly seeking an answer for why the CPRF was in crisis.[114] The lines of conflict were clear: the party radicals led by the Marxist-Leninist modernisers led a renewed assault on the CPRF leadership for 'colourless' party work, which had degenerated into sloganeering, and a 'weakness in mastering Leninist strategy and tactics' which had allegedly led the party to electoral defeat.[115] Spearheading the outcry of the party critics was party theoretician Viktor Trushkov, who lamented the lack of reference to socialism in Zyuganov's pre-electoral documents and insisted the party 'take a cold shower' by excising from the programme 'bourgeois democratic' elements such as the envisaged parliamentary path to power through the 'government of national trust'.[116]

Added force was given to party complaints by the character of the newly elected president himself. Unlike Boris Yeltsin, whose declared aim was to finish communism in Russia and for whom the communists felt a reciprocal visceral loathing, Putin was a far more ambiguous figure who had come to power on a platform of Russian patriotism.[117] In words he called for a new national idea based on such elements as patriotism, social solidarity and Russian Orthodoxy. In deeds he presided over measures such as the war against Russia's troublesome southern republic of Chechnya, designed to restore popular faith in the capacities of the Russian state. Communist leaders rightly complained that Putin had stolen many of the slogans of the CPRF's 'state patriotism'.[118] This posed a problem for the party. Had Zyuganov unwittingly given the party's opponents renewed ideological weaponry, while the CPRF itself had failed to implement even the basic elements in its programme? Or, as Zyuganov preferred to put it, was the emergence of a 'patriotic' opponent actually a sign of the defeat of ideological liberalism and anti-communism, and so of the victory of the party's ideas?[119]

The May 2000 Plenum, 'the most self-critical in recent years' vividly showed Zyuganov and the party hierarchy under attack.[120] Zyuganov's downbeat keynote speech admitted leadership responsibility for recent losses and called for widespread party theoretical work.[121] At the same time, he counselled against altering the party programme since none of its main aims had so far been achieved. He reaffirmed his view that all the party's main opponents had now been forced to use 'state patriotism' and insisted this concept needed only redefinition to make it unambiguous that it meant patriotism towards a 'strong state of the working people'. He reiterated his insistence that the party innovate, arguing that its primary task of inculcating workers' class-consciousness was vitiated by the degradation of the industrial proletariat. This demanded that the party change its approach to deal with post-industrial problems. In a new twist to his well-worn references to the transnational threats presented by the global 'New World Order' Zyuganov argued that since the modern productive class was moving from the machine-tool to the computer, communists needed to learn to use new technologies to their benefit. A vivid example, he added was the 'Love' email virus, which had caused so much (albeit temporary) disruption to businesses world-wide.[122] By such means workers could use the Internet to overthrow the New World Order and end workers' exploitation. However, criticism from the floor was not quelled. The first secretary of the party's Kamchatka *oblast* (region) committee accused Zyuganov of sounding like the famous Russian nationalist Aleksandr Solzhenitsyn, while Trushkov and Moscow city party leader Aleksandr Kuvaev demanded state patriotism be removed from the party programme. Yurii Belov sought to regain some ground for the statist-patriotic communists, arguing that the modern essence of Marxism was in its method, since many of its traditional ideas had been discredited by the liberal media and were no longer attractive to the masses.[123]

In response to the party backlash, the leadership organised its broadest intra-party discussion since 1994, focusing on questions of tactics, party organisation, campaigning and ideology. 'The immediate tasks of the CPRF' were published at June 2000 and formed the focus of party discussion until the party's Seventh Congress that December.[124] This document was intended to set out the party's tasks for the next two to three years. As with previous party ideological documents, it was prepared by a composite group of party leaders embracing all ideological trends.[125]

The 'Immediate tasks' were written in a sober and defensive style, and elucidated both the problems confronting the party and the tasks for overcoming them. While admitting specific weaknesses in the party's work both in parliament and among the masses, they conceded that the party had not achieved even the aim of 'removing from power the mafioso-comprador bourgeoisie, and establishing the power of the workers and patriotic forces' outlined in the first of its three stages to communism. Describing the situation it faced in

Russia, the CPRF asserted that the main social contradictions were between exploited and exploiter, labour and capital, and between attempts to revive Russia and the efforts of international capital to dismember the Fatherland, clearly a formulation which synthesised the positions of the party's internationalist and statist-patriotic trends. The document made a distinction between national patriotism and the attempts of the regime to 'privatise' love for the Motherland. So the party made an attempt to reclaim patriotism from Putin and, by its intention to adopt a 'Soviet constitution', tried to make clear that it was a distinct workers' patriotism it had in mind.

As an exit from its current predicament, the CPRF proposed a 'renewal of its own ideological, political, intellectual and organisational arsenal', and a socialism 'revived and . . . taking into account the achievements and mistakes of the past'. The exact essence of this socialism was left open, but it was to be a 'modern socialist ideal', aiming to develop personal creativity, while still led by 'materialist dialectic'. Compared with earlier internal party documents there was greater emphasis on specific demonstrable tasks – the party was to gain influence in the trade union movement, to undertake a 'programme of social defence' and to 'become necessary to people in their daily deeds, problems and tasks'. As in the party programme this provided a blend of the positions of the party tendencies. However, the influence of the statist-patriotic communists was less evident (in the absence of extended insistence on Russian exceptionalism, concepts such as *sobornost* or any reference to state patriotism). The emphasis on renewed socialism and 'defence of civil and socio-economic human rights' indicate that the ideas of the Marxist reformers had recovered some ground lost in 1995. At the same time, the Marxist-Leninist modernisers could agree most wholeheartedly with two injunctions that parliamentary deputies and party leaders should not diverge in deeds or action from the programmatic aims of the party.[126] Overall, the Marxists within the party appear to have reasserted their position, with the moderates benefiting most. This is consistent with other developments that will be dealt with in ensuing chapters – the diminishing returns of Zyuganov's national front strategy and the increasing hold of the party apparatus (headed by the Marxist reformer Kuptsov) over the party base.

Discussion over the 'Immediate tasks' proceeded apace in party organisations and the party press. The Marxist-Leninist modernisers continued to push the party towards a more orthodox position, with the statist-patriotic communists largely silent in public. On the eve of the Seventh Congress, Trushkov warned that attempts to renew ideology were a pretext to push Marxism-Leninism to the periphery of party ideology. Any talk of the crisis of Marxism-Leninism in his view said more about the attitude of the party's Marxists than Marxism itself![127] The Marxist reformers were split. In a development detailed later in this book the Duma chairman, Gennadii Seleznev, created a new centre-left movement, Rossiya (Russia), to push for ideological rejuvenation, and the threat to party unity appeared to weaken attempts to reform the CPRF from within. Party deputy leader Kuptsov defended state patriotism, but insisted it needed to be complemented with a Marxist analysis of socio-economic processes and, contradicting Zyuganov, claimed the 'Immediate tasks' could form the basis for a new party programme 'reaching a qualitatively new level in the Marxist evaluation of modernity'.[128] Viktor Zorkaltsev wrote a number of articles supporting the CPRF's closer ties to religion, for which he was attacked by party theoreticians and the Marxist reformer ideological secretary, Aleksandr Kravets.[129] More adventurous approaches such as the one-line contribution of one party member calling for a democratic, multiparty socialism were conspicuous by their absence from open party debate.[130]

Culminating this fraught ideological discussion, Zyuganov's report at the Seventh Congress of 2–3 December 2000 was a masterpiece of tactical flexibility. It was delivered as the report of the CC as a whole, and was described by a party colleagues as the collective work of the whole party, particularly expressing the basic wishes of its regional organisations.[131] This quite clearly indicated that Zyuganov's autonomous role in formulating ideology had been somewhat limited but, by taking an accommodating position from the outset and so openly involving the wider party in the new ideological direction, the leadership could share responsibility for solving its difficulties more widely and so defuse criticism directed at Zyuganov personally.

Zyuganov's speech aimed to balance the demands of the party expressed in recent months with a clear demand for ideological modernisation.[132] An attack on 'imperialist globalisation', earlier outlined by party leaders as one of the main elements of ideological innovation, found full expression in Zyuganov's report.[133] He explicitly linked globalisation with his concept of the exploitative division between the 'golden billion' and the rest of the world. Globalisation he argued, was a policy of Western diktat, enforced through Western organisations such as the IMF, the World Bank and the World Trade Organisation. However, only a world without exploitation in conditions of genuine socialism such as that offered by the CPRF could create a balanced and flourishing global society. This, as Zyuganov admitted, was 'a new term concealing the old, openly imperialist policy'. As for the linked concept of 'sustainable development', Zyuganov was appropriating a term which had 'come from nowhere to almost everywhere'.[134] 'Globalisation' does not map on to any traditional ideological view, since it describes common issues confronting the international community, particularly the problems of state sovereignty and porous state borders in an era of increased information. To many outside Europe and North America, the apparently untrammelled influence of transnational capital could look like an excuse for Westernisation, and it was understood by many on the left as such.[135] Globalisation's attractiveness for Zyuganov was as a term with radical and contemporary relevance with which to attack transnational capitalism. This was compounded by its increasing prominence among the radical young, as shown by large anti-globalisation demonstrations in Seattle and Prague.[136] But globalisation also opened up new possibilities: Zyuganov challenged the party to innovate, to use new technologies and to demonstrate it could propagate its basic ideas of social justice in creating a flourishing world and not the 'planetary concentration camp' of the New World Order.

Another thrust of Zyuganov's report was his re-elaboration of his understanding of patriotism. With some audacity considering his arguments of previous years, he underlined that patriotism was not a separate ideological system, but one of the deepest feelings that had existed through millennia. As Lenin had shown, patriotism was important because it could guide non-socialists to socialism if the communists could demonstrate that Russia's survival as a civilisation could not exist outside the socialist choice. However, in case this concession indicated that he had completely renounced his earlier views, Zyuganov later spoke of the spiritual elements of the communist world-view as a 'popular commune' that encompassed the dream of social justice, goodness and Holy Russia – a reformulation of his earlier views of communism as a synthesis of Russia's cultural and religious traditions.

Zyuganov's compromising and extremely eclectic style won the day. Despite Trushkov's warning from the Congress floor of the dangers of 'right opportunism' (read Zyuganov's position), Yurii Belov defended Zyuganov at length, equating a lack of understanding of patriotism with the policies of Trotsky.[137] The 'Tasks' were adopted with relatively minor modifications.[138] The most significant were stylistic changes, marking a more radical and less self-analytical tone appropriate to the evolution from discussion document to a guide to action.[139] The most significant addition (Section 14) was a plan of specific tasks designed to show that the party was 'ready to take responsibility for bringing the country out of crisis', including a war against crime and corruption, and, in a self-conscious evocation of Lenin, a modern NEP. The main elements of this were the nationalisation of strategic industries and national banks to stop capital flight from Russia, protectionist measures against importers, the 'legal' return of illegally privatised ownership, investment in the army and law-enforcement organs. This was backed up by a foreign policy which declared a united and powerful union state and opposition to Western diktat to be its main aims. In other words, this was barely a new departure, but a more specific while slightly less intemperate restatement of the party's long-held aims.

In the theoretical sphere the accent on ideological innovation was more muted than the earlier draft, with attacks on dogmatism removed, and fewer references to a renewed socialism. The question of 'state patriotism' was dealt with by reiterating Zyuganov's insistence that loyalty to a strong state meant a state governed in the interests of working people. A declaration that communists must study in depth the Marxist-Leninist classics and actively defend Lenin's works and name both upbraided the leadership and reflected more completely the concerns of party activists, while the attack on globalisation did not make it into the final document and was confined to the resolutions, indicating that this had not found overwhelming acceptance.

Overall the result was a document whose main effect was a psychological boost – this 'allows the party confidently to move forward' said Zyuganov. Moreover, by taking a more Marxist, defensive position from the outset, Zyuganov was able to emerge with a document which stressed innovation and a 'renewed socialism' in vague enough terms that few could object, while orientating the party towards more pragmatic goals. The claim that the 'Tasks' were to be subordinated to the party programme would reassure party members, while problematic debates over amending the party programme were avoided and the leadership got a document that was merely a 'guide to action' and did not much restrict their manoeuvre in the short term.[140] It was once more a clear compromise of positions, and if the Marxist-Leninist modernisers were still prominent and Zyuganov's own ideological position was most clearly weakened, the moderates remained in the ascendant. Yet the question of incompatibility between the party's strategic and tactical aims was postponed and not resolved. The leadership both conceded that their immediate programmatic aims had not been achieved and refused to amend these aims, which allowed no clear resolution of doctrinal dispute. Moreover, by producing a document which promised progress towards these aims in two or three years, and by giving more explicit (if still vague) criteria by which progress might be judged, the leadership gave their critics valuable ammunition to resume dissent in years to come.

Conclusion

The CPRF's ideological response to the problems of post-communism was clearly a more nuanced approach than a return to 'orthodox' communism or wholehearted embrace of nationalism. From the moment of the party's refoundation, the leadership was aware of the need both to utilise opportunities presented to them to maximise their influence in Russia against the threat of a declining constituency, and to overhaul their strategic and ideological options in order to survive. The defining characteristic of their approach to these problems was the contradictory attempt to conserve a communist identity and simultaneously to maintain and to renew it. The ambivalence and inconsistency of this attempt reflected not just inherent problems in conserving communism but specific features of the Russian context. The CPRF leaders were asking many tasks of communist ideology at once: to innovate, to become electorally attractive and to lose some of its former comprehensiveness. The choice of 'state patriotism', and of prioritising state interests over class interests arose as a compromise response to the combined pressures of perceived 'imperialist' aggression on the weakened Russian state and working-class passivity, and sought to make communism electorally attractive without radically compromising its key values. This was a circle which was difficult to square, particularly as the formation of an electoral strategy occurred simultaneously with the party's ideological development – 'party' ideology and 'public' ideology were intended to serve separate tasks but were confused in practice, a development not lost on many in the party. Party ideology itself appeared to conform ever less to abstract theoretical validity, and more to short-term electoral and tactical considerations, particularly those aimed at maintaining the party's internal equilibrium.

This chapter has also shown the continuing importance of ideology for the party. Much of the programmatic debate centred around the three main ideological trends identified by Urban and Solovei: the 'statist-patriotic communists' who were the keenest supporters of the national-patriotic front and ideological compromise, but who were numerically weak in the party leadership; the 'Marxist reformers' whose focus on pluralism and anti-bureaucratism rarely found expression in party documents; and the 'Marxist-Leninist modernisers' who had most reservations about ideological and tactical change. However, the overlapping distinction between the moderates and radicals was also strongly influential. The moderates, uniting statist-patriotic communists such as Zyuganov and Marxist reformers such as Kuptsov, were united in seeking relative ideological innovation, flexibility and realism in the search for tactical and electoral gain. The radicals, embracing such disparate figures as the democratic socialist, Boris Slavin, and the Marxist-Leninist modernisers, Kosolapov and Trushkov, found common ground in demanding a more theoretically consistent and rigid application of Marxism to practice. The party leaders' need to consult and compromise with the party base made programmatic evolution a very complex and slow business, and tactical changes proved difficult to disengage from ideological questions. Indeed, the extent of the CPRF's self-proclaimed ideological 'innovations' might be questioned. The espousal of the mixed economy, limited pluralism, constitutionalism and the rejection of militant atheism were changes which had already been initiated in Soviet ideology in the Gorbachev era. The failure of such concepts and of the main new emphases (state patriotism, sustainable development and globalisation) to receive unequivocal party endorsement was symptomatic of the resistance even minor changes encountered.

Finally, this chapter has indicated that forming a new communism directly challenges communist identity. Despite the leaders' protestations that a renewed socialism was their aim, in the eyes of his radical critics Zyuganov's actions were variously 'bourgeois', 'social democratic' or 'nationalist', but certainly not 'communist.' Such criticisms increased with time and were only exacerbated by Zyuganov's association with such people as Podberezkin and the party's increasing responsiveness to electoral imperatives. The most important question behind much of the party discussion and voiced openly by such people as Viktor Trushkov became: was the leadership reforming communism out of existence? If so, what was taking its place? It is to this question we will now turn.

Notes

1   M. J. Bull, 'The West European communist movement: past, present and future' in M. J. Bull and P. Heywood (eds), *West European Communist Parties after the Revolutions of 1989* (Basingstoke, Macmillan, 1994), pp. 203–22.

2   J. Olsen, 'Germany's PDS and varieties of "Post-Communist" socialism', *Problems of Post-Communism*, 45:6 (1998), pp. 42–52.

3   J. D. Nagle and A. Mahr, *Democracy and Democratization* (London, Sage, 1999), p. 182.

4   R. Sakwa, 'Left or right? The CPRF and the problem of democratic consolidation in Russia', *Journal of Communist Studies and Transition Politics*, 14:1&2 (1998), 145.

5   Bull, 'The West European communist movement: past, present and future', p. 205.

6   H. Kitschelt, *The Logics of Party Formation* (Ithaca, NY, Cornell University Press, 1989), p. 48.

7   N. McInnes, *The Communist Parties of Western Europe* (London, Oxford University Press), 1975, p. 169.

8   L. Holmes, *Politics in the Communist World* (Oxford, Clarendon Press, 1986), p. 98.

9   McInnes, *The Communist Parties of Western Europe*, pp. 12, 34.

10 J. Barth Urban and V. Solovei, *Russia's Communists at the Crossroads* (Boulder, CO, Westview, 1997), p. 73.

11 From the party statutes, *IV sezd Kommunisticheskoi partii Rossiiskoi Federatsii 19–20 aprelya 1997 goda (Materialy i dokumenty)*, (Moscow, ITRK RSPP, 1997), p. 93.

12 Kuptsov, *P*, 13–17 February 1998.

13 Q. Hoare and G. Nowell-Smith (trans and eds), *Selections from the Prison Notebooks of Antonio Gramsci* (London, Lawrence and Wishart, 1986), p. 195.

14 Zyuganov, *SR*, 30 July 1992.

15 E. Ligachev, *Sovetskaya kultura*, 7 July 1987. Noticeably both had moved to more nationalist positions by 1990.

16 Space precludes full treatment of this theme and it has been dealt with extensively elsewhere. A good place to start is J. Devlin, *Slavophiles and Commissars* (Basingstoke, Macmillan, 1999), ch. 4.

17 Zyuganov, *Den*, 10–16 January 1993.

18 G. Zyuganov, *Derzhava* (Moscow, Informpechat, 1994), pp. 102–3.

19 *SR*, 19 December 1991.

20 Zyuganov, *SR*, 11 February 1993.

21 W. Slater, 'Russia's imagined history: visions of the Soviet past and the new

'Russian Idea', *Journal of Communist Studies and Transition Politics*, 14:4 (1998), 69–86.

22 *P*, 14 February 1998.

23 *MN*, 27 July–3 August 1997.

24 Author's interview with N. Bindyukov on 18 December 1997.

25 N. McInnes, *The Communist Parties of Western Europe*, p. 12.

26 *MN*, 27 July–3 August 1997; *P*, 14 February 1998.

27 *P*, 14 February 1998; *Sovremennyi Rossiiskaya idea i gosudarstvo* (Moscow, Obozrevatel, 1995), pp. 48–9.

28 A. Podberezkin (gen. ed.), *Chto takoe 'Dukhovnoe nasledie', i pochemu ono podderzhivaet na prezidenskikh vyborakh G. A. Zyuganova* (Moscow, Obozrevatel, 1996), p. 59.

29 Author's interview with A. Filippov on 6 December 1997. Gennadii Seleznev was one of the few leaders with a good relationship with Podberezkin.

30 *P-5*, 20–27 December 1996; *S*, 19 December 1996.

31 Yurii Belov, *Ne tuzhi, Rossiya* (Moscow, 'Znanie', 1997), p. 64; G. Zyuganov, *Rossiya – rodina moya: ideologiya gosudarstvennogo patriotizma* (Moscow, Informpechat, 1996), p. 52.

32 Author's interview with Bindyukov on 18 December 1997.

33 J. F. Femia, 'Marxism and communism', in R. Eatwell and A. Wright (eds), *Contemporary Political Ideologies* (London, Pinter, 1993), p. 111.

34 *PR*, 3 (1995), no date given.

35 Zyuganov, *SR*, 26 February 1994.

36 Interview with Zyuganov 25 September 1997 from web site: www.intellectualcapital.com/0925/icinterview.asp.

37 *SR*, 26 February 1994.

38 G. Zyuganov, *My Russia: The Political Autobiography of Gennady Zyuganov* (Armonk, NY, M. E. Sharpe, 1997), p. 137.

39 Author's interview with CPRF CC secretary for ideological work, A. Kravets, 20 November 1997.

40 *SR*, 22 July 1993; Belov, *Ne tuzhi, Rossiya*, pp. 50, 121.

41 Author's interview with Kravets on 20 November 1997.

42 *SR*, 22 July 1993.

43 *Den*, 10–16 January 1993.

44 Zyuganov, *SR*, 23 November 1995.

45 Belov, *Ne tuzhi, Rossiya*, p. 34.

46 G. Zyuganov, *Za gorizontom* (Orel, Veskie vody, 1995), p. 67.

47 Zyuganov, *P*, 10 August 1994.

48 *SR*, 17 June 1993.

49 *PR*, 5 October 1995.

50 J. Lester, 'Overdosing on nationalism: Gennadii Zyuganov and the Communist Party of the Russian Federation', *New Left Review*, 221 (1997), 38.

51 A. Walicki, *A History of Russian Thought: From the Enlightenment to Marxism* (Oxford, Clarendon Press, 1980), pp. 1024. For Zyuganov on *sobornost* see *PR*, 5 October 1995.

52 G. Zyuganov, *Veryu v Rossiyu* (Voronezh, 'Voronezh', 1995), p. 31.

53 *Ibid.*, pp. 43, 232.

54 Zyuganov, *Rossiya – rodina moya*, p. 22.

55 *SR*, 22 September 1994.

56 Zyuganov, *Derzhava*, p. 15.

57 *SR*, 11 February 1993, 17 June 1993.
58 Zyuganov, *Veryu v Rossiyu*, p. 137; G. Zyuganov, *Drama vlasti* (Moscow, Paleya, 1993), p. 50.
59 Zyuganov, *Derzhava*, p. 66.
60 Belov, *Ne tuzhi, Rossiya*, p. 97.
61 Zyuganov, *Za gorizontom*, p. 12.
62 *Ibid.*, pp. 21–7.
63 *P*, 10 December 1993.
64 G. Zyuganov, *Uroki zhizni*, (Moscow, 1997), p. 366.
65 Zyuganov, *Rossiya – rodina moya*, p. 282.
66 Zyuganov, *Za gorizontom*, p. 21.
67 For the sheer number of sources, Western, Slavophile, Marxist, past and present, upon which Zyuganov draws, see Zyuganov, *Rossiya – rodina moya*, pp. 34–8.
68 Bob Davies points out that Zyuganov could not fit Lenin and Stalin into this schema, because Lenin created the Soviet state but endorsed world revolution, while Stalin built up the USSR's military and industrial might but was responsible for atrocities against the Russian people (among others) on a vast scale. See R. W. Davies, *Soviet History in the Yeltsin Era* (Basingstoke, Macmillan, 1997), p. 65.
69 *SR*, 26 February 1994.
70 Zyuganov's books and articles expound a limited number of themes at great and repetitive length. Most important are *Drama vlasti* (Moscow, Paleya, 1993), a collection of his earlier utterances and articles, *Derzhava* (Moscow, Informpechat, 1994), *Za gorizontom* (Orel, Veskie vody, 1995), *Rossiya i sovremennyi mir*, (Moscow, Obozrevatel, 1995) and *Rossiya-rodina moya: ideologiya gosudarstvennogo patriotizma* (Moscow, Informpechat, 1996). An accessible English language introduction (though compiled with a Western audience very much in mind) is *My Russia: The Political Autobiography of Gennady Zyuganov* (Armonk, NY, M. E. Sharpe, 1997).
71 *SR*, 2 March 1993.
72 Urban and Solovei, *Russia's Communists*, pp. 121–45.
73 For Judith Devlin's views, see her *Slavophiles and Commissars* (Basingstoke, Macmillan, 1999), pp. 162–70.
74 Kuptsov, *Glasnost*, 7, 1993; Zyuganov, *SR*, 17 February 1994.
75 Urban and Solovei, *Russia's Communists*, pp. 123–4.
76 See the CPRF's draft 1993 electoral platform in *SR*, 22 July 1993, and the leadership's open letter to CPRF members in *P*, 28 August 1993; Yu Belov, *Russkaya sudba* (Moscow, Soratnik, 1995), pp. 34–5.
77 *SR*, 17 March 1994.
78 Urban and Solovei, *Russia's Communists*, pp. 123–4.
79 Belov, *Russkaya sudba*, p. 38.
80 The concept was developed for the CPRF by the late CEC member, academician and environmentalist Valentin Koptyug. See *SR*, 1 April 1995.
81 Author's interview with N. Bindyukov on 18 December 1997.
82 See Kosolapov, *P*, 18 August 1993; B. Slavin, *Posle sotsializma . . .* (Moscow, 'Flinta', 1996), p. 369.
83 Such views are expressed by many other theoreticians. For example, see P. Lopata, 'Na puti ideinogo obnovleniya', *Dialog*, 2 (1997), 23; R. Gabidullin, 'O klassovom podkhode i gosudarstvennom patriotizm', *Dialog*, 10 (1997), 12.

84 B. Slavin, 'Otkaz ot marksizma pogubit kompartiyu – otkrytoe pismo
    Zyuganovu G. A.', *Mysl*, 10 (1994). Author's interview with Boris Slavin on
    29 November 1997.

85 The influence of the extra-CPRF radicals was still potent at this time; led by
    Aleksei Prigarin of the UC, they were fighting a rearguard action to reverse
    their membership decline, and membership was still fluid between parties.
    See M. Kholmskaya, 'Kommunisticheskoe dvizhenie Rossii: sovremmenyi
    etap razvitiya', *Alternativy*, 2:5 (1994), 92.

86 *SR*, 26 April 1994.

87 *SR*, 2 March 1993.

88 Author's interview with Kravets on 20 November 1997.

89 Author's interview with Bindyukov on 18 December 1997.

90 A. Shabanov, *Izm*, 1:6 (1995), 20; *SR*, 27 October 1994.

91 The RSSO included radical communist leaders such as Anatolii Kryuchkov
    and Oleg Shenin, and representatives of the democratic left such as Boris
    Slavin and Aleksandr Buzgalin. The majority of RSSO members criticised the
    CPRF's alleged deviation from Marxism. See *Izm*, 1:6, 95, 83.

92 R. Kosolapov, *P*, 18 August 1993; P. Lopata, 'Na puti ideinogo obnovleniya',
    20.

93 Author's interview with Bindyukov on 18 December 1997.

94 *SR*, 2 February 1995.

95 *Programma Kommunisticheskoi partii Rossiiskoi Federatsii, prinyata III sezdom
    KPRF, 22 yanvarya 1995 goda,* (Moscow, Informpechat, 1995), p. 27. Boris Slavin
    claimed that his own contributions to the programme were expunged, partic-
    ularly its anti-bureaucratic elements (Slavin, *Posle sotsializma . . .*, pp. 375–80,
    391–3).

96 Slavin, *Posle sotsializma . . .*, pp. 375–80, 391–3).

97 Urban and Solovei, *Russia's Communists*, pp. 140–1.

98 Author's interview with Boris Slavin.

99 Urban and Solovei, *Russia's Communists*, p. 162.

100 *SR*, 19 March 1996.

101 *SR*, 10 August 1996.

102 For example, the platforms of the NPUR in 1996, and of Zyuganov in both the
     1996 and 2000 presidential campaigns were published in the party press
     apparently without advance discussion except in the CPRF's top echelon.

103 Zyuganov, *Rossiya – rodina moya*, pp. 15, 72, 355.

104 *PR*, 19 December 1996.

105 Kuptsov, *PR*, 15 August 1996.

106 Kuptsov, *PR*, 15 August 1996; Zyuganov, *Rossiya – rodina moya*, p. 14.

107 *Dialog*, 2 (1996), 69–74, and *Iz*, 17 April 1996.

108 Igor Bratishchev, *P-5*, 3 February 1998. Also see *PR*, 19 December 1996.

109 V. Trushkov, 'Russkaya ideya v rossiiskom politicheskom prostranstve',
     Dialog, 5 (1997), 13; L. Petrovskii, *P-5*, 31 October–7 November 1997.

110 R. Kosolapov, *Idei razuma i serdtsa* (Moscow, 1996), p. 4.

111 *SR*, 25 March 1997.

112 *IV sezd Kommunisticheskoi partii Rossiiskoi Federatsii 19–20 aprelya 1997 goda,* pp.
     58–9.

113 *Glasnost*, 9 (1997).

114 *P*, 23–24 May 2000.

115 *P*, 20 April 2000, 21–24 April 2000.

116 *PR*, 17–23 May 2000.
117 For Yeltsin's ultimate ambition to destroy the CPRF, see Boris Yeltsin, *Midnight Diaries* (London, Weidenfeld and Nicolson, 2000), p. 24.
118 Author's interviews with CPRF CC members N. Bindyukov and A. Kravets on 20 and 22 September 2000 respectively.
119 Zyuganov in *P*, 18 May 2000; *PR*, 26 April–2 May 2000.
120 Mikhail Andreev, *P*, 25 May 2000.
121 Discussion of the 20 May Party Plenum is taken from *PR*, 24–30 May 2000.
122 This virus, allegedly produced by an East Asian computer hacker and distributed in May 2000, destroyed files and jammed computer systems in businesses in the USA, the Far East and Europe.
123 *SR*, 23 May 2000.
124 *Ocherednye zadachi KPRF* (Moscow, ITRK RSPP, 2000). See also *Dialog*, 8 (2000), 1–8.
125 For the composition of the programme commission see *P*, 25 May 2000.
126 For example, these statements echo those of Trushkov in *PR*, 17–23 May 2000.
127 *PR*, 43, 8–13 November 2000.
128 Kuptsov, *P*, 26–27 September 2000.
129 *P*, 24–25 October 2000 to 31 October–1 November 2000.
130 *P*, 19–22 May 2000.
131 *P*, 5–6 December 2000.
132 For the speech see the CPRF website: www.kprf.ru.
133 Kuptsov, *P*, 30 November 2000.
134 A. Giddens, *Runaway World*, (London, Profile, 1999), p. 7.
135 R. Burbach, O. Nunez and B. Kagarlitsky, *Globalization and its Discontents: The Rise of Postmodern Socialisms* (London, Pluto Press), 1997.
136 Zyuganov, *P*, 21–22 November 2000.
137 *P*, 14 December 2000.
138 The final version was published in *Sovetskaya Rossiya* and *Pravda* on 7 December 2000.
139 As Zyuganov revealed at the Congress, discussion of the 'Immediate tasks' had been held in nearly twenty thousand PPOs, with 152 written amendments taken into account in the Congress documents. See *P*, 5–6 December 2000.
140 See the resolutions of the Seventh Congress in *P*, 5–6 December 2000.

4

Evaluating the CPRF's ideology: backwards to socialism?

So was the CPRF's ideology communist at all? That the party was moving 'forward to socialism, not backwards to socialism' became Zyuganov's mantra, but the degree and direction of movement was questioned by analysts both inside and outside the party. We now look at the various alternatives which have been suggested to describe the CPRF's ideology, and find them wanting. The 'communism' of the CPRF was indeed paradoxical, reflecting the problems of 'conserving' communism, the blurring of public and party ideologies, the ideological defensiveness of the party leaders, deep internal party divisions and the pressures of the political context. It was increasingly difficult to speak of any comprehensive ideology which was shared by all party members, and made more sense to talk of 'socialisms' which the party espoused, some more nationalist, some more orthodox and some potentially social democratic, while the inability to resolve these contradictions increased the party's 'crisis of communist identity'.

Left or right? The duality of the CPRF's communism

So what ideology did the CPRF espouse? According to the most popular descriptions it was 'hardline' or 'unreconstructed' communism, social democracy, conservatism or nationalism. Of these, most common was the claim that the CPRF was a nationalist party, either of a more conservative or a quasi-fascist tint – Geir Flikke is not alone in asserting that the CPRF 'adheres to a purified nationalist ideology'.[1] This view denies that the CPRF was even left wing, still less 'communist', and concentrates on the regressive nature of its policies. Indeed, Aleksandr Tsipko has no hesitation in calling the CPRF's conservatism 'right-wing'.[2] Owing to its leaders' acknowledgement of the crisis of Marxism-Leninism, the CPRF's ideology had become so corrupted by the appropriation of 'rightist and restorationist' values that it amounted to an attempt 'to pass Marxism on the right'. It remained 'red' (left wing) only in outward form, but was 'white' (right wing) in substantive content.

Many others concur. Sergei Markov argues that the CPRF espoused a nationalist conservatism alien to Leninist practice, reliant on nation, not class, national specificity and not Hegelian universalism, incrementalism and not revolution.[3] This view was shared by many of the CPRF's critics on the Russian left, alleging that the CPRF's nationalist deviations and acceptance of nationally orientated capitalism in the 'mixed economy' meant its 'communism' was little different from the socially and economically hierarchical views of the Yeltsin regime. More disturbingly still, Zyuganov's 'state patriotism' had allegedly become indistinguishable from the xenophobic and chauvinist nationalism of Zhirinovskii and other extremists like Zyuganov's friend Aleksandr Prokhanov, whose sense of paranoia and humiliation it shared.[4] Veljko Vujacic has no hesitation in branding Zyuganov a fascist with 'national-socialist theory and praxis' as the basis of his activity.[5]

Boris Kapustin puts forward a more positive view. He sees Zyuganov's use of nationalism as just 'mimicry'. It is a political cocoon arising from the CPRF's lack of confidence in the appeal of left-wing ideas immediately after the collapse of communism, which will be shed by the party when such ideas regain popular appeal in Russia. Thus, although 'white in form' the CPRF's communism is a genuinely left-wing conservatism that is 'red in content'.[6] Nationalist themes such as the Russian Idea are used in a 'deeply socialist way' and 'leftist' aspirations towards progressive patriotism and radical socio-economic redistribution remain vital. So Zyuganov has managed to steal the nationalist banner from real dangermen like Zhirinovskii, while converting it into a more benign conservatism with similarities to that of Mannheim or Burke.

What all the above approaches tend to ignore is the extent to which Soviet communism itself could be described as nationalist and conservative, and embraced the ideas of both left and right. Sakwa notes a constant tension in the conduct of Soviet policy 'between the internationalism of communism and the form in which it was contained, the national state'.[7] When the world revolution had failed to appear, as Harding states, it was just a small step to identifying the interests of the global proletariat with the national group which had been foremost in organising anti-imperialist struggle, and defending the revolution in its Russian homeland, a tendency taken to its fullest from the Stalin era onwards when proletarian internationalism was identified directly with 'the sacred egoism of the Soviet state'.[8]

Such conservative tendencies were only increased in the Brezhnev era, when communism reflected the need of the elite for personal and social stability and has been regarded as 'bureaucratism elevated to the rank of an idea', with the might of the state as its central value.[9] The reliance of communism upon national bolshevism saw an increasing use of emotional and spiritual incentives and a departure from materialism. Rhetorically communism always maintained its revolutionary nature, and commitment to 'leftist' goals such as egalitarianism, participatory democracy, welfarism and materialism. In practice it also incorporated elements more usually espoused by the right, such as social hierarchy, state paternalism, elitism and, of course, state nationalism. However, because of its role as state ideology and its stress on social unity, it did not even recognise such notions as 'conservatism', associating it with social regress.[10] The Gorbachev era intensified this process, when the tension between communism's revolutionary and reactive elements was only exacerbated by the attempt to 'conserve a tradition which was itself revolutionary'.[11] It is thus correct to call the CPRF's communism 'conservative communism' to encapsulate its ambiguous nature, containing potentially contradictory elements of both traditions.

So to say that the CPRF deviated from 'pure' Marxism-Leninism misses the point. Ideological indeterminacy was a direct result of the Soviet system's suppression of coherent ideological articulation. Now there was no longer a 'correct' state ideology in Russia, communist ideology had at least the *potential* to develop into a more coherent 'left-wing' political position. The analysts mentioned above all conflate Zyuganov's views with those of the rest of the party and so fail to distinguish the CPRF's 'public' and 'party ideologies'. The CPRF was not aiming simply to nationalise its socialism or renounce communism. Rather, it was trying to forge a new communism reminiscent of the 'left-wing conservatism' noticed by Kapustin. In the process, however, it was veering towards the 'right-wing' conservatism described by Tsipko and others. This process was driven not just by the ideological preference of leaders like Zyuganov, but also by the pressure of events and escaped the full control of the party. The ultimate predominance of the 'left-wing' or 'right-wing' elements and the 'party' or 'public' ideologies is by no means yet resolved.

The majority of party *members* were clearly more left-wing than generally noted. The 'Marxist-Leninist modernisers' were aptly called so, with their misgivings about 'state-patriotism', interclass alliances and any move away from dialectical materialism. The 'Marxist reformers' were more ambiguous. They shared Zyuganov's support for both the mixed economy and tactical compromise, while they were keenly aware of the decline of the working class in Russia, and the need to innovate ideologically.[12] However, their avowed atheism, internationalism and scepticism towards the patriots showed a markedly different emphasis.[13] Their political conduct showed the cautious pragmatism of elite conservatives, with an ambiguous attitude to revolution; unlike Zyuganov, they insisted that revolutions were still valid, but saw peaceful 'velvet revolutions' as the aim.[14] This ideological position with its emphasis on pluralism, multipartism and incrementalism, was a modernised and democratised communism increasingly reminiscent of Eurocommunism (described below). The party programme was itself still a left-wing document: even though concepts like *sobornost* showed an eclecticism not strictly consistent with dialectical materialism, most nationalist elements were relegated to the tactical necessity of the national-liberation struggle. Overall, the CPRF programme and the views of most party members accorded with Kapustin's view. The party attempted to use the Russian Idea in 'a deeply socialist way' and if its ideology was conservative, this was a left-wing conservatism.

Such clarity was not the hallmark of the party chair and his strategy. That the original aim of the 'national-liberation struggle' was to utilise nationalism largely instrumentally has already been made apparent. State patriotism was to supplement and thereby save communism by linking it indelibly with national consciousness, or as Zyuganov put it: 'to reveal [Russia's] 'socialist predisposition . . . lies at the heart . . . of analysis'.[15] As Kapustin argues, the CPRF recognised that circumstances virtually force it to play on the nationalist field and to make virtue of necessity.[16] Hence the wide consensus for the national-patriotic front: 'if nationalism is what it takes to elect the communists . . . then so be it'.[17] Simultaneously, communists could appeal to Lenin in justifying an alliance with the progressive anti-imperialist 'national bourgeoisie' against imperialism and its domestic supporters (the 'comprador' capitalists).[18]

But what amounted from the twin use of public and party ideologies aimed simultaneously at the CPRF and an often strongly anti-
communist electorate was incoherence. As Tsipko remarked,
Zyuganov's thought balanced two mutually contradictory ideologies.[19] One was a 'white' non-communist patriotism advocating hierarchy, spirituality and a strong, nationally orientated state. This
appealed to those who had no truck with Marxism-Leninism, but
mourned the stability of the union state and who did not accept the
new liberal orthodoxy. This ideology attempted to offer a collective
identity beyond class and to assuage citizens' psychological needs.
Communism thereby ceased being utopian, and connected with real
human feeling. The other ideology (according to Tsipko, symbolic
only but politically impossible to renounce) professed loyalty to traditional 'red' communist symbols and commitments such as the red
flag, the Communist Party name, restoration of the USSR and all-
inclusive state welfare policies. This offered supporters the promise of
restoration of the entire communist 'social cosmos' which the 'reformers' had sought to destroy. No longer could anti-communists tell them
that 'you lived in vain, all your life has led to nothing'.[20]

Originally, both ideologies were intended to be mutually supportive. Zyuganov's declared aim was to synthesise 'red' values of social
justice and equality and 'white' values of 'nationally conceived statehood'.[21] He followed ideologies such as Italian fascism in transcend-
ing left and right in the search for national consensus, moving beyond
the 'class struggle' to the terrain of the 'popular-democratic' struggle.[22] That nationalism and communism are philosophically incompatible at the level of their most basic unit, class or nation, was
probably not important to Zyuganov. It was shared animosities to the
West, liberal democracy and capitalism and shared preferences such
as collectivism and authoritarianism which were emphasised in the
search for cross-class unity. This was consistent with Soviet ideological practice in that it maintained the militant separatism of Leninism
from liberal democracy. Even if the ideological synthesis was blurred,
this fostered consensus. As Tsipko notes, Zyuganov could 'look like a
communist in the eyes of those who are still Communists and . . . look
like a patriot in the eyes of those who consider themselves ethnic
Russians'.[23]

Yet such eclecticism had clear drawbacks, and rather than
forming a new higher synthesis, it subverted the principles of both left
and right, giving them incoherent and dual meaning. Such dualism

that we have noted in 'state patriotism' was present throughout Zyuganov's thinking and was most marked in his 'nationalism'. Contrary to Urban and Solovei, this was not pure, ethnic nationalism, yet nor was it 'Soviet' supra-ethnic nationalism.[24] Rather it combined both. Zyuganov's ultimate aim was a multiethnic state, whose borders would not 'be significantly different from the borders of the USSR'.[25] Yet at the same time, his nationalism was ethnocentric – the state would 'unquestionably encompass all territories where Russians or Russian speakers live . . . [it] would be based on the indissoluble brotherly union of the Great Russians, Little Russians and White Russians'.[26] A certain logic lay behind such contradictions. The communists' strategy for the revival of the USSR was two-staged. The first stage would be to prevent Russian state collapse, for which the revival of Russian national consciousness was necessary as an emotional community which had mobilising potential. Only then would the gradual, voluntary reconstruction of a larger union be initiated through the appeal to supra-ethnic historical ties, initially through the Slavic core of Ukraine and Belarus, later to incorporate the majority of other states.[27] The ultimate aspiration was still to a supra-ethnic community.

The result was a highly confused notion of 'nation'. More than once the 'statist-patriotic communists' differentiated their nationalism from pure ethnic forms. Belov took exception to (nationalist politician) Vladimir Zhirinovskii's 'narrow nationalism' – Russians 'were never the master-race' but, 'an all-national family encompassing other nations' and 'to divide people up by blood is racism'.[28] So patriotism and internationalism were allegedly complementary. Yet Zyuganov himself had difficulty distinguishing consistently between the term *russkii* (ethnic Russian) and *rossiiskii* (Russian citizen, irrespective of nationality).[29] Moreover, the notion of ethnic Russians as first among equals, backed by the statist-patriotic communists' reverence towards Russian culture, Orthodoxy and history contradicted their supranational aspirations. More than once Zyuganov referred approvingly to the writer Lev Gumilev's concept of *passionarnost*, referring to the biological and ethnic uniqueness of the Russian race.[30] Statist-patriotic communism was thus loosely connected to ethnicity, but lacked an unambiguous concept of nation at its very core. It was too concerned with the nation to be truly supra-ethnic, and too concerned with the former empire to be truly nationalist.[31] Zyuganov's admiration for Count Uvarov illuminates this paradox. The statist-patriotic communists aspired to an 'official nationalism' where, as for Uvarov, Russia's status as a powerful state (in particular), civic order and socio-economic community were more important than ethnicity or nationalism as such.[32] Likewise, the preference for the term Russian 'civilisation' rather than 'nation' implied harmonious multinational unity in an authoritarian state in a manner reminiscent of Soviet proletarian internationalism.

It became increasingly apparent in Zyuganov and Belov's writings that the transcendence of 'red and white' had resulted in an unequal synthesis. Gone were commitments to many fundamental principles of the communist world-view such as dialectical materialism, the class struggle, expansionist internationalism and the hegemony of the working class, to be replaced by emphasis on spirituality, national unity and distinctiveness, and support for 'national' or state capitalism. Zyuganov rarely quoted Lenin, still less Marx (except under internal party pressure), and talked of 'socialism' rather than 'Marxism-Leninism', even then most usually in tandem with notions like 'patriotism' and 'social justice.' It was not clear how such 'socialism' was different from the communal collective peasant conservatism of thinkers such as Konstantin Leontev and the *narodniki*.[33] Although the statist-patriotic communists continued to uphold the outward forms of traditional communism these were important primarily as symbols. The guiding philosophical values of Zyuganov's ideology were right-wing mysticism and 'official nationalism', and his ideology was indeed 'red' only in form, and 'white' in content.

So, although many communists continued to believe that Zyuganov and Belov's ideology was propaganda designed for non-communists, and he insisted on Marxism-Leninism's importance for examining socio-economic questions, all the indications were that they believed their own propaganda. This espousal of nationalism has been viewed as merely a matter of cynical opportunism in the manner of a Russian Milosevic.[34] Yet, although his personal motivations must remain a matter of speculation, it was difficult to believe that Zyuganov was ever a convinced Marxist-Leninist. His earliest public utterances, such as his denunciation of Gorbachev's advisor Aleksandr Yakovlev in 1991 were marked by the espousal of patriotic themes.[35] As a member of the CC CPSU's ideological department that had cultivated strong ties to Russian nationalists for decades he would have had much experience of the CPSU's 'patriotic' policies.[36] His writings are consistent in this regard, and give the impression of a convinced national Bolshevik, who joined the party not because of belief in Marxist scientific verity, but because 'the communist idea . . . coincided with . . . centuries-old Russian traditions . . . and answered the deepest interests of the Fatherland'.[37] Zyuganov's views doubtless moved 'rightwards' after 1991, but it appeared that he was always a statist by inclination and that in any clash between his socialism and patriotism, 'the pretences of the former would very quickly be sacrificed on the altar of the convictions of the latter'.[38] In sum, although state patriotism was supposed to supplement Marxism-Leninism, the suspicions voiced by many that Zyuganov wanted to supplant it were well founded.

Zyuganov and fascism

If Zyuganov's 'communism' was right wing, was it then fascist? His public concern with constitutionalism and legality could be seen as a façade concealing a real extremist, either national-socialist or secret Stalinist.[39] There was strong evidence for critics in the paranoid xenophobia and conspiracy theories which made up such a large part of Zyuganov's thinking and heavily compromised his usual public moderation. It seemed that the façade could slip and the real extremist appear. Moreover the parallels to fascism were there – the latent ethnocentric elements and, more significantly still, the aspiration to state-directed class harmony, collectivism and anti-liberalism reminiscent of Mussolini's fascism and evident in concepts like *sobornost* which were utterly inimical to the concept of healthy social diversity. Indeed, the synthesis of the 'social values of the left with the political values of the right' has historically been the starting point in the 'nationalisation of socialism' which makes fascism an explosive force.[40]

However, the contraindications were stronger. Zyuganov did not, as Vujacic alleges, have a 'combat or heroic mentality', unlike other national-patriots like Sergei Baburin, who called for a new 'anticomprador revolution', and Prokhanov who showed just such a love for conflict and confrontation, which is typical of fascism.[41] Some of the CPRF's radical 'red patriots' such as Makashov and Ilyukhin indeed professed a virulent form of 'red patriotism' akin to fascism (see below), although their lingering commitment to Soviet dogmas made branding them fascists problematic. Yet Zyuganov's emphasis on stability, consensus and social order were not mere lip-service, but the core of his world-view and showed him as a conservative, as evidenced by his duality towards the very concept of 'revolution'.[42] A conservative 'national-liberation movement' is rather a paradox. Unlike true fascist ideologies, Zyuganov's static 'official nationalism' prevented him having a transformative vision which could augment the mobilising potential of his nationalism. It lacked a 'dynamo', a concept of struggle, combat and radical social change, violent revolution and concepts such as the 'new man', a revolutionary fascist hero prepared to spill blood for the cause.[43] Similarly, his imperialism was less aggressive than usually understood. Although 'empire' was seen as the dictate of history, this would not expand beyond the former USSR, which is to be reconstituted 'voluntarily'.[44] The coercive geopolitical expansionism of the nationalists Aleksandr Dugin or Zhirinovskii was absent from Zyuganov's geopolitical tracts. If the West allowed Russia influence in its historical Eurasian heartland, Zyuganov argued, Russia would not harm the West, and a cooperative foreign policy based on 'healthy national pragmatism' could be achieved.[45] Admittedly, such a policy implied a reassertion of Russian geopolitical hegemony, but it was more defensive and isolationist than at first appearance.

The most significant difference between fascism and the CPRF's conservatism was its sense of movement. Fascism was able to keep its inconsistencies submerged because it was an anti-movement. Hitler and Mussolini decried abstract theorising and were interested in ideas only in so far as they were able to mobilise the masses against enemies.[46] Their vehement anti-liberalism, anti-capitalism and anti-communism were more evident than the affirmation of positive values. However, the conservatism of the CPRF moderates betrayed a 'retrospective pragmatism' that related change to existing tradition, and began to accept aspects of the prevailing order which were considered 'organically rooted' in Russian society.[47] Such was the acceptance of electoral realities in 1993. Zyuganov indeed was moving towards a form of national socialism in 1992 when he participated in the fascistic NSF, but his views thereafter moderated. In later works, he stressed the need to proceed from social realities, and more explicitly supported pluralism. He voiced a view of 'healthy conservatism' as a 'natural immunity and defence', with which many Western conservatives would concur.[48] As he did so, he moved further from the real extremists.[49]

Whereas fascist ideologies need a mythologised version of the past, they also need a dynamic vision of the future. Yet Zyuganov's ideology was past orientated, defining the future through the prism of the past, and much was concerned with reinterpreting this past.[50] Despite his iconoclasm, the symbols and rituals of communist power seemed important to him at an emotional level, and it was unlikely to be purely party pressure that prevented him from renouncing them. Above all, Zyuganov's role as an electoral politician and party leader cannot be excluded from consideration, and the ensuing chapters will show that in practice the CPRF assumed a role in Russian politics far from the revolutionary role of a fascist party. Ultimately, Zyuganov's need to balance his party and public faces, and his incremental nostalgic conservatism, meant he was unable to form a new synthesis of ideas with the cross-class mobilising power of fascism. Indeed, many of the CPRF's partners saw its reliance on communism as hindering the development of a true patriotism.[51]

A progressive or a dangerous patriotism?

There is evidence for Kapustin's view that Zyuganov's statism-nationalism was a relatively moderate and potentially beneficial form of 'Burkean' conservatism. Much was concerned with preserving symbols and history with meaning for the population, about cherishing roots and preserving continuity in time of crisis. The CPRF's use of nationalism was strongly reminiscent of that of the East German PDS. This was a restorative and not Messianic nationalism which sought to provide a sense of collective belonging for all those who suffered economically, socially and psychologically during transformation.[52] The CPRF sought to answer post-Soviet Russia's value disorientation. Public opinion surveys regularly showed that there was no social consensus over Russia's future direction, with no dominant support for either democratic or market values or socialist ideas, but with a majority (54 per cent in 1997) of the population believing that the pre-1985 Soviet system had been preferable to the present system in terms of security and stability, and 75 per cent regretting the collapse of the USSR in 1995, although without the wish to see it re-created.[53]

The communist critique of the post-Soviet order can certainly appear prescient, given that it has so far produced little to recommend itself to the majority of the population: it has presided over a multifaceted social catastrophe 'with no precedent outside of war or famine', an economic depression greater than in the Second World War and (in Chechnya) an immensely brutal war against elements of its own population.[54] Cohen's description of a sustained demodernisation with long-term catastrophic consequences for Russian society cannot lightly be dismissed.[55] The Russian population's view was more ambiguous, favouring advances in civil liberties since 1985 but seeing the Soviet system as more accountable and less arbitrary, and showing a disaffection from the new political institutions greater than any of the post-communist countries.[56]

Moreover, the communist injunctions against the 'comprador' bourgeoisie reflected the situation of many of post-communist elites, whose need for the Western model of reference to develop their relatively backward political and socio-economic structures placed them in a position of 'dependent modernisation', exceedingly vulnerable to the charge of selling out national interests to a new form of colonialism.[57] The Russian political elite's particularly precarious domestic support after economic reform bit hard compounded their tendency to consolidate their position by playing the 'anti-communist' card at times of crisis. The early 1990s saw an intensive campaign against communist history directed by the state, which was not always a balanced reappraisal of the Soviet past. Rather anti-communism became a new orthodoxy for historical publication, with official depictions of the entire Soviet period as a tragic mistake backed up by grim revelations from the Soviet archives (particularly about the cruelty and arbitrariness of Lenin).[58] The Yeltsin regime sought to exaggerate the image of the CPRF's 'communo-fascist' image to justify less than democratic behaviour in the name of the greater good of bolstering democracy against extremism.[59] Such practices as Yeltsin's summary abolition of the Supreme Soviet in 1993 were often tacitly overlooked by the West. Not only did this blacken the name of democracy in Russia, but showed that the 'democrats' were as capable of perpetuating authoritarian practices as their communist opponents and predecessors, who had also sought to impose a teleological and ideological project on society from above, and continually blamed all deficiencies and shortcomings on their enemies.

In this light, Zyuganov's proposal that consensus over national values and ideals might consolidate and restore balance to a highly ideologically polarised society was not a priori an unwelcome phenomenon. A process of long-term historical revaluation would appear beneficial after years of Soviet propaganda, a campaign of anti-communism in the 1990s, and the travails of democratic 'reform'. Vladimir Putin took this approach, his assertion that one would be heartless to regret the passing of the Soviet Union, brainless to want it back in its previous form encapsulating the ambivalent feelings of much of the Russian population.[60] Yet the major problem continually complicating the formation of a 'healthy conservatism' in Russia was that many of the national traditions upon which it would draw were themselves 'extremist' and authoritarian. Indeed, to some Russian liberals, Vladimir Putin's pride in his KGB background was like a German Chancellor eulogising the Gestapo.[61]

Similarly, Zyuganov's conservatism retained a militancy which vitiated any attempt to form a more 'progressive' conservatism. Nowhere was this more clearly illustrated than in the party's attitude to Stalin, marked usually by silence, denial or a 'return to Leninism'. The communists' dilemma was that they exalted the institutions of the Soviet state for their authority and stability, without necessarily being pro-Stalin, yet since almost all these institutions derived directly from him, indirect approval was inevitable. Even some of the moderates regarded Stalin as one of the 'classics'.[62] When the party outlined its position publicly, it was somewhat 'catch-all', basically positive in its evaluation of Stalin's role as a patriot and war leader, while admitting that the purges were a real national tragedy which inflicted serious harm on the socialist cause.[63] However, for the statist-patriotic communists who exalted state power and the fusion of nationalism and socialism in the Great Patriotic War, Stalin was a much more positive figure. Zyuganov was sensitive to his high public profile and usually refrained from public comment. However, in party fora, he approved of Stalin's 'ideological *perestroika*' during 1944–53, the national communism which was only stopped by his untimely death and the advent of Khrushchev and Gorbachev.[64] This was a position likely to go down well with the war veteran constituency, although it polarised public opinion.[65] At its worst, this resulted in a form of holocaust denial. Zyuganov railed against the 'great lie' of discrediting Stalin and claimed that there were more victims of 'genocidal' repression (in terms of Russia's demographic decline) in contemporary Russia than under Stalin.[66] Such thinking showed a reliance on the conspiracy theory and no understanding of the structural problems causing the Soviet Union's greatest crises.

A similar emphasis on Stalinist themes was evident in the CPRF's attitude to anti-Semitism. Historically, overt anti-Semitism reflected a nationalist tradition that had avoided the Enlightenment and openly declared its irrationality. Since anti-Semitism combines racial and religious prejudice and offers a simplistic emotional outlet for people at times of disorientating social change, it was explicable that anti-Semitic statements were among the nationalist themes tapped by Stalin. Although Zyuganov's direct allusions to the Jewish question were few, and the crudest conspiracy theories were avoided, the need to 'play the gallery' to basic irrational instincts was not. Zyuganov's division of Soviet history into a Manichaean battle between the heroic party of 'our country' and the treacherous party of 'their country' had an unpleasantly racist subtext, given that the patriots' party were all ethnic Russians, and the traitors' party included Caucasians and Russians of Jewish origin.[67] Elsewhere, Zyuganov described the Jewish diaspora as the backbone of the Western capitalist economy, and referred to 'cosmopolitan' (a Stalinist term) or 'mondialist' capital (a term seemingly borrowed straight from the ultra-nationalist Aleksandr Dugin).[68] Most infamously, the CPRF's anti-Semitic tones were highlighted by the inflammatory statements of party radicals Albert Makashov and Viktor Ilyukhin in autumn 1998.[69] Although Zyuganov belatedly denounced their statements as 'inappropriate' and 'incorrect', the communist-dominated Duma refused to reprimand either and, although the party later sidelined them, they remained members of its leading cadres.[70] A similar pattern was repeated with the statements of newly elected Kursk governor and CPRF member Aleksandr Mikhailov in 2000.[71] Similarly, one of the communists' most prominent allies, the Governor of Krasnodar *krai* (territory), Nikolai Kondratenko, became notorious for tirades against Jewish global conspiracies (allegedly responsible for introducing homosexuality to Russia and starting the Chechen war) and fostering ethnic tension in his province. Several other communist-aligned governors (such as Ivan Shabanov of Voronezh and Aleksandr Chernogorov of Stavropol) were noted for their tolerance of radical nationalist sentiments, media, individuals and groups such as the neo-Nazi Russian National Unity (RNU).[72]

It would be a mistake to see all communists as anti-Semites. Several leading communists condemned anti-Semitic and ethnocentric statements, albeit *sotto voce*.[73] Nor were communists the only offenders. Russian officialdom in general was permissive of anti-Semitism and created a culture of impunity for anti-Semites. The intolerance Moscow Mayor Yurii Luzhkov showed towards anti-Semitism and radical nationalist groups was conspicuous by its rarity, and yet Luzhkov's Moscow police force were themselves notorious for their harassment of Caucasian nationalities. Some Yeltsin-affiliated governors were little different from communist governors. Egor Stroev, Governor of Orel and chair of the Federation Council, allegedly expressed his admiration for Sergei Nilus, author of the archetypal statement of Jewish world conspiracy, the Protocols of the Elders of Zion.[74] The Russian legal system's general weakness contributed to the inability to implement federal anti-extremism laws, but the federal government's silence over outrages perpetrated by figures like Kondratenko might reflect the mood of the Russian electorate, with a significant racist minority and ambivalent majority.[75] In contemporary Russia in general the post-holocaust moral imperative to denounce anti-Semitism is weaker than in the West. This owes much to the Soviet treatment of the Second World War as a war in which the general civilian suffering was so great that that Jewish sensibilities were hardly deserving of any special protection.[76] But it is also feature of a political culture which still shows significant disregard for minority rights.[77]

As Urban and Solovei note, for the communists, 'Jewishness' was less an ethnic or racial category than the ultimate popular symbol of alien Judaeo-Christian civilisation and global capitalist malevolence.[78] For the communists the notion was relevant since some of Russia's widely despised business magnates, the 'oligarchs' (such as Vladimir Gusinskii and Boris Berezovskii) were Jewish. As communist Yurii Nikiforenko asserted, 'Makashov's no anti-Semite. He's just fighting Zionist capital. And it exists'.[79] Yet this was an untenable distinction, which blighted a supposedly internationalist party, and showed the communists among the worst offenders. It replicated Stalinism's specious use of 'Zionism' (the generally held neutral phrase denoting the movement to build an Israeli homeland in Palestine) as camouflage for conspiracist thinking, and tapped an ancient seam of Russian anti-rationalism. The historical identification of a nationality with such malevolent intentions must be seen as 'an irrevocable verdict against the Jews'.[80]

Similarly, while Zyuganov's nationalism was not the 'psychosis of revenge' that Sakwa talks of, but was a more defensive and isolationist 'psychosis of humiliation', Jeremy Lester points out that any nationalism grounded in national humiliation and the sense of nation as victim is immensely risky.[81] The movement of national-patriotism from the margins to become almost the lingua franca of Russian politics was a process in which Zyuganov played a huge role. The liberals helped: because of an apparent belief that democratic behaviour would follow the establishment of market rationality and their initial neglect of issues related to national identity, they effectively ceded control of the discourse of national identity to the national-patriots during 1992–93.[82] The regime increasingly relied on symbols and policies suggested by the opposition, seen most openly in early 2001 with the re-adoption of the Soviet tune for the national anthem. Whereas firebrands such as Zhirinovskii were relegated to the sidelines in the process, the most extreme repercussions of policies advocating state-directed national unity could be seen in Chechnya and were hardly indicative of a 'progressive nationalism'. Similarly, Makashov's uncensured statements were 'the opening salvo' in a trend towards increased anti-Semitic incidents in Russia during 1998–99, showing once again anti-Semitism's purchase in times of social stress, in this case exacerbated by such events as the August 1998 crash of the rouble.[83]

All in all, the 'state patriotism' espoused by Zyuganov was a highly ambiguous phenomenon. As Sakwa notes, it combined in one movement all the 'various bloody spectres haunting European political philosophy,'[84] drawing on a tradition known for extremes of statism, imperialism, chauvinism and anti-Semitism. There was certainly an attempt to civilise this tradition and move it away from the extremes, to reorientate communism towards existing realities and to accept entrenched social change. Such an attempt remained half-hearted. As Jeremy Lester further argues, why bother to attempt to 'tame' the dangerous statism of Stalin and Uvarov when the grass-roots democratic socialism of the early Soviets was an equally valid tradition for communist conservatism?[85] That such an attempt was made indicated how little of the *perestroika*-era critique of state socialism the communists accepted. Attempts to civilise this tradition appeared to be squaring the circle, and resulted in a highly eclectic ideology which was too conservative to be fascist, too nationalist to be communist and yet too statist to be truly nationalist.

The CPRF and social democracy

The conservatism which accepts entrenched change was best seen in the CPRF leadership's acceptance of such non-communist ideas as 'pluralism', 'multipartism' and the 'mixed economy', on which expectations that the CPRF might develop towards social democracy were based. Social democracy is difficult to define and has traditionally been a heterogeneous, hybrid tradition because it attempts to realise socialism through the institutions of liberal-democratic society and thereby combines elements of liberalism and socialism. A minimalist definition of social democracy would however include the six following elements: full commitment to parliamentary democracy and the electoral process, political liberalism, the mixed economy, the welfare state and a belief in equality.[86] The successor parties in Hungary, Poland and Lithuania, with their emphasis on socially orientated reform within the political systems of the post-Soviet order, fulfilled these broad conditions. How likely then was the CPRF's evolution in the same direction?

Many Marxist reformers were certainly aware of the potential of social democracy. The CPRF actively studied the social democratic parties in East-Central Europe, and learnt much in 'forms and methods of work' such as experience of the mixed economy, creating coalitions and working in pluralist politics.[87] The moderates (unlike the radicals) did not view social democracy as a priori heretical – it was at least seen as part of the left and, given that 'the crucial demarcation Leninism set out to draw was that between revolutionary Marxism and revisionist social democracy', this was significant.[88] Moreover, the main reasons give by moderate communists for rejecting a social democratic turn were pragmatic and showed an accurate awareness of the problems of forming a democratic left in Russia, ones echoed by Russia's inchoate democratic left itself.[89] They argued that Russia simply did not have the present socio-economic foundations for social democracy (although in future it is not foreclosed). There was no middle class or bourgeoisie who might support wealth redistribution, no strongly developed workers' movement, no highly developed economy. Moreover, social democracy needs stability, consensus and compromise – some kind of 'golden mean' between full-blown neo-liberal capitalism and communism. While Russian society remained sharply polarised between rich 'new Russians' and the 'proletarianised mass' there was little point in subtlety, softening their slogans and attacks on the regime.[90] This explained a disdainful attitude towards the democratic left movements, whom they observed, but regularly branded as being ineffectual 'appeasers'.[91]

However, those communists sympathetic to social democracy were not social democrats according to the criteria outlined above. They talked increasingly of 'social justice' and 'socialism', not communism. They had a commitment to the welfare state, equality and the mixed economy (a process to be seen most clearly in the Keynesian elements of the 2000 election economic programme) and thereby moved towards social democratic economics, although concerns to keep collective ownership on land and state ownership of banks still marked them as much more left wing than modern Western social democratic parties. Yet the extent to which the CPRF accepted social democratic politics was very questionable. Pluralism, multipartism and freedom of belief were openly endorsed, but the liberal philosophy which sustains them was not.[92] Yet simultaneous espousal of direct 'Soviet' fused executive and legislative power was still commonplace. Communist proposals for redistributing power from president to parliament appeared more concerned at redistributing power among the political elite than creating a genuine parliamentary republic.[93]

Gennadii Seleznev, often believed to be all but a social democrat, might appear to be an exception. He supported forming a parliamentary law-based state adopting Western theories of the division of powers.[94] Yet he also strongly praised the Chinese model of socialism and made it clear he regarded 'state capitalism' as merely a 'transitional phenomenon.'[95] For most communists, such developments appeared primarily tactical and dictated by the need to work in new conditions. They argued that they did not involve a revision of the *values* of communism in favour of social democracy – most believed such changes were fully in accordance with their tradition and not forced upon them.[96] Most held to the view that there was an extra-systemic alternative to capitalism – it was not to be modified but replaced.[97] So even the moderates saw themselves as merely trying to 'rid [communism] of its mistakes and move forward'.[98]

Such a mixed picture was also apparent in party fora. New concerns like 'globalisation' and 'sustainable development' indicated that the party was taking on a postmodern 'new left' aspect. It echoed the concerns of the Western European left since the late 1970s, needing to respond to the decline of industrial working-class militancy and the rise of new social movements (such as ecological groups), which threatened to replace the working class as radical alternatives. The need arose to go beyond the Marxist concept of the 'proletariat', to express other forms of social inequality such as 'contemporary anti-capitalist ecological questions', particularly those which resonated with the young.[99] This notion was strengthened by contacts with such parties as the PDS, which has also espoused ecological anti-capitalism.

As ever, Zyuganov sought to synthesise this with more nationalist inspirations emphasising the spiritual and moral reasons for Russia's opposition to capitalist development.[100] This imbued sustainable development with a declaratory quality and it was difficult not to agree with its critics that it was merely a 'set of good intentions', for which internal party dissent also bore significant responsibility.[101]

Indeed, party ideological innovation remained strongly restrained by its Marxist-Leninist heritage. The work of RSSO was far from dogmatic, yet was undertaken within very narrow parameters, largely concerned with the reinterpretation of the Marxist classics and of the crisis of state socialism.[102] The CPRF's organisational origins as a repudiation of democratic socialism seemed likely to leave a lasting legacy impeding its movement towards what it had earlier rejected. The continued presence of many members strongly committed to the party's official goals would force leaders (whatever they thought privately) continually to make ritual references to these goals lest they be accused of betrayal, and this behaviour certainly marked the Marxist reformers.[103] In the CPRF's case, espousal of social democracy would amount to admitting Gorbachev was right, and would be regarded by many as the betrayal of the 'social cosmos' which the party had guarded since 1991, as well as of the rejectionist position which glued party tendencies together. The party leaders, as conservatives professing internal party democracy, were very aware of the sentiments of their members, and were loath to challenge this heritage directly.[104] Significantly, it appeared that changing the party's name was proposed just once.[105] In this atmosphere, democratic socialists like Boris Slavin continued to leave the party, and those who were left had little influence on the formulation of party ideology.[106]

So, although there were countervailing tendencies, there was no unambiguous attachment to the 'move from abstract collectivism to possessive individualism' and personal freedom which began *perestroika*'s move towards social democracy from 1989 onwards.[107] After all, the communists' original aim was to exploit pluralism to subvert it. Yet despite this, the incipient 'crisis of communist identity' so dreaded by the CPRF's radicals was apparent in the declining confidence in the overall comprehensiveness of Marxism-Leninism. This was increasingly replaced by an eclecticism of theories which was also one of the first stages of Gorbachev's *perestroika*.[108] For many in the leadership, tactical changes such as the acceptance of the mixed economy and pluralism seemed to become accepted as integral parts of the communist model, and possibly as ends in themselves. Yet, as we have seen, there are limits to the extent to which communist parties can both incorporate elements of pluralist doctrines and compete in pluralist politics before they lose distinctiveness and coherence. The CPRF compounded this problem by trying to do both simultaneously.

Indeed, the experience of communist parties in Western Europe serves as a salutary lesson to communist successor parties like the CPRF today. Challenged by the erosion of collectivist, working-class identities and the degeneration of Marxism-Leninism's viability as a coherent alternative, an intense crisis was sparked which encompassed simultaneously the 'societal' dimension of communism (party links with society and electoral performance) and the 'teleological' dimension of communism (party ideology, strategy and organisation), presaging an inexorable decline in party support, structure and identity.[109]

The experience of Eurocommunism in particular has parallels with what was occurring in the CPRF. This movement, promoted from the 1970s primarily by the Italian, Spanish and French communist parties (the Communist Party of Italy or PCI, the Communist Party of Spain or PCE and the PCF), amounted to communism's acceptance of pluralism, often with ambiguity or reluctance (particularly in the case of the PCF), and the gradual breakdown in coherence of communism itself. Eurocommunism marked the congruence of two major changes. First, in response to the above crisis phenomena, Eurocommunists sought to reorientate themselves from Soviet towards national development and to seek alliances and support beyond the traditional working class.[110] This led to tactical changes: after long periods of post-war ambivalence, there was the final acceptance of the legitimacy of electoral politics and evolutionism as a means of creating a non-capitalist society.[111] Second, these tactical changes eventually fed into theoretical changes, such as the rejection of the dictatorship of the proletariat.

However, such theoretical changes began to weaken the Eurocommunist critique of capitalism, thereby eroding the distinctiveness of their 'extra-systemic' vision and the ontological distinction between communism and social democracy.[112] Eurocommunist parties found themselves impaled upon the dilemma of evolutionary socialism. When parties such as the PCI became grudgingly reabsorbed into national polities 'what had been regarded as the transition found itself elevated to the status of settlement'.[113] With their tactics *becoming* their aims, the revisionist Marxist Eduard Bernstein's dictum, 'the ultimate aim of socialism is nothing, but the movement is everything', came back to perplex the communists.[114] Apart from organisational traits such as PPOs and Leninist democratic central-ism, their policies and practice became de facto almost indistinguish-able from those of convinced social democrats.

The effect of political context

The Russian political system developed several features which much abetted the CPRF's ideological indeterminacy. Chief of these was the unstructured party and ideological landscape. The post-Soviet legacy was an inchoate civil society, with poorly developed socio-economic cleavages in comparison to most pluralist industrialised societies, for which reason ideologies remained largely estranged from their poten-tial social subjects and constituencies. Given this instability, there was every incentive for parties to pitch their appeals to the broadest pos-sible audience, adopting 'catch-all' strategies rather than appealing to particular strata and thereby risking political irrelevance.[115] This con-tributed to an ideological 'free-for-all' marked by volatility, populism, shifting loyalties and ideological inconsistency. The career of politi-cians such as Aleksandr Rutskoi (who migrated from nationalist, to democrat and back to nationalist in the post-Soviet era) illustrated that although ideological indeterminacy proved unviable in forming stable party organisations, it much aided political manoeuvrability and benefits for opportunistic politicians in seeking political office.[116] All in all, it seemed that 'pragmatism has replaced philosophy' and orientation to power became more important to Russian politicians than adherence to a particular set of political values.[117] Russian electo-ral politics was thus marked by a rapid blurring of party electoral platforms, with parties of most types showing consensus over state regulation and welfarism in the market economy, a move away from minority positions such as pure liberalism and towards patriotic themes.[118]

Ideological confusion was further exacerbated by the effects of what Sakwa calls the 'regime system' – the transitional political system that was the residuum of the authoritarian party-state and survived the incomplete democratic revolution.[119] The regime followed a path of co-optation, incorporation and neutralisation of political opposition through clientelistic routines and networks, and remained largely supra-ideological. The co-optation of opposition impeded parties from gaining mass character, forcing them into a 'cadre' party system based on intra-elite negotiation rather than roots in civil society, further diluting the ideological opposition and coherent political discourse usually generated by political parties and programmes competing in the public arena. This was a process that we have already seen was characteristic of formerly patrimonial communist states.

Strongly presidential systems like Russia have compounded the incoherence of parties which are torn between the meagre rewards of running for seats in a weak parliament and becoming broader coalitions for personalities to gain the 50.1 per cent of the vote needed to become president. In the CPRF's case the dilemma was exacerbated by its attachment to a rigid party organisation, which could not simply be discarded. As we have noted, organisation is as integral to communist identity as ideology, and pressure from the rank and file further limited the leadership's options. Yet, since the CPRF was to get only 23 per cent of the vote even when it 'won' the parliamentary elections of 1995, the communist leadership became convinced that the party could not win elections independently.[120]

Such conflicting pressures confronted the CPRF with an unenviable choice between restricting itself to its core constituency and risking marginalisation or embracing catch-all electoral competition and thus maximising the discordance with its core constituency and party identity. The tactic of running separate party and public ideologies might have had a greater chance of success in a less presidential system and with greater control over the party ranks. Instead, the twin pressures of constituency vs. electorate acted to push party ideology and public ideology further apart. Zyuganov's volte-face after the 1996 presidential elections was a case in point. Talking of incorporating 'democratic' and 'social democratic realities' into the new state ideology directly contradicted his long-standing anti-democratic and anti-liberal position.[121]

So the particular crisis affecting ex-ruling communist parties in post-communist systems had specificities: one could speak of a general crisis of political parties in countries once dominated by the CPSU, with most fragmented in ideology and organisation, and having to consolidate in rapidly changing conditions. Compared with these, communist parties such as those in Russia and Ukraine might appear relatively strong, owing to the ideological and organisational capital inherited from their past. Nevertheless, it was precisely this inheritance that intensified their crisis. Like the Eurocommunists, parties like the CPRF were increasingly riven between loyalty to the past and adaptation to a 'bourgeois' system, trying to use 'systemic' methods without weakening their critique of the system and to remain true to radical extra-systemic ends. Yet, because the political system was developing so rapidly and their ideology losing its dynamism simultaneously, this made defining a coherent 'anti-system' position still harder and led to a more intense crisis than gradually confronted the Eurocommunists over the space of decades.

Yet the CPRF could with justification be accused of colluding in its own exploitation. Critics such as Boris Slavin had a point when they said that downplaying the class critique and movement towards a 'catch-all' purely electoral strategy deprived the CPRF of important arguments with which to attack the regime. It blunted the party's criticism of capitalism and led to an increasing acceptance of national capital. When communists participated in parliamentary politics in the past, an extended 'war of position' involving extra-parliamentary pressure on the regime from below and the maintenance of a strict class critique of the state were seen as the key to avoiding eroding communist identity, although the balance between simultaneously assisting and undermining bourgeois-democratic national liberation movements was inherently difficult to strike.[122] Yet Zyuganov's national-liberation front was still more contradictory than the models it aspired to. After all, in the Great Patriotic War, Stalin had sought national unity around a socialist state, not a bourgeois one, and all previous 'national fronts' in Western Europe had been subservient to the internationalist aims of the Comintern.

Ensuing chapters will show that the CPRF's 'war of position' was to be weakened by the weak leverage of the Russian parliament and the CPRF's failure to mobilise popular pressure on the regime.[123] All in all, the CPRF threatened to repeat the Eurocommunists' main failure – to maintain a critical and ideological distance from the system they aspired to replace. State patriotism, nationalism, unity and consensus provided a ground for rapprochement with the regime, but at the expense of weakening the communists' own aspirations and arguments, while their continuing attachment to Soviet-era symbols and their party organisation made their patriotism less electorally attractive than that of figures who could espouse a nationalism not so tainted by the communist past.

Conclusion

So was the CPRF actually a communist party? There was no definitive answer to this question, given that the CPRF was a coalition of various ideological tendencies, themselves in transition and with the potential to develop along different lines. However, all CPRF members could be justifiably called 'communist' in their adherence to a 'conservative' form of communism which retained revolutionary elements alongside a strong conservative commitment to the institutions, symbols and traditions of Soviet power. Similarly, communism's claim to represent a distinct coherent alternative was still held and evident in Zyuganov's choice of state patriotism as an attempt to preserve many aspects of the 'special path' of the former ideology as its key mobilising and electoral strategy. Simultaneously, the party programme acted as a statement of faith to reaffirm the ideological probity.

Yet, at the same time electoral politics, regime co-optation and the leaders' own cautious outlook blurred tactical and strategic aims and made it still less possible to talk of a communist 'ideology'. While the majority of the party still subscribed to Marxism-Leninism the increasing acceptance of notions such as 'pluralism' and 'multipartism' marked a methodological and philosophical pluralism which eroded the distinctiveness of the Marxist-Leninist world-view, and left the door ajar for future further ideological transition.

But if the CPRF was not unambiguously communist, nor was is it national socialist or unambiguously nationalist, with its ethnocentrism still compromised by residual internationalist sentiment. Rather the CPRF should be seen as representing several new nationally specific post-Soviet socialisms. It was clearly not unreconstructed or orthodox. On one level it was engaging with realities affecting the left globally such as the decline of traditional class cleavages and coherent integrated alternatives to capitalism. Boris Kagarlitsky points out the similarities between Zyuganov and leaders such as Tony Blair, Massimo D'Alema and Gerhard Schröder, who moved their parties away from class activism towards a consensus politics which transcended traditional social divisions and attempted to form a 'third way' between traditional left and right.[124] Thus, though they preserved many outward forms of left-wing politics, just as Blair was no longer a traditional social democrat, Zyuganov was no longer a traditional communist. Similarly the CPRF was neither completely left nor right but expressed the attempts of the left to harness some lessons of its systemic crisis and to co-opt but not capitulate to the ideas of the right. This process was given added complexity by the historical obfuscation of these categories by the Soviet system, and the further challenges of the post-Soviet political and ideological landscape.

The CPRF was also 'post-Soviet' in its attempts to form a 'nationally authentic socialism' which sought to provide historical continuity for its supporters, and an idiom in which its previously discredited values might compete in Russian electoral politics. In this it had similarities with other 'successor' parties, but the differences in the respective socialist traditions in each country explained many of the differences also. The evolution of parties like the Polish SDRP in a social democratic direction was largely explicable as the victory of the reformist wing in a decades-long struggle to 'decommunise' the Polish left.[125] The weakness of the social democratic tradition in the CPRF originated in the relative success of Leninism in supplanting democratic socialisms in Russia. The movement towards national bolshevism and the culturally conservative ethos of much of the party reflected historical tendencies and, despite increasing Eurocommunist elements, there was nothing like Eurocommunism's 'embrace of pluralisms'. The CPRF's attitude towards pluralism was eclectic and more hesitant than even of the less convinced Eurocommunists like the PCF, although the CPRF leaders exhibited a disillusion with traditional Marxist-Leninist paradigms typical of the early stages of Eurocommunism or the evolution of the Polish and Hungarian former ruling parties, who gradually moved towards a democratic socialism for more pragmatic reasons. This indicated that the CPRF's movement in a more democratic socialist direction was far from foreclosed, but would be long and difficult.

Another key difference from Eurocommunism was that the CPRF's identity was not being worn down by incorporation in a wholly democratic regime whereby the acceptance of regime values might lead directly to a transition to social democracy. Indeed, the experience of democracy in Russia had hardly been a convincing demonstration of the virtues of multiparty politics and pluralism, an attitude many Russian voters shared.[126] So it appeared premature to envisage the social democratisation of the CPRF without the full liberal democratisation of the regime, the emergence of political leaders who saw democracy as more than a few pieces of paper to put in 'something called a ballot box', a strong civil society, and the wide penetration of democratic ideas that might 'civilise' and dilute the CPRF's residual militancy.[127]

Yet clearly the CPRF's ideological position did not take the lead in encouraging democratic ideas. There was a danger that the adoption of patriotism and authoritarianism in a political system which still preserved patrimonial tendencies might only perpetuate its worst traits. The communists' weakened critique of a quasi-democratic regime indicated that they had prioritised the paternalist tendencies of state socialism over their rhetorical aspirations towards socio-economic and democratic reformism, and when combined with quasi-fascist elements, Zyuganov's 'socialism' risked discrediting left ideas for good.[128] Arguably the biggest service the CPRF provided the regime was failing to provide a coherent alternative vision with which to replace it. Even the communists admitted their lack of future-oriented vision.[129] There were many contradictory elements. To the moderates, a putative communist regime would involve a switch of economic course, not system and a change of nothing more than 'methods of management', preserving the mixed economy, pluralism and multipartism.[130] Zyuganov's future vision appeared to amount to little more than collectivism, spirituality and a socially orientated economy.[131]

There were indeed clear questions over what the party might do in power: would the moderate or radical faces prevail? It was fully possible that since Zyuganov's alliance-building conduct was always more flexible than his rhetoric and, since the communists recognised their weak social support, they would moderate positions which alarmed the elite and international community – including national-isation, non-co-operation with the 'fascist' North Atlantic Treaty Organization (NATO) and support for anti-Western leaders such as Alyaksandr Lukashenka, of Belarus, and Slobodan Milosevic. The career of moderate communists such as the Russian Human Rights Commissioner (from 1998), Oleg Mironov, was indicative of the ability to moderate in power. Initially paying scant concern to abuses of personal liberty, he built up a working relationship with the Russian human rights community and became increasingly critical of the Chechen war.[132] Nevertheless the tendency of communists to remain more extremist than the regime, and to attack it more for being insufficiently nationalist than for being insufficiently democratic or just was shown by Zyuganov's putative 1998 'shadow cabinet'. This contained controversial appointees such as ex-putschist Vasilii

Starodubtsev, and the aforementioned chauvinists, Viktor Ilyukhin
and Nikolai Kondratenko, alongside (relative) moderates such as the
head of the Federation Council, Egor Stroev, and Kemerovo governor,
Aman Tuleev.[133]

Overall, any coherent movement 'forwards to socialism'
remained deeply problematic for the CPRF. The move 'rightwards'
towards state patriotism accorded with historical tradition, the
current development of the political regime and Zyuganov's own
preferences, but should not be seen as inevitable. Certainly, other
CPRF leaders were well aware of the dangers of strong statism.[134] The
party's inchoate and divergent ideological tendencies were variously
potentially social democratic, orthodox communist, Stalinist, nationalist and even fascist. Yet the autonomous development of such tendencies and significant ideological innovation was hampered by the
continuing commitment to shared Leninist symbols and traditions,
and to the unity of the party organisation, while no coherent political
face emerged. Comparison with other communist parties after the
crisis of communism might offer the CPRF little cheer. Electoral break-
throughs such as those achieved by the SDRP and the PCI (which
achieved electoral success in 1996 as the social democratic 'Democrats
of the Left') seemed to require the transcendence of Leninist politics
altogether, party schisms and reformation prior to resurgence. The
party's adherence to Leninist politics in its party organisation will be
a key topic of analysis in the next chapter.

Notes

1 G. Flikke, 'Patriotic left-centrism: the zigzags of the Communist Party of the
   Russian Federation', *Europe-Asia Studies*, 51:2 (1999), 275. For just some other
   views of the CPRF as predominately nationalist or Stalinist/national socialist
   see J. Devlin, *Slavophiles and Commissars* (Basingstoke, Macmillan, 1999), pp.
   179–80; D. Remnick, 'Hammer, sickle and book', *The New York Review of Books*,
   23 May 1996, 45–51; V. Vujacic, 'Gennadiy Zyuganov and the "third road"',
   Post-Soviet Affairs, 12:2 (1996), 118–54. For views which see the CPRF as actually or potentially social democratic see, S White, R. Rose and I. McAllister,
   How Russia Votes (Chatham, NJ, Chatham House, 1997), p. 209; *Novoe vremya*,
   22 (1996).
2 *NG*, 9 November 1995.
3 *Vek*, 6–13 November 1997.
4 J. Lester, 'Overdosing on nationalism: Gennadii Zyuganov and the
   Communist Party of the Russian Federation', *New Left Review*, 221 (1997), 44.
5 Vujacic, 'Gennadiy Zyuganov', p. 151.
6 *NG*, 5 March 1996.
7 R. Sakwa, *Soviet Politics in Perspective* (London, Routledge, 1998), p. 254.

8 Isaac Deutscher, cited in N. Harding, *Leninism* (Basingstoke, Macmillan, 1996), pp. 198–218.
9 A. Amalrik, 'Ideologies in Soviet society', *Survey*, 2 (1976), 6; V. Shlapentokh, *Soviet Ideologies in the Period of Glasnost: Responses to Brezhnev's Stagnation* (New York and London, Praeger, 1988), pp. 82, 95.
10 S. F. Cohen 'Introduction: Ligachev and the tragedy of Russian conservatism', in E. Ligachev, *Inside Gorbachev's Kremlin: The Memoirs of Yegor Ligachev* (Boulder, CO, Westview, 1996), p. xxiv.
11 R. Sakwa, 'Left or right? The CPRF and the problem of democratic consolidation in Russia', *Journal of Communist Studies and Transition Politics*, 14:1&2 (1998), p. 142.
12 Author's interview with deputy head of CPRF CC department for international affairs, A. Filippov, on 31 January 1998.
13 V. Kuptsov, *Summary of World Broadcasts* (*SWB*), SU/2899/B/2 (22 April 1997).
14 Author's interview with A. Filippov on 6 December 1997.
15 Zyuganov, *SR*, 24 January 1995.
16 *NG*, 5 March 1996.
17 J. Lester, 'Overdosing on nationalism', 41.
18 Kuptsov, *SWB*, SU/2899/B/2 (22 April 1997).
19 *NG*, 9 November 1995.
20 Yurii Belov, *Ne tuzhi, Rossiya* (Moscow, 'Znanie', 1997), p. 44.
21 G. Zyuganov, *Derzhava* (Moscow, Informpechat, 1994), p. 33.
22 C. Mercer, 'Fascist ideology', in J. Donald and S. Hall, *Politics and Ideology* (Milton Keynes, Open University Press, 1986), p. 214.
23 *NG*, 9 November 1995.
24 J. Barth Urban and V. Solovei, *Russia's Communists at the Crossroads* (Boulder, CO, Westview, 1997), p. 98.
25 Zyuganov, *Derzhava*, p. 67.
26 *Ibid.*
27 Urban and Solovei, *Russia's Communists*, p. 125.
28 Belov, *Ne tuzhi, Rossiya*, pp. 35, 38, 82.
29 See, for example, when he talks of 'rossiiskii patriotizm' and the 'russkaya natsionalnaya ideya' synonymously. G. Zyuganov, *Rossiya – rodina moya: ideologiya gosudarstvennogo patriotizma* (Moscow, Informpechat, 1996), pp. 231, 285.
30 G. Zyuganov, *Rossiya i sovremennyi mir* (Moscow, Obozrevatel, 1995), p. 65.
31 M. Molchanov, 'Russian neo-communism: autocracy, orthodoxy, nationality', *Harriman Review*, 9:3 (1996), 70–1.
32 M. Steven Fish, quoted in Sakwa, 'Left or right?', 140.
33 J. Lester, *Modern Tsars and Princes: The Struggle for Hegemony in Russia*, (London, Verso, 1995), p. 217.
34 V. Vujacic, 'Gennadiy Zyuganov'.
35 *Ibid.*, pp. 131–6.
36 Y. M. Brudny, *Reinventing Russia: Russian Nationalism and the Soviet State 1953–1991* (Cambridge, MA, Harvard University Press, 1998), p. 255.
37 *SR*, 19 March 1996. See also the classic national Bolshevik argument that Russian socialism facilitated the preservation of state integrity and Russia's emergence as a great power in Zyuganov, *Rossiya i sovremennyi mir*, p. 6.
38 J. Lester, 'Overdosing on nationalism', 47.
39 Vujacic, 'Gennadiy Zyuganov'.
40 *Ibid.*, 122.

41 Quoted in A. Yanov, *Posle Eltsina: 'Veimarskaya' Rossiya* (Moscow, KRUK, 1995), p. 154.

42 October 1917, while it raised society to a new social level was nevertheless an 'irreparable geopolitical catastrophe', responsible for discord, bloodshed and artificial social division – Zyuganov, *Rossiya – rodina moya*, pp, 127, 147, 219.

43 C. Mercer, 'Fascist ideology', p. 218.

44 Zyuganov, *Rossiya – rodina moya*, p. 224.

45 *Patriot*, 49 (1997); Zyuganov, *Za gorizontom* (Orel, Veskie vody, 1995), p. 82.

46 A. Heywood, *Political Ideologies: An Introduction* (Basingstoke, Macmillan, 1992), p. 174.

47 *NG*, 5 March 1996.

48 This was Zyuganov sounding very like Podberezkin (*Rossiya – rodina moya*, pp. 14–15, 72, 145).

49 This was revealed starkly when a group of Zyuganov's erstwhile allies such as Eduard Limonov, Yurii Vlasov and Sazhi Umalatova accused him of stealing their ideas to 'stab Russian nationalism in the back' before the election in 1996.

50 R. Scruton, *The Meaning of Conservatism* (Basingstoke, Macmillan, 1990), p. 39.

51 Sergei Baburin, head of the 'Russian All-People's Union' and State Duma deputy for the 'Popular Power' group, *NG*, 14 August 1996.

52 According to PDS party chair Bisky: 'For much of the older generation we are a last remnant of the homeland'. See J. Olsen, 'Germany's PDS and varieties of "Post-Communist" socialism', *Problems of Post-Communism*, 45:6, (1998), 42–52.

53 M. Wyman, 'Political culture and public opinion' in M. Bowker and C. Ross (eds), *Russia after the Cold War* (London, Longman, 2000), pp. 111–13; and S. White, *Russia's New Politics* (Cambridge, Cambridge University Press, 2000), pp. 269–75; J. Dunlop, 'Russia in search of an identity', in I. Bremmer and R. Taras (eds), *New States, New Politics* (Cambridge, Cambridge University Press, 1997), p. 55.

54 Judith Shapiro, quoted in T. Gustafson, *Capitalism Russian-Style* (Cambridge, Cambridge University Press, 1999), p. 183.

55 S. F. Cohen, 'Russian studies without Russia', *Post-Soviet Affairs*, 15:1 (1999), 37–55.

56 White, *Russia's New Politics*, p. 274.

57 J. D. Nagle and A. Mahr, *Democracy and Democratization* (London, Sage, 1999), pp. 182, 274.

58 R. W. Davies, *Soviet History in the Yeltsin Era* (Basingstoke, Macmillan, 1997) pp. 41–59.

59 T. McDaniel, *The Agony of the Russian Idea* (Princeton, NJ, Princeton University Press, 1996), p. 17.

60 *Komsomolskaya pravda*, 11 February 2000.

61 Sergei Kovalev, *RFE/RL Newsline*, 19 January 2001 from web site: www.rferl.org.

62 Author's interview with deputy head of CPRF CC department for international affairs, A. Filippov, on 6 December 1997.

63 See the declaration of the CPRF Presidium, *SR* 17 December 1999 (web version: www.sr.park.ru), and Kosolapov's view of Stalin as 'neither a demon nor an angel', R. Kosolapov, *Idei razuma i serdtsa* (Moscow, 1996), pp. 3–4; *P*, 19–26 December 1997.

64 Notably Zyuganov does not even mention Stalin in his book, *Derzhava*. For other more positive treatment of Stalin, see Zyuganov, *SR*, 11 February 1993.

65 The most popular view of Stalin in 1998, held by nearly one in three, was that he should be remembered for his role in helping the USSR to victory in war rather than for the injustices of his rule, whereas a slightly smaller number felt the reverse (VTsIOM survey in M. Wyman, 'Political culture and public opinion', p. 115).

66 *SR*, 13 January 1996, 14 March 1996.

67 Davies, *Soviet History in the Yeltsin Era*, pp. 64–5.

68 Zyuganov, *Za gorizontom*, pp. 17–18.

69 For Makashov's derogatory remarks about 'yids' at party rallies in Samara and Moscow see *Zavtra*, 42 (1998). For Ilyukhin's remarks on Jewish responsibility for large-scale genocide against the Russian people, see *Kommersant* (*K*), 12 November 1998; *S*, 16 December 1998.

70 For the immediate reaction and Zyuganov's comments see *SWB*, SU/3370 B/5 (29 October 1998); *SWB*, SU/3381 B/5 (11 November 1998); *SWB*, SU/3434 B/6 (16 January 1999).

71 *Johnson's Russia List*, 4 December 2000.

72 *Anti-Semitism, Xenophobia and Religious Persecution in Russian's Regions 1998–9* (Washington, DC, Union of Councils for Soviet Jews, 1999), p. 68.

73 See Gennadii Seleznev, *SWB*, SU/3412 B/2; Yurii Maslyukov, *SWB*, SU/3412 B/1; Aleksandr Kravets, *Duma*, 24, 2000.

74 *Anti-Semitism, Xenophobia and Religious Persecution*.

75 *Ibid.*, p. 60. For example, in 1998 a VTsIOM survey found just 30 per cent of Muscovites polled believing that criminal charges should be brought against Makashov for his statements against Jews, while 64 per cent expressed a negative reaction if a Jew were to become president of Russia (*K*, 12 November, 1998).

76 W. Slater, 'Imagining Russia: the ideology of Russia's national patriotic opposition, 1985–1995' (PhD thesis, University of Cambridge, 1998), pp. 53–9.

77 M. Wyman, 'Political culture and public opinion', p. 114.

78 Urban and Solovei, *Russia's Communists*, p. 103.

79 *Vechernyaya Moskva*, 5 April 2000.

80 David Goldstein, in P. Duncan, *Russian Messianism: Third Rome, Revolution Communism and After* (London, Routledge, 2000), p. 34.

81 Lester, 'Overdosing on nationalism', 45.

82 Brudny, *Reinventing Russia*, pp. 262–5.

83 *Anti-Semitism, Xenophobia and Religious Persecution*, p. 21.

84 Sakwa, 'Left or right?', 152.

85 J. Lester, 'Overdosing on nationalism', 43.

86 This definition is adapted from S. Padgett and W. E. Paterson, *A History of Social Democracy in Postwar Europe* (London, Longman, 1991), p. 3.

87 Author's interview with A. Filippov on 6 December 1997.

88 Harding, *Leninism*, p. 113. Author's interview with Filippov on 6 December 1997.

89 For example, see the views of Kagarlitsky, Slavin and Buzgalin, in 'The Russian left debates its future', *Labour Focus on Eastern Europe*, 50 (1995), p. 43.

90 Author's interviews with Filippov on 6 December 1997, with Bindyukov on 18 December 1997 and with Slavin on 29 November 1997.

91 Kuptsov, *PR*, 15 August 1996.

92 Author's interviews with Bindyukov on 18 December 1997, with Kravets on 20 November 1997 and with Filippov on 6 December 1997.

93 For example, Zyuganov called for the president to be appointed by a select body of regional and party representatives in the two houses of parliament (i.e. not necessarily reflecting a parliamentary majority) and for Russia's elected governors to be appointed (*RFE/RL Newsline*, 8 February 1999).

94 G. Seleznev, *Vsya vlast zakonu* (Moscow, Gosudarstvennaya Duma, 1997), pp. 11, 13, 14.

95 *Glasnost*, 20 (1997), 3.

96 Author's Interview with CPRF CC secretary for ideological work, A. Kravets, 20 November 1997.

97 Therefore the communists may argue that social democracy is simply a feature of the developed capitalist economy. (Author's interview with Filippov on 6 December 1997 and with Bindyukov on 18 December 1997).

98 Semago, *S*, 28 June 1995.

99 For example, Raymond Williams, 'Towards many socialisms', *Socialist Review*, 16:1 (1986), 62.

100 *Politicheskii otchet Tsentralnogo Komiteta KPRF VII sezdu i ocherednye zadachi partii*, from web site: www.kprf.ru.

101 P. Lopata, 'Na puti ideinogo obnovleniya', *Dialog*, 2 (1997), 23.

102 One of the exceptions was RSSO member Boris Kurashvili, who argued for a new socialism, envisaging a law-based state and enshrining the principles of personal liberty, though he, like most RSSO members, remained resolutely opposed to private property. See B. Kurashvili, *Kuda idet Rossiya?* (Moscow, Slovo, 1994), p. 223.

103 A point made by A Panebianco in *Political Parties: Organisation and Power* (Cambridge, Cambridge University Press, 1988), pp. xiii, 27–30.

104 A 1997 poll performed by the communist-affiliated Centre for Studying the Political Culture of Russia found that two-thirds of communist supporters wanted the party to continue to synthesise communist and patriotic ideas, while almost one-third wanted a very orthodox communist position and only 4 per cent wanted the party to become social democratic. See V. Peshkov (ed.), *Kommunisty: pravo na vlast* (Moscow, Inform-znanie, 1998), p. 79.

105 Author's interview with N. Bindyukov on 18 December 1997 and with Boris Slavin on 29 November 1997.

106 Slavin left the party in protest immediately after its Third Congress. His arguments are still echoed by many on the Marxist democratic left as a reason not to co-operate closely with the CPRF.

107 See M. Sandle, 'Gorbachev's ideological platform: a case study of ideology in the USSR' (PhD thesis, University of Birmingham, 1993), p. 242.

108 *Ibid.*, pp. 170–253.

109 M. Lazar, 'Communism in Western Europe in the 1980s', *Journal of Communist Studies*, 4:3 (1988), pp. 243–57. For more on this, see L. March, 'For victory? The crises and dilemmas of the Communist Party of the Russian Federation', *Europe-Asia Studies*, 53:2 (2001), 263–290.

110 T. Bottomore, *A Dictionary of Marxist Thought*, 2nd edn (Oxford, Blackwell, 1991), p. 180.

111 L. Holmes, *Politics in the Communist World* (Oxford, Clarendon Press, 1986), pp. 20, 22.

112 M. J. Bull and P. Heywood (eds), *West European Communist Parties after the Revolutions of 1989* (Basingstoke, Macmillan, 1994), p. xviii.
113 A. Wright, 'Social democracy and democratic socialism' in R. Eatwell and A. Wright (eds), *Contemporary Political Ideologies* (London, Pinter, 1993), p. 89.
114 E. Bernstein, *Evolutionary Socialism* (New York, Schocken, 1967), pp. 202–6.
115 M. Steven Fish, *Democracy from Scratch: Opposition and Regime in the New Russian Revolution* (Princeton, NJ, Princeton University Press, 1994), p. 11.
116 S. E. Hanson, *Ideology, Uncertainty and the Rise of Anti-System Parties in Post-Communist Russia* (Glasgow, University of Strathclyde Centre for the Study of Public Policy, Studies in Public policy 289, 1997), pp. 22–5.
117 P. Rutland, 'Russia's broken wheel of ideologies', *Transitions*, 4:1 (1997), 48.
118 S. Oates, 'Party platforms: towards a definition of the Russian political spectrum', *Journal of Communist Studies and Transition Politics*, 14:1&2 (1998), 87–91.
119 R. Sakwa, 'The regime system in Russia', *Contemporary Politics*, 3:1, 7–25.
120 Author's interview with N. Bindyukov on 18 December 1997.
121 G. Zyuganov, *Uroki Zhizni* (Moscow, 1997), p. 372.
122 Harding, *Leninism*, pp. 210–14. For the CPRF's justification see *Informatsionnyi byulleten*, 19:60 (December 1997), pp. 12–14.
123 J. Townsend, *The Politics of Marxism: The Critical Debates* (London, Leicester University Press, 1996), pp. 193–5.
124 B. Kagarlitsky, 'Five years of the Communist Party of the Russian Federation', *Labour Focus on Eastern Europe*, 59 (1998), pp. 45–52.
125 Nagle and Mahr, *Democracy and Democratization*, p. 182.
126 Wyman, 'Political culture and public opinion'; White, *Russia's New Politics*, pp. 269–75.
127 See the statement by Yeltsin's bodyguard Korzhakov during the 1996 elections, cited in White, Rose and McAllister, *How Russia Votes*, p. 254, and the comments of Liliya Shevtsova in Sakwa, 'Left or right?', 144.
128 Author's interview with B. Slavin on 29 November 1997.
129 I. Melnikov, in *Materialy IX plenuma tsentralnogo ispolnitelnogo komiteta KPRF* (Moscow, 1994), p. 20.
130 In the author's interview with Andrei Filippov, on 6 December 1997, he assured the author that the communists would not change the political system at all; similar intimations, although not so direct, were made in the author's interviews with N. Bindyukov on 18 December 1997 and with A. Kravets on 20 November 1997.
131 See *IV sezd Kommunisticheskoi partii Rossiiskoi Federatsii 19–20 aprelya 1997 goda (Materialy i dokumenty)*, (Moscow, ITRK, 1997), p. 35.
132 For example see *Moscow Times* (*MT*), 29 February 2000 and 7 December 2000.
133 *Iz*, 4 March 1998, 2. Independent Television (NTV), 6 March 1998.
134 Author's interview with A. Kravets on 20 November 1997.

5

Organisational development and membership

The CPRF was commonly referred to as the only genuine political party in Russia with a mass membership, regional representation and programmatic structure. This chapter confirms this general character-isation but notes that the CPRF derived its organisational strength mainly from its Soviet-era organisational blueprint, rather than from its adaptation to post-Soviet political conditions. While the evidence of adaptation is often underestimated, particularly in the behaviour of the moderates and in the development of the CPRF's membership base, the CPRF remained attached to a constituency and organisa-tional forms that might have poor long-term viability.

What kind of party?

The word 'party' must be used carefully in the Russian context. Most Russian political 'parties' appeared so far from the Western under-standing of the word that according to some, a communist 'one-party' system was replaced by a pluralist 'no-party' system.[1] Yet even the 'one party', the CPSU, only partially fulfilled the cardinal functions usually ascribed to a party, such as interest aggregation and articula-tion, and providing a two-way link between civil society and state.[2] Rather, it was a 'quasi-state' organisation which enmeshed itself in the state and dominated civil society, performing many of the key admin-istrative functions that in pluralist societies normally accrue to the non-partisan bureaucracy and executive arm of the government.[3]

The result of such dominant state power was understandably weak autonomous social groups that might sustain political parties. The evolutionary decades-long process by which parties arose in the West as defenders of specific social interests in pluralist society, be they class, regional, religious or ethnic, was only recently able to develop, and voting in the sense of choosing between programmes rather than between officially approved candidates was new.[4] Furthermore, the prevalence of a 'lop-sided power balance' in expatrimonial systems and clientelist intra-elite relations might impede the development of genuine political parties, by perpetuating dependence on the regime's patronage and financial resources and complicating the evolution of genuine programmatic positions. So most Russian political parties were usually seen as leader dominated, institutionally weak and electorally fragile, with poor linkage between leadership and social base and weak ideological articulation.[5] Zhirinovskii's Liberal Democratic Party was the archetypal example. Dominated by Zhirinovskii and his closest relatives, and neither liberal, nor democratic, and only ambiguously a party, it moved from a clear Russian nationalist stance to a evasive centrist position masking opportunist defence of criminal business elements. Parties such as the (genuinely) liberal/social democratic Yabloko, which sought to stake out a clear policy position and succeeded in reaching a core support base remained marginal to the policy process, with a relatively weak national organisation and poor links to regional elites.[6]

Given such conditions, analysts have surmised that Western-style political parties are unlikely to develop in post-communist countries, where it appears likely that 'catch-all' parties with indeterminate platforms will seek to compete on an open political field. The absence of stable social constituencies and traditions of popular mobilisation means that mass parties, which arose in the West to defend the interests of clearly defined social strata and were strongly organised around a programme and an activist mass membership, might have little purpose. They may even be counterproductive in an age where increased information technology can increasingly substitute for traditional forms of party organisation. In post-Soviet societies, where the role of the state and elite remain dominant in distributing political resources, 'cadre' organisations with smaller mass memberships, a pronounced role for the party elite and dependency on state resources are likely, although a general weakness of party organisation and links with civil society is the overwhelming feature.[7]

This was not to say that traditional forms of party organisation were not useful. Indeed, successor parties possessed two major advantages vis-à-vis their potential competitors which allowed them to remain comparatively large and viable actors in post-communist politics:

1   Advantages of *identity*. All political organisations need to form a collective identity – defining the major philosophical bases of an organisation, political programmes and specific goals, as well as identifying potential constituencies are cardinal tasks even before crucial organisational, financial and strategic problems can be resolved.[8] In societies where autonomous political identities were suppressed, establishing such an identity was problematic for all political forces, but leftists at least had the advantage of nationally authentic socialist traditions and the potential of a working-class constituency to draw upon, such as we have seen with commitment to 'the communist idea' in Russia.

2   Still more profitable to successor parties were the advantages of *organisational heritage*. Skills learnt in a state-bureaucratic communist party might give no particular advantages in electoral politics, but management and leadership skills learnt in a large organisation gave significant experience which competitors lacked.[9] More significant still were continuities in organisational divisions of labour and leadership. Generally, non-communist successor parties shed their workplace organisation and Leninist democratic centralism (for which see below).[10] However parties such as the Hungarian HSP and Polish SDRP retained a commitment to 'organisational communism' – political-cultural discipline which allowed them to remain coherent as organisations despite ideological divisions.[11] Also crucial were intra-elite personal, organisational and financial connections which accrued to these parties from their past as curators of the state. The ability, despite loss of property and attempted lustration, to re-form cross-crass alliances with former communist trade unions, the ex-*nomenklatura* elites, and even benefit financially from the opaque and illicit processes of *nomenklatura* privatisation was vital to the re-emergence of the successor parties.[12]

The CPRF's evolution will be seen to echo this process, but the party's comparative (to the 'social democratic' successor parties) organisational and ideological rigidity prevented it finding what may be seen as its 'natural' home as the representative of business and labour interests, despite its attempts to court them. Moreover, the origins of the Russian transformation as a split in the governing elite, rather

than the defeat of the communist elite by new social forces, imbued
its evolution with specificities. Communist political capital was distributed unequally, and many of the advantages obtained by successor parties elsewhere accrued to the Russian 'democratic' regime.
Indeed it could be said that this regime, not the CPRF, was the true
'successor party' to the CPSU, albeit its reformist wing.[13] Whereas the
East-Central European successor parties represented the relative
'winners' of transition, these were represented by the new 'democratic' elite in Russia. This explains the paradox that the CPRF was relatively strong vis-à-vis its competitor parties, but was utterly unable to
surmount the united opposition of the new political elite in the elections of 1996. Moreover, like the Soviet state, the CPRF was 'decapitated' in 1991, losing key personnel, institutions, organisational
control and, above all, property and capital.[14] Although the party
obtained mileage from its residual personal, institutional and elite
contacts, and worked assiduously to cultivate those it had lost, in
practice these attempts were vitiated by the centrifugal, tendencies in
Russian society.

Internal party structure – the CPRF as a 'vanguard parliamentary party'

Organisational development

The political capital to which the CPRF made most explicit claim was
its Leninist organisational heritage – indeed the party was proud of
its genealogy from Lenin's Social Democratic Working Party via the
CPSU.[15] The CPRF can be conceptualised as a form of post-Soviet
party called here a 'vanguard parliamentary party' to encapsulate the
way in which it tried to adapt Leninist practices like the 'vanguard
party' to post-Soviet circumstances. As party leader Kuptsov admitted: 'we are aiming for a [vanguard party] but it is impossible in
current conditions'.[16] This interaction between Leninist organisational heritage and post Soviet possibilities imbued the party with a
hybrid nature and deep internal tensions. The CPRF only partially
shed its Leninist heritage and adapted to its new conditions, and
while it became gradually 'parliamentarised' (a process described in
greater detail in Chapter 7), it maintained a commitment to Leninist
non-parliamentary methods which significantly complicated this
process.

At the core of this heritage was the conception of a party of dedicated revolutionaries which the CPSU professed right to the end. Party members were to be knowledgeable activists stimulating revolutionary consciousness in the working masses. As Harding notes, the Leninist concept of 'party' was deeply elitist and anti-democratic. The party was not just the objective expression of class interest, but through its greater knowledge of the laws of history, it defined and shaped this interest.[17] Though it claimed to represent the wishes of the working mass, it was the revolutionary elite who defined them. So the party's right to its exalted position as the 'leading and guiding force' of the communist system was based on its self-fulfilling claim to be the revolutionary 'vanguard' force best able to interpret the scientific truth of Marxism-Leninism and mobilise the unenlightened in the correct direction.

This implied tension between mass and elite gave CPSU activity some of its other distinguishing features. The CPSU contained both a cadre 'inner party' of dedicated activists who ran the party, most evident in the *nomenklatura* functionaries who were selected by the party hierarchy to fill important posts, and a broader mass party of ordinary members.[18] The party gained mass influence and was at its peak nineteen million strong, but could never allow its mass character to dilute its vanguard role, for which reason it imposed strict criteria on party membership. Furthermore, it balanced its needs of social support and social control through a policy of 'entrism', the penetration and domination of ostensibly independent groups which acted as 'transmission belts' transmitting the party's wishes to society. These included the trade unions, the youth organisation (*Komsomol*) and a network of party cells, the PPOs. The CPSU was structured internally on the principle of democratic centralism, emphasising democratic discussion before the decision of a higher party body and binding obedience and unity of action in implementing a decision once taken. In part borne from an awareness that under Tsarist repression a revolutionary body needed unity of thought and will and had little opportunity for the luxury of extended debate, the practice owed much to Leninism's elitist belief that the knowledge of a few adepts at the apex of the party could substitute for input from below.

We will return to some of the implications of these practices below. Suffice it to say now that Leninism's organisational practice shares the weakness of its ideological practice. Its strength is as a revolutionary model, capable of producing disciplined and mobilised revolutionary organisations. The weakness lies in its inflexibility and tendency to reach crisis point in pluralist politics, prone to constricting internal options and degeneration.

The CPRF's debt to the CPSU as its organisational blueprint was everywhere evident in its formal structure. Except for the addition of republican committees (*reskomy*), the full structure of party committees was re-established from the seventeen thousand PPOs upwards to the 159–member CC which governs the party and meets regularly at plenums. The party adhered to a modified form of democratic centralism, with lower bodies electing only those immediately above them. There was in addition a Central Control-Auditing Commission of approximately thirty members responsible for party discipline, twelve CC commissions with responsibility for ideology, women's affairs and so on, subordinated to the Secretariat since 1995, and even the institution of probationary candidate membership (see Figure 1). The General Secretary was now renamed the 'chair of the Central Committee' and the seventeen-person Presidium replaced the Politburo as the main organ working day to day. These new names reflected the CPRF's claim to be a new party but were a cosmetic change. Indeed, the Central Executive Committee was renamed the Central Committee at the Third Congress in 1995 as a tilt towards the party's traditionalists. The CPRF's adherence to traditional methods was shown in its foreign connections, where despite the absence of anything approximating the former Communist International, and the increasing marginality of Shenin's UCP-CPSU, the party maintained a series of bilateral links with (predominately) orthodox communist parties such as those of Cuba, China and Greece. Links with socialist parties tended to be those such as Milosevic's Serbian Socialist Party, while formal links with social democratic successor parties were all but absent.[19]

Such organisational forms gave the CPRF a significant head-start over its competitors in building a viable organisation. The majority of new Russian parties reacted *against* democratic centralism with a strong commitment to an idealised internal democracy, often with collective leadership structures governed by a body of twenty to sixty members, and no hierarchy or discipline. Despite the weakness of the CPRF's own 'hyper-democratic centralism' described below, it did not breed the 'collective irresponsibility' which plagued and split many other Russian parties.[20] Instead, the CPRF emerged very quickly as the only party in Russia with a universal regional presence and strong local structure in eighty-eight federal units.[21] Its mass

Figure 1 The CPRF: organisational structure after Seventh Congress
(2–3 December 2000)

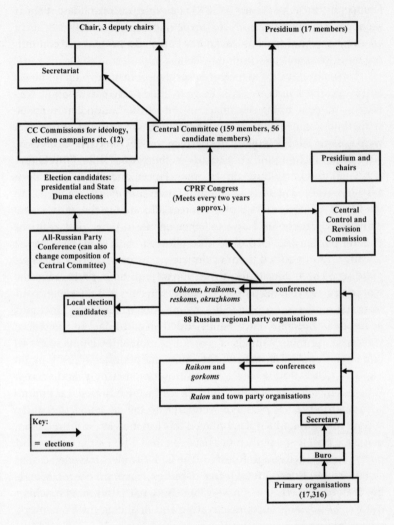

membership of over five hundred thousand was probably twice as
large as the real membership of all the other parties combined, and its
commitment both to programmatic documents and regular party
meetings was matched by no other Russian political movement.
Latterly, there were signs that the field was becoming more even.
Successive elections stimulated party organisation and the gradual

emergence of stronger connections between parties and social bases, with such relatively stable parties as Yabloko and the Liberal Democratic Party of Russia (LDPR) beginning to consolidate distinct sections of the population.[22] However, in comparison with the CPRF all other political 'parties' lacked nation-wide presence, structural, organisational and programmatic cohesion.[23]

The main stimulus to the party's organisational development was entry into the Duma in 1993. Prior to this, party organisation was friable and prey to the schismatic efforts of the radical communists, with fluid membership and weak central control. Organisational weakness certainly hindered the party in the 1993 elections. However, after these elections and particularly in the period of the Fifth Duma (1993–95), the party built up its organisation, and strove to build a grass-roots political party with representatives in every locality.[24] Like the LDPR, CPRF leaders took resources allocated to the party's parliamentary fraction and devoted themselves to party development outside parliament. Deputies were allowed by law five assistants, but the CPRF required them to donate up to four to tasks of party-building. These assistants, usually also full-time party officials, worked in the regions as part of approximately 800 assistants paid from state coffers who formed the organisational core of the CPRF and its unofficial *apparat*.[25] Party funds added an additional 100 paid activists who used the channels of communication of the Duma to maintain operational contacts between centre and periphery.[26]

The CPRF leaders used their resources sparingly and wisely. Whereas most other factions' chiefs of staff were non-political juniors who often served as personal secretaries to the faction leader, party second in command Kuptsov played this function in the Fifth Duma, using the post to strengthen ties between the CPRF Duma faction and party organisers through Russia.[27] The CPRF leaders travelled extensively around Russia on their free deputies' travel privileges, spending 'a third of their time' on re-establishing party links and reaching out to new social groups, reactivating and financing the Komsomol, strengthening links with trade unions, and beginning to court businessmen. Panebianco argues that parties created outside power have a tendency to develop strong organisations, whereas those created in power rely on the state and remain institutionally weak.[28] The CPRF's relative organisational strength compared with 'parties of power' created by the political elite such as Russia's Choice and Our Home is Russia was thus stimulated by three factors: being initially denied access to power, by having a ready-made organisational blueprint to adopt, and by careful use of its resources.

So, by the time of the 1995 elections, after CPRF candidates had contested nearly every legislative election at *oblast* and city level throughout Russia, the party organisation was tested and ready. A concerted campaign to tighten party discipline, aided by Duma funds, national presence and communications advantages that the radical extra-parliamentary communist parties did not possess, allowed the CPRF to whittle down their membership and face down their challenge.[29] The party was able to reconstitute its *apparat* at its Third Congress in 1995 to exploit its new opportunities, but in part because of the CPRF's aversion to 'bureaucratism', in part because of lack of resources, this remained a pale shadow of its former self.[30] This Congress further enlarged the leadership apparatus, creating two deputy chairs and a five person Secretariat to supervise work in the commissions. Above all, the Duma became the CPRF's national head-quarters, indispensable for its resources and material supplies, and its campaign headquarters during elections. The inextricable link between the party and the Duma was further strengthened by the mass entry of prominent CPRF leaders into the Duma. In December 2000, for example, all but one of the CPRF's Presidium were deputies, while fifty-four of the party's Duma fraction of eighty-six in September 2001 were CC members, a factor which, it must be ima-gined, helped consolidate party discipline and leadership control over the parliamentary caucus.

Yet, while the CPRF was to become enmeshed in the Duma and thereby the electoral process it maintained an ambivalent attitude towards parliamentary politics per se. The party maintained aspira-tions towards hegemony in areas not appropriate to a genuine parlia-mentary or electoral party, and the aims of 'entrism' were openly acknowledged by CPRF leaders.[31] The leadership, pressurised by the radicals, continued to insist that parliamentary activity was a tactic and not an end in itself. This fact was emphasised structurally by the dominance of the party Congress and Plenum over the parliamentary fraction in the party hierarchy.[32] Adherence to extra-parliamentary methods was also evident in the continued existence of PPOs. These were historically primarily situated in the members' workplace (the so-called 'territorial-production principle') and aimed to keep workers mobilised for party tasks, supervise the role of enterprises and recruit, train and discipline new members.

Their role came under increasing threat during *perestroika*, as Gorbachev sought to withdraw the CPSU from its direct role in managing the economy, while radical democrats argued that the party should work through elections and give up its privileged position in the workplace.[33] As new local and republican state bodies sought to unburden themselves from party directives, many PPOs dissolved themselves or were excluded forcibly from the workplace, a process which culminated with Yeltsin's banning their presence in state administration on 20 July 1991. Yet many apparently avoided dissolution and continued to exist on a territorial-production basis. Local CPRF organisations surmounted the ban by insisting that joint-stock or private enterprises were exempt, and many were reconstituted on the invitation of sympathetic 'red directors' in communist localities. Thus in Volgograd, PPOs existed in the Volgograd tractor plant, the teacher-training university, the technical college and elsewhere. There was an influential PPO in Moscow's State University, and even in the Kremlin (or so the CPRF claimed).[34]

Membership: better fewer but better?

Although the CPRF tried to reinvigorate the structure of the CPSU with content, the post-Soviet context resulted in an organisation totally different in scale and effectiveness. Hegemonic aspirations were vitiated by the quality and quantity of its membership. Reflecting processes in its broader electorate, by 1995 the party had ceased being simply the party of 'losers' of transition or the 'pensioners' party' and became the party of the 'relatively deprived', increasingly representing managers, the Military Industrial Complex (MIC), educational and white-collar workers who had all experienced a status decline since the Soviet era, but some of whom were slowly adapting to post-Soviet conditions.[35] In 1996 its membership composition was reputed to be 20 per cent workers or collective farmers, 23 per cent engineering and technical personnel, and 31 per cent cultural, scientific, health, education and military personnel.[36] Among the party's most important new supporters were 'red businessmen', based in structures of the old Soviet economy, predominately in the defence, energy and engineering sectors, such as the 'red millionaire' and casino owner, Vladimir Semago, and the ex-head of Gosplan, Yurii Maslyukov, who soon occupied prominent positions within the CPRF.[37] The influx of businessmen grew after Yeltsin's liquidation of local soviets in 1993 had forced local functionaries to seek new work.

Many who had earlier hidden their party cards now attempted to 'jump on the bandwagon' once the CPRF was legalised, adding to the party's successes in regional legislatures up to 1995.[38]

While these new members helped rapidly to re-create the CPRF's financial and regional network, severe problems remained. The party had a stable social base, but it was not strongly rooted in ideologically sensitive groups such as the young and the working class. Rather its membership base (even more so than its electorate) was predominately the former CPSU *apparat*.[39] Only some twenty thousand of the party's half a million membership in 1994 were not ex-CPSU and this had risen only to seventy thousand by 1998.[40] Even in December 2000, twenty-one of the CPRF's twenty-four top leaders were from CPSU *apparat* positions of various levels.[41] Moreover the party membership (average age fifty-two in 1996) was even older than an ageing electorate, younger members having left the CPSU in droves in its final years.[42] Concentrated efforts to enlarge youth support resulted in some success, with the influx of some seventy thousand younger members under forty between 1993 and 1998, and forty-eight thousand new members in the three years to December 2000, twenty thousand of those in the previous twelve months. The majority of new recruits were said to be in the twenty-five to forty year range, with some third of all new members under thirty.[43] But the long-term trend was still bleak, with Kuptsov declaring the party needed forty thousand new members a year just to offset those dying from natural causes, and the general picture of a slowly declining and ageing membership seemed borne out by figures (see Table 5.1).[44]

Relatively weak political activism of workers and youth is common to most post-communist societies. This owes in part to organisational reasons (the weakness of post-communist labour unions and their marginalisation in transition in the case of the former, high unemployment, and problems in the post-communist education system in the case of the latter). Also important and linked is political apathy owing to long-term alienation followed by dashed hopes in the post-Soviet era.[45] Yet compared with parties such as the DLA and HSP, which moved from a grounding in ex-ruling party members in 1991 to a broad cross-class and cross-generational support by 1993, the CPRF's reliance on the ex-*apparat* and lack of representation among the young and workers was marked, and the reasons will be further explored below.[46]

Table 5.1   Trends in party membership, 1993–2000

Date	Number of members	Number of PPOs	Average age of delegate to CPRF Congress
1993 (February)	450,000[a]		50[b]
1994		20,000[a]	
1995			47[b]
1996	600,000[a]		
1997		27,000[b]	46[c]
1998	550–560,000[b]		
1999	530,000[d]		
2000 (December)	547,000[e]	17,316[e]	49[b]

Sources: [a] J. B. Urban and V. Solovei, *Russia's Communists at the Crossroads* (Boulder, CO, Westview, 1997); [b] CPRF documents and interviews with the author; [c] Sakwa, *The Communist Party of the Russian Federation and the Electoral Process* (Glasgow, University of Strathclyde Centre for the Study of Public Policy, Studies in Public Policy 265, 1996); [d] S. Chernyakovskii, in M. McFaul *et al.*, *Primer on Russia's 1999 Duma Elections* (Washington, DC, Carnegie Endowment, 1999); [e] *Kommersant*, 2 December 2000.

Such problems not only affected the CPRF's long-term future but were obviously pivotal for the CPRF's self-definition as a vanguard of society's radical sections. Much of the CPRF's early membership stability appeared to have been maintained through drawing on inactive CPSU members and members of the radical parties, and with these sources increasingly exhausted, the leadership sought to relax its rules, allowing more nominal membership. In 1997 the party allowed candidate members to be sponsored by party members of just one rather than three year's standing, while leaders called for new recruits to be drawn from existing members' families, and reduced the general duties of membership.[47] Indeed, with some 60 per cent of party members over sixty and national demonstrations seldom mustering more than a third of the party's membership, they had little choice.[48] This relaxation may well have helped stabilise membership. But such attempts implicitly jettisoned the Leninist notion that the number of communists were 'better fewer but better'. No consensus was reached in the party. Whereas some members realised that the party's electoral support was more important than its precise membership, the quality and quantity of the party ranks still appeared a major concern to most.[49]

The CPRF's internal devolution

The CPRF replicated the CPSU's interaction of mass and cadre tendencies, but these co-existed in greater tension than before. The mass tendencies were increased by the CPRF's radicalised membership, the cadre tendencies by the bureaucratic background of the leaders and the incentives of the post-Soviet scenario. Though stronger than many of its competing organisations, the CPRF remained a very fractured organisation whose unity was a pale shadow of its predecessor.

As Fish notes, Russian party organisations reflected the regionalism and centrifugal tendencies prevalent in Russia as a whole. Parties were Moscow-centric, with their leadership based in the capital. However, they were not truly centralised. They had only weak control over their regional cadres, and constantly struggled to retain their allegiance.[50] The CPRF illustrated these tendencies, with its leadership group struggling to control its local activists. However, control problems were magnified because the CPRF was not solely a party built from the top down as Fish implies, although most other significant Russian parties have been. Rather, its refoundation in 1993 was a combination of central initiative from the relatively consolidated leadership group and strong autonomous grass-roots initiative which largely bypassed the former CPSU party functionaries.[51] The spontaneous radicalism of the communist rank and file was well demonstrated by the hundreds of thousands who took to the streets in protest during 1992–93.

Such beginnings left an organisational imprint. The 'decapitation' of the CPSU apparatus forced second-echelon CPSU officials to take leading positions in the new party and many of the former rank and file to enter leadership positions at the regional level.[52] Dual membership was largely erased, but some CPRF organisations (for example in Chelyabinsk) fused together with radical communist organisations at local level.[53] These factors only exacerbated the moderate/radical split and resulted in a structure where the horizontal cleavages between party institutions were marked and each successive stage of the party apparatus from the PPOs upwards was progressively more moderate.[54] When combined with the radicals' insistence on the primacy of extra-parliamentary politics this provided continued upward pressure on the party's Duma fraction, and disagreements between CC and fraction were to remain an ongoing problem.

Similarly, the CPRF's regional organisations retained autonomy and key party organisations such as in Dagestan, Bashkortastan, Tatarstan and Yakutia showed signs of 'republicanisation'. The leadership was able to bring the latter two back into the fold in 1997, although half of the Tatar party remained independent.[55] Many local party organisations developed their own regional name recognition such as 'Comrade' in Kamchatka *oblast* or 'For Social Justice' in Orenburg *oblast*, and formed their own electoral coalitions with groups such as the Agrarian Party independently of the party leadership.[56] The CPRF was forced to accede to this de facto devolution and its statutes stipulated significant autonomy for its regional organisations.[57]

So far from presiding over a unified, disciplined revolutionary organisation, party leaders continually complained about weak discipline, factionalism, poor internal links and communications.[58] The party's friable organisation was demonstrated by its ideological apparatus, where rather than favoured policy centres emerging there were a profusion of competing groups. The most influential single group was RSSO, which was well organised with a number of party leaders in its ranks, and held regular conferences and theoretical seminars with party leaders.[59] Yet its leaders felt that the CPRF leadership actively blocked it taking a greater role, and CPRF leaders themselves insisted that it was not an official party body.[60] Zyuganov preferred to use the national-patriotic organisation, Spiritual Heritage, and its sponsor organisation, 'RAU-Corporation', a patriotic policy centre set up in 1990 with its own prolific patriotic journal *Obozrevatel* (Observer), for propagating 'state patriotism'.[61] The party's own ideological commission (created in 1995) remained largely a co-ordinating centre with little direct policy-making input in reflection of the party's 'collective ideologist' role.[62] In practice, the party consulted a wide variety of organisations, seeking to manoeuvre between them while remaining beholden to none, and built up working relationships with many other non-party analytical centres and forecasting groups.[63] While this increased the leadership's manoeuvre it did little to avoid eclectic and contradictory policy positions.

A similar situation was prevalent in the party press. The CPRF presided over a significant number of media resources, with some 470 affiliated regional newspapers, and three radio stations. Most significant were the federal papers *Sovetskaya Rossiya* (claiming a print run of three hundred thousand copies), *Zavtra* (one hundred thousand), and the official party papers, *Pravda* (sixty-five thousand) and *Pravda Rossii* (seventy-four thousand). But in practice a unified information line was not achieved. *Sovetskaya Rossiya*, officially affiliated to the RCP in 1990, promoted a strong Zyuganovite statist-patriotic line, while *Zavtra* promoted an even more virulently nationalist line anathema to many in the party. After a long battle over several competing successors to the CPSU's official mouthpiece, *Pravda*, the CPRF regained the right to its name in 1998, but it remained a pale shadow of its illustrious party predecessor. Neither the thrice-weekly *Pravda* nor the weekly *Pravda Rossii* were under the direct control of the party Presidium, and the party had little say in producing an editorial line, reflecting internal wrangling.[64] The Secretariat, set up in 1995 and including officials with significant experience of professional party work in the 1980s, such as Viktor Peshkov and Aleksandr Kravets, gradually raised the standard and frequency of the party press, but poor subscription rates among party members continued to bedevil party propaganda. The party increasingly moved towards Internet technologies, setting up a highly professional official web site in 1997 (www.kprf.ru), as well as over fifty regional sites, and actively encouraging members to 'log on'. Whereas this offered a potential way of obviating the party's communication difficulties, surveys revealed poor wages and telecommunications drastically impeded Russian Internet potential. At the same time, the CPRF's continued financial difficulties (see below), meant that ambitions to unite the party press and increase circulation into the millions remained ambitious indeed.[65]

Internal party democracy and dissent

There were clear internal divisions between the party's various subgroups, principally regional and central interests, which appeared to raise the likelihood of a major split.[66] Such internal feuds, hostilities and personal rivalries within the CPRF appeared vastly exaggerated and should be seen in the light of the over-politicisation of the media, particularly during the 1996 presidential election campaign, yet nor should the party's claims of monolithic unity be taken at face value. What internal challenges did the leaders face and how did they maintain control?

The CPRF's use of a relaxed democratic centralism was somewhat ambivalent, and the balance of forces between leadership and rank and file proved mutable. Initially, as we saw in Chapter 2, it appeared that the weakness of central control had resulted in a kind of 'hyper-democratic centralism', a level of democracy unusual in a communist party, and not necessarily advantageous for party functioning. Compared with the statutes of the CPSU in 1986, the CPRF's statutes allowed freedom of internal party criticism, and more emphasis on the rights rather than the responsibilities of party members.[67] The rank and file had significant access to and leverage over the leadership. The CC's structural superiority to the fraction forced rank-and-file pressure to be taken into account before any key decision. The CPRF's tendency to hold lengthy plena before major Duma decisions such whether to confirm Kirienko and Chernomyrdin as premiers in 1998 showed this.[68] The party was also prepared to give the leadership a bloody nose. Zyuganov was prepared to sign Yeltsin's 1994 Civic Accord agreements (whereby key political forces promised to cooperate), but was refused permission by the All-Russian Party Conference in April that year.[69]

Nevertheless, long-term developments proved less democratic, and appeared to result from the complexities of democratic centralism itself. Shore notes how, despite the best intentions of its founders, any kind of democratic centralism ends up prioritising centralism over democracy.[70] Tiersky goes further. Democratic centralism replicates Leninism's disparagement of free politics. The emphasis on free criticism plus unity of action implies real limits to open discussion of (even disastrous) leadership decisions, acceptance of 'correct' political leadership and a morbid concern with factionalism which imbues communist politics with a 'crunching inertia' and bureaucratic dogmatism.[71] The interdiction on party factions and horizontal communication between party structures also encourages conformist and oligarchic tendencies in the leadership and a docile membership incapable of mounting any organised challenge to the leadership. The practice of indirect election cements this with the rank and file having very little say in the election of top leaders. All political change in the party has to come from a very narrow apex of self-selecting leaders, as the leadership has to renew revolutionary fervour or respond to previous mistakes, imbuing party policy with an erratic or precipitate quality.[72]

We can see such processes in microcosm within the CPRF. The party leadership reversed some of its earlier concessions, progressively tightened discipline, and regained a strong grip on the party's organisational levers.[73] The period of ideological debate in the 1993–95 period was considered divisive, as the leadership sought to avoid degeneration into a 'discussion club' and to gain more leeway for political action.[74] Party number two, Valentin Kuptsov, shouldered the main responsibility for the party's organisational development. He was the main link between the party masses and the leadership and held daily meetings with party representatives of all levels, allowing him to gauge party feeling.[75] Such relatively open channels of top to bottom communication, allied with the regular 'report and election' campaigns involving the majority of the membership, and regular meetings with party members, allowed the leadership to test the waters with initiatives, hear grievances and ultimately to pre-empt them, a tendency clearly seen in the CPRF's discussion of its 'Immediate tasks' in 2000.

In addition, the leadership elite developed the tendencies of a co-optive oligarchy, relatively unified, despite its personal differences. Having jettisoned its most prominent dissidents at the Second Congress in 1993, the moderates, and specifically the 'Marxist reformers' and 'statist-patriotic nationalists', predominated. A predetermined leadership list had helped secure this outcome, showing the continuation of *nomenklatura* tendencies.[76] This pattern continued, and the leadership attempted to minimise discontent by the progressive co-option of more loyalist Marxist-Leninist modernisers (such as Lukyanov and Bindyukov) and more tractable radicals (such as Viktor Ilyukhin) on to the Secretariat and Presidium while leaving real intransigents (such as Shenin or Kosolapov) out of the central leadership. Zyuganov showed himself an adroit, manoeuvring consensus-builder, making concessions to the other ideological positions in the party and co-opting different political tendencies on to his own personal team.[77] He thereby mollified much potential opposition.

Leadership rivalries existed, but were often less serious than claimed. Most attention focused on the allegedly bitter and competitive relationship between Kuptsov and Zyuganov.[78] Kuptsov's more left-wing emphasis towards allies and ideology may have been an issue. There may certainly have been friction over the role of Podberezkin, whom Zyuganov increasingly consulted over ideological questions in preference to Kuptsov and his party colleagues.[79] Moreover, Kuptsov, as mouthpiece of the party apparatus, ensured that Zyuganov's public position did not conflict with responsibility to the party collective. Despite his ideological moderation, Kuptsov was a harsh and traditionalist disciplinarian. He used his responsibility for party cadres to install his own people in key positions, raising accusations of dogmatism from former colleagues.[80] However, the aforementioned division of labour between Kuptsov the party organiser and Zyuganov the public politician did not appear to have been infringed and, given Kuptsov's organisational hold on the party and its personnel, it was difficult to see how Zyuganov could have survived as leader without his support. After all, Kuptsov stood aside for Zyuganov in 1993 and thereafter showed little evidence of ambition for a greater public profile.[81]

More traditionalist and opaque methods of control were in plentiful evidence, such as the alleged 'falsification' and rewriting of the 1993 party programmatic declaration. The co-ordination of the party's ideological proposals by some forty to fifty members of the central leadership allowed the leaders to dilute the concept of 'collective ideologist'. There were allegations of muzzling the party press.[82] Similarly the CPRF sought a tight grip on the reins over its Duma fraction.[83] Although party platforms were allowed in the CPRF's programmatic campaigns, permanent party factions remained banned and opposition thereby failed to organise. The most influential party platform, Kosolapov's leftist 'Leninist Platform' fell into abeyance after the programmatic debates of 1993–95.[84] The principles of democratic centralism often remain a routinised part of communist political culture despite a party's loss of ideological militancy.[85] So although the CPRF's adherence to party unity was weaker than the CPSU's, it still had purchase. With a cult of party unity, the power of informal sanctions, *apparat* intrigues and behind-the-scenes arm-twisting by the hierarchy became enhanced, and the leaders increased such methods against dissidents.[86] Within the CPRF, those who already had administrative or *apparat* experience were far wiser to such methods than those who had not, causing the pragmatists to win at nearly every Plenum.[87]

Similarly, there was a continuing tradition of deference to the leader. Most of Zyuganov's potential rivals either showed little sign of independent ambition (Kuptsov, Seleznev until 1998) or developed little public authority and recognition outside the communist electorate (Tatyana Astrakhankina, Aleksandr Kuvaev).[88] The party leadership was well aware of the danger of splits, given both the experience of the Gorbachev years and continued public attention on them, and maintained public unanimity. Despite widespread discontent with Zyuganov and the 'leadership vacuum' in the party, critics asserted that inertia and fear of speaking out meant that Zyuganov was re-elected almost unanimously at every party Congress, despite electoral defeats in 1996 and 2000.[89] In such circumstances, the long awaited party split remained just that.

So the CPRF's internal organisation was a mixed blessing. It imbued it with a stability that was the envy of other Russian party organisations, and compensated for the party's internal divisions, yet paradoxically the party's very structure seemed to militate against the resolution of such divisions. Zyuganov's leadership was a case in point. His much remarked lack of charisma actually marked him as an ideal communist 'collective leader' with little independence from the party hierarchy, thereby well representing the party's collectively worked-out political position.[90] Therefore, the CPRF's 'leadership vacuum' was more a function of the party's organisation than any personal mediocrity on Zyuganov's part, and might not be easily overcome even with a different leader. However, Zyuganov's consensus-seeking leadership and use of symbolic and unrealised radicalism as a 'safety valve' to placate the immediate passions of the party base repeatedly enflamed party discontent.[91]

The party and organised interests

The CPRF's diluted adherence to practices of 'entrism' will be seen in coming chapters as a constant in its formation of political coalitions, from its active participation in the formation of the Agrarian Party of Russia (APR), formed in 1993 to co-ordinate the collective farm lobby, to the electoral bloc the NPUR in existence from 1996. The conflict between the CPRF's aspirations for and ability to achieve hegemony over non-parliamentary institutions was seen most clearly in its relationship with organised interests. The fractured nature of the post-Soviet state meant that social organisations and national and local elites tended to pursue independent interests and resist efforts at control, not only from political parties but also from the federal authorities.[92] This tendency continually thwarted the CPRF's reliance on its traditional allies and techniques and the party's vanguard capabilities became significantly attenuated through time.

The CPRF and workers – the vanguard lagging

Most painful and challenging to the CPRF's self-perception was its weak relationship with the workers' movement. Here the party long acknowledged that 'the vanguard is lagging', and leaders showed little confidence in their ability to call the workers to the barricades, to provoke or lead social protest.[93]

The weakness of labour activism in Russia in the face of a deep socio-economic slump that so astounded the communists had deep roots in the political passivity encouraged by communism, as well as fear induced by the results of such recent manifestations of mass activism as the bloody events of October 1993.[94] The rapid involvement of much of the workforce in an atomised 'struggle for survival', which the state alleviated through selective bargaining, further militated against broad labour solidarity, at least in the short term.[95]

But structural factors also limited popular protest. Since Soviet trade unions were 'transmission belts' of party directives downwards, there were few means of airing collective grievances upwards.[96] Most trade unions remained hierarchically structured with weak horizontal links able to organise and co-ordinate workers nationally. Such problems were replicated within the largest union, the Federation of Independent Trade Unions of Russia (FITUR) (comprising some sixty million people, or 95 per cent of union members), and between unions and enterprises across the country.[97] Moreover, as was noted, such links and connections with the unions that remained accrued to the post-communist regime rather than to the CPRF, and were assiduously cultivated by the former. Trade union leaderships were co-opted in quasi-corporate arrangements such as the annual tripartite commissions, where they bargained with government and management over economic policy. Within the enterprise, trade unions remained dependent on management for patronage, and had more to lose by opposing management than by joining enterprise directors in seeking state support for industry and actually supporting the privatisation process.[98] As for other post-Soviet organisations, the political muscle of FITUR was dissipated. It appeared allergic to coherent political organisation or party affiliation, and preferred opportunistic lobbying towards centrist and pro-government groups such as Our Home Is Russia (OHIR), or Fatherland-All Russia (FAR) in 1999. Union members themselves remained distrustful of their leadership's ability effectively to defend their interests, and split their political preferences, and thereby the potential of organised protest.[99] So the emergence of even a democratic left movement was complicated by the absence of a united labour movement to which to appeal.

Overall, the claim of critics that the CPRF avoided active engagement with civil society forces such as trade unions was exaggerated.[100] It was not a case of lack of intent but rather a lack of ability to influence groups which remained beyond the reach of any one political group. However, the CPRF's party structure and culture appeared to exacerbate the problems and defy immediate resolution. The CPRF leaders at times (particularly in 1993) saw spontaneous social upris- ing more as a threat than an opportunity to be exploited and led.[101] More fundamentally, the PPOs appeared to perpetuate their Soviet role as organisations better suited to directive than discussion. They had a tendency for abstract sloganeering, and could offer no concrete proposals for workers' concerns.[102] Party workers were generally unsuited by age and training for mass activism and preferred to con- centrate on internal party matters and avoid work with 'bourgeois' social strata.[103] The CPRF did manage to co-ordinate some demands with trade unions, particularly regional and minor groups such as 'Defence', and achieved joint actions with them on the proviso that the communists did not try to dominate.[104] But renewed attempts from 1998 to infiltrate FITUR and gain the election of more pro-communist union leaders backfired, with many communist activists simply removed from the unions by their irate leadership, who estimated sig- nificant communist influence at no more than 2 per cent of work- places.[105] Such problems only reinforced the CPRF leaders' pessimism, and strengthened their tendency to preserve influence through lobbying the state, as described below.

Relations with youth

Symbolic of the CPRF's problems with attracting the young were its relations with left-leaning youth organisations. The Soviet *Komsomol* had played a major role in the socialisation of youth in communist values while providing a first step up the party career ladder. Its dis- solution in 1991 after the ban on the CPSU was followed by a fight for its heritage by successor organisations. Its main successor was the non-communist Russian Union of Youth (RUY), which remained aloof from the CPRF.[106] The remaining fragments fought for revolu- tionary purity, and the CPRF vied for hegemony over these. The most traditionalist and least influential organisation was the Vladimir Lenin Communist Union of Youth (VLCUY), affiliated to Shenin's UCP-CPSU, and preferring not just the name of the former *Komsomol*, but its style of work (organising cultural and sport activities).[107] A more radical offshoot, the Russian Communist Union of Youth (RCUY), was formed in 1993 with the CPRF's participation, and came to number (allegedly) some twenty-one thousand members. This group focused on street agitation and itself produced a more extreme scion, the Revolutionary Communist Union of Youth (Bolsheviks)

(RCUY (b)) headed by Pavel Bylevskii, which was close to the Russian Communist Workers' Party and the radical nationalist National Bolshevik Party of Eduard Limonov. It modelled itself on North Korean and Cuban communism, and its negligible social impact was to some degree compensated for by its declared involvement in the bombing of Moscow monuments.[108]

The CPRF's relationship with the more moderate RCUY broke down permanently in 1997 over tactical differences, and the CPRF's attempts to control the *Komsomol*, which then supported Anpilov's radical 'Stalinist Bloc' at the 1999 elections and later made overtures to the pro-Putin Edinstvo.[109] After this the CPRF created its own loyalist Union of Communist Youth (UCY), allegedly by using supporters in regional administrations to restrict youth leadership positions to CPRF members and to smear the RCUY.[110] The UCY claimed thirty-eight thousand members, organised pickets, participated in regional elections, set up organisations in schools and universities, and organised charitable donations to the needy.[111] It had a more pragmatic orientation, as the CPRF recognised that it had to concentrate on new methods of working with youth, avoiding ideological slogans and solving specific problems such as state support of young families and professional training.[112] That the CPRF had a sizeable youth wing at all might be seen as a success, given that such youth organisations were conspicuous by their absence in Russia. Yet the UCY remained beset by financial and ideological differences. While the CPRF had problems in keeping even the most doctrinaire youth, non-communists were distinctly sceptical about an organisation known in Soviet times for bureaucratism, conformism and the careerism of its higher echelons.[113]

Relations with the military

The party's relationship with the military followed a similar pattern of limited infiltration and politicisation. Those associated with the still bloated and heavily disaffected military-defence constituency made up some 20 per cent of the overall electorate, and their concerns were voiced by many political movements.[114] The CPRF logically enough sought to present itself as the best defender of the military's heritage, and the prominence of former Soviet officers in its ranks (such as Generals Makashov and Varennikov) reinforced its patriotic ideological stance, and seemed to help it win significant military support in the elections of 1993–95.[115] Yet, as the events of autumn 1993 indicated, the army preferred to follow an independent agenda, and the army officer corps still preferred to work out its problems with top brass rather than through politics.[116] Lectures from the presidential chief of staff, Egorov, during the 1996 elections increased pressure on senior officers not to support the CPRF.[117] But the CPRF's own ability to exploit military grievances appeared weak. The communists appeared to benefit most in 1997 when the popular General Lev Rokhlin formed the Movement in Support of the Army, the Defence Industry and Military Science (MSA) with the assistance of the CPRF regional *aktiv* and Spiritual Heritage, and declared his readiness to 'march under a red flag'.[118] The MSA's aim to create a truly broad and vehemently anti-government military bloc meant that its potential was greater than many previous military-political organisations, although the overall number of active servicemen in the MSA did not prove to be high. Yet in practice its relations with the CPRF were fraught. Rokhlin's militancy and his courtship by party radicals such as Ilyukhin alarmed the CPRF leadership, who managed to persuade Rokhlin to stand down as Duma Defence Committee chair (under regime pressure) and not to form a separate Duma defence fraction. After Rokhlin's murder in July 1998 the MSA (now headed by Ilyukhin) was given little support from the CPRF and faded into obscurity.[119] Within the Duma, the CPRF generally tended to give welfare issues and civilian industry subsidies greater priority than defence spending, and although the party still commanded 18 per cent of the military vote in 1999, 48 per cent supported the Edinstvo bloc and, by implication, Putin's greater ability to turn military rhetoric into action.[120]

The CPRF and the Church

At first glance, the Russian Orthodox Church might seem a profitable ally for Zyuganov's communist party. His explicit appropriation of religious morality and nationalist themes even culminated in his taking baptism.[121] There was strong common ground between Russian nationalism and the Church's traditional identification with the state, its values of *sobornost* and collectivism, as well as over the opposition to the increasing influence of foreign sects. Communist Zorkaltsev's stewardship of the Duma Committee for Public Associations and Religious Organisations from 1993 onwards showed the priority the communists put on this sphere. However, as for many other Russian institutions, the Church did not have a unified infrastructure and was riven by internal rivalries between pro-Western and anti-Western wings. The activities of sympathetic nationalist priests in groups such as the Union of Orthodox Brotherhoods (these were originally set up in 1990 as charitable and education groups, but took an increasingly xenophobic slant) remained isolated.[122] They were estranged from Patriarch Aleksii himself, who preferred to steer the church on an independent course, and tacitly supported Yeltsin towards the latter stages of the 1996 election campaign.[123] The virulently nationalist and anti-Semitic Bishop Ioann (Snychev), who was long the figurehead of the anti-Western wing in the church hierarchy and repeatedly courted by Zyuganov in the communist press, was replaced after his death in 1995 by Vladimir (Kotlyarov) who became extremely negative towards the CPRF.[124]

Elite rapprochement and accord

Although the CPRF failed to regain an influential position in any of the above institutions, its success in achieving influence within the political elite was more marked, while still subject to many limitations. The marked clientelistic and 'state-seeking' tendencies within the CPRF's higher echelons were prompted by several factors, chief of which was financial necessity. Deprived of property and isolated as a pariah after August 1991, the party had to bargain and negotiate with banks and entrepreneurs to ensure its continued survival, which would overcome the failure to pay membership dues and help set up a party press.[125] Undoubtedly the urgent need to appeal to such strata lay behind state patriotism and its weakened critique of capital.

The question of the CPRF's financial support was controversial, and it became clear that elite bargaining worked to a degree. The party did get some mileage from *nomenklatura* connections and the transition from 'plan to clan', albeit not to the degree of the Polish, Hungarian or Bulgarian successor parties. Finance from the *nomenklatura* system helped set up the Komsomol, and the party appeared to benefit from funds placed in commercial structures before 1991 and channelled back to the CPRF through intermediaries who had benefited from the *nomenklatura* capitalism process.[126] Such individuals included Vladimir Semago (an early participant in the formation of co-operatives in the late 1980s, and head of Rosbiznesbank), and Nikolai Ryzhkov, ex-Soviet prime minister, former chair of Tveruniversalbank and one of many former party officials who had gravitated to key economic posts.[127] The 'red businessmen' became major party sponsors, and were rewarded with prominent posts in the leadership. Among many examples the most important were president of the Rosagrompromstroi corporation, Viktor Vidmanov, who joined the party Presidium in 1997 and helped establish connections with industrial companies in the MIC, energy and machine-building sectors, and Valerii Vorotnikov, Spiritual Heritage member, former KGB General and director of the security agency VZOR (with ties to important banking circles such as MOST-bank), who was twelfth on the CPRF party list in 1995.[128] The orientation towards national capital helped the CPRF develop connections with many large banks which were keen to back all winning horses in regional and national campaigns, such as Kredobank, Inkombank, Promstroibank, Agroprombank and even ONEKSIMbank.[129] The party was rumoured to have access to the budgets of communist-controlled regions, and received donations from other friendly institutions such as the Russian Academy of Agricultural Sciences, which reportedly owned an extensive network of agricultural and commercial structures.[130]

Financial considerations further tied the CPRF to the Duma. In 1997 over 95 per cent of its funding allegedly came from the state, more than sufficient for its central staff.[131] The reliance on state funding was only increased by the poor material position of party members. Well-off party members were required to donate 1 per cent of earnings to party coffers each month, while pensioners and others gave what they could.[132] But those who had themselves not been paid for months could be unwilling and unable to contribute, forcing severe financial crisis in some areas.[133] Altogether, it seemed that the party was not as impoverished as it claimed to be, particularly since many thousands of campaign activists and veterans worked for free. Nevertheless, financial problems became a major factor in the party's dependency on the state.

A key concern of the communists in increasing their national influence was overcoming the so-called 'information blockade' against them – their pariah status as 'communo-fascists' so beloved of the mainstream Russian media. Initially leaders concentrated on bypassing the state media, resurrecting their own press and mobilising their members by addressing hundreds of meetings and writing dozens of articles.[134] Their favoured 'door-to-door' campaigning, whereby CPRF members avoided state media altogether and canvassed the public personally for votes or in support of their legislative proposals, not only saved money but allowed the party to cultivate an image both as an activist and omnipresent organisation, and as one abused by the central authorities.[135] Simultaneously, the whole thrust of the CPRF's ideological and propagandist innovations and active public profile was aimed at demonstrating that it was a new, legal, democratic and constitutional force that was not the 'party of revenge', but a significant counterweight to the unpopular ruling regime. This strategy was later to prove a clear failure in the 1996 elections, when the party's reliance on door-to-door methods and poor relationship with the state media came to the fore.

After this defeat, the party sought to rectify its poor image by increasing its resources spent on propaganda and presence in the press.[136] While the party branched out into Internet technologies, its most prominent leaders (especially Zyuganov and the party's ideological secretary, Kravets), became regular interviewees, particularly with non-communist and non-state media such as NTV and *Nezavisimaya gazeta*. The party undoubtedly gained propaganda value by default as the largest party in the State Duma and, thereby, coverage on the Duma's television show, 'Parliamentary Hour', broadcast on RTR, Russia's second national television station.[137] Although the CPRF's diminished electoral challenge was also responsible, such improved image techniques certainly helped the CPRF get more positive election coverage during 1999–2000, when anti-communism was much less apparent. This should not be overstated however: CPRF actions such as its March 1999 approval of a law creating a council to regulate morality on the media convinced the journalists' union and the heads of television networks that the party's promises to respect media freedoms were far from sincere.

From the outset, a strategy of inculcation into the elite was likely because of the bureaucratic mentality of moderates in the CPRF leadership. In terms of life histories, social experience, ideology and interests, these were no revolutionaries, and they seemed happier at elite politics than grass-roots activism.[138] This was evident as early as February 1992 in the formation of the small nationalist group, the RNC, by Zyuganov and KGB General, Aleksandr Sterligov. The RNC's chief difference to many of the similar nationalist groups of the time lay in its attempt to subvert the democratic inclinations of the regime from within in a 'creeping coup' rather than from the street.[139] The CPRF had moreover been attempting infiltration of the state itself since as early as September 1991, when qualified party loyalists had entered government service in the localities en masse and incognito.[140]

Such a strategy was feasible given that elite continuity in Russia was so marked. Following the August 1991 'revolution', Yeltsin's' prioritisation of economic reform meant no new elections to local Soviets and no clearout of former communist party personnel in many enterprises and administrative levels.[141] Irrespective of their ideological position, many of the bureaucratic elite (including the communist 'moderates') were formed in the same school, often shared the same mentality and recognised certain common interests, while the vast network of personal relationships and clans within the *nomenklatura* was maintained.[142] At the same time the new elite's allegiance to democracy was tenuous, thereby encouraging the communists that the democratic choice was not final and could be reversed. After the near calamitous divisions of 1991–93, a certain 'balance of interests' took over intra-elite relations as various groups combined through self-interest to promote the values of statehood, patriotism and civic peace. All this was aimed at consolidating the (often ill-gotten) economic gains of the new financiers and officials and preventing any further redistribution or revenge.[143] This 'self-limiting revolution' was to draw on the skills of the old elite and secure their loyalty to the new order, thus prioritising stability over any further progress with the anti-communist revolution.[144]

Forced to acknowledge these constraints, and recognising that even a capitalist state was probably better than none, the CPRF leadership moved towards a 'strategic compromise' with the regime during 1994–95, although they maintained their aim of subverting the regime from within.[145] The moderates were increasingly forced to recognise the difficulty of swiftly changing the post-1991 political and economic arrangements, and restoring the Soviet system. The overriding goal became not the achievement of full political power, but the gradual assumption of power through power-sharing arrangements such as the 'government of national trust'. This aimed at giving the communists a share of political power and concessions in policy, such as a parliamentary political system and a retreat from free market monetarism towards statist protectionism.

The first manifestation of this was the 'Accord for Russia' movement of early 1994, which was a trial balloon for Zyuganov's favoured 'national front strategy' but also had the aim of offering an alternative elite and supra-party consensus politics to Yeltsin's parallel Civic Accord. Compared with earlier incarnations such as the NSF, it had a narrower scope and moved from radicalism towards the centre. The majority of its members belonged to 'the old or new elite and [were] connected with one another and with their political opponents through long-standing business and personal relations'.[146] Zyuganov increasingly offered olive branches to centrist political forces such as Women of Russia and even Yabloko.[147] The president and his entourage talked of incorporating the communists in government. The Communists rebuffed attempts to co-opt them, but notably did make attempts to bargain with the regime.[148] A more sophisticated effort at infiltrating the elite was attempted by Spiritual Heritage, which used its pre-existing connections with the state apparatus and security services to re-establish links between the patriots and CPRF, power ministries and banks.[149] Its ex-KGB chairman, Podberezkin, consolidated links with both regime and opposition.[150] As a public proponent of the 'strategic compromise' he openly declared its aim to replace the intelligentsia, business, military, president and prime minister's adherence to liberalism with state patriotism.[151]

In the Russian political context such processes were highly ambivalent. As we shall see in later chapters, it became clear that many in the political elite saw the moderate communists as more reliable partners than radicals, even of the liberal sort. The top-down technocratic approach of the ex-*nomenklatura* raised fears for the development of an autonomous civil society even in relatively democratic East-Central Europe.[152] In Russia, in the absence of completed democratisation and marketisation, the danger remained that elite rapprochement might take on a corporatist, clientelist and deeply anti-democratic character. After all, the CPRF was backed by organisations whose real *raison d'être* was the desire of certain key sections of the former Soviet elite to preserve their old dominant status, now based on a new set of ideological/motivational reasons. This ideology drew on variants of authoritarian modernisation, all of which shared scant concern for 'the niceties of democratisation'.[153] This threat was graphically revealed in the 1996 election campaign, when Podberezkin and Zyuganov allegedly joined Yeltsin's bodyguard Aleksandr Korzhakov and thirteen bankers and industrialists in proposing to postpone or cancel free elections.[154]

That such a compromise did not occur showed that a corporatist outcome remained frustrated by the continuing fragmentation of the elite into groups with their own interests, on the basis of economic-branch, apparatus, functional and regional dividing lines.[155] But the ramifications for the CPRF were still pernicious. The party was increasingly enmeshed in a less than democratic system it ostensibly aimed to replace. This was nowhere more evident than in the party's relationship to capital and the 'oligarchs' against which the party spouted so much venom. Participation in the State Duma as the largest fraction exposed the party to unregulated business lobbying activities and the pronounced tendency for Duma deputies of all fractions to use state funds for personal and party tasks. Semago, who left the CPRF in 1998, accused virtually all Duma groups of participating in a routine of selling votes and distributing favours between government, Duma and major corporations. The CPRF was apparently a serial offender, with Duma chair Seleznev distributing favours to his colleagues in the Duma and taking payments for putting bills on the Duma agenda.[156] Deputies were regularly 'bought' to lobby for business and regional interests during legislation, or to support the government on key decisions like the 1999 impeachment of Yeltsin or, indeed, the budgetary process.[157]

The CPRF's implication in corruption allegedly stretched to defending the oligarchic Gazprom gas monopoly from break-up in return for kickbacks, and receiving budget funds channelled for other purposes through commercial partners such as Rosagropromstroi.[158] They even defended privileges to Russia's numerous closed cities, whose lack of budgetary transparency apparently concealed donations from the military to the CPRF.[159] Kulik and Maslyukov, the CPRF's allies in the Primakov government of 1998–99, had allegedly diverted state funds to party coffers. Their departure from government dealt the party a heavy financial blow to which Kuptsov (in charge of party finances) responded by selling party list places in 1999 at a price of up to $1.5 million.[160] Such processes were becoming increasingly difficult to conceal and communist critics decried the presence of dozens of previously unknown businessmen on the party list. Some such as Gennadii Semigin (who soon became vice-chair of the Duma) appeared to receive prominent positions in return for cash.[161] Such allegations might be politically motivated, and were impossible to prove conclusively in a political system whose distinguishing features are the inter-linking of capital and politics and the absence of a clear line between legal and para-legal. Indeed communist deputies denied impropriety and asserted that their lobbying activities of parliament would stand up to clearer regulation.[162] Even Semago asserted that some communists were immune from suspicion. Nevertheless, the party's enmeshment in an inherently corrupt political system meant that its creeping coup was vitiated even as it was vindicated, and gave real substance to the radicals' allegations of bourgeois-*nomenklatura* tendencies in the leadership. Strategic compromise became a compromised strategy.

Conclusion

So to what extent was the CPRF a genuine party able to slough off its past as a state organisation? The answer is somewhat ambivalent; organisational advantages bestowed on it from the CPSU and residual leadership and management experience gave it a head-start in its emergence as the largest and most organised political party in Russia. Its strong and relatively stable connection with its party constituency was to become one of the few examples in Russia of a connection between an elite grouping and the spontaneous democratic insurgency of civil society. In this respect the CPRF played the key intermediary role of a genuine political party.

Yet features common to many post-communist political parties were present in the CPRF, particularly in its friable structure, pronounced dependency on the state, cadre tendencies and decreasing role for mass membership. However, the party's heritage endowed the party with unique features, and whereas these may have given it an initial political advantage, many were arguably not optimal for the party's longer-term future. The CPRF's original foundation can be seen as an attempt to refill the structures of the CPSU with mass content, but Katz and Mair note that mass parties which aim to defend the interests of well-delimited and internally well-organised segments of the population tend to an inflexible structure which may outlast the social community it is used to mobilise.[163] Kitschelt agrees that 'historical baggage' such as party structures and ideology can limit a party's 'path-dependent learning' and may promote strategic inertia which may only be overcome by momentous events such as an electoral defeat.[164] Indeed, the CPRF's historical baggage was large. The party remained very 'Soviet' in membership and internal structure, particularly the latter. The initial weakness of leadership control over a committed radical membership was to create constant upward pressure on the upper echelons, which it seemed could be placated or suppressed, but not surmounted.

The CPRF's response to this pressure reflected its ambivalent internal democracy and more broadly the ambivalence of the democratisation of the Russian system as a whole. By using authoritarian methods to override their more intransigent members the party leadership looked to modernise the party. But by subverting the spontaneous activism of the party mass and negotiating with a regime which itself was not fully democratic, they threatened to perpetuate the dominance of elite politics over mass which continually marked politics in Russia. What is more, by using Leninist methods to re-establish leadership control the CPRF's leaders indeed threatened to replicate the strategic inertia and inflexibility of earlier Leninist parties. Although the CPRF leadership was clearly aware that the party's organisation itself might become a serious brake on development and needed reform, their apparent unwillingness to move beyond the Leninist template meant that the solutions were not obvious.[165]

So the CPRF was a hybrid party described here as a 'vanguard parliamentary party', becoming increasingly inculcated into the political system while protesting the validity of parliamentary politics and retaining much residual vanguardism. It retained structure, ideology and much behaviour from the Soviet era. Although it was the only approximation to a national mass party in Russia it remained stamped with clientelistic and cadre elements and Leninist organisational forms. The implications of this went beyond the matter of the party's internal cohesion, where mass and cadre tendencies were in tension. As we have seen the CPRF's continued aspirations for hegemony over civil society were constantly frustrated by a combination of the party's organisational structure, its ideology and the superior political capital of the post-communist regime, suggesting serious limits to its potential for continued political renewal. We shall see the same interaction in the party's electoral behaviour. As the ensuing chapters will show, the hybrid nature of this 'vanguard parliamentary party' with its only partial acceptance of parliamentary politics combined with its clientelistic tendencies explains much of its performance in the presidential elections of 1996 and its erratic behaviour thereafter.

Notes

1 R. Sakwa, *Russian Politics and Society*, 2nd edn (London, Routledge, 1996), p. 80.

2 For a summary of the main functions of a political party, see K. von Beyme, *Political Parties in Western Democracies* (Aldershot, Gower, 1985), pp. 11–13.

162 The Communist Party in post-Soviet Russia

3 G. Gill, *The Collapse of a Single Party System: The Disintegration of the Communist Party of the Soviet Union* (Cambridge, Cambridge University Press, 1994), pp. 4–6.
4 S. White, *Russia's New Politics* (Cambridge, Cambridge University Press, 2000), p. 34.
5 S. White, M. Wyman and S. Oates, 'Parties and voters in the 1995 Russian Duma election', *Europe-Asia Studies*, 49:5 (1997), 775.
6 G. Golosov, 'Who survives? Party origins, organizational development, and electoral performance in post-communist Russia', *Political Studies*, 46 (1998), 529–39.
7 P. G. Lewis, *Political Parties in Post-Communist Eastern Europe* (London, Routledge, 2000).
8 M. Steven Fish, *Democracy from Scratch: Opposition and Regime in the New Russian Revolution*, (Princeton, NJ, Princeton University Press, 1994), pp. 81, 84.
9 M. Waller, 'Adaptation of the former communist parties of East-Central Europe: a case of social-democratization?', *Party Politics*, 1:4 (1995), 482.
10 *Ibid.*, 476.
11 A. Bozóki, 'The ideology of modernization and the policy of materialism: the day after for the socialists', *Journal of Communist Studies and Transition Politics*, 13:3 (1997), 61.
12 V. Zubek, 'The phoenix out of the ashes: the rise to power of Poland's post-communist SdRP', *Communist and Post-Communist Studies*, 28:3 (1995), 284.
13 S. White and O. Kryshtanovskaya, 'From Soviet nomenklatura to Russian elite,' *Europe-Asia Studies*, 48:5 (1996), 711.
14 R. Sakwa, 'Left or right? The CPRF and the problem of democratic consolidation in Russia', *Journal of Communist Studies and Transition Politics*, 14:1&2 (1998), 137.
15 *IV sezd Kommunisticheskoi partii Rossiiskoi Federatsii 19–20 aprelya 1997 goda (Materialy i dokumenty)*, (Moscow, ITRK RSPP, 1997), p. 90.
16 *SR*, 2 February 1995.
17 N. Harding, *Leninism* (Basingstoke, Macmillan, 1996), p. 173.
18 For more on the structure of the CPSU, see R. J. Hill and P. Frank, *The Soviet Communist Party*, 3rd edn (London, Allen and Unwin, 1986), and R. Sakwa, *Soviet Politics in Perspective* (London, Routledge, 1998), ch. 6.
19 Author's interview with Boris Zarankin, parliamentary aide to Ivan Melnikov, 21 September 2000: *P*, 2–3 February 1999.
20 Fish, *Democracy from Scratch*, pp. 113–17.
21 The party has a regional organisation even in Chechnya, but its St Petersburg and Leningrad *oblast* organisations have been amalgamated.
22 M. Steven Fish, 'The advent of multipartism in Russia, 1993–5, *Post-Soviet Affairs*, 11:4 (1995), 340–83.
23 F. J. Fleron, Jr, R. Ahl and F. Lane, 'Where now in the study of Russian political parties?', *Journal of Communist Studies and Transition Politics*, 14:1&2 (1998), 230.
24 M. McFaul, *Russia between Elections: What the December 1995 Results Really Mean* (Moscow, Carnegie Moscow Center, 1996), p. 21.
25 *Komsomolskaya pravda*, 26 March 1996.
26 *S*, 21 May 1994.
27 McFaul, *Russia between Elections*, p. 21.

28 See Fish, 'The advent of multipartism', 360.
29 J. Barth Urban and V. Solovei, *Russia's Communists at the Crossroads* (Boulder, CO, Westview, 1997), pp. 128, 138.
30 Each local organisation had at least one full-time employee devoted to organisational work, but many other members combined their party work with other paid activity (*Iz*, 20 March 1996).
31 Kuptsov, *SR*, 2 February 1995.
32 *IV sezd*, p. 105.
33 S. White, 'Background to the XXVIII Congress', in E. A. Rees (ed.), *The Soviet Communist Party in Disarray* (Basingstoke, Macmillan, 1992), p. 12.
34 *Rossiiskie vesti*, 16 July 1996; *Iz*, 20 March 1996.
35 A. Makarkin, *Kommunisticheskaya partiya Rossiiskoi Federatsii* (Moscow, Tsentr politicheskykh tekhnologii, 1996), p. 1.
36 *Kto est chto: politicheskaya Rossiya 1995–6* (Moscow, Ministerstvo ekonomiki RF, 1996), p. 78.
37 Many became CPRF Duma deputies and members of the CPRF CC from 1995 onwards.
38 *Iz*, 20 March 1996.
39 A. Buzgalin, *Budushchee kommunizma* (Moscow, 'Olma-press', 1996), p. 91.
40 Zyuganov, 13 February 1998 from web site: www.kprf.ru/pmes.htm.
41 See the biographical information on the Presidium, Secretariat and related commissions after the December 2000 Congress on the CPRF's web site: www.kprf.ru.
42 Zyuganov, *SR*, 17 December 1996.
43 *P*, 30 November 2000, author's interview with A. Filippov on 6 December 1997; Kuptsov, *SWB* SU/2899 B/2 (22 April 1997).
44 *P*, 30 November 2000.
45 J. D. Nagle and A. Mahr, *Democracy and Democratization* (London, Sage, 1999), chs 5 and 6.
46 M. Orenstein, 'A genealogy of communist successor parties in East-Central Europe and the determinants of their success', *East European Politics and Societies*, 12:3 (1998).
47 For example, Zyuganov at the Eighth CC CPRF Plenum on 20 June 1998, from web site: www.kprf.ru/news/buleten.htm.
48 *Russia*, 7 (1997).
49 Author's interview with A. Filippov on 31 January 1998; report of Vladislav Yurchik, chair of the party's Central Control-Auditing Commission at the Seventh Congress, December 2000 from web site: www.kprf.ru.
50 Fish, 'The advent of multipartism', 357.
51 For the role of the grass roots, see Urban and Solovei, *Russia's Communists*, pp. 49–50.
52 *Ibid.*, p. 175, n. 42.
53 *Informatsionnyi byulleten*, 7:48 (1998) (accessed from web site: www.kprf.ru).
54 *P-5*, 31 October–7 November 1997.
55 Sakwa, 'Left or right?', 13.
56 G. Golosov, 'From Adygeya to Yaroslavl: factors of party development in the regions of Russia, 1995–1998', *Europe-Asia Studies*, 51:8 (1999), 1333–66.
57 *IV sezd*, p. 98.
58 *Ibid.*, pp. 32, 36–41.
59 *Izm* 1:6 (1995), 83; *Dialog*, 12 (1996), 61–3.

60 *Dialog*, 2 (1996), 69–74; author's interview with N. Bindyukov on 18 December 1997.

61 *Russia Review*, 17 June 1996.

62 Author's interview with Bindyukov on 18 December 1997.

63 These include the left-leaning Centre for Researching the Political Culture of Russia, which produced opinion polls for the CPRF, the Institute of Economic Affairs, the Institute of National-Economic Forecasting, the Russian Union of Industrialists and Entrepreneurs (*Kapital*, 29 May–4 June 1996).

64 J. Barth Urban, 'The communist parties of Russia and Ukraine on the eve of the 1999 elections: similarities, contrasts, and interactions', *Demokratizatsiya*, 7:1 (1999), 126.

65 A. Kravets, *P*, 29–30 August 2000.

66 *Moscow News*, 21–27 August 1997.

67 Compare G. Gill, *The Rules of the Communist Party of the Soviet Union* (Basingstoke, Macmillan, 1988), p. 235, and *IV sezd*, p. 95.

68 Kuptsov, *SWB* SU/3208 B/2 (23 April 1998).

69 M. Kholmskaya, 'Kommunisticheskoe dvizhenie Rossii: sovremmenyi etap razvitiya', *Alternativy*, 2:5 (1994), 99.

70 C. Shore, *Italian Communism: The Escape from Leninism* (London, Pluto Press, 1990), pp. 131–6.

71 R. Tiersky, *Ordinary Stalinism: Democratic Centralism and the Question of Communist Political Development* (London, Allen and Unwin, 1985) p. 49.

72 M. Waller, *Democratic Centralism* (Manchester, Manchester University Press, 1981) p. 127.

73 *IV sezd*, p. 32, p. 105.

74 E. Razumov, *Krushenie i nadezhdy: politicheskie zametki* (Moscow, Politekh–4, 1996), p. 154.

75 *PR*, 3–10 December 1997.

76 Urban and Solovei, *Russia's Communists*, p. 54.

77 *K*, 16 May 1996.

78 For example, S. Chugaev, *Iz*, 21 March 1996.

79 *MN*, 27 July–3 August 1997.

80 Vladimir Semago, *S*, 2 August 1998.

81 *Novoe vremya*, 22, 1996.

82 *P-5*, 29 October 1997.

83 Vladimir Semago, CPRF Duma deputy, alleged that voting cards were collected after every Duma meeting and locked in a safe, with no members of the faction allowed to vote personally. Furthermore, absentees' voting cards were used by their comrades to fulfil the party line (*K*, 10 April 1997).

84 Author's interview with R. Kosolapov on 10 February 1998.

85 Tiersky, *Ordinary Stalinism*, p. 53.

86 Many long-term dissidents were removed from leadership positions. The RSSO leaders Ivan Osadchii and Richard Kosolapov were removed from the CC at the Fourth Congress in 1997, along with *Komsomol* leader Malyarov. Kosolapov asserted that those who wrote letters of protest about the party leadership were put under great pressure by the leadership to leave the party or publicly retract their statements (*P-5*, 31 January 1998).

87 *KPRF mezhdu umerennostyu i radikalizmom* (Moscow, Tsentr politicheskykh tekhnologii, 1997), p. 1.

88 One of the other leadership rivals, Viktor Ilyukhin, was considered too con-

frontational even for his own colleagues. See V. Bondarev, *Kto est kto–politicheskaya elita Rossii v portretakh* (Moscow, NTS Russika, 1995), p. 223.

89 Richard Kosolapov asserted that no one was willing to support his protests at the December 1996 CC Plenum, despite their approval. (Author's interview with Kosolapov on 10 February 1998; see also *Molniya*, 21, October 1997; *PR*, 7 May 1997.)

90 For the traditional features of communist party leaders see N. McInnes, *The Communist Parties of Western Europe* (London, Oxford University Press, 1975), p. 121.

91 *Trudovaya Rossiya*, 18 (1997), 2.

92 Sakwa, 'Left or right?', 137.

93 Zyuganov, *SR*, 17 January 1996, and 20 November 1997: 'the CPRF in the Duma simply cannot be more radical than the moods of the people and people simply are not going on to the streets in sufficient numbers'.

94 Author's interview with A. Filippov on 6 December 1997.

95 G. Gill and R. Markwick, *Russia's Stillborn Democracy? From Gorbachev to Yeltsin* (Oxford, Oxford University Press, 2000), pp. 226–30.

96 S. Clarke, *Labour Relations in Transition: Wages, Employment and Industrial Conflict in Russia* (Cheltenham, Edward Elgar, 1996), p. 34.

97 T. F. Remington, 'Democratization and the new political order in Russia', in K. Dawisha and B. Parrott (eds), *Democratic Changes and Authoritarian Reactions in Russia, Ukraine, Belarus and Moldova* (Cambridge, Cambridge University Press, 1997), p. 106.

98 S. Ashwin, *Russian Workers: The Anatomy of Patience* (Manchester, Manchester University Press, 1999) pp. 89, 182.

99 L. J. Cook, *Labor and Liberalization: Trade Unions in the New Russia* (New York, Twentieth Century Fund Press, 1997), pp. 63–4.

100 Gill and Markwick, *Russia's Stillborn Democracy?*, p. 246.

101 *Materialy Vsesorossiiskoi konferentsii Kommunisticheskoi Partii Rossiiskoi Federatsii* (Moscow, 1994), pp. 70–8.

102 Author's interview with Boris Slavin on 29 November 1997; CC CPRF secretary Vladimir Tikhonov, *PR*, 4–10 February 1998.

103 Zyuganov, *SR*, 17 February 1994.

104 Author's interview with A. Filippov on 6 December 1997; *NG*, 27 March 1997.

105 See the comments of Andrei Isaev, head of FITUR's parliamentary wing the Union of Labour in *NG Stsenarii*, 21 April 2000.

106 *K*, 17 February 1998, 2; *Rossiya–95: Nakanune vyborov* (Moscow, 'Akademia', 1995), p. 221.

107 A. Verkhovskii (ed.), *Levye v Rossii: ot umerennykh do ekstremistov* (Moscow, Panorama, 1997).

108 *Bumbarash 2017*, 6 (46) (1997); and *Ne Dai Bog*, 6, (1996).

109 *P-5*, 6–13 March 1998; *Johnson's Russia List*, 16 February 2000.

110 Renfrey Clarke, web site: www.international.se/sp/maj5.htm.

111 *P*, 15 June 2000.

112 Author's interview with A. Filippov on 31 January 1998.

113 See *Transitions Online*, 13 November 2000 at web site: www.tol.cz.

114 R. Barylski, *The Soldier in Russian Politics 1985–1996* (New Brunswick, Transaction, 1998), pp. 280–5.

115 *Ibid.*

116 *NG*, 3 July 1997.

117 Barylski, *The Soldier in Russian Politics*, p. 11.
118 *S*, 10 July 1997, 3; *General Lev Rokhlin i perspectivy Rossiiskoi oppozitsii* (Moscow, Tsentr politicheskykh tekhnologii, 1997), p. 1.
119 For more on Rokhlin's highly suspicious murder, for which his wife was convicted in 2000 then released by the Russian Supreme Court in June 2001 on the basis of insufficient evidence, see A. Rogachevskii, 'The Murder of General Rokhlin', *Europe-Asia Studies*, 52:1 (2000), 95–110.
120 *NG*, 25 December 1999.
121 *SR* (version on web site: www.sr.park.ru) 14 March 2000.
122 J. Devlin, *Slavophiles and Commissars* (Basingstoke, Macmillan, 1999), pp. 82–8.
123 E. T. Bacon, 'The Church and politics in Russia: a case study of the 1996 presidential election', *Religion, State and Society*, 25:3 (1997), 260.
124 A. Makarkin, *KPRF i ee soyuzniki posle vyborov* (Moscow, Tsentr politicheskykh tekhnologii, 1996), p. 4.
125 *Materialy Vserossiiskoi konferentsii*, p. 49.
126 *P-5*, 23 January 1997.
127 *S*, 28 June 1995.
128 Urban and Solovei, *Russia's Communists*, p. 161; *Zavtra*, 50 (1997). For the many other party donors see www.nns.ru/elects/izbobyed/finansy.html.
129 *K*, 6 November 1997; and *Vek*, 1 September 1995.
130 *Delovie Lyudy*, 101 (1999); *Argumenty i fakti* (*AiF*) 6 October 1999; and *Novaya gazeta*, 21–27 February 2000.
131 *K*, 6 November 1997.
132 *Iz*, 20 March 1996.
133 *IV sezd*, pp. 36–7.
134 *Materialy Vserossiiskoi konferentsii*, p. 49.
135 S. Chernyakovsky, 'The Communist Party of the Russian Federation', in M. McFaul *et al.*, *Primer on Russia's 1999 Duma Elections* (Washington, DC, Carnegie Endowment, 1999), p. 82.
136 *NG Stsenarii*, 8 October 1999.
137 Chernyakovsky, 'The Communist Party', p. 80.
138 A. Fadin, *Obshchaya gazeta* (*OG*), 29 February–6 March 1996.
139 B. Clark, *An Empire's New Clothes: The End of Russia's Liberal Dream* (London, Vintage, 1995), pp. 171–2.
140 Urban and Solovei, *Russia's Communists*, p. 151.
141 For example, in 1994, 75 per cent of the presidential administration, 74.3 per cent of the Russian government and 82.3 per cent of the local elite were former members of the communist ruling group (O. Kryshtanovskaya, *Iz*, 10 January 1996).
142 Sakwa, *Russian Politics and Society*, 2nd edn, pp. 160–1.
143 L. Telen, *MN*, 17–24 December 1995.
144 Sakwa, *Russian Politics and Society*, 2nd edn, p. 161.
145 J. Barth Urban and V. Solovei, 'Kommunisticheskoe dvizhenie v postsovetskoi Rossii', *Svobodnaya Mysl*, 3: (1997), 21.
146 Members included nationalists Aleksandr Rutskoi and Sergei Baburin, film director Nikita Mikhalkov, writer Aleksandr Tsipko and several CPRF figures. See *MN*, 29 May–5 June 1994.
147 *Megapolis-ekspress*, 22 December 1993.
148 *S*, 6 October 1994.
149 The RAU-corporation upon which Spiritual Heritage was based was an

organisation set up to further the adaptation of the CPSU's statists to the post-Soviet era. The majority of its workers were former members of the MIA, KGB and CPSU *apparat*. See *NG*, 5 June 1996; *MN*, 27 July–3 August 1997.

150 Podberezkin's connections with the 'democrats' went back at least to his work with Yeltsin's aide Tsaregodtsev in 1990–91. He furthered contacts between the CPRF and prime minister Chernomyrdin, and co-wrote the programme of his Our Home is Russia bloc (*NG*, 28 December 1996).

151 *PR*, 27 April 1995.

152 Bozóki, 'The ideology of modernization and the policy of materialism', 61.

153 J. Lester, *Modern Tsars and Princes: The Struggle for Hegemony in Russia* (London, Verso, 1995), pp. 140–3.

154 V. Clark, *Observer*, 19 May 1996, p. 21, 26 May 1996, p. 23. This was most likely under acute regime pressure, for which see Chapter 6.

155 L. Shevtsova, *Iz*, 22 December 1995.

156 *MT*, 19 August 2000 (version on web site: www.moscowtimes.ru).

157 *Novaya gazeta*, 17 July 2000. Allegedly, some sixty to eighty people were paid $5000 to vote against impeachment.

158 R. C. Otto, 'Gennadii Zyuganov: the Reluctant Candidate', *Problems of Post-Communism*, 46:5 (1999) 37–47.

159 *NG*, 23 May 2000.

160 *Kommersant vlast* (*KV*), 6 July 1999.

161 Semigin was an ex-president of the Russian Financial-Industrial Group and the Congress of Business Circles, and a Mercedes owner. The recruitment of businessmen was apparently arranged by Kuptsov and his business manager (*upravdelami*), Evgenii Burchenko (*Moskovskii komsomolets*, 30 September 1999).

162 *Parliamentskaya gazeta*, 2 August 2000 (version at web site: www.pnp.ru).

163 R. S. Katz and P. Mair, *How Parties Organize: Change and Adaptation in Party Organizations in Western Democracies* (London, Sage, 1994), p. 105.

164 H. Kitschelt, *The Transformation of European Social Democracy* (Cambridge, Cambridge University Press, 1994), p. 36.

165 Zyuganov, *PR*, 19 December 1996.

6

Electoral ascent, 1993–96

Having looked at the CPRF's organisational adaptation, we now look at its electoral adaptation. The election cycle of 1993–96, when the CPRF developed as an electoral force to become the main (and to many eyes, the favoured) challenger in the presidential elections of June–July 1996, is our focus of analysis, considering the party's effectiveness in electoral politics and the significance of its eventual defeat in the 1996 elections after a period of increasing electoral momentum. Features we have already alluded to form much of the explanation: the CPRF's early electoral gains were made largely against weaker opponents, while its ideological, organisational and electoral rigidity ceded the electoral advantage to a far stronger opponent, Yeltsin, in the presidential race.

The communist electorate and electoral performance

We can see the CPRF's gradual movement beyond a party of 'losers' and 'pensioners' in its broader electorate. Certainly CPRF support, as for the Agrarians and the radical communists, was heavily drawn from the most marginal and excluded strata of the population – those on lower incomes, ordinary workers, rural voters and the less educated.[1] The party's social base among the elderly (among those who had lost most in values, savings and state support since 1991) was shown by it being the most popular party for the over fifty-fives in November 1995, while being significantly weaker among the under forty-fives and not even in the top five most popular parties among those under twenty-five.[2] This pattern was replicated on a regional level. The CPRF generally fared poorly in large and relatively well-off urban centres, such as Moscow and St Petersburg, while it performed markedly better in the provinces south of the fifty-fifth parallel known as the 'red belt', particularly in the Central Black Earth Zone around Moscow, along the Volga and in the North Caucasus, with pockets of support in West Siberia and the Far East (see Figure 2).[3] Most of these areas were ailing regions, either agricultural or based on unproductive heavy industry, dependent on state subsidy and/or where the communist *nomenklatura* remained entrenched. Here Zyuganov's economic paternalism and conservative patriotism could find fertile soil.

However, across the Russian electorate as a whole, attitudes were a surer predictor of party vote than social characteristics, as we might expect in a system with still fluid social strata.[4] We can see this clearly with the CPRF electorate, which, as we alluded to in the last chapter, was gaining a cross-class appeal and improving its vote share in many social strata by 1995 (see Table 6.1). Simultaneously, the impoverished and elderly did support other parties, particularly the LDPR. What was most distinctive about the party was its ideological and programmatic appeal. All other Russian parties showed 'charismatic' elements, but among the CPRF electorate, support for the party programme was far higher than support for the party leader.[5] This is unsurprising – CPRF voters tended to be drawn disproportionately from those who both belonged to the CPSU *and* believed in it.[6] Of the Russian electorate, communist supporters were the most authoritarian, most opposed to marketisation, most collectivist and supportive of the return of communist rule (which no less than 88 per cent wanted in 1995).[7] Although by no means all 'communist' voters supported communism as an ideology, conservative nostalgia for the security of the Soviet system and Soviet values showed evidence of a Soviet-era value culture with strong sub-cultural elements.[8]

This distinctiveness had important consequences. Most important was that the CPRF vote had too hard a core and too hard a ceiling.[9] Its supporters were the most strongly ideologically committed in the Russian electorate, which even in conditions of marked voter volatility guaranteed it a core vote of 15–20 per cent, and thereby a strong showing in Duma contests.[10] Yet these Soviet-era attitudes were self-isolating and perceived negatively by much of the rest of the electorate. In 1995, the communists had high negative ratings among the supporters of all other parties, with voters of the allied Agrarian party the only exception.[11] Even the similarly anti-Western and collectivist electorate of nationalist parties such as the LDPR was almost as anti-communist as it was anti-Western.[12]

Figure 2 Regional vote for the CPRF in the 1995 Duma elections

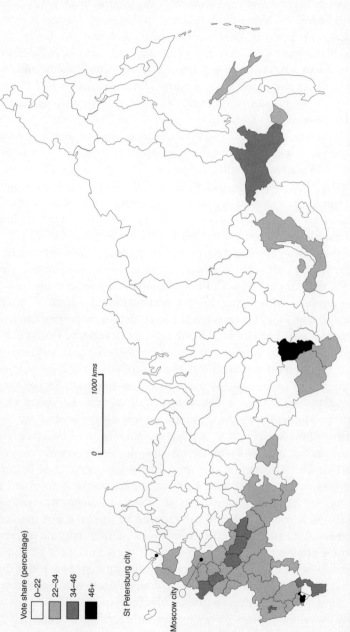

Vote share (percentage)

- 0–22
- 22–34
- 34–46
- 46+

St Petersburg city

Moscow city

0   1000 kms

Source: M. McFaul, N. Petrov and A. Ryabov (eds), *Rossiya na dumskikh i prezidentskikh vyborakh* (Moscow, Moscow Carnegie Center, 2000), Appendix 8 (Chechnya not included in data).

Table 6.1 Party list vote cast for CPRF, 1993–95, by age, social group and income (percentage)

	1993	1995
18–29 years	1	9
30–54 years	9	20
55+	21	31
Self-employed, managerial, professional clerical	9	12
Worker	9	25
Retired, housewife	21	32
Full-time student	0	4
Unemployed, disabled	4	19
Low income	13	24
Moderate income	12	25
High income	4	15

Source: M. Wyman, 'Elections and voting behaviour', in S. White, A. Pravda and Z. Gitelman (eds), *Developments in Russian Politics 4* (Basingstoke, Macmillan, 1997), p. 120.

The seriousness of the CPRF's negative image was magnified by the peculiarities of the Russian electorate. As McFaul and Petrov persuasively argue, Russian voters during 1991–96 were profoundly polarised between 'reform' and 'anti-reform' camps, reflecting a fundamental lack of social consensus over the nature of the post-Soviet system.[13] All so-called 'pocketbook' positions on specific issues were subsumed to irreconcilable differences between supporters and opponents of post-Soviet political change, while a more consensual politics failed to emerge. This feature of the electorate was muted by Russia's 'twin-track' mixed presidential-parliamentary system. Elections to the State Duma, half of which was formed by a proportional representation party list, tended to diffuse votes among a large selection of candidates and mask this bipolarity.[14] Moreover, since the parliament established by the 1993 Constitution had little executive power (the prime minister being selected by the president), voters grew adept at using Duma votes to express concern with 'pocketbook' issues, and vote retrospectively on the record of government and Duma factions, most often as a protest vote against and 'not in favour of anyone'.[15]

Table 6.2 The polarised electorate, 1991–96

	'Reform' vote (Yeltsin)	'Anti-reform' vote
June 1991 (presidential election)	58.6	36.0[a]
April 1993 (referendum)	58.7	39.3
December 1993 (constitution)	58.4	41.6
July 1996 (presidential second round)	53.8	40.3

Note: [a] Ryzhkov, Makashov, Tuleev, Zhirinovskii.
Source: M. McFaul and N. Petrov, 'Russian electoral politics after transition: regional and national assessments', *Post-Soviet Geography and Economics*, 38:9 (1997), p. 510.

Yet, public support for anti-reform forces in Duma elections and acute nostalgia for Soviet times when polled did not apparently translate into a desire to return to communism. When presented with a series of stark choices in binary votes from Yeltsin's first presidential campaign in 1991 (when he competed with the communists Ryzhkov, Tuleev and Makashov and the nationalist Zhirinovskii) through to his eventual victory in 1996, there was a significant majority preferring 'reform' to 'anti-reform', albeit with a slight migration to latter over time (see Table 6.2).

Whereas this suggested that some twenty-eight million people who voted for communists and nationalists in 1991 did not endorse the 'democratic revolution' even at the peak of anti-communist sentiment, it also suggested that the anti-reform vote might have real limits, even at times of acute socio-economic crisis. Furthermore, presidential elections themselves, particularly when the prize is such a dominant presidency as in Russia (with the right to form the government and the basic contours of domestic and foreign policy), create a 'forced choice' between two individuals competing in a winner-takes-all election and thereby maximise the bipolarity of the electorate. This tends to give voters a choice of 'the lesser of two evils' and causes many to vote for those for whom they would not in a parliamentary system, where choices are spread between competing blocs.[16] Such factors were to mean that, contrary to impressions given by the good performance of anti-reform forces in preceding parliamentary elections, presidential elections might favour reform forces regardless of the concrete policy performance of reformist forces preceding the election.

The 1993 Duma elections

The Duma elections of 12 December 1993 were unique in many ways. They were to elect a transitional parliament to serve just two years and simultaneously adopt a strongly presidential constitution, and directly followed the bloody events of 3–4 October 1993. Consequently, the political atmosphere was highly charged, and a 'strong pro-government reform climate pervaded official public discourse'.[17] The opposition was disorganised, demoralised and harassed. The CPRF itself was briefly banned between 3 and 18 October 1993, and from 3 October until the election its newspapers were published only very intermittently.[18]

Consistent with its renunciation of the radicals' extra-constitutional manner of 'deciding everything on the Moscow asphalt', the CPRF decided to contest the 1993 elections under protest, while resisting radical calls for a boycott.[19] Its platform's central theme was its slogan of 'resistance to violence and illegality'. The party presented itself as the advocate of civic peace and stability, and justified participation in the elections as necessary to prevent the Duma becoming an instrument of 'dictatorship'. It campaigned to maximise the 'no' vote in the constitutional referendum, while proposing its own constitution with legislative supremacy over the executive.[20] Simultaneously, the party articulated two themes that were to become constant. It presented itself as the party of 'new communists, people with new thinking', and distanced itself from aspects of the Soviet past, particularly corruption, authoritarianism and religious repression. Meanwhile, the party tested its new 'national front' strategy, aiming for a broad 'communist-patriotic bloc' which would form a 'government of national trust'.[21]

However, organisational chaos torpedoed the national front strategy. Communists and 'white' nationalists such as Sergei Baburin (head of the nationalist RAPU), Mikhail Astafev and Viktor Aksyuchits traded mutual recriminations over the failure in October of the NSF, whose members were now banned from standing except as individuals. Consistent with its later behaviour, the CPRF ran separately, while the 'whites' preferred to form their own blocs. Plausible allegations arose that these groups were hounded and that their registration signatures were stolen, and so none of them passed the 5 per cent barrier for entry into the Duma.[22] Lack of co-operation between the radical communists and the CPRF also doomed its campaign against the constitution, with too few either voting against it (as the CPRF advocated) or boycotting the vote altogether to invalidate it outright (as the radicals advocated). For years to come the radicals were to argue, not without foundation, that the CPRF had helped secure the necessary turnout to validate a constitution it ostensibly opposed. Lack of confidence further splintered the CPRF's efforts. The party appeared to believe it was virtually finished after October 1993, and was being driven underground.[23] In these circumstances, many of its organisers and activists defected to other parties such as the APR or RAPU, exacerbating the CPRF's parlous financial and organisational position.[24] Organisational weakness explains why the CPRF was able to get only sixteen seats in the regional single mandate districts (SMDs), although this was second only to the reformist bloc 'Russia's Choice'.[25]

The 1993 parliamentary elections first showed the 'protest' nature of the Duma contests, with the nationalist and anti-communist LDPR's 23 per cent first place being construed as 'a protest against all the establishment political parties' in the wake of the October fiasco.[26] The LDPR was the chief beneficiary of the fractionalisation of the opposition vote in 1993, as the banning of other nationalist groups left it with little competition, while the CPRF's poor organisation meant that it lost this protest vote and some of its core support to newer opposition competitors, such as the APR (with twenty-one seats on the party list and twelve in the constituencies) and, indeed, to the LDPR. So although the CPRF came first on the party list in three republics and Amur *oblast*, it was relegated to second place behind the LDPR in normally (since 1989) 'red belt' areas such as Pskov, Voronezh and Smolensk *oblasts*.[27] Overall, although the CPRF gained the most support in republics and small towns, it was the LDPR which got the votes of those alienated by economic decline, the end of superpower status and the perceived hostility of the former Soviet republics.[28]

Yet despite this the CPRF attained third place with 12.4 per cent of the party list vote and thirty-two seats. This, along with the sixteen SMD seats, gave it the third largest Duma fraction with forty-five seats, or approximately 10 per cent of the total. The party interpreted this attainment in adversity as an unexpected victory and as a sign that communism was not dead after all.[29] Indeed, without such unusual electoral conditions the CPRF might have performed even better. This election marked the beginning of the comeback for the

CPRF, through the organisational advantages of the Duma and the ability to broadcast its message. The elections gave the CPRF a respectability and legitimacy it had not possessed in the Supreme Soviet or on the street, and allowed it to bolster its image as a post-Soviet political force, while the radical communist groups atrophied in comparison.

The 1995 elections – the return of the left?

So if the 1993 elections had provided the opening for the CPRF to return to national political influence, then this was confirmed by the Duma elections of 17 December 1995. The CPRF was the clear winner with 22.3 per cent of the party-list vote, nearly twice the share the party had received in 1993 and twice that of its nearest rival, the LDPR, with 11.2 per cent. This was aided by a combination of economic deterioration, the CPRF's improving electoral image and the organisational strength of the party vis-à-vis its competitors.

By 1995, Russian economic activity was less than half that recorded under late communism.[30] Unemployment, social stratification, life expectancy and crime had all increased catastrophically. All over East-Central Europe, such conditions had resulted in a marked move 'leftwards' as voters began to prioritise economic security over political values such as freedom and democratisation. This did not mean that voters had forgotten about past communist injustices, but reflected the continuation of a welfarist culture supportive of the social guarantees and stability of the old system. Particularly after the second post-communist elections when the post-Soviet regime had begun to share blame for the most recent economic calamities, there was a demand for forces which could guarantee security, stability and 'clean hands', which criteria the professional, organised and hitherto marginalised successor parties were often best placed to fulfil.[31] In Russia, the socio-economic devastation and inequalities which had seemed temporary in 1991–93 had entrenched themselves by 1995, increasing the incentives for previously privileged and now increasingly impoverished groups such as skilled workers, and the academic and technical intelligentsia, to gravitate towards the CPRF as illustrated in the figures above.[32] While the divided 'reformist' forces in government and the liberal opposition attacked each other over such issues as Chechnya as much as they did the communists, they became increasingly blamed for the fiasco in the country. Support for the post-Soviet order fell rapidly, from 36 per cent of Russians in 1994, down to 25 per cent by spring 1995.[33]

So the economic 'feel-bad' factor was being felt intensely by the Russian electorate by 1995, and a general move 'leftwards' among the opposition electorate was borne out by the increased vote for the combined 'left' groups (32.2 per cent in 1995 as opposed to 20.4 per cent in 1993) and the strong showing in December 1995 (4.5 per cent) of the ultra-radical communist bloc 'Communists–Working Russia–for the Soviet Union', headed by Tyulkin and Anpilov and professing a radical Marxist-Leninist programme, using electoral democracy to 'send the Duma to hell' and establish a workers' regime.[34]

The CPRF's own propagandist methods played their role. The party used its new position in the Duma to good electoral effect. Its fraction was by far the most disciplined fraction in the Fifth Duma of 1993–95.[35] Although it eventually supported the 1994 budget to demonstrate its new respectability, nearer the 1995 elections it took a more resolute position, supporting votes of no confidence in the government in October 1994 and July 1995 and refusing to support the 1995 budget.[36] This position allowed other Duma fractions to take the strain. The APR, a mixture of ideological oppositionists and single-issue lobbyists for the agrarian sector, and the LDPR, seemingly held together by little more than a liking for pork-barrel benefits and Zhirinovskii's leadership, both succumbed to government pressure, and finally supported the 1995 budget in February 1995. Given the weak powers of the Duma and the unpopularity of the executive, a single-minded, disciplined position had clear advantages. By the time of the December 1995 parliamentary elections, groups such as the LDPR and APR had become compromised in the view of the opposition electorate, whereas the CPRF had demonstrated 'clean hands' and only increased its prominence and respectability as *the* opposition party, aided by Yeltsin's portrayal of the communists as the principal opponents of both government and president.[37] With the radical communist groups now out of the limelight it had assumed visible leadership of the communist camp as well.

The 1995 CPRF platform made clever adjustments to the party's image. In 1995, most Russian parties produced platforms with anti-market and patriotic stances, reflecting both popular disillusionment with 'reform' and Zhirinovskii's success in 1993.[38] The CPRF also sought to extend its constituencies by adopting a populist patriotism that was strong in sentiment and vague in specifics.[39] Its platform was more Soviet than socialist, invoking Soviet-era slogans, while avoiding any reference to Marxism-Leninism. Socialism was barely mentioned, still less 'communism', while Lenin got only a single passing nod. The policy aims were familiar. The party targeted the feel-bad factor with promises of full welfare guarantees and price controls, a mixed economy with state control of the 'commanding heights' but some private property, and property seized 'against the law' renationalised. Its vague political programme envisaged a national-patriotic government introducing a Soviet constitution and abolishing the presidency, and annulment of the Belovezha accords leading to the gradual, voluntary resurrection of the USSR. So, compared with 1993, the 'state patriotic' slant was much further developed. Appeals to hurt national pride made up the core of the party's appeal, with pride of place given to the 'two parties – two countries' thesis, and much emphasis on the CPRF as the heir to the national greatness of the eras of Peter the Great and the Second World War. Stress was put upon the communists' realism, with tackling crime and corruption among the party's overriding tasks. In a novel development the party defended its parliamentary record: it made a pitch for Zhirinovskii's voters by contrasting his empty promises and support for the regime in the Duma with the communists' patriotic and welfarist credentials, demonstrated to the limits of their small fraction's capabilities. All of this contributed to an overall tone of indignant but moderate, principled but pragmatic opposition, despite many of the populist measures outlined.

Such image-making appeared to reap benefits. By, 1995 the CPRF was seen as strong on the economy, crime and 'rule of law', and one of the most sensible and balanced parties, less authoritarian than nationalists like Zhirinovskii and General Aleksandr Lebed.[40] Its self-image as the heir of Stakhanov and Gagarin, 'true patriots', who had always tried to oppose the break-up of the USSR was a selective nostalgia that deflected blame for the socio-economic crisis, avoided many unpleasant memories and clouded any meaningful criticism of the Soviet past. The CPRF appeared to be reinvented not as the party of repression, but as the party of stability, economic protectionism and conservative patriotism. Although its moderation may have cost votes to the radical communists (whose anti-CPRF message made up much of their electoral strategy, and who polled 4.5 per cent) it gained at the expense of the LDPR and APR (both of whom lost over half their votes in 1995) and those who did not vote in 1993, although it took some votes from all its competitors.[41]

In countries such as Poland, the organisational strength of the successor party contrasted with the relative *naïveté* of their opponents, who effectively lost the election before the ex-communists won it.[42] In Russia, too, this election was a victory for the CPRF's organisation. As Moser notes, such mixed plurality and proportional systems as used for Russia's Duma elections may favour parties with nation-wide recognition, a developed grass-roots organisation and a network of well-known local candidates.[43] This system suited the CPRF well and its organisational work over the preceding two years paid off. Since 1993 there had been a string of communist local election victories in 'red belt' areas like Volgograd and Penza, where the CPRF tested its organisation and campaign skills and reformist parties were continually unable to unite.[44] It thus developed the experience to run a cleverly targeted election campaign. Whereas other parties often listed unknowns on the regional list section, the CPRF had a selection of prominent local party leaders and local notables noted for implacable opposition credentials alongside its top party leaders (such as Eastern Siberia's Svetlana Goryacheva and Kemerovo's Aman Tuleev, who were second and third on the central list behind Zyuganov).[45] The neighbourhood effect of community and workplace presence proved self-generating and greatly helped the CPRF in 1995, allowing it to draw back many of those who had voted Agrarian in 1993.[46] Above all, in a situation of widespread party proliferation, the CPRF could use its disciplined core vote to win in single mandate seats (where the average number of candidates was twelve) with a low proportion of the vote. This allowed it to become the 'party of the provinces' in 1995. It came first in sixty-two of Russia's eighty-nine regions on the party list, and a strong second in seventeen regions, while gaining fifty-eight seats from single mandate districts, over twice as many as its nearest rival the APR (with twenty).

Simultaneously, the CPRF's competitors wasted their advantages. In 1995, unlike 1993, the timing of the Duma election before the presidential race turned it into something of a presidential primary. The ultimate aim of many participants was not to win the largest share of seats in a weak parliament, but to use the elections as springboards for promoting individual candidates and blocs as credible presidential candidates. This clearly exacerbated party proliferation, even when the supposedly 'rational' choice for minor parties would have been to form consolidated coalitions to overcome the 5 per cent barrier. Unsurprisingly then, whereas thirteen electoral associations contested the 1993 elections, forty-three appeared on the ballot in 1995. Because of the diminished incentives for party consolidation, rivalries and political *naïveté*, the CPRF's main competitors failed abysmally at party organisation. Zhirinovskii failed to co-ordinate organisational work in the party effectively and to cement ties with other nationalist organisations, or the public in general.[47] More startling still was the reformers' failure. Whereas four pro-government and liberal parties contested the 1993 election, in 1995 they split into thirteen, and since none of them had put much effort into regional organisation or mass membership, none had national presence.[48] Only OHIR and Yabloko, with a combined 17 per cent of the party list vote, passed the 5 per cent barrier. But the combined reformist and pro-government party list vote in 1995 was 27.9 per cent, which hypothetically might have drastically altered the balance in the Duma had such forces combined.

The CPRF also followed this selfish logic, but since it possessed a consolidated organisation, running for election without allies would not be a disaster. The CPRF's organisation early on proved a magnet attracting other presidential hopefuls to whom the CPRF was able to dictate terms. Although Zyuganov himself seems to have wanted a broad national-patriotic bloc until early 1995, nearer the election the CPRF's dominance of the opposition gave it little incentive to compromise with its smaller competitors (particularly the radicals, whom it saw as a distinct minus).[49] There was much to be gained from enhancing its own role as the nucleus of the opposition prior to the presidential elections, to the detriment of its national-front strategy, and all negotiations with potential allies broke down over the CPRF's conditions.[50] Theoretically, the 32.2 per cent total 'leftist' vote united in a bloc could have been converted into a significant parliamentary majority able to envisage the 301 votes necessary to challenge the Yeltsin constitution. Yet, having run separately, the party preferred to exercise control over its putative allies by lending deputies to form Agrarian and Popular Power fractions in the new Duma. These eventually had thirty-five and forty-three deputies in the new Duma, and with a combined strength of around 211 seats, the opposition remained short of even the 226 votes needed for a simple majority.

As it was, with only four parties clearing the 5 per cent barrier, the largest party was disproportionately benefited. The CPRF was able to convert 22.3 per cent of the party list vote into nearly 44 per cent of party list seats and over a third (157) of Duma seats as a whole, 149 after its initial donations to its allies. This was indeed a victory for the CPRF, as it was confirmed as the nucleus of the left and the opposition as a whole. Zyuganov emerged as the 'man to beat' in June 1996 as he became top choice for president almost at once. Potential competitors Zhirinovskii and the nationalist General Aleksandr Lebed, whose bloc the Congress of Russian Communities (CRC) got a mere 4.3 per cent, were disadvantaged by their showing in the December elections.

The CPRF's performance indicated not just a bloody nose for the government and the liberals, but deep disenchantment with the political and economic values of the post-communist regime. Successor parties in East-Central Europe had combined a welfarist appeal with continued support for the post-Soviet order. Given its platform and the deep alienation of its electorate, the CPRF's victory was in contrast a strong setback for liberalism and market economics. Given that the LDPR's success in 1993 had been on a platform which was simultaneously anti-government and anti-communist, the CPRF's result did amount to a partial rehabilitation of communism. This was, however, a heavily qualified victory and should be seen as a victory for conservatism, Soviet values and socialist welfarism rather than communism per se. Even 22 per cent of communist supporters in 1995 did not support the restoration of communism.[51] Significantly, this result was largely achieved by a redistribution of voters within the anti-reform camp (from the APR and LDPR) rather than by a shift from reform to anti-reform.

More significant was the way in which the structure of the vote and the CPRF's organisation interacted to magnify its apparent success. The failure of its opponents to unite, the CPRF's reliance on its organisational and name recognition, and a 5 per cent barrier had combined to multiply its share of Duma seats. Moser claims that institutional factors alone account for much of Yeltsin's eventual success in 1996. He was paradoxically able to produce a reformist victory out of roughly the same distribution of the vote that produced an anti-reformist majority in the 1995 parliamentary elections.[52] This is because the support for pro-government, liberal or centrist forces combined was still 43.7 per cent in December 1995, a fact obscured by their failure to be represented in the Duma. Furthermore, the amorphous centrist vote, which tended to vote for the reformist side in binary votes, was spread among several parties in 1995, compounding the effect.[53] Similarly, although communist and nationalist support combined rose to 51.9 per cent in 1995, we have noted that many nationalists are anti-communist. So although the 1995 election was rightly portrayed as a 'referendum on Yeltsin',[54] the indications were already present that anti-communism was only dormant as an election issue. Should the presidential election follow the pattern of other binary votes in Russia, and turn into a referendum on 'reform' itself rather than the consequences of reform, it could force a 'systemic' choice between reform and anti-reform. In these circumstances, the divisions of the reformist forces might not be repeated, and they could benefit from the swing of centrist and anti-communist nationalist voters.

The 1996 presidential elections

Given that Zyuganov entered the presidential race as clear favourite with the CPRF's main objectives so far achieved, we must ask why this head-start was not translated into a corresponding success only seven months later. The key reasons were Yeltsin's carefully targeted campaign strategy and superior elite resources, and Zyuganov's flawed strategy which ceded him the political initiative and failed to provide an effective rebuff to the thrust of his strategy.

Yeltsin's campaign: maximising the forced choice

To win the presidential election required completely different tactics from winning the parliamentary elections. It placed a premium on nation-wide appeal and popularity, rather than the local notoriety and grass-roots organisation that had allowed the CPRF to do so well in the parliamentary elections.[55] Similarly, 'catch-all' strategies aiming to secure the loyalty of a majority of the electorate became paramount and partisan appeals were of limited utility. Since neither reformist nor communist forces in the parliamentary elections had come close to getting the 50.1 per cent required for victory in a presidential contest, the cardinal issue for both the presidential team and opposition was how to expand their potential electorate to encompass the disparate 'centrist' vote who had supported neither camp in the parliamentary contest.

Yeltsin's campaign had the harder task initially, needing to consolidate the dozen disparate reformist forces around its own candidate even before he could add new voters to this coalition. It was the Yeltsin campaign's main strength to recognise the dynamics of the 'forced choice' of this election and achieve the objectives it set itself. After initially flirting with a strategy of campaigning on the communist and nationalist field rather than as a 'democrat', the presidential team finally realised it thereby risked winning a handful of nationalist votes at the expense of losing most of the liberal vote.[56] The change in late March 1996 to a 'liberal' campaign team headed by Anatolii Chubais brought his noted administrative skills to bear on the rest of the campaign. Less transparently, Chubais' ascendancy reflected a temporary alliance of Russia's leading 'oligarchs', around the concern that a communist victory was well nigh inevitable, and would lead them 'to hang us from the lampposts'.[57] As such, it brought a web of covert financial and administrative resources on to the side of the president. Publicly, the most noted change was that Yeltsin's team sought to divert attention from the abject results of reform in Russia on to on the question of reform itself. By shifting from the concrete to the abstract, Yeltsin sought to hold a 'referendum on communism', not simply a choice between two candidates, but between two regimes, and two world-views. This exploited the polarising tendencies of the presidential election, and raised the likelihood that Yeltsin could win if he consolidated the (majority) reform vote.[58]

Yeltsin's campaign now adopted a sophisticated catch-all strategy in five main directions:

- The continued appropriation of communist and nationalist themes. Thus Yeltsin exploited Soviet nostalgia by signing a (largely symbolic) Union of Russia and Belarus, promised aid to agricultural centres and made decrees to end pension arrears.
- The proclaimed 'solution' of long-running sore points in his own record, such as the war in Chechnya, where federal forces had been engaged in a bloody, unsuccessful and unpopular conflict since December 1994, and there was a lull in fighting in the critical electoral period of 1 June–3 July.
- The elimination of any alternatives to the two front-runners. The most significant effort was co-optation of the third-placed candidate, Lebed, with tacit financial, media and logistical support. His appointment as Yeltsin's security chief between election rounds prevented much of the nationalist vote defecting to Zyuganov.
- The Yeltsin camp targeted the least committed centrist vote and the young with the portrayal of their candidate as the guarantor

of stability, continuity and progress, as well as the unifier, consensus figure and the 'father of the nation'.

- Finally, the overriding theme of the whole campaign was the media-led attempt to terrify the population into uniting behind Yeltsin as the only choice against the spectre of communism. This attempt focused on all the repressive, extremist, Stalinist and stereotypical features of the communist record and portrayed a potential communist victory as a victory for instability and civil war.

The campaign's success began soon after its inception. In late April 1996, Yeltsin overtook Zyuganov in the polls and stayed there. By April, approximately two-thirds of Russians believed a communist return to power would mean censorship of the media or repression of other political parties.[59] Above all, the bipolar effect of the election was evident in the clear distance the two leading candidates had put between the rest of the candidates in the first round of the election, when between them Yeltsin and Zyuganov got two-thirds of the votes cast.

Zyuganov's campaign (1): flawed strategy

Zyuganov's electoral campaign was the latest development of his 'national front' strategy, given a greater 'catch-all' twist to reflect the needs of capturing a broader electorate. Accordingly, national-patriotism was seen as the main idea to cement the non-communist electorate around Zyuganov. He campaigned as leader of the national-patriotic bloc and not the CPRF. The only thing communist about his programme was a sole reference to communism as consonant with *sobornost* and collectivism, while the patriotic tone was insistently repeated, with terms such as Fatherland, spirituality and morality.[60] Much was done to build up Zyuganov's credentials as a genuine Russian *muzhik*, a man of peasant upbringing, honest and hardworking. Indeed, the peasantry was considered the greatest pillar of the state and no mention was made of the working class! In turn, specifically communist (and therefore contentious) commitments were erased, while the socio-economic emphasis of the 1995 platform was made vague enough to appeal to communists and non-communists alike – such were the aims of rebuilding a strong military and raising the minimum wage, and gradually restoring 'popular power' and the union state. Welfarism and state ownership of the 'commanding heights' and land were professed as ever. Notably, the long-term aim of abolishing the presidency mentioned in 1995 and creation of 'soviet democracy' was replaced by preference for an elected presidency under legislative control (a strong presidency appealing to nationalists). There was no mention of nationalisation or the priority of state ownership, while the mixed economy was emphasised more than ever.

Simultaneously, Zyuganov sought to demonstrate statesmanlike moderation. He promised to avoid 'eliminating' owners, and 'historical revenge'. He claimed he would continue reforms, and respect political pluralism and freedoms. He appropriated social democratic rhetoric, talking more of the socially orientated market and of allowing national capital.[61] In order to substantiate this moderate patriotic image, the communists chose not to use their dominant Duma fraction to enact 1995 campaign pledges like restoring welfare benefits and price controls. Zyuganov's campaign team pursued an outreach strategy of attempting to court and placate various hostile financial and military-industrial elite groups.[62] At the World Economic Forum in Davos in February, Zyuganov made headway in convincing international capital that he would respect investors' rights and pursue a moderate although domestically orientated foreign policy.[63]

In many ways, Zyuganov's campaign was a mirror image of Yeltsin's. He aimed to make the vote a 'referendum on Yeltsin's tenure'.[64] His team portrayed Yeltsin as the main instigator of the disintegration of the USSR and Russia through his disastrous socioeconomic reforms. They attacked him personally as a man prone to dictatorship and 'genocidal' policies such as in the Chechen war, as weak, ill and incompetent, altogether incapable of resolving Russia's problems. He was seen as a stooge of crony capitalist and Mafia influences, his Western pals and their anti-Russian interests.[65] Zyuganov countered Yeltsin's profligate campaign promises by lambasting his past trustworthiness, and claiming that his best ideas were stolen from the patriots.[66] By demonising Yeltsin, Zyuganov also sought to make himself appear the 'lesser of two evils', and the 'stability candidate'. He was also a quasi-'father of the nation', standing for the majority of the country, and not the privileged and criminal few.[67] The communists were the sole force around which competing groups could unite, as their parliamentary record had shown them as the sole bulwark of social stability against an unpredictable Tsar-like president.

Prima facie, this was not an inconceivable strategy – there was much headway to be made by attacking Yeltsin's record and avoiding their own. Even the communists' policy inconsistencies were arguably little worse than Yeltsin's attempt to win votes by solving problems which his own regime had caused. Why then did Zyuganov lose by 13 per cent of the vote, a significant margin in a bipolar contest?

The CPRF leadership made its biggest mistake of the campaign right at the outset. Analysing the results of the 1995 parliamentary elections in January 1996, Zyuganov asserted that the single most important result of the elections was that 'anti-communism did not succeed'.[68] Rather, the increased vote for the nationalist and communist opposition (51.9 per cent), combined with an increased proportion of this for the 'leftist' parties (32.2 per cent), led Zyuganov to conclude that society was moving decisively 'leftwards'.[69] These conclusions led to the theme of the campaign. The communists believed they could win an outright majority simply by consolidating the leftist share of the vote and by winning over the rest of the noncommunist opposition with a patriotic theme, as it turned out largely at the expense of courting the centrist vote and democratic opposition. In the aftermath, it was acknowledged that this judgement was shared by many in the CPRF and was one of the main reasons Yeltsin had won.[70] Given that such a miscalculation disarmed the communists against just the sort of campaign that Yeltsin would wage against them and that they had been well aware of anti-communist sentiments in the electorate in the past, one must ask why they so drastically underestimated it on this occasion.

Zyuganov's analysis that anti-communism was dead was based on the fact that it had been a key campaign theme for Russia's Democratic Choice and OHIR in 1995. The latter's campaign manager, Sergei Belyaev, even asserted that if the communists won they would put the initiators of reform on trial.[71] But anti-communism clearly did not benefit either of these two parties, with 3.9 and 10.1 per cent of the vote respectively. Yet we have noted the different effects of electoral institutions. In the parliamentary elections anti-communism was diffused. Not only were the CPRF and the ultra-radicals competing on rival ballots, but the nationalist vote was split between nine nationalist candidates and thus anti-communist appeals made little difference to how nationalists voted. However, the presidential contest brought such minor issues to prominence. Given a bipolar choice between in the second ballot of the presidential elections, the anti-communist sentiments of some nationalists would play a more significant role – a fact Zyuganov overlooked entirely when looking at the December 1995 results.

Undoubtedly a key contributing factor to the communists' loss was their relatively poor campaign technology, including methods of contact with the electorate, and their access to voting data per se. During the campaign the CPRF's ally, Baburin, highlighted the communist tendency to work only with ideologically correct strata, and to indulge in philosophical and not practical questions.[72] The party's preferred campaigning of 'door-to-door' leafleting, grass-roots agitation, meetings and rallies might be perfect for mobilising the party's traditional supporters, but was labour intensive and not necessarily ideal for attracting the uncommitted. Given the unwillingness to work with the bourgeois, information feedback from strata who were already partisan would be of little help in objectively evaluating the opinions of the electorate as a whole. Similarly, the CPRF's affiliated survey organisation, the Centre for Researching Russian Political Culture could not match the Yeltsin campaign's use of a number of polling organisations, focus groups and Western image-making advice. This allowed the Yeltsinites to profile the key centrist 'swing' voter as an anti-communist Yeltsin critic, concerned overall with stability, and defined their campaign themes.[73] Zyuganov, however, had little knowledge of the centrist voter and could only guess, based on past election experience, that nationalist preferences such as 'patriotism' and 'law and order' were the way to expand his electorate.

This in turn affected respective tactics. Whereas the Yeltsin campaign spent much time visiting key marginals as well as its own core areas, the Zyuganov campaign concentrated on winning over areas where the nationalist vote was strong in 1995, largely neglecting areas where the non-nationalist centrist vote was at stake and completely neglecting Yeltsin's heartland. The effect of this was reflected in the final results when Zyuganov failed to win any of the regions in which support for liberals and centrists was between 40 and 50 per cent in 1995, trailing Yeltsin by an average of nearly 25 per cent in these regions in the second round.[74]

Ultimately, a more fundamental reason behind this misreading of the electorate was the CPRF's residually ideological world-view, which was to drastically restrict its electoral options, and the flexibility of its campaign. At the heart of this world-view was an economic determinism which appeared to mean that the communists interpreted society's movement 'leftwards' in December 1995 as an 'objective' and permanent phenomenon, showing that the 'social basis of capitalism had narrowed'.[75] In their view, the socio-economic misery under the Yeltsin regime (in addition to the incumbent's ailing health) meant that the regime was 'historically doomed', almost preordaining a communist victory as the vanguard of the socially oppressed.[76] Indeed, the fact that workers did not show the expected 'class-consciousness' in 1996 appeared to them in retrospect one of the major disappointments and mysteries of the whole campaign.[77] Given that the communists were well aware of the recent victory of reformed leftist Aleksander Kwasniewski in the 1995 Polish presidential elections, there appeared to be a general mood that history was on their side again, a reversal of their previous pessimism, and consequently a drastic overconfidence which they took into the campaign.[78] Certainly this would explain why the communist campaign appeared cautious, even inert, not fundamentally changing its strategy of 1993–95, and appearing to wait for power to come to it by default.

A further effect of the communist world-view was a Manichaeanism which resulted in the election being seen as a bipolar conflict. In January 1996 Zyuganov had announced the death of centrism, while his campaign manager Shabanov regarded all other forces except the capitalists and the opposition as merely peripheral.[79] This explains why the communists spent little effort on courting key centrist groups – moderate leftist groups, trade unions, the 'Third Force' (Lebed, Yavlinskii and the democratic leftist, Svyatoslav Federov), until far too late in the campaign. So the communists did little to counteract Yeltsin's conversion of the contest into a battle of systems – rather they took up the challenge with optimism.

It has been suggested that the social democratic strategy practised by Kwasniewski was the most rational strategy for the CPRF to capture the moderate swing votes, and particularly the young, while capitalising on the socio-economic distress of the population.[80] But the converse adoption of a national-patriotic strategy was almost preordained by the communists' ideological world-view. As we have seen, this was an ideological strategy rather than simply an electoral one, long predating Zhirinovskii's electoral success, as well as being the undeviating strategic line of Zyuganov personally. For most Russian communists social democracy was closer to democracy than socialism, and it was a case of 'better nationalism than democracy'. The ideological mindset of the communist electorate as a whole further restricted the communists' electoral options. Even if Zyuganov and the CPRF leadership were secret social democrats (which most were not) a social democratic strategy could not have brought them victory in 1996. The polarised nature of the Russian electorate needs to be taken into account. Social democracy is a compromise between the values of state socialism and liberal democracy. But, since the polarised electorate saw such subtleties as either too close to state socialism or to liberal democracy, there was little electoral space for genuine social democracy despite the paradox that, in economic terms at least, much of the Russian electorate is social democratic, favouring a mixed economy and interventionist state.[81]

Moreover, this electoral bipolarity much aided Yeltsin. Support for reform may have been shallow, but it was potentially wider than Zyuganov's if Yeltsin managed to unite disparate liberals, centrists and nationalists under the reformist banner. The looser ideological commitment of Yeltsin's electorate meant that he could more easily concoct a catch-all platform without upsetting his supporters, combining social democratic promises to increase state subsidies with promises of continued reform while stealing patriotic themes from Zyuganov. However, Zyuganov's support was much narrower and much deeper. If he had run as a social democrat, or even as a moderate nationalist appropriating democratic or market slogans, he was even more likely than Yeltsin to offend his core electorate and risk being outflanked by a competitor. Zyuganov's platform was not purely nationalist, as some have argued.[82] Indeed, his pledges to guarantee political freedoms were more moderate than ever before, but the 'hard-core' of the electorate was to prove repellent to the centrist electorate and torpedo Zyuganov's catch-all strategy. Thus Zyuganov actually had little option but to adopt the strategy he eventually took – appealing to the centrists with a populist but evasive patriotism which blurred contentious issues, rather than choosing an overtly nationalist or social democratic strategy. Yet this strategy was to run up against the apparently insurmountable 40 per cent hard ceiling of the communist electorate. Once more, the initiative was conceded to Yeltsin. If he managed to mobilise his 50–55 per cent potential electorate, Zyuganov would almost certainly lose.

Above all, as Boris Kagarlitskii plausibly asserts, the CPRF's main weaknesses in tactics and strategy in the 1996 elections were a symptom of the communists' ideological confusion as a whole.[83] Conditions in 1996 certainly made it appear that success for the left was even more likely in Russia than in countries like Poland, where communism had little domestic legitimacy. In Russia, there were many more issues to exploit, such as loss of statehood and empire, bottomless economic depression and the ongoing bloodshed in Chechnya. Yet it was precisely the lack of propitious issue opportunities for parties like the Polish SDRP in the early 1990s that had been the catalyst for thorough organisational and ideological renewal. The new image of a commitment to democracy, the market economy, welfarism and managerial experience allowed Kwasniewski to take the votes of key centrist groups and the young in the Polish presidential elections of 1995.

In contrast, the CPRF's recent successes had been much aided by the mistakes of its opponents and the huge problems of transition, giving it a wide issue space to exploit without forcing it to compromise its fundamental values and be asked too many searching questions. Despite tactical innovations and the astute marshalling of limited resources, the party's ideological divisions remained merely concealed but not resolved. If the party was forced into the spotlight and its opponents now fought the communists rather than each other, such divisions offered many issues to exploit. Was the CPRF social democratic or Stalinist? Just what would it do in power?

Zyuganov's campaign (2): flawed execution

The most significant effects of the ideological mindset during the campaign were an incoherent electoral message, an electoral bloc which restricted Zyuganov's options and caused acute tensions within the communist camp, and drift towards the end of the campaign.

Throughout Zyuganov's campaign, what he was against was clear, but what he stood for was much less obvious.[84] His vacuities and inconsistencies prevented him providing an unambiguous reply to many of his opponents' most damaging allegations, and added to the difficulty he had in stressing the moderate elements of his platform. His promises to continue reform were vague and evasive. For example, on NTV on 21 April he said he respected all forms of property, but declined to give explicit guarantees about how much he would renationalise, and he equivocated when asked how to control inflation or whether he would meet IMF conditions.[85]

Similarly, when Zyuganov's detailed economic programme was finally produced it was derided by the pro-government press. This was once more an attempt to strike a moderately patriotic pose and rebut charges that the communists were 'unrestructured'. So it was not communist or even anti-capitalist in inspiration or detail, but rather offered support for domestically orientated capital against the 'comprador bourgeoisie' and rejected calls for widespread renationalisation. Indeed much of it was based on bona fide capitalist models (such as the developmental capitalism of Japan and Korea, with nods to the investment-led growth of Keynesianism and Roosevelt's New Deal). Yet there were many unanswered questions, in part because this was an eclectic amalgamation of two separate programmes formulated by competing research groups.[86] Much of the media was concerned with the question of how much private property was permitted, while even more balanced analysis conceded that Zyuganov's economic plans might promise chaos. They envisaged massive investment-led growth. Even if it were shown where investment might come from without inflation (it was not), Russia's ineffective bureaucracy and the conflicting demands of military, industrial and welfare funding could reduce this to incoherence.[87] All in all, despite its innovations, this programme failed to demonstrate that the communists had become completely economically literate.

For the Zyuganov campaign overall, the situation was similar – a little moderation but not enough. Zyuganov and Seleznev talked positively about social democracy but later retracted their statements, always denying that they were social democrats.[88] Often, the nationalist message undercut the potential to exploit social injustice. Zyuganov criticised Yeltsin for instigating bloodshed in the Chechen war, and demanded its immediate end, but offered no means as to how, because he simultaneously supported upholding Russia's territorial integrity at all costs, as well as preserving the prestige of the armed forces.[89] Because Zyuganov was no democrat, his attacks on the media's subservience to Yeltsin seemed motivated by its failure to be fair to him in particular, rather than because of its implications for democracy in general, and thus Yeltsin's anti-democratic tendencies were lost as a potent campaign issue.

Many of these inconsistencies resulted from the nature of the national-patriotic bloc. Its ideological spectrum was too narrow and never moderate enough to appear a genuine wide coalition. Zyuganov's campaign aimed both to consolidate and mobilise his core supporters while actively courting new ones. The marked success at the first of these objectives, and the abject failure at the second, confirms our view that the CPRF had too hard a core to its vote and that the radicalism of many of its core supporters was a near insurmountable barrier to attracting a wider stratum of sympathisers. At the same time, because of the communist legacy, the bloc was too organisationally wide and cumbersome, because it allowed too many disparate (and sectarian) voices to cloud Zyuganov's moderate image.

Consolidation of his core support was one of Zyuganov's early achievements. The 'Bloc of National-Patriotic Forces of Russia' was rapidly set up, relying on the CPRF's grass roots. Zyuganov was the first candidate to collect the million signatures to required to register as a candidate by 23 February, a month ahead of Yeltsin. Moreover, Zyuganov was successful at getting most of his ambitious rivals to step aside and emerge as the bloc leader, capitalising upon the poor performance of competitors like the Agrarians and Sergei Baburin and Nikolai Ryzhkov's left-nationalist 'Power to the People!' in the 1995 elections.[90] The campaign's momentum created a bandwagon forcing other opposition candidates such as Aleksandr Rutskoi and Petr Romanov to join. But for all the fanfare, in true communist tradition most 'independent' individual or group signatories to the bloc were either already the CPRF's members, or fellow travellers of long standing such as Podberezkin and Lapshin. There were too few non-communists or centrists to counteract the (true) impression of the bloc as the CPRF in disguise with a few insignificant and often hardline satellites in train.[91] Indeed, the CPRF had consolidated its core too early and too well. It caused the electorate to take note of the real threat of a communist revanche. Local election results, until 1995 so successful for the CPRF, began to swing against them. The party had won 16 per cent of the vote in Omsk in December 1995, but in April 1996 lost three separate second round races for the regional legislature. It also lost ten seats in Altai *krai*, and did poorly in Moscow and Sverdlovsk.[92]

The 'radical' nature of the opposition bloc created continual problems. On the stump, in front of his own supporters, Zyuganov sounded much more extremist, revelling in cold war rhetoric and nationalist-religious mysticism.[93] The most notable concession to the radicals was the CPRF-sponsored Duma resolution denouncing the Belovezha accords on 15 March 1996, designed to stress the union of nationalism and communism and to persuade vacillating radicals such as Baburin and Anpilov to join the bloc.[94] This gesture was very counterproductive, inciting a universal outcry from the ex-union republics, and denunciation by the communists' favoured foreign minister Primakov.[95] The media gleefully reported all of Zyuganov's radical statements and ignored his moderate ones. Although the state-run media apparently published a plethora of fake, extremist communist 'secret' programmes, they barely needed to, as the spontaneous actions of radical loose cannons were a godsend to them.[96] Most famously, Valentin Varennikov alluded to a secret CPRF 'maximum programme' to restore full communism being worked on by the party's analysts. Zyuganov refuted this admission, but Varennikov never retracted it and, given the party's programme intentions and the theoretical work of RSSO, it is not implausible.[97] Viktor Anpilov, whom Zyuganov had promised to appoint as head of Russian Public Television (ORT) in the event of his victory, promised quotas for the number of Jews and foreign soaps (such as the popular 'Santa Barbara') allowed on television. Comments like these are alleged to have lost Zyuganov some 3 per cent of the vote and gave credence to the idea that even if he was a moderate, he was beholden to radical forces beyond his control.[98]

The patriotic bloc was riven by disputes and the sheer number of competing claims on Zyuganov hindered its effectiveness. His campaign platform's vagueness appeared to result from insurmountable differences between ten groups working on it, resulting in a final version drawn largely from Zyuganov's speeches and articles.[99] The economic programme's delay and inconsistencies resulted from the amalgamation of competing programmes and multiple drafts.[100] These non-communist documents were so far removed from party ideology that they met uproar within the party.[101] Moderates who supported the electoral platforms argued with radicals, whose propositions were those usually left out in the cold, and with each other. It goes without saying that all disputes, real or imaginary, were pounced on by a press eager to show that Zyuganov's policies would cause civil war in his party and country.

Zyuganov often appeared a better committee person than presidential candidate, always compromising with and never confronting his radicals. Again, the problem appeared to lie with communist 'front' politics. Even as a presidential candidate, Zyuganov remained beholden to the party collective, not given nearly as much leeway as Yeltsin make ad hoc policy with apparent impunity, which limited his ability to react quickly and improve his campaign performance. Similarly, Zyuganov never criticised Stalin, and often had to qualify most statements by reference to the bloc. When questioned publicly about who would comprise a communist government, all he could say was 'the bloc has its own laws . . . we must gather together and discuss it'.[102]

Theoretically Zyuganov might have strengthened his moderate image by excluding altogether radicals such as Anpilov from the coalition – few of the other radical communists had endorsed him anyway, and they could not make the second round on their own. But Zyuganov had his own radicals within the party, and Anpilov's participation was presumably a way of preventing embarrassing defections and minimising dissent. Perhaps the CPRF could have been dissolved more completely in a non-party bloc. Such methods might have included having a sympathetic independent (perhaps someone like Aman Tuleev) as the bloc's overall leader in a manner reminiscent of the 'Olive Tree' left bloc in Italy's elections of 1996. This could have diminished allegations that the bloc was a purely communist front, and opened the way to coalition with other groups. But releasing the communist grip on the bloc was contrary to 'entrist' practice. This impeded negotiations with the 'Third Force'. Even if the radicals had not protested (which they did), all the communists could offer someone like Lebed was participation in a heavily communist 'government of national trust'. Zyuganov markedly did not promise Lebed a specific post such as prime minister, which was always less attractive than an offer from Yeltsin, with incumbency on his side and fewer constraints from his electoral coalition. Similarly, the Patriotic Bloc's own 'shadow' candidate Aman Tuleev ran independently and withdrew in support of Zyuganov at the last moment. But the communists did not allow Tuleev enough independence to make the effect of his endorsement of Zyuganov anything like as effective as Lebed's last minute support of Yeltsin.

In the final stage of the campaign, the communists' earlier mistakes came back to haunt them and caused the campaign drastically to lose momentum at a critical moment. Although all indications are that many in the communist camp had thought victory was assured until April–May 1996, thereafter Zyuganov's rating began to stagnate while Yeltsin's surged ahead. The communists' former overconfidence was now punctured with the realisation that they had peaked too early and that Yeltsin could score points off them.

More significant was the growing realisation that Yeltsin simply would not give up his position even if the communists won freely and fairly. The presidential team (prompted by Yeltsin himself) discussed dissolving the Duma, using the 15 March Belovezha vote as a pretext to evacuate the Duma and search the CPRF's offices, prior to possibly banning the CPRF and cancelling or postponing the elections.[103] The president's hardline bodyguard, Aleksandr Korzhakov, informed a visibly intimidated CPRF representative that the regime would not concede defeat.[104] Even though the president backed away from this scenario because of opposition from Chubais and the Interior Minister Anatolii Kulikov's doubts over military loyalty, the CPRF hierarchy appeared to concede defeat. A series of meetings with Chernomyrdin, Korzhakov and Luzhkov tried to avert violence and come to compromise. Although none was publicly reached, the rest of the CPRF's campaign was marked by inertia, panic and disputes within the party over whether to continue the electoral fight or come to a pre-electoral pact.[105] The communists' instinctive caution seems to have increased their demoralisation. Not only did they realise that much of the elite was solidly against them, but they appeared to lack the will to win. Given their resources and experience they knew they could gain nothing by taking responsibility for the catastrophic situation in the country alone.[106] Moreover, although many of Russia's regional bosses had stayed above the fray, by late April they were clearly moving towards Yeltsin, fearing that Zyuganov had candidates to replace them, and that his ambitious economic plans might mean more centralised resource allocation.[107]

In the first round on 16 June 1996, Zyuganov won 32 per cent of the vote to Yeltsin's 35.3 per cent. This confirmed that the patriotic bloc had only just succeeded in consolidating the leftist vote of the 1995 elections (with 0.2 per cent less than the 'leftists' had polled then) and had not reached centrist voters at all. It was only at this stage that Zyuganov put all of his efforts into presenting a moderate image and removing the radicals from view, making strong efforts to appeal to the religious vote and non-communist leaders and organisations.[108] He proffered a new coalition 'government of popular trust' discarding the most radical members of his coalition, and appealing to centrists, government and regional leaders. Given that leaders such as Luzhkov and Federation Council chair, Stroev, had worked for Yeltsin, this came across as a last desperate attempt to save face which backfired when many of those named disowned the project, and confirmed the impression that Zyuganov had already lost.[109] Indeed, the communist campaign ground to a halt between the two election rounds. After the Congress of National Patriotic Forces on 8 June, Zyuganov made no campaign stops outside Moscow, even those previously planned, and confined himself to press conferences designed to keep himself in the public eye. He did not exploit fruitful issues in the last days of the campaign, including Yeltsin's public disappearance due to a heart attack or a financial scandal involving Yeltsin's aides.[110]

Conclusion

The CPRF's electoral performance in the elections of 1993–96 remained clearly marked by its residual ideological and organisational legacy. This had ambiguous effects. In the parliamentary elections of 1993 and 1995 it clearly benefited the party's performance, with its relatively disciplined national and regional organisation and committed membership giving the party major advantages over competitors, which in turn gave it leverage in the presidential contest, but the ideological nature of the CPRF and its electorate were the main factors explaining why the party failed to translate this leverage into victory in June–July 1996, and lost in apparently highly propitious circumstances for a left-wing victory.

Clearly the Yeltsin regime used the advantages of incumbency, especially financial and media resources, in a way which did serious damage to its democratic credentials. The bias of the press was so significant in the view of the European Institute for the Media that it 'undermined the fairness of the election'.[111] Real or veiled threats to cancel the election and create a wave of anti-communist hysteria had a drastic effect on the whole atmosphere of the election. Not only was the vast majority of the media against the communists, but they were systematically excluded from most radio and television networks even at local level. Yeltsin was able through local loyalists to put pressure on state employees and military commanders to avoid helping the CPRF.[112] The regime's financial and media resources, backed by bankrolling from the oligarchs and access to the state budget, towered over those of the CPRF, who had no way of matching the propaganda techniques such as the anti-communist paper *Ne dai Bog*, distributed free to ten million homes.

Clearly this election was not solely a conflict between 'reform' and 'anti-reform' as it was portrayed in the public arena. Parallel to this fight between regimes was a conflict between the new and old elites. As Judith Devlin succinctly puts it, for many 'what was at issue was not ideology but interests: competing networks of patronage and privilege, closed or open economic systems'.[113] For many of those in the new pro-Yeltsin elite, the issue was who could best guarantee financial and information access to world markets and consolidate their economic and political gains. Conversely, the communists appeared split between their elite agricultural and industrial backers who preferred merely to lobby within the new elite for influence and subsidy, and many who preferred a more full-blooded restoration of what they had lost in 1991. For many in the regime, such restoration, rather than communist ideology per se that was to feared. It was the superior ability of the Yeltsin camp, backed with the resources of incumbency, to consolidate the post-Soviet elite around this fear of restoration through fair means and foul that explained much of its victory.

Russia's electoral system also clearly discriminated against the communists from the outset. A different electoral system such as full parliamentary proportional representation might have defused the bipolar nature of the contest, and needed a lower share of the vote for victory, thereby weakening Yeltsin's 'anti-communist' strategy and benefiting the communists. But, as Sakwa states, the Janus-faced nature of the mixed presidential-parliamentary system forces Russian parties to develop simultaneously as parliamentary parties for Duma elections, and catch-all organisations supporting presidential contenders, thus preventing them developing successfully as either.[114] With such a strong presidency, a disparity of political capital and an unstructured party landscape, the role of government financial and media resources and elite alliances was intensified in elections. Flexible organisations which had less fixed programmatic identities and concentrated on winning elections through 'catch-all' strategies and charismatic electoral appeals rather than building up a membership base had advantages over parties with an inflexible mass character like the CPRF. The sequencing of elections further benefited the incumbent, with Duma elections acting as a 'safety valve' allowing the anti-reform forces to 'win' without significant consequences, and giving the incumbent time to formulate a counter-strategy.

The communist position was to blame their defeat on the 'information terror' unleashed against them and falsification and fraud in some regions, where vote rigging and vote ballot-box stuffing appeared to be rife.[115] From this point of view they could take comfort from the fact that they had held together their coalition in the face of extreme pressure; their second round vote was the most they had ever received, and the simple fact that a communist challenger could be the main rival to the man who had apparently ended communism five years earlier was a feat in itself. Yet, whether media and financial pressure was in itself decisive is to be doubted. It undoubtedly had an effect in preventing the CPRF reaching out far beyond their traditional electorate to centrist voters who got much of their information from television. Had Yeltsin's hushed-up heart attack been publicised before the final vote, this might have made a major difference. However, financial and information bias towards the pro-Yeltsin forces in Duma elections had not duped the electorate. The majority of them even said that the media had not played a part in their final decision in 1996.[116] It is unlikely that falsification could have drastically altered the result when ten million votes separated the two candidates.

More important to the final result is the way in which the communists' ideological and organisational heritage lost them the election from the outset. Brudny claims that the CPRF could use its regional press and national papers to offset such disadvantages, could have minimised the disparity in financial resources because of their loyal electorate, and so could spend money on the undecided voters.[117] This possibility is overstated, because of the poor financial and informational possibilities of the CPRF's media. But what is more important is that the CPRF did not even try. Papers such as *Sovetskaya Rossiya* and *Zavtra* were not aimed at the undecided voter, and communist preference for traditional methods of grass-roots campaigning meant that they avoided buying television time or producing helpful information for the media, which only made a bad situation worse.[118] The communists found that their declarative opposition of the previous few years would not suffice for a modern media-dominated electoral campaign where party statements were meant to be substantiated, confirmed or denied, and their failure to engage the non-communist media more proactively encouraged suspicions of their intentions.[119]

Moreover, the media did not create the divisions and inconsistencies in Zyuganov's camp and ideology – rather they hit upon a real weak spot. There *were* Stalinists and revanchists in Zyuganov's team, there *were* major questions over the communists' platform and promises, and justified doubt about their respect for the status quo.

Although there were arguably as many searching questions to ask of Yeltsin as well, the communists failed to ask them. After all, in 1995 Alexander Kwasniewski had been beset by an anti-communist smear campaign but he was able to protest that he was a real social democrat.[120] Zyuganov could make no such claim. Ultimately he failed to convince as a moderate, while vituperative zeal of the communists' own papers matched those of the regime, and personnel choices such as Anpilov as Television Tsar were enough to persuade much of the print and broadcast media to support Yeltsin entirely of their own accord.[121] Ultimately, even if the communists had had fuller and fairer coverage, it may well have exposed their inconsistencies still more.

Most seriously, Zyuganov's strategy failed on the tasks it had set itself. The targeted nationalist vote did not vote overwhelmingly for Zyuganov in the second round. Rather, Zhirinovskii voters voted equally for Yeltsin and Zyuganov, and most of Lebed's voters for the incumbent also, just demonstrating how much the communists had underestimated the anti-communist appeal to the nationalists. Yeltsin's strong performance among Yavlinskii supporters and the minor reformist parties showed how the CPRF had failed with the centrist vote.[122] Many of the CPRF's successes in 1995 were reversed. In July 1996, Zyuganov had more support than Yeltsin among only the oldest and least educated part of the electorate.[123] If the 1995 elections had shown the CPRF as the party of the regions, with a majority in over sixty federal members, in the first round in 1996 the party won forty-five and in the second round only thirty-one, with a strong majority in only nineteen as the local elites feared upheavals under communism.

Above all, the elections had been fought on Yeltsin's agenda, and had become a referendum on communism, and not a referendum on Yeltsin. By stealing communist rhetoric and policies, while in addition proving a more convincing guarantor of economic and political reform, Yeltsin guaranteed that he could achieve all that Zyuganov could and more without the uncertainty he brought. Yeltsin thus won the contest to appear the 'lesser of two evils'. This was underlined by the fact that, according to opinion polls, 70 per cent of his final second round vote put 'dislike of the opponent' as the main reason for their vote.[124] The inelasticity of the communist vote was shown: Zyuganov's 40.2 per cent consisted of even fewer votes than voted against Yeltsin in the April 1993 referendum, despite the continued socio-economic cataclysm.[125] Indeed, the CPRF seemed caught in a 'classic constitutional bind' with little room for ideological, organisational or electoral manoeuvre.[126] Placating 'leftists' such as Anpilov alienated the centrist vote, tacking right to court centrists threatened party dissent, which owing to communist organisational loyalties, the party seemed prone to placate but not eradicate. The party only partially adapted from being an ideological party concerned above all with the needs of its core supporters towards a purely electoral party able to respond to electoral demand and maximise its opportunities in a presidential system.

Given the substance of Yeltsin's campaign and the forced-choice nature of the election, this was above all a victory for anti-communism. The Yeltsin campaign had polarised the vote into a choice between a communist past or an anti-communist future. But, given that Yeltsin voters voted negatively in 1996, it was not so clear what the vote was positively *for*. Because of the democratic and liberal elements in Yeltsin's campaign, and the clearly illiberal and anti-democratic elements espoused by Zyuganov, it was at least a vote for 'non-anti liberalism', and for 'reform' loosely defined.[127]

However, it was harder to see the result as an unambiguously positive vote for democracy, liberalism, even less 'the Europeanisation of Russian political culture'.[128] Certainly, there was no clear endorsement of Yeltsin's personality or programme, and he could claim the strong or usual support of less than a quarter of the electorate.[129] The election campaign itself showed two segments of the former Soviet elite in symbiosis, both with dubious democratic credentials, and using the democratic process in a less than fully democratic way. The reformist elite, despite their rhetorical commitment to democracy, adopted an information policy that appeared to replicate the worst practices of Soviet propaganda, manipulated state resources in a way which prejudiced electoral fairness and apparently only recognised the necessity of elections when it was clear they would be won. The anti-reform elite appeared in practice to be the better democrats, respecting the electoral process and graciously accepting defeat, but arguably only when it was clear that they had no alternative. Meanwhile they remained rhetorically ambivalent about what they aimed to achieve through democratic politics.

While this demonstrated strong continuities in Soviet political culture even among the democrats, that the elections of 1996 occurred at all and that their results were not contested by the main participants marked a significant step in the establishment of routinised and quasi-constitutional political practice in Russia. McFaul and Petrov further argue that the anti-communist vote in the 1996 election marked the beginning of the end of the revolutionary polarisation of Russian politics, and the break-down of the 'umbrella' issues of reform and anti-reform.[130] This might herald the emergence of a more consensual, less ideological and certainly more stable polity. It might increase the tendencies towards compromise and negotiation shown in the latter stages of the campaign, even though these appeared driven more by fear of destabilising alternatives than democratic conviction. This would be a necessary, but not sufficient step in establishing the 'rules of the game' and the give and take of a developed democracy. We will return to this issue in future chapters.

Whatever the longer-term prognosis for Russian democracy in 1996, the prognosis for Russia's communists looked bleak. The CPRF's erstwhile ally, Sergei Baburin, savaged the party's strategy after its defeat, on the grounds that it had fundamentally misjudged the Russian electorate and had failed to prove the progressiveness of its positions to those segments of the electorate who had accepted the end of communism, particularly the young and the intelligentsia.[131] Certainly the communists' electoral strategy had proved flawed from the outset, by underestimating the anti-communist and overestimating the nationalist appeal, and then proving too inflexible to change strategies or court new allies midway. The ramifications of this misguided strategy outweighed the effects of the Yeltsin campaign's use of media manipulation, fraud, or superior resources and elite connections. The residual and confused communism of the communists gave Yeltsin a campaign issue which he exploited to the full. Ultimately then, it was this ideological inflexibility that cost the communists their best opportunity to exploit the near bankruptcy of the Yeltsin regime. If the communists could not win in these conditions, it seemed probable that they never would and that the 1996 elections would mark the high water mark of their influence, given the ageing of their support base, and their apparent unwillingness to risk exchanging this base for pastures new. If 1996 showed the victory of anti-communism, where did this leave the communists?

Notes

1 T. J. Colton, 'Economics and voting in Russia', *Post-Soviet Affairs*, 12:4 (1996), 306–7.
2 *MN*, 5–12 November 1995.

3 R. W. Orttung, 'Duma votes reflect north-south divide', *Transition* (23 February 1996), 12–14.

4 S. White, R. Rose and I. McAllister, *How Russia Votes* (Chatham, NJ: Chatham House, 1997), pp. 131–51.

5 M. Wyman, 'Developments in Russian voting behaviour: 1993 and 1995 compared', *Journal of Communist Studies and Transition Politics*, 12:3 (1996), 287.

6 White, Rose and McAllister, *How Russia Votes*, p. 145.

7 *Ibid.* pp. 230–3.

8 *NG*, 17 October 1997.

9 White, Rose and McAllister, *How Russia Votes*, pp. 230–3.

10 The communist core vote in 1999 was 17.7 per cent. See L. Byzov, 'What about the voters?', in M. McFaul, N. Petrov, A. Ryabov and E. Reisch (eds), *Primer on Russia's 1999 Duma Elections* Washington, DC, Carnegie Endowment, 1999), p. 14.

11 L. Belin, 'Are the communists poised for victory?', *Transition* (1 December 1995), 26.

12 R. Rose, E. Tikhomirov and W. Mishler, 'Understanding multi-party choice: the 1995 Duma election', *Europe-Asia Studies*, 49:5 (1997), 811.

13 M. McFaul, 'Russia's 1996 presidential elections', *Post-Soviet Affairs*, 12:4 (1996), 318–50; M. McFaul and N. Petrov, 'Russian electoral politics after transition: regional and national assessments', *Post-Soviet Geography and Economics*, 38:9 (1997), 507–49; M. Myagkov, P. Ordeshook and A. Sobyanin, 'The Russian electorate, 1991–1996', *Post-Soviet Affairs*, 13:2 (1997), 134–66.

14 R. G. Moser, 'The electoral effects of presidentialism in post-Soviet Russia,' *Journal of Communist Studies and Transition Politics*, 14:1&2 (1998), 54–65.

15 *NG*, 9 April 1995.

16 Moser, 'Electoral effects', 65.

17 R. J. Brym, 'Voters quietly reveal greater communist leanings', *Transition* (8 September 1995), 32.

18 J. Barth Urban and V. Solovei, *Russia's Communists at the Crossroads* (Boulder, CO, Westview, 1997), p. 106.

19 *SR*, 23 June 1994.

20 *Megapolis-ekspress*, 17 November 1993.

21 See Appendix in P. Lentini (ed.), *Elections and Political Order in Russia: The Implications of the 1993 Elections to the Federal Assembly* (London, Central European University Press, 1995), p. 275.

22 *Megapolis-ekspress*, 17 November 1993.

23 M. McFaul, *Russia between Elections: What the December 1995 Results Really Mean* (Moscow, Carnegie Moscow Center, 1996), p. 20.

24 *Megapolis-ekspress*, 17 November 1993.

25 The CPRF did not manage to field candidates in many dozens of *okrugs* (I. Osadchii, 'Vybory v Rossii: vozmozhnosti i perspektivy levykh sil', *Dialog*, 9 (1995), 44).

26 V. Tolz, 'Russia's parliamentary elections: what happened and why', *RFE/RL Research Report* (14 January 1994), 1.

27 *Ibid.*

28 R. Sakwa, 'The Russian elections of December 1993', *Europe-Asia Studies*, 47:2 (1995), 215–16.

29 *SR*, 16 December 1993.

30 S. White, M. Wyman and S. Oates, 'Parties and voters in the 1995 Russian Duma election', *Europe-Asia Studies* 49:5 (1997), 768.
31 *Rossiya–95: Nakanune vyborov* (Moscow, 'Akademia', 1995), pp. 92–5.
32 A. Makarkin, *Kommunisticheskaya partiya Rossiiskoi Federatsii* (Moscow, Tsentr politicheskykh tekhnologii, 1996), p. 1.
33 White, Rose and McAllister, *How Russia Votes*, p. 181.
34 *Moskovskii Komsomolets*, 12 September 1995. The groups making up this slate were Tyulkin's RCWP, Kryuchkov's RPC and Anpilov's 'Working Russia'. Those which made up the 'left' were this bloc, the CPRF, the APR and 'Power to the People!'.
35 M. Urban and V. Gelman, 'The development of political parties in Russia', in K. Dawisha and B. Parrott (eds), *Democratic Changes and Authoritarian Reactions in Russia, Ukraine, Belarus and Moldova* (Cambridge, Cambridge University Press, 1997), p. 199.
36 Zyuganov, *PR*, 29 June 1995.
37 Urban and Gelman, 'The development of political parties', 204.
38 S. Oates, 'Party platforms: towards a definition of the Russian political spectrum', *Journal of Communist Studies and Transition Politics*, 14:1&2 (1998), 86–94.
39 *SR*, 31 August 1995.
40 S. Oates, 'Vying for votes on a crowded campaign trail', *Transition* (23 February 1996), 27; Makarkin, *Kommunisticheskaya partiya Rossiiskoi Federatsii*, p. 1.
41 White, Wyman and Oates, 'Parties and voters', 785.
42 V. Zubek, 'The reassertion of the left in post-communist Poland', *Europe-Asia Studies*, 46:5 (1994), 275–306.
43 Moser, 'Electoral effects', 61–2.
44 *NG*, 21 February 1994.
45 Urban and Solovei, *Russia's Communists*, pp. 160–2.
46 White, Wyman and Oates, 'Parties and voters', 785.
47 V. Andreev, *Jamestown Foundation Prism*, 5 April 1996.
48 M. Steven Fish, 'The predicament of Russian liberalism: evidence from the December 1995 parliamentary elections', *Europe-Asia Studies*, 49:2 (1997), 201.
49 *SR*, 1 April 1995.
50 McFaul, *Russia between Elections*, p. 22.
51 *Iz*, 11 January 1996.
52 Moser, 'Electoral effects,' 56.
53 McFaul and Petrov, 'Russian electoral politics after transition', 511.
54 White, Wyman and Oates, 'Parties and voters', 793.
55 Moser, 'Electoral effects', 64.
56 For the most detailed treatments of Yeltsin's campaign, see McFaul, 'Russia's 1996 presidential elections', and Y. M. Brudny, 'In pursuit of the Russian presidency: why and how Yeltsin won the 1996 presidential election', *Communist and Post-Communist Studies*, 30:3 (1997), 255–75.
57 B. Yeltsin, *Midnight Diaries* (London, Weidenfeld and Nicolson, 2000), p. 21.
58 McFaul, 'Russia's 1996 presidential elections', 329.
59 Brudny, 'In pursuit', 260–3.
60 *SR*, 19 March 1996.
61 *OG*, 29 February–6 March 1996.
62 Urban and Solovei, *Russia's Communists*, p. 168.
63 This led Chubais to rage that this was an outright lie designed for foreign con-

sumption, and was the catalyst for the oligarch's alliance. See C. Freeland, *Sale of the Century: The Inside Story of the Second Russian Revolution* (London, Little, Brown and Co., 2000), p. 185.

64 McFaul, 'Russia's 1996 presidential elections', 336.
65 *OMRI Russian Presidential Election Survey*, 1, 3 May 1996.
66 *SR*, 22 June 1996.
67 *SR*, 19 March 1996.
68 *SR*, 16 January 1996.
69 *Ibid.*
70 E. Ligachev, *P-5*, 30 July 1996.
71 *OMRI Special Report*, 9, 28 December 1995.
72 *OMRI Daily Digest*, I, 83, 24 April 1996.
73 McFaul, 'Russia's 1996 presidential elections', 332.
74 Brudny, 'In pursuit', 271.
75 V. Trushkov, *PR*, 21 December 1995.
76 'RUSO–Rekommendatsii konferentsii "Rezultati i uroki vyborov v gosdume. Strategiya i taktika levykh sil v predstoyashchikh prezidentskykh vyborakh"', *Izm*, 2 (10) (1996), 42–4.
77 Kuptsov, *PR*, 15 August 1996.
78 *MT*, 22 November 1995.
79 *PR*, 23 May 1996.
80 Brudny, 'In pursuit', p 267; McFaul, 'Russia's 1996 presidential elections', 335.
81 T. F. Remington, *Politics in Russia* (London, Longman, 1998, p. 75).
82 Brudny, 'In pursuit', 267.
83 B. Kagarlitskii, 'Posle vyborov: O prichinakh porazheniya levykh" *Svobodnaya mysl*, 9 (1996), 3.
84 L. Belin, 'Zyuganov tries to broaden an already powerful left-wing coalition,' *Transition* (31 May 1996), 14.
85 *Jamestown Foundation Monitor*, II, 80, 23 April 1996.
86 *Kapital*, 29 May–4 June 1996.
87 *OG*, 29 February–6 March 1996.
88 *MT*, 18 April 1996.
89 For a useful treatment of the CPRF's policies towards Chechnya see J. Devlin, *Slavophiles and Commissars* (Basingstoke, Macmillan, 1999), p. 177.
90 *NG*, 10 January 1996.
91 Other groups or individuals whose membership overlapped with the CPRF included RSSO, the Komsomol and the editors of *Pravda* and *Sovetskaya Rossiya*.
92 *OMRI Daily Digest*, 72:1, 11 April 1996.
93 For example *P*, 1 July 1996.
94 Urban and Solovei, *Russia's Communists*, p. 170.
95 *OMRI Daily Digest*, 56:1, 19 March 1996.
96 Freeland, *Sale of the Century*, p. 204.
97 *Iz*, 19 March 1996, 20 March 1996.
98 *NG*, 11 July 1996.
99 *Iz*, 13 April 1996.
100 There were up to sixteen drafts – *P*, 25 May 1996.
101 I. Osadchii, *Dialog*, 12 (1996), 69.
102 Said to Yevgenii Kiselev on NTV, *Russia Review*, 17 June 1996.
103 Freeland, *Sale of the Century*, pp. 198–200.

204 The Communist Party in post-Soviet Russia

104 A. Korzhakov, *Boris Eltsin: ot rassveta do zakata* (Moscow, Izdatelstvo 'Interbuk', 1997), pp. 368–75.
105 Seleznev, Lukyanov, Podberezkin and Zyuganov apparently tried to forward a compromise, possibly allowing Zyuganov into government as prime minister. Many radicals (and Kuptsov) are said to have disagreed (*Iz*, 21 May 1996).
106 *P-5*, 16 April 1997.
107 *OMRI Russian Presidential Election Survey*, 3, 11 May 1996.
108 *SR*, 11 June 1996.
109 *SR*, 25 June 1996.
110 *OMRI Russian Presidential Election Survey*, 12:2, 2 July 1996.
111 *Jamestown Foundation Monitor*, 131, II, 5 July 1996. Yeltsin had 75 per cent of coverage in the print media and 90 per cent of television coverage. Of the national press, only *Sovetskaya Rossiya*, *Pravda* and *Zavtra* supported Zyuganov.
112 McFaul, 'Russia's 1996 presidential elections', 340.
113 Devlin, *Slavophiles and Commissars*, p. 195.
114 R. Sakwa, 'Russia's permanent (uninterrupted) elections of 1999–2000', *Journal of Communist Studies and Transition Politics*, 16:3 (2000), 109.
115 Kuptsov, *PR*, 15 August 1996.
116 *S*, 26 July 1996. According to VTsIOM (Russian Center [*sic*] for Public Opinion and Market Research) only 6 per cent of Yeltsin voters said that the media changed the way they had voted. OHIR outspent the CPRF by 605:1 in the 1995 elections, but was outpolled by it by 2:1.
117 Brudny, 'In pursuit', 265.
118 McFaul, 'Russia's 1996 presidential elections', 339
119 J. Lloyd, *Rebirth of a Nation: An Anatomy of Russia* (London, Michael Joseph, 1997), p. 76.
120 A. Smolar, 'Kwasniewski's legitimacy deficit', *Transition* (22 March 1996), 18.
121 L. Aron, *Yeltsin: A Revolutionary Life* (London, HarperCollins, 2000), p. 624.
122 R. Rose and E. Tikhomirov, 'Russia's forced-choice presidential election', *Post-Soviet Affairs*, 12:4 (1996), 369.
123 *S*, 26 July 1996.
124 Rose and Tikhomirov, 'Russia's forced-choice presidential election', 358.
125 In April 1993 30.4 million voters voted against Yeltsin's socio-economic policies, compared with 30.1 million for Zyuganov in the second round. See Brudny, 'In pursuit', 273.
126 R. Sakwa, 'Left or right? The CPRF and the problem of democratic consolidation in Russia', *Journal of Communist Studies and Transition Politics*, 14:1&2 (1998), 145.
127 Fish, 'The predicament of Russian liberalism', 214.
128 Urban and Solovei, *Russia's Communists*, p. 172.
129 Rose and Tikhomirov, 'Russia's forced-choice presidential election', 374.
130 McFaul and Petrov, 'Russian electoral politics after transition', 507.
131 S. Baburin, *NG*, 14 August 1996.

7

Electoral decline, 1996–2001?

After the defeat in June 1996, the Communist Party was expected to
split, reform or march into obscurity.[1] Some five years later this expectation was still being raised, but in the interim the party had managed
to perform creditably in regional elections, come first in the Duma
elections of December 1999 with a greater vote share than in 1995 and
put forward its candidate Zyuganov as the main challenger to
Vladimir Putin in the presidential elections of March 2000. So to what
degree did the party remain a viable electoral force? How realistic
were the repeated expectations of the party's demise? This chapter
will find that such expectations were vastly exaggerated.
Nevertheless, despite some countervailing tendencies, the party's
electoral problems had multiplied, threatening its long-term electoral
viability.

Regional performance

The 1996 election was shortly followed by a wave of elections for
thirty-three of Russia's regional governors. Elections to these posts
had been introduced only belatedly, reflecting Yeltsin's unwillingness
to allow reform opponents to entrench themselves at local level.
Theoretically at least, the new round of elections would allow the
communists to consolidate their good showing in regional legislative
elections during 1994–95, gain representation in Russia's Upper
House, the Federation Council (where Russia's eighty-eight regional
executives held ex officio seats), and gain some recompense for the
recent electoral defeat. In practice, these elections held little correla-
tion to the national elections held in 1995 and 1996. As Slider notes,
Russian regional elections have tended (even more so than national
elections) to be a competition between elites over resources rather

than a struggle between coherent ideologically based parties.[2] With minimal elite turnover at local level, chaotic decline in central leverage after 1991 and the first party-based elections only in 1993, neophyte political parties faced an uphill struggle to challenge entrenched elites, such as chairs of collective farms, the regional bureaucracy and local business, who all competed in regional elections. These elites in turn had little incentive to engage in party-building since they already had ample access to political and economic power through influencing votes or clientelistic personal networks.[3] Indeed, pluralistic competition for resources was a positive disadvantage for entrenched interests, particularly when elites needed to unite in bargaining with Moscow, and so parties were used instrumentally by local elites, if at all. Weak party penetration became self-perpetuating with 83 per cent of regional legislative candidates during 1995–97 having no party affiliation at all.

Such tendencies were only strengthened by the dilution of polarised politics after the anti-communist vote of 1996.[4] Recognising this, the communists sought to turn their electoral national-patriotic coalition into a far more 'catch-all' bloc than hitherto. The NPUR, founded on 7 August 1996, comprised the CPRF, the Agrarians, Spiritual Heritage and several dozen other organisations. This was a pragmatic and non-ideological movement, whose aim was to convince Russia's sceptical regional elites that the communists would no longer challenge the foundations of the political system, and aimed to 'unite them around a neutral ideology'.[5] Its platform espoused similar populist patriotic ideas to Zyuganov's presidential campaign platform, but marked a new departure. Its aims of building 'a powerful, truly democratic, law-governed, socially just state, consolidating civil accord and social stability', with emphases on humanist values and constitutionalism showed a mishmash of nationalist, democratic and social democratic values rather than a simple continuation of Zyuganov's national-patriotic line.[6]

The overall tendency of these elections was for the apolitical economic manager (the *khozyain* or 'boss') to prevail outside 'red belt' areas. Such candidates suited the interests both of the local elite (in strengthening connections with other politicians and business) and of the centre (in finding a 'professional' with whom it could work). These factors proved more important than political affiliation.[7] Moreover, neither regime nor the demoralised opposition sought an all-out battle, almost agreeing to postpone the elections.[8] Since Yeltsin was then so ill, the CPRF chose to run a low-key campaign to save its scarce resources, confirm its status as the respectable but weighty opposition and to hone its organisation for possible presidential elections.[9] As for the regime, the primary aim became to support any likely winner irrespective of their ideological purity to increase local influence. Such candidates included Vadim Gustov in Leningrad, Leonid Gorbenko in Kaliningrad and Valentin Tsvetkov in Magadan.[10] So the party targeted areas where Zyuganov outpolled Yeltsin in 1996 or where the incumbent was vulnerable, often supporting pragmatic 'managerial' candidates, particularly in the second round of elections when the victor was clear. Even in 'red belt' areas like Smolensk the communists sought the agreement of the local industrial and financial elite. They made little effort in 'lost causes' like Saratov, often seeking a role in the local power structure in exchange for not running a strong campaign.[11]

Overall these elections proved ambivalent for the CPRF. Despite regime and opposition's claims to the contrary, no side won. This was at best a 'velvet revanche' – the regime was defeated in many areas, but found a working language with most new victors, the vast majority of whom were distinctly 'non-ideological'.[12] The communists claimed victories for twenty-six CPRF and a further twenty-one NPUR-backed candidates in sixty-nine contests held from 1995 to 1997.[13] They consolidated their hold over 'red belt' areas (the number of ideologically communist governors increased from three to nineteen but was not even a quarter of the total) and claimed victories in non-communist areas, such as Magadan, Vladimir and Chelyabinsk.[14] The CPRF's claims to be the premier opposition force proved justified. However, many victorious candidates would have won even without its support and, so, were not dependent on the party after victory, even though they often chose not to ignore the CPRF entirely.[15]

However, the NPUR's promise as an umbrella front was not ultimately fulfilled, due to the age-old problem of organisational, ideological and personal rivalries. Even from the outset, its organisation remained weak, while constituent groups competed. The largest non-communist component was the Agrarian Party, whose leader Mikhail Lapshin sought autonomy within the NPUR. Agrarian candidates often competed with communists, most notably in the July 1997 gubernatorial election in Nizhnii Novgorod when the APR supported the winner Ivan Sklyarov and the NPUR supported his opponent Gennadii Khodyrev.[16] The CPRF's inability to attract significant non-communist notables left the NPUR with a cumbersome top-heavy organisation that was largely dependent on the CPRF in the provinces.[17] This did not satisfy either non-communists like Baburin (who saw the bloc as an even narrower front than before) or the radical communists, who refused to join it, while many CPRF members saw the bloc as an ephemeral alliance with electorally weak and ideologically dubious allies, and the very purpose and efficacy of the NPUR was constantly questioned.[18]

Yet it was the poorer areas that tended to elect more radical governors and these were the most dependent on the centre for subsidy, often making radical turnabouts in their opposition behaviour. This tendency for formerly radical governors (such as Aleksandr Rutskoi in Kursk, who left the NPUR and repeatedly denounced communism and his former communist colleagues) to turn loyal to the regime when faced with the 'exigencies of power' and financial dependency meant than many of them were in practice little different from centrist or industrialist managers.[19] The more the CPRF tried to gain regional manoeuvre, the greater the triangular tension between 'communist' governors, the Moscow leadership and local communists, as in Kursk when the local leader Aleksandr Mikhailov had been forced by the Moscow leadership to stand aside for 'renegade' Rutskoi. As election cycles repeated there were clear signs even in the 'red belt' that communist support was dependent not just on ideological affinity but administrative capability, with communists in Volgograd losing influence owing to inexperience in resolving intractable issues such as pension arrears.[20] From 1997 even loyalist governors such as Aman Tuleev of Kemerovo lamented the party's weak record in the Duma and locally of producing concrete rather than declarative benefits for their supporters and began to distance themselves from both the CPRF and the NPUR. Governors such as Tuleev and Kondratenko sought to subordinate local left movements to personalised governors' blocs.[21] So, of the NPUR's nineteen 'ideologically conscious' governors, the number of those who strongly supported the CPRF in 1999 had dropped to ten.[22] All in all, it was not clear whether the communists gained enough respect from their pragmatic approach from new supporters to offset the potential loss of their old supporters, and ultimately such tensions were to break the NPUR asunder.

Repeated gubernatorial elections saw these trends increasing significantly. Yeltsin's long-term ailments and the economic crash of

August 1998 gave a major spur to regional autonomy, while experienced governors developed skills at so-called 'administrative resources', including control over local finance and media, patronage at regional and electoral commission level, to the detriment of political parties or opposition more generally, forcing regional candidates to develop still more fuzzy or non-existent ideological and party affiliations.[23] In seventeen gubernatorial elections in 1998 and 1999, only two candidates had clear party affiliation, the communist victors in Smolensk and Belgorod.[24] Although President Putin sought to reduce the autonomy of the governors by removing their right to sit in the Federation Council, in the forty-six elections of 2000 and early 2001, the greatest victory (with thirty-three) was apparently incumbency, with both regime and opposition struggling to maintain influence in the political elite. The communists ran a more flexible campaign than hitherto, not running candidates at all where they could reach agreement with the incumbent. They claimed twenty-six victories out of forty-one, and their regional first secretaries won in non-communist Kursk, Ivanovo and Kamchatka. This was apparently a significant boost for the party, although it must be noted that in none of these cases was the incumbent standing.[25] A resounding victory for communist Gennadii Khodyrev over Ivan Sklyarov in 'reformist' Nizhnii Novgorod on 29 July 2001 and a near miss for Sergei Levchenko in the Irkutsk gubernatorial election of 19 August suggested the CPRF was better able to consolidate the protest electorate, although in both cases the elections were marred by low turnout, which may have disproportionally benefited the disciplined communist vote.

In the 'red belt', consolidated communist support was still very useful for the governor. For example in Volgograd, communists in the *oblast* Duma and regional electoral commission stacked electoral conditions in incumbent governor Maksyuta's favour, although support from the regional division of the firm LUKoil was arguably as significant.[26] However, new communist governors generally won on a platform promising stability and allegiance to Putin rather than communist slogans, and Moscow proved quite willing to help communist candidates.[27] Simultaneously the party lost its governors in Marii-El, Voronezh, Tambov and Amur. In non-communist areas the party was often reduced to supporting candidates in the second round along with other parties, while if they opposed the incumbent governor (as in Samara and Sakhalin), they lost. Once more, the communists were the main party victor with eighteen confirmed victories versus eleven to the pro-Putin Edinstvo (Unity) bloc in 2000, but even compared with the earlier election round, the CPRF's connections with 'its' candidates were likely to prove very weak, indicated by Khodyrev's decision to resign his party membership on taking office.

The 1999 election campaign

The stakes of the election marathon of 1999–2000 were even higher for many Russian political forces than that of 1995–96. Despite the absence of the threat of a return to communism, Boris Yeltsin's physical frailties and his diminishing support among the political elite made the question of who would succeed him of vital importance. Making even the nature of the post-Yeltsin system unclear were the after-effects of the August 1998 collapse of the rouble, closely followed by international tensions over NATO involvement in the Yugoslav republic of Kosovo, the cumulative effects of which amounted to increased social insecurity and diminished support for the Western-dependent liberal model of reform. Analysts have since noticed a tentative social consensus forming around the belief that political and economic 'reform' needed amendment in favour of greater state intervention in economy and polity.[28] Mild anti-Westernism and increased prioritisation of stability and 'strong government' over democracy (though with little support for the suspension of democracy) also marked this new 'left-patriotic consensus', which appeared to mark a stage of necessary social consolidation after a period of revolutionary change. It appeared that society was 'tired from the last decade of reforms and the reformers themselves'.[29]

For the communists this offered both opportunities and threats. The opportunity was present to move beyond the electoral ghetto that they had found themselves in 1996, since the communists' views were increasingly mainstream. However, the competition for the 'left-patriotic' vote was fierce, with even Moscow Mayor Yurii Luzhkov staking out an eclectic position which sought to draw from Russian traditions and even Blair's New Labour. The CPRF was no longer in an impregnable position in the opposition camp, as opinion polls showed Zyuganov's rating to be stagnant, and also that he would lose to almost any serious challenger in a presidential second round. When compounded by severe internal problems within the CPRF itself (described further in Chapter 7), this meant that the CPRF approached the 1999 elections in some disarray, with maintaining its hegemony over the opposition camp and ending its fragmentation to right and left a priority, even before radically extending its vote could be addressed. Therefore the CPRF repeated its 1995 policy of running independently both to maximise its leverage over other anti-government forces in the state Duma and to attain the role of backbone of the opposition for the presidential campaign, though this time with a still keener concern to preserve hegemony over the opposition niche.

So the party concerned itself first with internal discipline, removing some of its more troublesome members.[30] From the outset, the CPRF sought to dictate terms to its allies in the NPUR, the most significant of whom were seeking a looser centrist coalition in order to broaden support in larger towns.[31] Zyuganov himself was considering a 'grand coalition' with Luzhkov (with whom the party had cordial relations since 1994) in autumn 1998, but he was upbraided by the party hierarchy, who were concerned that their allies' independence could lead to Luzhkov himself being nominated as presidential candidate at the NPUR congress at the end of 1998.[32] The CPRF pre-empted this by holding a party Plenum *before* the NPUR congress in October 1998 and asserting that it would contest the 1999 elections independently. This answered the ideological critics of the NPUR and the more self-interested demands of those party secretaries who did not want to cede their position to others on a common list.[33] Overall the 1999 election campaign appeared to show Kuptsov's party apparatus strengthening its position over Zyuganov, and the latter's diminished independence in formulating ideology and tactics.[34] Indeed, he was forced to distance himself from Podberezkin, whose independent voting conduct in the Duma and attempts to court Luzhkov in the CPRF's name appeared to be the last straw for the apparatus. Podberezkin's calls for Kuptsov's circle to resign were eventually followed by his expulsion from the party fraction in August 1999. Ultimately the anti-Semitic outbursts of Makashov and Ilyukhin drove Luzhkov away from a possible union and toward the moderately patriotic FAR alliance he formed with ex-prime minister Evgenii Primakov in late 1999.

At the NPUR congress in November 1998, Zyuganov sought to mollify criticism of the CPRF's decision by concocting the thesis of three electoral columns. The CPRF would run independently alongside the 'enlightened patriots' (Spiritual Heritage and the Agrarians, possibly with the increasingly independent Gennadii Seleznev) and the radical patriots (Ilyukhin and his MSA). This was presented as a way to maximise the patriotic bloc's electoral support. Each column would maximise its own independent electorate in the Duma elections and then support a single candidate from its enlarged electorate for the presidential elections. In practice, this was more like a party purge designed to manage the split and 'keep it from turning into a fully-fledged chasm'.[35] The CPRF leadership knew that even if this strategy did not force troublesome allies into line then the 'enlightened patriots' could have little electoral influence. They therefore left the patriots to 'sink or swim', while giving minimal support to Ilyukhin's MSA.[36] This organisation would give a home to those radicals discontented with the CPRF's strategy while its independence from the CPRF might diminish accusations of the party's anti-Semitism. The CPRF also knew that the MSA would only take votes from the CPRF's rivals such as Zhirinovskii and the radical communists, and that if it did pass the 5 per cent barrier it would be completely dependent on the CPRF.[37]

The NPUR congress postponed a definitive decision for three months, but did not reach one. After contradictory statements from the party leaders and confusion from CPRF party members, in July 1999 the CPRF then suddenly announced its reversion to the formation of one bloc – the 'For Victory!' patriotic bloc.[38] Initiated by an appeal for patriotic unity from CPRF member and retired General Valentin Varennikov, and answered in the affirmative by Zyuganov and a selection of patriotically minded governors and public figures a few days later, the aim appeared to be to force the party's allies to unite on the CPRF's terms.[39] The Agrarians and Podberezkin's Spiritual Heritage refused to sacrifice their independence, but numbers of both blocs split and sought spots on the CPRF list. The APR split seriously between party leader, Mikhail Lapshin, who feared that an alliance with the CPRF would reduce the party's lobbying potential with the government, and the CPRF-loyalist Duma fraction leader, Nikolai Kharitonov. This led to about two-thirds of the APR candidates joining FAR, and the rest finding places on the CPRF list.[40] Now the CPRF 'For Victory!' bloc existed largely in name only. The party appeared resigned to sacrificing a wider bloc to obtain a smaller, absolutely loyal fraction. This may be regarded as a significant blow to Zyuganov. The NPUR, Zyuganov's long-cherished national-patriotic bloc, still existed, but had lost any significant component bar the CPRF. According to critics, it was now no more than the CPRF's 'department for work with social organisations'.[41]

The CPRF's 'For Victory!' election platform followed a similar strategy to that of 1995: a radical attack on the problems of the day designed to project the image of the CPRF as the nucleus of the anti-regime opposition.[42] Therefore the party appropriated the symbolism of Stalinist Second World War military patriotism, epitomised by its adoption of the Order of Victory awarded to war heroes as its bloc symbol. As for previous campaign platforms, the theme of the patriotic 'national-liberation struggle' uniting all patriots against the 'genocidal ruling regime' meant that socialist and class language was all but absent.

However, the party platform did mark a very significant evolution from all earlier platforms. As a party critic noted, it was still more declarative and ideologically 'eroded.'[43] Despite the vitriol heaped on the 'criminal oligarchy', the measures proposed were markedly more moderate and pragmatic than in 1995. The party's purge and the diminished challenge from the radical left allowed the party to emphasise its peaceful and legal image. If in 1995 its key slogan was 'Russia, Labour, Popular Power, Socialism', in 1999 it was 'Order in the Country, Prosperity in the Home'. Whereas the earlier platform explicitly promised the abolition of the presidency, renationalisation and the resurrection of the USSR, in 1999 the aims were more cautious – a reduction in presidential power and the creation of a Slavic union. There was little about the economy in the programme but a separate economic programme for the parliamentary and presidential elections drafted by Sergei Glazev showed a still more marked evolution. If the electoral platform was national-patriotic in inspiration, this programme was social democratic. In a strongly Keynesian vein, it still called for state ownership of the commanding heights and 'managed money issuing', but now talked of how to enforce property and investors' rights, defend small and medium businesses and of a pragmatic acceptance of private ownership in a 'socially-orientated socialist market economy'.[44] The communist Duma fraction proposed amendments to the Russian constitution to limit presidential power, to demonstrate they meant business.[45] The party's praise of Stalin just before polling day seemed designed to reassure the party faithful, calling for 'strong party unity' in an 'anti-Hitler coalition'.[46]

Moreover, just as in 1995, the CPRF ran a strongly targeted regional campaign, with regional notables prominently placed in the regional *troika*. A prominent development in 1999 was that the candidates were becoming still less party based. The presence of around

100 non-party candidates on the party list of 270 upset the party ranks.[47] Only half of the main section of the party list were party members, and only about two-thirds of its single mandate candidates.[48] The CPRF sought to distance itself from allied governors who had lost popularity and to improve its contacts with popular regional leaders even in areas outside its control. So the party sought rigidly to audit its deputy candidacies prior to the campaign. It expressly nominated well-known candidates and initiated flexible contacts with regional administrations. Its regional campaigns sought to respond to local concerns and avoid generalities.[49] Ultimately, and reflecting the increasing power of the newly elected governors, who paid far greater attention to the regional composition of parties than in 1995, the CPRF's candidates represented the interests of regional leaders as much as the party itself.

Better financing and elite contacts (which we noted in Chapter 5) certainly helped the CPRF to mount an improved information campaign. While concentrating on its traditional grass-roots campaigning, the CPRF regional party committees had greater access to television and media, particularly in areas where it had governors.[50] Compared with 1995, the party made far greater use of national campaign broadcasts, which sought to balance the vehement and moderate tones, and portray the CPRF as the only serious opposition party with a constructive programme for the revival of domestic industries.[51] Significant also was the CPRF's improved treatment from the central media. No longer was there a solid wall of anti-communism, but the central media diverted most of their attacks on Primakov and Luzhkov, the former for his age and health, and the latter for his alleged criminal connections, leaving the CPRF unscathed. This reflected the CPRF's improved image – fewer people were now scared of it.[52] But it reflected something more fundamental. The regime saw the communists as a declining force, while Primakov's anti-corruption credentials and intentions to redistribute power from president to parliament were a far greater threat. So the media coverage of the communists' negotiations with Putin over the budget were generally positive. Even accusations that the CPRF was ready to co-operate with FAR would more damage the latter and strengthen the CPRF's preferred image as the only solid opposition force with which everyone would have to reckon.

The party could claim considerable success in the final tally. Its share of the vote on the party list went up from 1995 (24.3 per cent against 22.3 per cent) as did the number of votes (16.2 million versus 15.4 million).[53] A feature of the 1999 elections was more sophisticated voting – far fewer votes were wasted on parties which failed to pass the 5 per cent barrier. Consequently Spiritual Heritage, the MSA and the remnants of the radical communists mustered 3.5 per cent between them. The party appeared to have successfully managed the split. Moreover, its success in SMDs in 1999 was actually greater than in 1995 when it got fifty-eight seats. In the CPRF and closely allied 'agro-industrial' fraction on 2 March 2000, the party had sixty-five single mandate members, albeit only forty-nine who ran on the communist ticket. This indicated some success in its flexible regional policy.[54] So party support appeared to be relatively stable. The increasing role for non-party figures in the party campaigns (seen most starkly in the presence of Glazev, formerly in Gaidar's government, on the party list) was indicative that the party managed to win support from non-communists and was slowly losing its 'programmatic' nature.

Yet there was evidence that the communist vote was beginning to lose some aspects of its hard core without making commensurate gains. In 1999, the party's base remained weak among the under thirty-fives and strongest in the over fifty-fives and socially excluded.[55] Business support for Zyuganov also remained relatively weak.[56] Preliminary results suggested the CPRF gained votes from some who voted for Yeltsin in 1996, but lost votes to both Edinstvo and FAR.[57] The regional picture was mixed (see Figure 3) At first glance the party certainly made impressive gains on the party list vote outside former 'leftist' regions in areas like St Petersburg, Perm, Murmansk and Primorskii *krai*, and improved its vote share overall in sixty-two federal subjects.[58] It certainly improved its positions in the Far East, West and East Siberia, the North and the North Caucasus.[59] However, gains in these regions were often from a very low base. For example, an 8.2 per cent gain in Yamalo-Nenets autonomous *okrug* resulted in a vote share of 13.8 per cent. Significantly, where the party increased its vote, in only five regions did it exceed or even capture the total leftist vote of 1995. This indicated that the party's major gains were from other 'leftist' parties who had run in 1995 such as the APR, 'Power to the People!' and the radical communists, rather from new converts from outside the leftist niche.[60]

More worryingly for the future, on the party list the communists lost in areas in the 'red belt' where they had won for years, usually to

Figure 3 Change in support for the CPRF in Duma elections, 1995–99

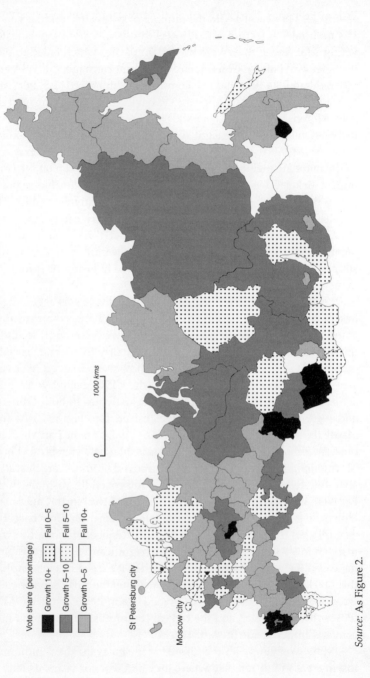

Vote share (percentage)

Growth 10+   Fall 0–5

Growth 5–10   Fall 5–10

Growth 0–5   Fall 10+

St Petersburg city

Moscow city

0   1000 kms

Source: As Figure 2.

FAR or Edinstvo. The CPRF suffered significant losses to Edinstvo in Kemerovo, Rostov, Volgograd and Voronezh.[61] Nation-wide, if in 1995 the CPRF had come first on the party list in 143 *okrugs*, in 1999 it achieved this in only seventy-eight.[62] A similar situation prevailed in the SMDs, where the party suffered some notable losses (including to hated oligarch Boris Berezovskii in communist-held Karachaevo-Cherkesiya). Similarly, most communist winners were either incumbents, or supported by incumbent communist governors, suggesting limits to the party's electoral potential. Overall, the vote for 'leftist' parties as a whole had decreased from 32 per cent to 28 per cent in 1999. Party leaders positively evaluated the results as showing that the CPRF had consolidated its support among the opposition and had thwarted potential rivals to this position.[63] However, the *kompromat* (compromising material) launched at FAR appears to have artificially boosted the CPRF's final vote by up to 5 per cent and so prevented a more damaging result.[64]

Perhaps more to the point, the CPRF's improved result had the appearance of a defeat, because compared with 1995, the party lacked momentum for the presidential race, with the real fight going on for second place between FAR and the pro-government Edinstvo, created only in September on a patriotic platform designed explicitly to steal votes from FAR. Edinstvo was the real winner of the campaign with 23.3 per cent of the vote, relegating FAR to third with 13.3 per cent and giving its patron, prime minister Vladimir Putin, momentum into the presidential campaign. The Putin-endorsed patriotic-liberal Union of Right Forces (URF) performed strongly with 8.3 per cent. Unity's rise was not anticipated by the CPRF at all. It was accompanied by the decision of opposition governors Tuleev, Ivan Shabanov of Voronezh and Aleksandr Chernogorov of Stavropol, to support Putin's presidential bid, along with indications that up to a quarter of the CPRF's voters were inclined the same way in a presidential second round.[65] Overall, the results for the CPRF in 1999 were equivocal. It appeared that the party's constructive approach was still not gaining it enough electoral manoeuvrability to move much beyond its niche. This left the party ill placed to mount a successful presidential bid in the short term and still vulnerable to the likely long-term decline in the pro-Soviet subculture.

Within the new Duma, the CPRF formed a communist fraction of eighty-eight and a satellite 'agro-industrial' fraction of forty-two, headed by the loyal ex-Agrarian Kharitonov.[66] However, with six parties passing the 5 per cent barrier, rather than the four in 1995, the party lost the 'multiplier effect' that had increased its party list seats in the previous Duma. The loss of its allied Agrarian and Popular Power fractions reduced the leftists' share of the seats from 211 (47 per cent) to 130 (29 per cent). Yet any suggestion that this would mark a new 'reformist' Duma were complicated by the communists' deal with the Edinstvo fraction. Seleznev was re-elected as speaker and the Edinstvo and communist fractions and their allies divided up the twenty-eight parliamentary committee chairs in violation of the previous convention of dividing them proportionally to fractions' strength. From this deal the communists obtained nine chairs, as opposed to the seven they should have received by convention.

This deal seemed to be a short-term electoral manoeuvre and not a long-term strategic alliance, although common interests between the regime and CPRF were visible in the benign media treatment of the CPRF in the campaign. The Seventh Duma gave no group a majority and forced each group to seek increased compromise in order to fulfil its aims. The executive wanted a stable majority and to preclude an obstructive Duma in the run-up to the elections. More notably, both executive and communists were concerned to avoid giving Evgenii Primakov a platform to challenge for the presidency, either as speaker or in a majority coalition. Primakov's appeal was broad and he could take votes from both camps.[67] Seleznev was a known quantity and through alliance with the relatively disciplined communist fraction the government could preclude an obstructive Duma in the run-up to the elections. Better for the regime to face the communists, whom Putin could almost certainly beat, and for the communists to stick with Zyuganov. For the communists, this deal was the safest option, although an electoral boycott or supporting Primakov as their presidential candidate were other options discussed.[68] Zyuganov had a chance of forcing Putin into a second round. This would prolong communist influence and the image of a 'red' Duma in the eyes of their supporters. The division of committee chairmanships certainly helped with such an image, and was also aimed at deflating the URF's claims that the reformers had won the election.[69]

The 2000 campaign – Russia's normal politics?

This presidential campaign was much less 'epochal' than that of 1996. Essentially, the question of succession had been decided by Edinstvo's victory in December, and confirmed by Yeltsin's resignation on New Year's Eve, 1999, thereby making Putin acting president and bringing the elections forward to 26 March. This was far from being the 'first peaceful, democratic transfer of power in Russia's 1000-year history' as claimed by Rutland, for which the idea of a Russian president losing an election would have to be entertained.[70] Rather it demonstrated again the overweening role of incumbency in Russia's polity. As Rutland himself admits 'Putin's democratic legitimacy was forged in war'. The invasion of Dagestan in August 1999, followed by explosions in Russia in September which left 300 dead, dramatically altered the tenor of the parliamentary campaign, forming a climate of fear which led to the need for decisive action against a common enemy, swiftly answered by the authorities' second campaign in Chechnya.[71]

Edinstvo exploited this skilfully, with extensive positive media coverage, access to public spending and governors' support.[72] When this was compounded by a strongly patriotic platform which asserted that critics of the military campaign were traitors, and endorsement from commander-in-chief Putin, a discourse of crisis was created by which all government opponents were stripped of manoeuvre and forced to support the government's Chechnya policy.[73] The 'succession' itself, while formally constitutional, truncated the election campaign, while bogging down challengers like Primakov in a time-consuming dispute over the parliamentary committees (itself provoked by supporters of the president). This was resolved only in February without concessions to the protesting deputies in FAR and URF, and after Primakov had unsurprisingly declined to run for president. Finally Putin's 'non-campaign' as a man of action, not words, his unwillingness to engage his opponents in debate or produce a detailed party platform, also denied opposition ammunition with which to attack him, and demeaned the campaign as a contest. Only Zyuganov even had a chance from the outset and, as we have seen, there was already evidence to suggest that he was being used a 'sparring partner' to ensure Putin's electoral victory over a weak opposition.

The television and print media gave overwhelming coverage to Putin, and much of it favourable.[74] However, although Zyuganov got much less coverage, it was 'almost tender', with Zyuganov granted long interviews on RTR and ORT.[75] Gone were the virulent anti-communist themes of 1996, with the exposure of party splits and the inconsistencies of the party platform. Putin himself never appealed to anti-communism. Rather most attacks on the communists were achieved by proxy. Former communist allies Tuleev and Podberezkin attacked the communists and Zyuganov's leadership explicitly, apparently with support of the Kremlin. Tuleev in particular sought to portray himself as a popular and effective leader of the left in contrast to the bureaucratic 'bigwigs' ensconced in the Duma, and as a direct rival to Zyuganov.[76] Both endorsed Putin late in the campaign. Putin had warned the CPRF of its need to change its programme to that of a left-wing party 'of the European type' if it were to retain influence.[77] These candidacies, as well as that of the nationalist Stanislav Govorukhin (also formerly of the NPUR), appeared to be backed by the Kremlin in an effort to push the CPRF further in this direction.

Contributing to the lack of electoral dynamism was Zyuganov's campaign. From the outset the party realised it had little hope of winning, but concentrated on maximising its second-place vote and developing new campaign methods. So Zyuganov sought to respond to the perception of himself as lacking leadership ability by presenting his platform as a moderate, realistic alternative to the existing leadership, with concrete proposals for governing, and less emphasis on criticising.[78] Gone on this occasion were attacks on the 'anti-national regime'. Zyuganov refrained from attacking the popular Putin directly. Instead he concentrated fire on Putin's lack of economic programme, and lack of concrete achievements to date.[79] He asserted that Putin's campaign lead was false, although he acknowledged he himself was behind.[80] Increased criticism of Putin in the latter stages of the campaign was designed to diminishing his winning margin.[81]

Zyuganov's concrete promises included constitutional reform aimed at liquidating the authoritarian power of the presidency and restoring the power of parliament and government, openness to alliance with the former Soviet republics, and state protection of the Orthodox church. These were all more modest versions of similar proposals aired in 1996, stressing Zyuganov's moderate patriotism. New emphases in a similar vein were promises promised to protect the middle class, and not to settle scores or renounce democratic achievements. He also stressed that the party's role in the 'patriotic belt' and State Duma showed that it was an effective force.[82] Stressing the party's economic experience was another lesson learnt from 1996, and Sergei Glazev was used to present a young, more moderate image to electors, with much mention made of his 'new economic course' and its successful antecedents: NEP, Roosevelt's economic policy, Chinese reform and the 'Primakov-Maslyukov' government of 1998–99, which had allegedly brought a concrete improvement to the economy.[83]

The CPRF made an explicit push to win over undecided voters, another area of weakness in 1996. Zyuganov, who visited twenty-two regions in 1996, visited only six in 2000, and concentrated instead on the youth and student vote and maintaining a profile in the mass media in Moscow.[84] He relied on traditional door-to-door campaigns to keep his core supporters happy. Some reports asserted that his regional campaign was relatively inactive, which would accord with the lack of will to win shown from the outset.[85] Meanwhile Zyuganov maintained a radical image in the party press, courting radical communists and nationalists alike. However, he had real difficulty in producing a clear campaign message when he no longer had a monopoly on patriotism. Putin explicitly made use of Soviet military patriotism, praising the army on the Day of the Defender of the Fatherland.[86] As a result, the national-patriotic paper *Zavtra* could not decide whether Putin was an ally or an 'agent of influence'.[87] Zyuganov accordingly sought to distinguish himself from Putin by reminding voters that Putin was Yeltsin's heir, and a tool of the oligarchs.[88]

In the final tally, Zyuganov's vote in 2000 was 29.2 per cent, 3 per cent less than he received in 1996, but 5 per cent more than in 1999, and far behind Putin's 52.9 per cent. This showed that despite the party's problems, its vote was still relatively stable in the aggregate, although increasingly volatile in components. Seventy-five per cent of the CPRF's 1999 Duma vote voted again for Zyuganov in 2000 and he gained votes from former FAR and Unity supporters, but lost 12 per cent of his 1999 votes to Putin and 3 per cent to Tuleev.[89] Further good news for Zyuganov was his performance in several regions in the north, the Far East and Siberia, where the CPRF had not traditionally done so well, and its leader improved upon his 1996 first round vote in forty regions, including in Moscow and St Petersburg (see Figure 4). Most remarkable was the party's showing in Primore, where Zyuganov's vote increased from 24.6 per cent in 1996 to 36.4 per cent, and in Omsk where Zyuganov got 43.6 per cent and beat Putin. Zyuganov's success in these regions could often be attributed to conflicts between governors and mayors against the background of a worsening economic situation (for example in Krasnoyarsk, Primore and Novosibirsk). In Omsk, for example, the unpopularity of the regional administration, and the collapse of the local machine-building and agricultural sectors increased protest tendencies.[90] This,

Figure 4 Change in support for Zyuganov in president elections (first round), 1996–2000

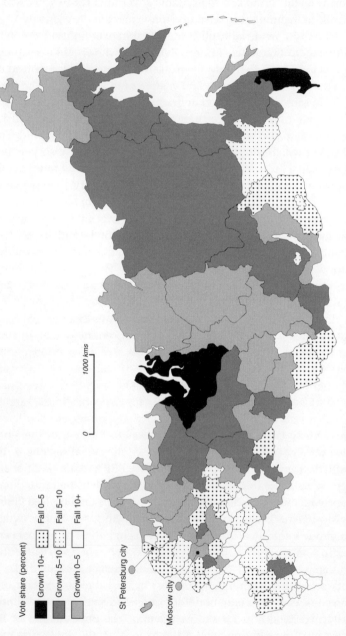

Vote share (percent)

- Growth 10+
- Growth 5–10
- Growth 0–5
- Fall 0–5
- Fall 5–10
- Fall 10+

St Petersburg city

Moscow city

0   1000 kms

Source: M. McFaul, N. Petrov and A. Ryabov (eds), *Rossiya v izbiratelnom tsikle 1999–2000 godov* (Moscow, Moscow Carnegie Center, 2000), Appendix 6 (Chechnya not included in data).

along with the declining competition from the Liberal Democrats, increased the protest vote that Zyuganov was able to exploit.[91]

However, while such successes beyond the Urals gave the communists a greater nation-wide presence, many losses in the southern red belt continued the trend noted in December 1999. The changed allegiances of many communist governors appeared significantly to affect Zyuganov's vote share. In Krasnodar, perhaps reflecting some ambiguity on the part of Governor Kondratenko, Putin got 51.5 per cent of votes while Zyuganov's vote dropped from 42 per cent to 37.4 per cent and there were similar stories in Stavropol, Saratov, Volgograd, Voronezh, Tambov and even Zyuganov's home region, Orel. In Tuleev's region, Kemerovo, Zyuganov's vote dropped by nearly 25 per cent. Putin's stance on the Chechen war also helped him win support in Russia's south.[92] In many other 'controlled regions' where the governors had influence over their electorate, Zyuganov's vote fell precipitously, such as in Dagestan (from 63.2 per cent in 1996 to 16.4 per cent in 2000), Ingushetiya (from 24.5 per cent to 4.6 per cent) and North Osetiya (from 62.3 per cent to 28.5 per cent). Whatever the local picture, the overall picture for the communists again appeared bleak. Having come first in forty-five regions in the first round of 1996 and thirty-one in the second, in 2000 Zyuganov managed this in just four (Lipetsk, Omsk, the Altai republic and Bryansk).

This defeat was even less unambiguous than it appears, given that the electoral statistics were plausibly alleged to be fraudulent, giving extra votes to Putin, particularly at Zyuganov's expense, and guaranteeing Putin victory in the first round. Thus we may imagine that Zyuganov's vote was closer to his 1996 result and more stable than it appears, although communist claims of seven million stolen votes were backed up by no demonstrable evidence and appeared designed mainly to explain the defeat to the party's supporters.[93] No one denies that Putin would have won handsomely in the second round.

Conclusion

The communists' election results after 1996 were not an unambiguous tale of decline, although the party's weaker representation in the Duma and weaker presidential challenge in 2000 was evidence enough of a loss of position. The CPRF much exceeded its own expectations of

22–27 per cent, but such low indications are indicative in themselves. By 2001 the party could still take comfort from the fact that it had preserved its status as the official opposition. The 3 per cent showing for Tuleev was particularly significant, suggesting that the CPRF had fought off challenges to a relatively stable electorate, while no national-level challenger for Zyuganov had yet emerged. Regional elections and electoral improvements during 1999–2000 showed that the CPRF was capable of adapting to local electoral conditions and did not just rely on nostalgia or its traditional supporters. Its electoral campaign itself showed a great progression from 1996. Despite attrition, the party preserved organisational coherence and a national and regional electoral presence.

Yet none of the CPRF's major problems apparent in 1996 appeared resolved: its ageing electorate, inability to attract major allies (rather it tended to repel them), tendency to put internal party problems before its electoral needs, preference for populist (if increasingly moderate) patriotism rather than a more defined centre-left orientation and, above all, inflexible organisation and electorate and passive campaigning, which made the party seem 'doomed to be the bridesmaid but never the bride' in presidential contests.[94] Of great significance was the depolarisation of the electorate after 1996. Whereas this offered the party the chance to move beyond its electoral 'ghetto', it threatened its stable constituency. Although the CPRF remained head of the 'opposition', it had not monopolised the protest vote. Although it outperformed its own expectations, one may ask why the party had not performed still better, particularly given the fact that it received benign media treatment relative to 1996. After all, in the wake of the August 1998 crisis, it had seemed that the resulting changes in public opinion would virtually guarantee the communists electoral success.[95] Yet, while the CPRF's disciplined electoral core was showing signs of softening, new 'patriotic' forces such as FAR and, still more successfully, Edinstvo and Vladimir Putin himself had also exploited the populace's desire for order and national self-reliance.

As Aleksandr Buzgalin notes, Zyuganov's appropriation of nationalist and patriotic themes left him vulnerable, and not just to internal party disquiet. If a politician with executive power and popularity stole his patriotic slogans and took action establishing him as a 'nationalist' head of state, then Zyuganov's trump cards would be rendered worthless.[96] Vladimir Putin proved more than able to play that role. At the same time FAR's showing, with Luzhkov's social democratic hints, and Primakov's respect among parts of the communist electorate, indicated at least a potential for a centre-left movement, despite the patriotic and eclectic idiom of this bloc's platform. The CPRF might ignore such trends at its peril.

More marked than ever after these elections were the general weaknesses of party politics in Russia, and the concomitant strength of incumbency resources and clientelistic networks at both local and national level. None of Russia's established political parties (the CPRF, LDPR and Yabloko) performed well, the former improving its vote share, but appearing further from power than ever, the latter two polling their worst yet in parliamentary elections with 6 per cent and 5.9 per cent respectively. The URF was a partial exception, but even this 'liberal' party discarded much of its liberalism in search of the amorphous patriotic 'centre'. Rather the main contestants in these elections were two blocs of the ruling elite 'party of power', FAR and Edinstvo, using their considerable media and patronage resources to fight for the presidential prize. Indeed it was this characteristic of FAR that explained its sudden demise, as many of its governors jumped ship to join Edinstvo and latch on to Putin's rising star. The rise of Edinstvo at least produced a regime able to identify and respond clearly to popular demand, and in this sense the elections presented a major advance. Putin's popularity was based firmly on his ability to respond to public desire for an active, energetic and decisive crisis leader. But there was evidence also of the elite's increased ability to mould electoral demand in a way not available to those with fewer elite resources, more cumbersome party organisations or even coherent party programmes (particularly in the case of overt falsification in loyal regions). When Edinstvo organisers believed that a personal endorsement from Putin had added a dozen percentage points to their total, and preferred to concentrate on an 'air war' rather than a 'ground war' even relying too much on governors, the message appeared clear: traditional parties were not necessary to reach the electorate.[97] More worryingly for the CPRF, it appeared that regional trends were being replicated on a national level, with parties being useful to the elite instrumentally as cheerleaders for election victories after which they then became mere onlookers. If regional trends were anything to go by, the CPRF's integration in the political elite, even as a 'sparring partner', might prove damaging to its long-term interests. It is to this question we now turn.

Notes

1 *Novoe vremya*, 35 (1996).
2 D. Slider, 'Regional and local politics', in S. White. A. Pravda and Z. Gitelman (eds), *Developments in Russian Politics 4*, (Basingstoke, Macmillan, 1997), pp. 257–8.
3 K. Stoner-Weiss, 'The limited reach of Russia's party system: under-institutionalization in the provinces', *PONARS Memo*, 122 (2000).
4 M. McFaul and N. Petrov, 'Russian electoral politics after transition: regional and national assessments', *Post-Soviet Geography and Economics*, 38:9 (1997), 507.
5 *NG*, 8 August 1997.
6 *SR*, 10 August 1996. For views of the NPUR as predominately a nationalist organisation in the mould of earlier blocs see Y. M. Brudny, 'In pursuit of the Russian presidency: why and how Yeltsin won the 1996 presidential election', *Communist and Post-Communist Studies*, 30:3 (1997), 274.
7 *OMRI Russian Regional Report*, I, 10, 30 October 1996, McFaul and Petrov, 'Russian electoral politics'.
8 A. Verkhovskii (ed.), *Levye v Rossii: ot umerennykh do ekstremistov* (Moscow, Panorama, 1997), p. 23.
9 *OMRI Russian Regional Report*, II, 4, 18 September 1996.
10 *K*, 1 November 1996.
11 *Financial Times*, 30 August 1996, p. 2, *Moscow News*, 21–27 May 1998.
12 *Moscow News*, 21 November 1996.
13 Information from web site at: www.kprf.ru.
14 McFaul and Petrov, 'Russian electoral politics'.
15 *KPRF mezhdu umerennostyu i radikalizmom* (Moscow, Tsentr politicheskykh tekhnologii, 1997), p. 7.
16 *OMRI Russian Regional Report*, 2:1, 8 January 1997; *Patriot*, 1 (1998); *OMRI Russian Regional Report*, I, 6, 2 October 1996.
17 It had a co-ordinating council of 150, with one representative from each of the eighty-nine regions plus representatives of all member blocs. In the regions the NPUR was formed on the basis of CPRF local cells. (Author's interview with deputy head of CPRF CC department for international affairs, A. Filippov, on 31 January 1998). See also *NG*, 19 September 1996.
18 T. Avaliani, *Molniya*, 9 (1997).
19 R. Sakwa, 'Left or right? The CPRF and the problem of democratic consolidation in Russia', *Journal of Communist Studies and Transition Politics*, 14:1&2 (1998), 137.
20 *NG*, 19 September 1997.
21 G. Golosov, 'Gubernatory i partiinaya politika', *Pro et Contra*, 5:1 (2000), 102; *SR*, 29 July 1999; *P*, 25–26 May 1999.
22 Those governors who eventually supported the CPRF in the 1999 election were Belogonov (Amur), Kondratenko (Krasnodar), Maksyuta, (Volgograd), Ryabov (Tambov), Vinogradov (Vladimir), Chernogorov (Stavropol), Starodubtsev (Tula), Lodkin (Bryansk), Shabanov (Voronezh) and Surikov (Altai). Of these only the last five might be regarded as very strongly ideological. See *EWI Russian Regional Report*, 4:37, 7 October 1999; V. Tolz and I. Busygina, 'Regional governors and the Kremlin: the ongoing battle for power', *Communist and Post-Communist Studies*, 30:4 (1997), 412.

23 *EWI Russian Regional Report*, 6:1, 21 March 2001.
24 Stoner-Weiss, 'The limited reach of Russia's party system'.
25 *Vybory glav ispolnitelnoi vlasti subektov Rossiiskoi Federatsii*, CPRF web site at: www.kprf.ru.
26 For example, by removing the requirement of a second round run-off election (which Maksyuta might have lost), and by censoring media opposition to the governor during the election (*OG*, 21 December 2000).
27 *Itogi*, 26 December 2000.
28 L. Byzov, 'Presidentskaya kampaniya – 2000 i novyi electoralnyi zapros', in M. McFaul, N. Petrov and A. Ryabov (eds), *Rossiya v izbiratelnom tsikle 1999–2000 godov* (Moscow, Moscow Carnegie Center, 2000), pp. 484–96.
29 N. Petrov, 'Broken pendulum, recentralization under Putin', *PONARS Memo*, 159 (2000).
30 For example, in early 1999, 18 per cent of party secretaries were changed as result of criticism (Sergei Potapov, CPRF CC Presidium member, *P*, 27–28 April 1999).
31 The Agrarian Party, Derzhava and Spiritual Heritage wanted a loose coalition rather than the disciplined union the CPRF sought, and sought alliances with centrists such as Yurii Luzhkov, the Union of Realists and S. Federov's social democratic Party of Workers' Self-Management (*NG*, 4 July 1998).
32 See Agrarian leader Lapshin's comments to this effect in *K*, 6 January 1998.
33 *Informatsionnyi byulleten*, 30 (1998), on web site at www.kprf.ru; *SWB*/SU/3375 B/5 (4 November 1998).
34 *Moskovskaya Pravda*, 66 (December 1999); *P-5*, 23 May 1998.
35 *MT*, 14 January 1999 (web version at: www.moscownews.ru).
36 The CPRF supported only nine MSA candidates, and refused to give a party list place to the MSA's Albert Makashov, thereby virtually forcing it to run independently. See *NG*, 3 September 1999; S. Chernyakovskii, 'Kommunisticheskie obedineniya', in M. McFaul, N. Petrov and A. Ryabov (eds), *Rossiya nakanune dumskikh vyborov 1999 goda* (Moscow, Moscow Carnegie Center, 1999), p. 102.
37 Ilyukhin said his aim was to pitch the MSA vote towards Cossacks and military personnel who were nationalists but who might object to the communist label (Ilyukhin at MSA website www.gull.ptt.ru/Asm).
38 Zorkaltsev, chairman of the NPUR's executive committee, said that the opposition would run in four columns – the APR, CPRF, and the moderate and radical patriots (*Jamestown Foundation Monitor*, 8 January 1999). Kuptsov insisted that Zyuganov and Seleznev would top a central CPRF candidate list. Many communists feared that the columns would split the party (*P*, 30 June–6 July 1999).
39 The timing of the formation of the bloc was dictated by the party secretaries, when it had become clear that none of the columns would pass the 5 per cent barrier (*NG*, 28 July 1999).
40 In Tula, Ulyanovsk, Rostov, St Petersburg and a number of other regions, regional organisations of Spiritual Heritage joined the CPRF (*NG*, 10 September 1999). For the APR split and leader Lapshin's views see *NG*, 20 August 1999.
41 *NG*, 22 September 1999. Derzhava had already left the NPUR because Zyuganov insisted it leave Luzhkov's Fatherland movement. Lapshin and Podberezkin, as well as Aman Tuleev were finally expelled from the NPUR in June 2000.

42 For the platform, 'Get up, Great Country!', see web site at: www.kprf.ru/
    zapobedu.htm; and for the seventy-five page campaign booklet see *RFE/RL
    Russian Election Report*, 2, 12 November 1999.
43 Darya Mitina, *Moskovskii komsomolets*, 30 September 1999.
44 For the economic programme 'By Means of Creation' see web site at:
    www.kprf.ru.
45 *RFE/RL Newsline*, 3:186, I, 23 September 1999.
46 *SR*, 17 December 1999.
47 The party list even contained one ex-OHIR Duma deputy (Zhores Alferov,
    tenth place on list), and thirty-seven Agrarians, as well as other groups (*PR*,
    15–21 September 1999).
48 *NG*, 23 September 1999.
49 S. Chernyakovskii in M. McFaul *et al.*, *Carnegie Bulletin 2: Parliamentary
    Elections in Russia*, from web site at: www.ceip.org/programs/ruseuras/
    Elections/elections.htm.
50 Valentin Kuptsov at CPRF Sixth Congress 15 January 2000 from web site at:
    www.kprf.ru.
51 See web site at: www.rferl.org/elections/russian99report/speeches.html.
52 The number of people who would not vote for the CPRF in any circumstances
    declined from 70 per cent in 1995 to 30 per cent in 1999 (S. Chernyakovskii,
    'The Communist Party of the Russian Federation', in M. McFaul, M. Petrov,
    A. Ryabov and E. Reisch (eds), *Primer on Russia's 1999 Duma Elections*
    (Washington, DC, Carnegie Endowment, 1999), p. 82).
53 Information from web site at: www.fci.ru.
54 Eleven were independents (most backed by the CPRF) and five nominated
    from other parties (information from web sites at: www.fci.ru and
    www.duma.gov.ru). The party had endorsed up to forty independent candi-
    dates.
55 Eleven per cent of under thirty-fives voted for the CPRF in 1999. See N. Petrov,
    'Vybory i obshchestvo', in McFaul *et al.*, *Rossiya v izbiratelnom tsikle*, p. 403; and
    New Russia Barometer VIII at web site at: www.russiavotes.org.
56 Seven per cent according to a ROMIR poll on 29 February 2000 from web site
    at: www.russiatoday.com.
57 Information kindly supplied by Neil Munro. A large share of the CPRF electo-
    rate in Voronezh, Kalmykiya and Volgograd shifted to Putin (*NG*, 17
    December 1999; *EWI Russian Regional Report*, 5:2, 19 January 2000).
58 S. Chernyakovskii, 'Kommunisticheskoe dvizhenie' in M. McFaul, N. Petrov
    and A. Ryabov (eds), *Rossiya na dumskikh i prezidentskikh vyborakh* (Moscow,
    Moscow Carnegie Center, 2000).
59 V. Kuptsov at CPRF Sixth Congress, from web site at: www.kprf.ru.
60 These regions were Magadan and Kamchatka oblasts, Krasnodar krai and the
    Khanty-Mansi and Yamalo-Nenets autonomous okrugs. See statistics in
    McFaul *et al.*, *Carnegie Bulletin 4: Itogi vyborov* from web site at: www.ceip.org/
    programs/ruseuras/Elections/elections.htm; and M. McFaul, N. Petrov and
    A. Ryabov (eds), *Rossiya nakanune dumskikh vyborov 1999 goda* (Moscow,
    Moscoe Carnegie Center, 1999), pp. 307–9.
61 *EWI Russian Regional Report*, 4:48, 22 December 1999. In Kemerovo, the com-
    munists won 29 per cent as opposed to 45 per cent in 1995, while Edinstvo
    took 34 per cent. Kemerovo governor Tuleev appeared on the communist list
    and simultaneously supported Edinstvo.

62 M. McFaul *et al.*, *Carnegie Bulletin 4: Itogi vyborov*.

63 *P*, 23 December 1999.

64 *S*, 22 December 1999.

65 On the CPRF's failure to anticipate Edinstvo at all see N. Bindyukov, *P*, 27 January 2000, and for the voting intentions of CPRF voters see *New Russia Barometer VIII*, survey data from 19–29 January 2000 (from web site at: www.russiavotes.org).

66 Figures on 2 March 2000 from web site at: www.duma.gov.ru.

67 From the Kremlin's point of view, if Edinstvo had a majority coalition with FAR, this would strengthen Primakov, but if it united with Yabloko and URF this would have raised the possibility of an opposition FAR-CPRF alliance. An alliance with the communists at least promised stability as the party's discipline meant that they were easy to work with. Seleznev's ability to compromise got his support from the Kremlin, oligarchs such as Berezovskii and a number of regional leaders. See *Harvard Election Watch*, 2 (2000), 8. For the communist view see *PR*, 26 January–1 February 2000.

68 S. Chernyakovskii, 'Kommunisticheskoe dvizhenie'.

69 *PR*, 23–29 February 2000.

70 P. Rutland, 'Putin's path to power', *Post-Soviet Affairs*, 16:4 (2000), 313–54.

71 L. Byzov, 'Parliamentskye vybory kak etap v formirovanie konsensusnogo obshchestva', in M. McFaul, N. Petrov and A. Ryabov (eds), *Rossiya v izbiratelnom tsikle 1999–2000 godov* (Moscow, Moscow Carnegie Center, 2000), 222–30.

72 See T. J. Colton and M. McFaul, 'Reinventing Russia's party of power: "Unity" and the 1999 Duma election', *Post-Soviet Affairs*, 16:3 (2000), 201–24.

73 A. Ryabov, 'The Putin factor', in M. McFaul, N. Petrov, A. Ryabov and E. Reisch (eds), *Carnegie Bulletin 2: Parliamentary Elections in Russia* (Moscow, Moscow Carnegie Center, 1999) (web site at: http://pubs.carnegie.ru/english).

74 Putin got about half of all air-time devoted to candidates on news programmes and received about a third of column space devoted to the presidential candidates. Zyuganov got just 13.2 per cent coverage in the media in February. See *Johnson's Russia List*, 27 March 2000; *RFE/RL Russian Election Report*, 5:13, 7 April 2000.

75 *Russia Today*, 29 March 2000; *RFE/RL Russian Election Report*, 1 (9), 3 March 2000.

76 See, for example, web site at: www.rferl.org/elections/russia00report/tuleev.html.

77 N. Gevorkyan, N. Timakova and A. Kolesnikov, *Ot pervogo litsa: razgavory s Vladimirom Putinym* (Moscow, Vagrius, 2000).

78 For experts' views view on Zyuganov's weak points, such as indecisiveness and 'lack of ability to accept responsibility' see *S*, 26 January 2000.

79 See interviews with Zyuganov on 10 February 2000 and 18 February 2000 on web site at: www.kprf.ru.

80 Interview on ORT 18 February 2000 on web site at: www.kprf.ru.

81 S. Chernyakovskii, 'Kampaniya G. Zyuganova', in M. McFaul, N. Petrov and A. Ryabov (eds), *Rossiya v izbiratelnom tsikle 1999–2000 godov* (Moscow, Moscow Carnegie Center, 2000).

82 For Zyuganov's 'Appeal to the People' see web site at: www.zyuganov.ru, 9 February 2000.

83 See *P*, 14–15 February 2000 on web site at: www.kprf.ru; and the interview with Glazev on Radio Rossii 9 March 2000, *Johnson's Russia List*, 4159, 10 March 2000.

84 N. Petrov, 'Politicheskii vkus i poslevkus', *Carnegie Bulletin 3: Itogam vyborov 26 Marta 2000 g.*, from web site at: http://pubs.carnegie.ru/english/elections/president2000.

85 *RFE/RL Russian Federation Report*, 2:7, 16 February 2000.

86 *Johnson's Russia List*, 4125, 22 February 2000.

87 See for example *Zavtra*, 11, 14 March 2000 and 13, 28 March 2000 from web site at: www.zavtra.ru.

88 Interview with Zyuganov on ORT 18 February 2000 from web site at: www.kprf.ru, www.russiatoday.com, 22 March 2000.

89 VTsIOM poll 31 March–3 April 2000 in *Johnson's Russian List*, 4241, 11 April 2000. Eleven per cent of FAR's supporters in December 1999, 6 per cent of Unity's and 13 per cent of the LDPR's voted for Zyuganov in 2000.

90 *Parliamentskaya gazeta*, 25 April 2000.

91 *Nezavisimaya gazeta-Stsenarii* (*NG Stsenarii*), 12 April 2000; *EWI Russian Regional Report*, 5:12, 28 March 2000.

92 *NG Stsenarii*, 12 April 2000.

93 *MT*, 9 September 2000. Five hundred and fifty thousand extra votes may have been given to Putin in Dagestan alone, and nine regions where Putin won 6.96 million votes had dubious returns. The official number of registered voters also mysteriously grew by 1.3 million between the Duma and presidential votes.

94 L. Belin, *RFE/RL Russian Electoral Report*, 5 (13), 7 April 2000.

95 For example Vitalii Tretyakov saw the CPRF as almost guaranteed an absolute majority in the next Duma and with a very strong chance of performing well in the presidential campaign. See *SWB* SU/3382 B/6 (12 November 1998).

96 *Johnson's Russia List*, 4205, 28 March 2000.

97 Colton and McFaul, 'Reinventing Russia's party of power', 208–11.

8

The CPRF and the political system

[The CPRF] can be only in irreconcilable opposition . . . the greatest task of the party is the change of the ruling regime in its entirety, the consistent build-up of popular resistance to the new ruinous round of shock 'reforms', presidential autocracy and betrayal of national interests.[1]

We now turn to the party's activities in the parliamentary arena, where the communists were dominant in the Sixth Duma of 1995–99 and commanded the biggest fraction in the Seventh Duma elected in December 1999. Communist participation in the Duma made explicit the theme of the CPRF's adaptability to post-communist politics implicit in our discussion so far. As shown above, the party always insisted that it aimed at a change of regime, not simply government, and was thereby the 'irreconcilable' opposition. Yet its actual practice proved to be more opaque, with an ability to deal with the ruling elite apparent in its deal with the Edinstvo fraction in 1999.

The nature of the opposition of Russia's biggest political party is of obvious broader significance, as the absence of a powerful anti-democratic opposition representing an 'explicit authoritarian alternative' is recognised as a key stage in the consolidation of a new democracy, while a within-system opposition which aims for a change of government, not regime, entrenches the principle of a democratic electoral alternation of power.[2] But Valerii Solovei identifies a key problem in analysing such oppositions: 'if an opposition plays by democratic rules or the rules of a system, does that mean that it recognises the values of democracy and the aims of the given system?'[3] Accordingly we look at the CPRF's convoluted performance in parliament, when precisely this question gave the party the hallmarks of a strategic crisis in its interaction with both regime and membership, before summarising the party's role in the evolution of the Russian polity. The CPRF's elite made the transition to a within-system opposition within the parliament of 1995–99, but the conflict this caused with the party's ideology, structure and mass membership seemed to provide an intractable obstacle to the party playing an unambiguously 'systemic' role, while adaptation to Russia's quasi-democracy did not yet make the CPRF a democratic opposition.

The dilemma of communist opposition

The behaviour of other communist parties in pluralist systems is instructive in understanding the problems confronting the CPRF since its decision to participate in a 'bourgeois' system after its re-foundation in 1993, although we must also take Russian specifics into account. Like the British Labour Party at the turn of the twentieth century, the CPRF recognised it faced the choice of being 'His Majesty's opposition' or 'opposition to His Majesty',[4] that is between within-system and anti-system opposition. As Sartori argues, within-system opposition parties aim to form 'responsible' alternative governments which do not seek to act outside the 'rules of the game', and confine their opposition to constitutional and legal forms.[5] However, anti-system opposition parties have very little chance of being called on to govern, tend to behave less responsibly and may make wild promises. Their actions need no acceptance of 'rules of the game', limits of the constitution or legality.

The communist parties of Western Europe long tended towards this type of opposition. As 'foreigners encamped in a hostile country', they followed Lenin's dictum 'the worse [for the bour-geois], the better [for the communists]' – all policies were seen as class actions, and so anything the ruling class did was to be con-demned, anything done in the name of the working class to be approved.[6] They preferred obstructive or non-committal opposition, refusing all but temporary compromises with the ruling regime. Using bourgeois parliaments as 'tribunes' for ideological demagogy and denunciation of their opponents, they offered purely demon-strative non-constructive demands meant to destabilise and ruin the capitalist system.[7] There appeared to be a limit to how much con-structive opposition a communist party could render. The gradual change from 'obstruction to amendment' in parliament marked the beginning of the incorporation of Western European communist parties in bourgeois systems and the start of the breakdown of their communist identity itself. The CPRF itself increasingly faced this risk the more successful it was and the closer it came to power within the political system, a tendency only increased by the co-optative and clientelistic tendencies of Russia's political system.

Opposition in evolution: constructive or irreconcilable?

The CPRF initially avoided facing serious problems over its participation in the 'bourgeois' Fifth Duma of 1993–95, simply because of the relatively small size of its faction (forty-five members). This allowed it to avoid sharing responsibility with the regime, much as the similarly sized Yabloko faction did in both the Fifth and Sixth Dumas. The party used the Duma as a 'tribune' for its non-constructive opposition. It sought to combine an image of responsible lawmaking (which would both boost its 'democratic' respectability and minimise the likelihood of a ban), with implacable opposition to the regime (to preserve its 'anti-system' image in the eyes of the electorate).[8] It continually denied the legitimacy of the parliament in which it sat and of the new constitution.[9] Any communist renegades were immediately expelled, such as fraction member, Valentin Kovalev, who became justice minister without consulting the party, and Duma speaker, Ivan Rybkin, who used his position in an excessively compromising fashion.[10] The CPRF's principled and largely uncompromising public position allowed it to disseminate the party message consistently and adhere steadfastly to positions despite government pressure to break it down.

Yet, the mere fact of participation in the Duma, where the majority of contentious issues were resolved through compromise and bargaining, tended to foster dialogue and contacts both between opposing factions and between legislative and executive power over a shared aversion to repetition of the events of 1993.[11] Lenin had insisted on the need for communists to remain true to their revolutionary purpose 'through all compromises', but it was not clear that the CPRF was so steadfast. In the absence of extra-parliamentary possibilities most CPRF Duma deputies accommodated to new realities and sought to maximise the parliamentary possibilities of the party.[12] Even at this stage the radical public face concealed a more moderate line, as the party's demands for higher welfare spending and for a vote of no confidence in the government (initiated in June 1995) were made in the full knowledge that these were unlikely to succeed.[13]

However the latent moderate-radical division in the CPRF was exacerbated by the increasing long-term incorporation of its higher echelons within the regime, and there was increasing divergence over the nature of opposition. Moderates, owing to their *nomenklatura* mentality, manifested tendencies towards 'constructive' opposition with the regime, in order to 'save what [could] be saved' of Soviet values.[14] The radicals were unwilling to take upon themselves even symbolic (in their terms 'moral') responsibility for reforms.[15] In their opinion the Duma was to be used only for anti-bourgeois agitation. Any constructive compromise strengthened the new political order and would lead to the collapse of the CPRF's rating among its electorate.[16] Moreover, the size of the CPRF's representation in the Sixth Duma of 1995–99 (211 seats with its allies, close to the parliamentary majority of 226 able to complete a no confidence vote in the government) started new problems: would the party promote compromise or conflict with its new-found strength? As we saw in Chapter 6 the party managed to avoid the implications of this dilemma until the latter stages of the 1996 election campaign, by refusing to 'flex its muscles' within the Duma.

However, with the 1996 election over, it was always likely that the overriding unity should begin to splinter, and that competing party groups should begin to seek blame for the defeat. The end of electoral polarisation would imply that divisions within blocs such as those between moderates and radicals should become stronger, and would pose significant problems for a party whose very identity was predicated on anti-system unity, but it did not necessarily imply that the deep mutual distaste between the communists and leaders like Yeltsin and Chubais would quickly diminish.

Acceptance of the election result, despite qualms about 'falsification', meant that the CPRF 'crossed the Rubicon' into constructive behaviour. It refused the urging of party radicals to make mischief such as a no confidence vote.[17] Zyuganov made the conclusion that the party lacked majority support even among workers, whereas the regime was stable and had popularity and 'vitality'.[18] Given the solidity of elite opposition to a communist revanche demonstrated during the election, the most profitable way to retain influence was extend the communists' 'creeping coup' to win sympathetic allies within the regime (such as prime minister Chernomyrdin, with whom the party developed contacts during the campaign) and to use parliamentary pressure to wring concessions from the executive.[19] Thus the communists offered their power-sharing initiatives such as the 'government of popular trust' and 'roundtables' with increasing frequency in the two years after the election as a way of insulating both the regime and the communists from the instabilities of a new election prompted by Yeltsin's ongoing incapacities, which some unpredictable figure like Aleksandr Lebed might win.[20] The political elite's need for stability was satisfied by the CPRF's moderation and the communists aimed to exploit differences in the government between 'nationally oriented capitalists' like Chernomyrdin and neo-liberals like head of the presidential administration Anatolii Chubais.

The party's new orientation was most obvious in its interaction with the Chernomyrdin government in the State Duma. Landmark decisions were the CPRF's confirmation of Chernomyrdin as prime minister on 10 August 1996, and the decision of the CPRF's then ally, Tuleev, to become minister for co-operation with the Commonwealth of Independent States (CIS) countries. He became the first CPRF ally to enter government with the full approval of the party leadership and without any government concessions over policy to the CPRF. In December 1996, the 1997 budget was approved by the CPRF faction, as were all subsequent budgets in this Duma. Simultaneously, the party leadership began to focus on changing the party's anti-systemic stance towards the regime. Thus leaders began to talk more and more of the CPRF as part of the 'systemic opposition' in a 'two-party system' alongside the 'party of power'.[21] Towards the end of 1996 the leadership sought to make this palatable to the membership by con-cocting the eclectic compromise formula 'responsible but irreconcil-able opposition' – responsible for affairs in the country but irreconcilable to the course of the regime.[22] But the aim, though denied, was apparent: the CPRF was increasingly defending the inter-ests of workers and state *within* the new political system.

However, from late 1996 until late 1998, the CPRF's 'responsible but irreconcilable opposition' phase was reduced to incoherence by a combination of party dissent and the poor leverage that the party could exert on the regime either through either mass demonstrations or the powers of the State Duma. One corollary of the gubernatorial elections of 1996–97 was the further incorporation of the CPRF in the regime. The CPRF aimed to use these elections to gain enough strength in the Federation Council to complement its legislative dom-inance in the Duma. Then it could envisage a constitutional majority in both houses of parliament and attempt to get a constitution giving more power to the Duma, so obviating the party's inability to win the presidency.[23] But the Federation Council was formed on a non-party basis where corporate and regional interests proved paramount, increasing the tendency of the new 'red' governors to turn loyalist. At the same time, the new governors pushed CPRF activists into local government, so that they too became de facto executives.[24]

Simultaneously the regime alternated 'psychological pressure' on the Duma (as in summer 1997 with a selection of neo-liberal budget cuts and rumours circulated of possible Duma dissolution) with concessions designed to get the opposition to share responsibility for economic policy. For example, in October 1997 the threat of a CPRF-inspired no confidence vote was averted when the president intervened with a face-saving compromise, whereby the communists were promised roundtable talks, the meeting of the 'big four' (heads of executive, government, Federation Council and parliament) and increased media access.[25] But such concessions were not formalised and soon fell by the wayside, meaning that the CPRF's opposition policy was in crisis as it contemplated its election campaign for 1999. A backlash among party ranks was fomented that checked the leaders' moves towards programmatic and tactical innovation. Emboldened radicals criticised the CPRF's weak parliamentary opposition to the regime, its ideological leanings towards 'Christian democratic' and 'social democratic' ideas, and demanded the removal of leaders such as Zyuganov and Podberezkin. This effort was to culminate in the formation of a 'Leninist-Stalinist platform within the CPRF' in 1998.[26] This opposition's strength was more rhetorical than real, but it forced the party into increasing policy zigzags, as it tried to combine an increasingly rhetorical radical opposition with de facto but unacknowledged weak opposition. The leadership sought to reiterate its hardline credentials to avoid serious threats of a split.[27] A case in point was the party's Fourth Congress in April 1997 where Zyuganov's littered his keynote speech with class terminology, quotes from Stalin and Lenin, and calls for extra-parliamentary strike committees[28] – to little avail. In late 1997, sixty of the CPRF's then eighty-nine regional organisations pressed for an end to compromise, even at the expense of Duma dissolution.[29]

The CPRF was loath to countenance this, despite most opinion polls showing it could gain seats, and its unwillingness to stand up for its anti-regime credentials was often attributed to a wish for cosy seats in the Duma, cowardice or, indeed, veniality, as we saw in Chapter 5.[30] In a resource-scarce society like Russia, purely self-interested motives cannot be dismissed. The material importance of the Duma to party funding, communications and election campaigns would in itself hamper the CPRF were it closed in pre-term elections.

However, the structure of incentives facing the communists was a more convincing explanation. The CPRF fraction was placed a complex double bind. It was too small to threaten the existing government with obstruction, yet too large to avoid sharing some responsibility for key government decisions such as the budget.[31] Moreover, the party was well aware that the Duma's leverage was blunt, limited and could lead to crisis. This reflected the general tendency that systems with elected hegemonic presidencies and elected but weakly representative parliaments have an inability to terminate a crisis of government without it becoming a crisis of regime.[32] Indeed, the Duma appeared well engineered to limit the legislature's real influence. Duma dissolution, as threatened by the no confidence motion in October 1997 or during the confirmation of Sergei Kirienko as prime minister in April 1998, would achieve little in terms of changing government policy. Voting down the prime minister (always a presidential appointee) three times would only lead to the prime minister being appointed anyway and new Duma elections held. Few critics of the communists asked what such kamikaze tactics would achieve for the communists themselves. In fact, they might give the government carte blanche to rule by decree until new elections, even permitting the sale of farmland and the break-up of natural monopolies, policies the communists had long fought hard.[33] Besides, during 1997–98 the executive was proposing to change the Duma's electoral rules from a mixed proportional representation system to a majoritarian system, which would have adversely affected most Duma groups.[34] Such were the administrative methods by which the regime kept the Duma docile.

Because the legislature was so dependent on the president, if the CPRF chose overtly constructive opposition, it had little way of claiming credit for initiatives which the president also supported. Yet, if the CPRF backed down, this made it look impotent in the eyes of its electorate. A critical occasion was Yeltsin's appointment of Kirienko, a political neophyte who had none of his predecessor Chernomyrdin's experience at mollifying the Duma. With no face-saving concessions offered from the executive, the party seemed prepared to countenance dissolution to retain opposition credibility. But simultaneously, it appeared to adopt a routine rehearsed in previous key votes in the

Sixth Duma: that is, of proclaiming absolute opposition, secretly negotiating with the executive and discretely allowing some of its deputies
to break party ranks on a secret ballot.[35] The party leadership was
deeply split, facing pressure from its Duma chairman Gennadii
Seleznev, governors Tuleev and Maksyuta, and some of its single
mandate deputies (such as Maslyukov) to preserve the Duma. In the
event perhaps twenty-five to forty communists voted for Kirienko
on the third vote as he was accepted by 225 votes to twenty-
five.[36]Although the actual preservation of the Duma may have suited
Zyuganov, the scale of the 'yeas' appeared to come as shock to him,
while his apparent inability to discipline any of the renegades meant
that his leadership indubitably lost authority.[37]

As even Zyuganov acknowledged, the party and its fraction were
openly split into a radical 'left' wing whose concerns were voiced by
chair of the Duma Security Committee, Viktor Ilyukhin, and a moderate 'right', whose views were most clearly expressed by Seleznev,
both of whom publicly challenged Zyuganov's leadership, Seleznev
even hinting at bidding for the presidency.[38] The party increasingly
looked like a 'centaur' with its moderate and radical sides utterly
antipathetic.[39] While Ilyukhin apparently called for illegal means to
be used against the 'criminals' in the Yeltsin regime, single mandate
deputies who represented particular constituencies, or those in parliamentary legislative committees were more likely to support 'professional work' and reject reflex discipline and the activities of
political 'outsiders'.[40] As a result fraction discipline was weakening,
with expulsions and defections of members from the party line and
party itself.[41] All told, the CPRF fraction fell from 149 members in 1995
to 128 in September 1999, many of these delegated to reinforce the
increasingly rebellious allied fractions, while radicals called on the
party to put the Duma fraction in order or 'die as an opposition organisation'.[42] The party's hastily called Fifth Congress of 23 May 1998 dissolved the Leninist-Stalinist platform.[43] But this did nothing to heal
the party's gaping fissures. In July Yurii Maslyukov joined the
Kirienko government as trade and industry minister, thereby becoming the first CPRF *member* (Tuleev was not a CPRF member, Kovalev
only a member of the fraction) to do so. This came just a day after the
Party Presidium had unanimously vetoed the move, and threatened
renewed infighting had the autumn events not intervened.[44]

However, the party received a temporary relief from its travails
from the August 1998 crisis and the resultant damage done to Yeltsin's

authority. Scapegoating Kirienko for a default he himself had earlier declared would not happen, the president replaced him with Chernomyrdin on 23 August. Since the latter had been premier for most of the post-Soviet period, and therefore could be held responsible for the fundamental problems underlying the crisis, he was opposed by much of the political elite. Then Yeltsin made himself appear weaker still by rapidly agreeing to a power-sharing agreement with the Duma and then withdrawing his agreement, which allowed the CPRF to 'smell blood', and withdraw from compromise negotiations.[45] The party's support was instrumental in the Duma approving the Yabloko-sponsored compromise candidate, Evgenii Primakov, whose realist policies as foreign minister and consensus-seeking style were fully congenial to the communists.

Primakov's government marked a new paradigm in Russian politics: a government dependent more on the Duma than the increasingly discredited and enfeebled president, although crucially no constitutional mechanisms were present to formalise this. In response to the widespread belief that the previous 'so-called reformers' had ignored state infrastructure and the 'social aspects of the economy', Primakov promised to establish a more state-oriented and consensual programme.[46] The CPRF initially took a cautiously supportive stance, allowing Yurii Maslyukov to join (as first deputy prime minister) only when the government's left-centrist political line became clear. It sought to claim credit for 'leftist' policies if they succeeded, and yet to be able to dissociate itself from relatively independent communists such as Maslyukov if they failed.[47]

Later, since Primakov oversaw a stabilisation of the economic crisis, and benefited from ever-rising public approval figures, the party's support for the government was far less ambiguous. Participation in government marked a crucial stage in the party's evolution, increasing its interaction with financial groups like ONEKSIMbank and its affiliated *Izvestiya* newspaper, and giving Maslyukov practical experience of market economics.[48] However, the increasing ascendancy of the CPRF's radical wing limited any dividends. Needing to demonstrate it was not 'collaborationist', the CPRF acted on one of the long-term demands of the radicals and supported a bill to impeach Yeltsin on five charges.[49] Yet highly politicised charges such as 'genocide against the Russian people', following so soon after the Makashov affair, damaged the fragile social compromise over which Primakov presided, while limiting the likely success of the venture. Primakov and Maslyukov themselves felt that impeachment was inflammatory, and gave the president ammunition to use against them.[50] Indeed this was the result. Ultimately, the CPRF's association with the Primakov government confirmed that the Duma was only strong against a weak president and was weak against a strong president. When Yeltsin returned from recuperation and fired Primakov in May 1999, the failure of impeachment was a major blow to the CPRF's prestige.[51]

Opposition under Putin: from constructive to cosmetic?

The party entered the Seventh Duma in a fundamentally different political situation. The initial deal with Edinstvo broke the taboo on public deals between the Kremlin and communists, and whereas this (temporarily) damaged Putin's reformist credentials among voters, it marked a significant step in the CPRF's return to the mainstream of political life.[52] Both Putin, his staff and the communists openly talked of the formation of a stable two or three-party system in which Edinstvo and the Communists might play a key systemic role, with liberals marginalised or engulfed.[53] Yet talk of a 'nomenklatura' Duma dominated by a 'Kremlin-communist bloc' was premature.[54] Through their deal with Edinstvo the communists got the chairs of nine parliamentary committees as in the previous Duma (plus two for the agro-industrialists). This immediately gave the party an important propaganda, gatekeeper and patronage role.[55] However, they lost the strategically important security committee and failed in negotiations for the budget and defence committees.[56]

Moreover, Putin's form of governing threatened political opposition per se. His action-oriented, consensus-based and anti-political style, backed with great popularity, was profoundly disorientating for the communists (and not just them). He appeared to support 'communist' great power politics with 'reformist' liberal economics simultaneously, and so presented opposition with an amorphous target. Moreover, with his emphasis on the 'dictatorship of law', he showed a far more manipulative approach to politics than Yeltsin, and so provided a major test of the ability of Russia's nascent democratic institutions to check and balance any concentration of executive power. We have already noted the Duma's lack of options between obstruction to and complete compliance with the executive. This was amply demonstrated in the new Duma, where Putin redressed Yeltsin's permanently conflictual attitude towards it and manufactured a compliant majority through a mixture of co-optation (such as shown towards the communists) coercion (by initially marginalising FAR), and consent (by regularly consulting the heads of Duma fractions). The endorsement of Putin's prime minister, Mikhail Kasyanov, by a record majority of 325 in May led some to lament the death of political opposition, as Duma forces betrayed a 'conformism bordering on lackeydom'.[57]

Overall, the dilemma posed for the CPRF was acute. With a smaller fraction, principled and uncompromising opposition might be easier than during 1995–99. Yet the party was now accustomed to influence, and if it were to preserve any in the new Duma, the need to make (possibly unprincipled) compromises would be intensified, which could reopen the party's internal strains. Indeed marginalisation threatened. Putin's policies gradually evolved in a moderately pro-Western and economically reformist direction, for which he was often able to command a Duma majority of over 270, even if the communist/agro-industrial bloc was resolutely opposed.[58] They alone refused to endorse two deputy speakers from liberal factions and opposed the Strategic Arms Reduction Treaty (START) II ratification in April.[59] The communist-endorsed readoption of the music of the Soviet national anthem in December 2000 notwithstanding, on more concrete policy positions the communists were increasingly in the minority, opposing the budget on all four readings in late 2000. Paradoxically, they found that their own statist rhetoric could be used against them, and at times they found themselves rejecting Putin's authoritarian proclivities. For example, they opposed Putin's proposal to deprive governors of legal immunity on the grounds that this lever might be used against the 'red' governors, so contradicting their long-held rhetoric about strengthening the power vertical.[60]

Although there was some truth in the allegation that the communists were casting round for an opposition role after the departure of the anti-communist Yeltsin, and resorting to reflex opposition for internal reasons (as seen below), their convoluted stance reflected real problems of opposition.[61] This was shown in spring 2001 when, after a two communist walkouts in January and February protesting proposals to widen private ownership of non-agricultural land and budget amendments permitting more privatisation, the fraction initiated a vote of no confidence in the government. The motion got 127 votes and so failed by over a hundred votes. This was no surprise to the communists, but it was more important to demonstrate their position.[62] The Edinstvo fraction threatened to join the communists to 'bring [the communists] down a couple of notches', and force the election of a new less leftist Duma, suggesting the Kremlin's new confidence in public opinion.[63] The lack of tolerance for even such toothless opposition was further demonstrated by renewed suggestions from Kremlin officials that the communists be deprived of some of the committee chairs they had won so unfairly, and Seleznev be replaced as Duma chair.[64] A proposed alliance of the Edinstvo and FAR blocs in late 2001 promised to consolidate the pro-government majority in the Duma, as well as to stimulate amalgamation around one pole of the party system. Such methods acted as further 'psychological pressure' on the communists.

Moreover it appeared that Putin's support for the communists was conditional: either they become a modern, left-wing and docile opposition as the other pole of the party system (the two are not inextricably linked!) or be consigned to history. Putin's lack of anti-communist animus was shown by an apparent close relationship with Zyuganov and frequent lengthy consultations with the party hierarchy, but his circle appeared to regard communist ideology itself as obsolete.[65] The clearest evidence of this was the formation of the 'patriotically-oriented centre-left organisation' Russia (Rossiya) by Gennadii Seleznev in July 2000, apparently with the blessing of the Kremlin.[66] Seleznev, who had been backed by Putin in his abortive attempt to become Moscow *oblast* governor in January 2000, then took an extremely pro-Kremlin line in the Duma, not supporting the vote of no confidence. This only exacerbated his frictional relationship with the CPRF hierarchy. Seleznev was disingenuous about Rossiya's aims, insisting that this was not an attempt to split or compete with the CPRF, or set itself up as an independent party, but was aimed at advancing new leaders and seeking new allies to improve the communist's electoral position.[67] Although probably not a direct attempt at a split, which would have made Seleznev's expulsion from the CPRF an inevitability, the forming of a centre-left bloc autonomously of the party structure had obvious implications for its leadership, and Zyuganov personally.

Consequently the CPRF's discussion of its 2000 electoral defeat, characterised by Zyuganov as 'one of the most difficult periods of our history', focused on questions of ideology, opposition strategy (becoming increasingly 'cosmetic' according to critics) and organisation, with renewed suggestions that Zyuganov's leadership was under threat.[68] How to respond to Rossiya occupied centre stage, and the party was clearly divided. Certain regional organisations (such as Moscow region) expressed open support, while some close to the party hierarchy privately expressed a tactful neutrality.[69] Many rank-and-file members were simply confused.[70] Officially the leadership took a tough line, denouncing Rossiya as a direct attempt to split the party and play on its electoral field, and directing its members not to join it.[71] Attitudes to Putin were similarly divergent. Ilyukhin remarked that Putin was a unifying force for the Fatherland, Volgograd first secretary, Alevtina Aparina, regarded Putin as a direct continuation of Yeltsin, while a regional leader perhaps summed up the trend best: 'there's no clarity in our attitude to Putin'.[72]

The December 2000 Congress resulted in at least the temporary reconsolidation of leadership around Zyuganov, with the threat of a party split paramount. Many of the tacit supporters of Rossiya appeared to prefer to work for change within the party, while Seleznev himself, resigning from *Pravda*'s editorial board at the Congress, claimed that it had censored information about Rossiya.[73] Ultimately to want Zyuganov's removal did not mean to relish the damage Seleznev's actions might bring. Significant also was the pre-emptive reanimation of the moribund NPUR, whose Third Congress in September 2000 re-elected Zyuganov as leader. The bloc was organisationally streamlined with a thoroughly non-ideological platform emphasising specific socio-economic tasks and the forming of a new 'shadow cabinet' in which Semigin and Glazev took prominent place.[74] The rules of the NPUR now allowed it to compete in elections independently. This was a clear attempt to outflank Rossiya in the race for a centre-left position, advance Zyuganov's protégés and, so it was rumoured, reverse the decline in the party's lobbying potential that had set in after its election defeats.[75] Threats to remove Seleznev from his party and Duma positions helped push him formally to join the NPSR in a subordinate position as one of five co-chairs.[76] This reflected stalemate. In the short run at least, the party was loath to lose the main symbol of its 'red' Duma. Yet the message was clear, the party alone took charge of expanding its electorate.

The Congress itself took the 'zero option'.[77] Zyuganov hardened his rhetoric with insistence on constructive opposition to Putin, with irreconcilable opposition to the 'Yeltsinism' of his liberal government, and called for the 'authoritarian presidential republic' to be replaced by a 'parliamentary Soviet republic'. Without naming

names he lambasted Rossiya as an attempt to infect the party with
'the bacilli of apostasy'.[78] Whatever was said behind closed doors
clearly worked, for in plenary sessions open dissent was rebutted in
turn by speakers warning against a party split. The head of the CC's
Control Commission, Vladislav Yurchik, vocalised a demand
increasingly heard in the party press, for the positions of party chair,
Duma fraction leader, NPUR chair and UCP-CPSU head to be
shared.[79] Ultimately this challenge to Zyuganov (who now held all
posts) was a proposal only promising new leadership infighting, and
thereby failed. Unity was paramount. Seleznev, absent most of the
Congress, was re-elected to the Presidium unanimously, while
several dissidents were removed, including Yurchik himself. The
Congress showed again the eccentricity of the party's opposition,
with the pragmatism of its new Presidium (evidenced by the election
of Leonid Ivanchenko, a classic 'red director' with regional knowledge, as the party's third co-chair) at a tangent with its vehement
Congress documents.[80] According to the leaders, the streamlined
Presidium and CC reflected a more effective organisation, but could
also reflect 'personnel famine'.[81] The removal of the moderate but
increasingly independent ideology secretary, Kravets, who had
objected to the party's apparent replacement of 'Marxism with
Machiavellianism', suggested as much. His post was abolished and
he was replaced by the secretary for 'information and analytical
work', Oleg Kulikov, in April 2001.[82]

Opposition and democracy

What did the tactical oscillations of the CPRF indicate about the
party's adaptation to the post-Soviet regime? Consensus that democracy is the 'only game in town' is democracy's basic starting point,
but as we have noted, such consensus over fundamentals was
lacking in a polarised transition when neither the 'democrats' nor
'communists' made a 'credible commitment' to abide by the decisions reached under the new political order nor believed in the end
of winner-takes-all politics.[83] The CPRF's behaviour reflected this: it
was willing to play by the rules of the political system (and thereby
become a stabilising, systemic opposition), while permanently
holding out the prospect of changing the system (thereby remaining
potentially subversive and anti-systemic). The *nomenklatura* background of its moderates increased its systemic trends, at the same

time as its radical ideology and membership prevented it fully integrating into the system. This was encouraged by an imperfectly institutionalised political system, where dissonance between ideological convictions and between leaders and led was prevalent. As we shall see, the CPRF was at best as a quasi-parliamentary, quasi-systemic and quasi-democratic force, whose role in furthering democracy in Russia was highly ambiguous.

At key periods, the CPRF's behaviour entrenched Russia's political institutions. The party's decision to contest its ban in 1991 through the courts and not the streets helped establish an impartial constitutional court, and avoided potential social unrest, and thereafter 'constitutionalism' became one of its key slogans. The party's participation in many national elections from 1993 through the landmark acceptance of the 1996 election results was also another major turning point. For the communists, acceptance of electoral politics came rather from instinctive caution and fear of the alternatives than credible commitment, but latterly there was explicit evidence of this. According to the party's election campaign manager, the 'electoral process is . . . beginning to lose the quality of a dangerous antagonistic clash among political organisations with conflicting viewpoints. A normal, healthy principle is finally emerging . . . in which some parties, then others, would democratically take turns ruling'.[84] Postcommunist Russia was at best an electoral democracy with formally democratic institutions and regular competitive elections, rather than a liberal democracy where democratic institutions are grounded in a pluralist civil society.[85] Nevertheless, in establishing the electoral framework the communists played no small role.

As shown above, parliament was a key area where compliance was forced on the communists and here their activity was more ambiguous. Initially joining the Duma instrumentally as its sole way of maintaining a legal presence in Russia, the party's increasing dominance of it raised fears that it was adapting to democratic political institutions and processes only formally while vitiating their substantive content.[86] Indeed, Anatolii Lukyanov's authoritarian dominance of the legislative committee which he headed raised fears of former Soviet practices.[87] As we noted, exposure to the Duma's unregulated lobbying implicated the party in the regime's corrupt practices, while its use of the Duma as its de facto party headquarters looked like classical communist entrism. Meanwhile, the party garnered a reputation as an obstructive force true to the principle of 'the worse, the better',

evidenced by such 'points scoring' as a May 1997 demand that the
government double money supply to pay overdue wages and pen-
sions. Such intransigence often paralysed legislative initiative and
allowed the president to set the agenda by decree.[88]

Yet, it would be a simplification to see communist Duma activity
as simply reflex opposition to reform. Declarative opposition had
reflected reciprocal ideological polarisation, whereby a utopian neo-
liberal welfare provision model confronted full-blooded socialist restoration, with little room for compromise. Whereas the government
demanded means-tested benefits and private insurance in the absence
of sufficiently developed procedures for testing or accurate allocation
of funds, the communists unilaterally refused welfare rationalisation
and demanded inflation-boosting resource allocations.[89] Also, as we
have alluded, the Duma's tendency to irresponsible opposition was
partially structural. As Huskey notes, the Duma 'exerts influence but
does not in any real sense share sovereignty with the chief executive'.[90] With the president able to bypass parliament by decree, and
with both government and president defiantly non-party, parliamentary factions had only blunt instruments such as the threat of no confidence votes to influence policy, enjoy the spoils of office and
demonstrate their own significance to their electorate. The question of
whether the CPRF might demonstrate more responsibility given
incentives in a balanced parliamentary system remained open. The
debacle over impeachment might suggest not, as the party proved
unable to reconcile its 'collaborationist' and intransigent faces, which
cost it participation in a popular government, and thereby its greatest
success yet. Yet even here the party demonstrated learning, not
raising such maximalist demands again.

Indeed, as the party fraction became drawn into the parliamentary process, it appeared that it was the most addicted to democratic
procedures and parliamentary discipline of any, which at least raised
the question of numbering it as a democratic force.[91] Its discipline
meant that it became somewhat of a dependable partner for other
fractions, an important consideration in Edinstvo's alliance with it in
2000. With their increased emphasis on 'professional' work, and
negotiation for extra budgetary resources for the state sector, moderate CPRF deputies looked increasingly social democratic, while radicals saw the limited time deputies spent in activist work as proof of
their fears that the party was de facto a parliamentary party.[92] If the
party had aimed to vitiate parliament, its opposition in turn was

increasingly vitiated by it, and for all the many and manifest faults of the Russian Duma as a representative institution the CPRF played an important, if not always consistent, role in nurturing it.

Yet if the party stabilised and entrenched electoral and parliamentary political institutions, and was increasingly a systemic force, this did not yet make it a democratic one. A failed communist Duma motion in late 2000 to reinstall the statue of the KGB's founder, 'Iron Feliks' Dzerzhinskii (torn down in August 1991 and an important symbol of the August revolution) outside the Moscow security service headquarters showed that they were still no instinctive friends of democracy.

Indeed, the party's democratic credentials were everywhere ambivalent. Huntington notes that political oppositions can play a major role in helping to consolidate a transitional democracy, first, by marginalising the extra-systemic opposition and, second, by socialising the disaffected in the norms of the new polity, and thereby institutionalising mass support for that polity.[93] The specific role for post-communist successor parties consists in channelling economic protest into support for the regime, and by forming a 'socialism of transition' based on an '"authentic" representation of interests rooted in a socialist value culture'. In doing so they can correct the implicit 'rightwards' bias of transitions to capitalist democracy, and thereby help form a more nuanced and balanced pluralist political spectrum, giving representation to the most excluded elements.[94]

The CPRF partly fulfilled the first criteria. As we saw in Chapter 4 its domination of the opposition bloc meant that it absorbed or sidelined potentially more dangerous opposition figures such as Zhirinovskii and the radicals in its own midst, while communist nationalism acted as a hindrance to the dominance of a purer, more dynamic form of nationalism. However, the CPRF had much less success in the second and third tasks of stabilisation and socialisation, which showed its incomplete adaptation to democratic politics. The electorate of the reformed successor parties was broadly supportive of the post-Soviet regime.[95] In contrast, as we have seen, the CPRF's electorate was deeply alienated from the post-Soviet order. The party sought to draw the venom of its intransigent members with symbolic radicalism and emphasis on incrementalism but simultaneously sought to replace regime norms with anti-Westernism and anti-liberalism. The party's calls for a fairer distribution of wealth and an end to corruption showed that the CPRF could play a positive role in articulating and defending the interests of the dispossessed social strata, and it thereby retained socialist elements, yet the development of communist ideology into a genuine 'socialism of transition' was hindered by its adoption of 'right-wing' conservative state patriotism and its discourse of extremism and hyperbole.

A most serious allegation levelled at the CPRF was that its peculiar form of self-contradicting opposition strengthened an undemocratic regime and, worse, strengthened those elements of the regime against which the party itself strove.[96] We have seen ample evidence of this throughout this book. It has been suggested that the results of the 1996 election might replicate the experience of post-war Italy, whereby the anti-system nature of the communist PCI consolidated the ruling elite around a wish to keep out the 'extremists', and thereby produce a form of blocked politics preventing the democratic transfer of power.[97] What emerged in Russia after 1996 was slightly different, if little more democratic. Both opposition and regime knew that the opposition was neither extremist enough to be completely marginalised, but extreme enough not to threaten an electoral turnover of power. The common bureaucratic, 'statist' mentality of many members of the regime and opposition, their shared fear of social disorder and disruption to their political or economic interests further limited their commitment to open political competition. This gave rise to an increasingly 'symbiotic' relationship, shown graphically in the course of the 2000 election, whereby the communist opposition was allowed into power as a very junior partner in order to block the emergence of more radical alternatives which might upset the elite status quo.

Andrei Piontkovsky's view of the two combatants of the 2000 elections ('Zyutin' and 'Puganov'), and the blocs they represented as being wholly interchangeable in 'background, social status, political instincts and even physical appearance' has some merit, but is overstated.[98] There were clear differences between Zyuganov's and Putin's professed policies over economics and constitutional reform. However, this opposition was increasingly conducted behind closed doors as the communists became merely one of the elite clans vying for the president's attention. This clearly deformed the concept of opposition and the language of politics itself as the communists railed against the 'anti-national regime', and the 'criminal bourgeoisie', while seeking the approval of the former and the finances of the latter, giving their opposition an increasingly virtual nature. This

contradiction shot through the party's structure and electoral performance – it remained a 'limbo opposition', neither the irreconcilable
opposition many of its supporters wished, nor a responsible opposition with a coherent and popular programme entrusted with enough
votes to gain political power.

Conclusion

So, what were the overall implications of communist opposition? We
can see that the party's hierarchy gradually adapted to the post-
communist 'rules of the game' and, so, could be called a systemic
opposition but, since these were the rules of a less than democratic
system, the party's espousal of democratic rules remained ambiguous. Simultaneously, the limited 'self-contradictory' nature of the
communists' opposition seemed to reflect and reinforce the elite-
dominated nature of the Russian transformation. For this reason
McFaul and Petrov's argument that the 1996 presidential election
marked the end of the revolutionary polarisation of Russian politics
and the emergence of a more consensual polity based on acceptance
of the 'rules of the game' looks far too optimistic.[99] They argue that
1996 amounted to the end of 'transition' in the way usually understood by political scientists, as a period of explicit abnormality and
flux over the rules of the game, meaning the emergence of an 'electoral democracy' with institutionalised structuration of competitive
elections. But we must beware focusing on electoral institutions alone,
since this commits the 'electoralist fallacy', saying little about how
these institutions are grounded in civil society or used by the political
elite in a possibly authoritarian way.[100]

Indeed, when these elements were taken into account the situation looked less optimistic: the lack of institutionalisation of the
Russian transformation has been its theme. The polarised dichotomy
between communists and democrats fundamentally reflected the
cyclical insecurities of a post-Soviet political elite whose origins lay
outside democratic politics (with much of the political elite surviving
1991 unscathed without going through free elections), and who
'failed to institutionalise either the political influence of social movements through party forms of representative government, nor its
own responsibility to society through a legislature or . . . other elements of a pluralistic civil society'.[101] So after 1991 it was easier for
politicians to motivate supporters and legitimate their rule through

rhetoric which demonised political opponents than through grounding their legitimacy in as yet unformed democratic institutions. Even
for the 'democrats', this was a 'mobilisation strategy' reflecting a
Soviet use of ideology as a top-down aggregator of social interest
rather than a bottom-up reflector of autonomous social mobilisation.
Meanwhile, tension between the regime's formal 'democratic legitimacy and the semi-authoritarian, semi-monarchical manner in
which it functioned' replicated the age-old inability of the Russian
state to govern by consent not command and endowed the regime
with instability.[102]

So with the decline of polarisation, consensus was indeed
revealed, but this was less a normative consensus over a positive
future-oriented programme, than a negative consensus, reflecting a
lack of choice with the exhaustion of ideological alternatives such as
communism and revolutionary liberalism. Putin's strong and stable
support could itself be seen in this light: 'because of the . . . vagueness
of the ideological-political appearance of the basic political forces and
figures, their lack of connection with the interests of large social
groups, and the lack of clarity of the programs and alternatives . . .
there is nothing left for the ordinary voter to do but personify his
choice'.[103]

This lack of institutionalised connection between state and
society was even more apparent after 1996. The CPRF-Edinstvo deal
appeared to illustrate this, showing 'a cynicism that no longer feels
the need to cloak itself in ideology, the remodelling of the political
center with little or no awareness (let alone participation) on the part
of the Russian public'.[104] In these circumstances, consensus between
regime and opposition was deeply ambivalent and also appeared
based less on normative values than a 'balance of interests' between
elites. Huskey felicitously calls the Russian transformation a 'permanently negotiated transition'.[105] With the absence of social consensus
or institutionalised rules, social peace was achieved through elite
compromise and bargaining, which, except briefly in October 1993,
avoided the full implications of an ideological stand-off. This compromise potentially offered a path to democracy, but unless rules were
quickly formalised, Soviet practices of co-optation, clientelism and
administrative pressure might reassert themselves, while the transition remained permanently negotiable and hence open-ended.
Certainly, bureaucratic elite consensus imposed a tentative stability
on the political system, but when civil society and the opposition

electorate remained poorly integrated and alienated from the regime, elite domination left open the possibility of a new anti-elite insurgency, particularly were it to be accompanied by renewed socioeconomic problems, and thereby contributed to the long-term instability of the Russian political system.[106]

Eventually, the gap between democratic legitimacy and authoritarian procedure would have to be closed, and until this period the regime remained potentially transitional and unstable. In the early months of Putin's term, the Chechen war seemed to demonstrate an authoritarian mobilisation strategy once more used to reconsolidate support for the regime, while the docile Duma showed that Russia's constitutional order itself still contained revolutionary elements. If the Duma was not quite a Leninist 'transmission belt', then as Bacon states, Russia's 'heavily presidential provisions clearly vitiate[d] opportunities for organised opposition'.[107]

It is against this background of the cyclical under-institutionalisation of Russian politics, the weak institutional opportunities for opposition, the 'amorphousness and omnivorousness' of Russian political ideologies, as well as deep internal party conflicts over the nature of the 'regime' that the CPRF's opposition should be measured.[108] The party's stance was complex, shape-shifting and contradictory. The incorporation of the CPRF in an under-institutionalised and partially democratic regime exposed it to paradoxical tensions between an anti-system ideology, rhetoric, membership and electorate, mass party organisation mobilised against the regime, and a leadership and parliamentary apparatus that were increasingly psychologically and financially enmeshed in the system. Party moderates' transformation from an anti-regime force to a within-system opposition exposed the party to further ideological, organisational erosion while vitiating its ability to oppose in any meaningful way. Against this background, the party's insistence on internal unity and leadership stability became more understandable, but it offered little solution to the party's inherent contradictions. It was the paradox of Russian 'democracy' that the CPRF could play fully by the rules of the system, without fully recognising the values of democracy or the aims of the political system. When such tendencies were replicated across the political spectrum and throughout the political elite, it was not clear that the evolution of the CPRF from a communist to a 'cosmetic' opposition was beneficial for the Russian polity as a whole.

Notes

1 'Resolutsiya IV sezda KPRF ob otnoshenii k pravyashchemu v Rossi politi-cheskomu rezhimu', *IV sezd Kommunisticheskoi partii Rossiiskoi Federatsii 19–20 aprelya 1997 goda (Materialy i dokumenty)*, (Moscow, ITRK RSPP, 1997), pp. 58–9.

2 S. Huntington, *The Third Wave: Democratization in the Late Twentieth Century* (Norman, OK, University of Oklahoma Press, 1991), p. 263.

3 V. Solovei 'Kommunisticheskaya i natsionalisticheskaya oppozitsiya v kon-tekste postkommunisticheskoi transformatsii Rossii', in L. Shevtsova (ed.), *Politicheskaya Rossiya* (Moscow, Moscow Carnegie Center, 1998), p. 195.

4 See T. Astrakhankina, *P-5*, 29 October 1997; and *Glasnost*, 10 (1997).

5 G. Sartori, *Political Parties and Party Systems: A Framework for Analysis* (Cambridge, Cambridge University Press, 1976), pp. 138–9.

6 M. Duverger, *Political Parties: Their Organization and Activity in the Modern State* (London, Methuen, 1964), p. 201; N. McInnes, *The Communist Parties of Western Europe* (London, Oxford University Press, 1975), p. 161.

7 McInnes, *Communist Parties of Western Europe*, p. 166.

8 M. Urban and V. Gelman, 'The development of political parties in Russia', in K. Dawisha and B. Parrott (eds), *Democratic Changes and Authoritarian Reactions in Russia, Ukraine, Belarus and Moldova* (Cambridge, Cambridge University Press, 1997), p. 199.

9 *S*, 29 December 1993, 8 December 1995.

10 Rybkin took a seat on the Security Council and signed Yeltsin's Civic Accord agreements without the permission of the CPRF leadership. He was removed from the Party's CC in April 1994 (*OG*, 12–18 October 1995).

11 T. F. Remington, 'Democratization and the new political order in Russia', in K. Dawisha and B. Parrott (eds), *Democratic Changes and Authoritarian Reactions in Russia, Ukraine, Belarus and Moldova* (Cambridge, Cambridge University Press, 1997), pp. 85–7.

12 *KPRF mezhdu umerennostyu i radikalizmom* (Moscow, Tsentr politicheskykh tekhnologii, 1997), p. 4. For Lenin's approach to compromise, see V. Lenin, 'On compromises', *Selected Works* 2 (Moscow, Progress, 1970), pp. 226–30.

13 Solovei, 'Kommunisticheskaya', p. 222.

14 Yurii Maslyukov, *Trud*, 30 July 1998.

15 A. Kuvaev, *Zavtra*, 43 (1997); A. Makashov, *Pravda Moskvy*, 78 (November 1997).

16 For example, see A. Prokhanov, *Zavtra*, 43 (1997).

17 A. Makarkin, *KPRF i ee soyuzniki posle vyborov* (Moscow, Tsentr politicheskykh tekhnologii, 1996), pp. 1–3.

18 Zyuganov, *SR*, 17 December 1996.

19 Foe example, Zyuganov, *PR*, 15 August 1996.

20 See *Iz*, 31 January 1997. During the first few months of 1997, the CPRF floated the idea of a vice-presidency, with rumours that Zyuganov would be sug-gested as vice-president.

21 See Podberezkin, *P-5*, 11 February 1997; Zyuganov, *P*, 6 July 1996.

22 See *PR*, 19 December 1996; Kuptsov, *PR*, 11 March 1997.

23 Solovei, 'Kommunisticheskaya', pp. 248–9.

24 However, only the governors of Bryansk, Ryazan and Stavropol permitted the CPRF local organisation to control key positions in administration (*Informatsionnyi byulleten*, 7 (48) (1998), from web site at: www.kprf.ru).

25 *Itogi*, 14 October 1997, 14.
26 The most vocal oppositionists were Teimuraz Avaliani, Albert Makashov, Richard Kosolapov and Tatyana Astrakhankina. For their complaints see *Molniya*, 9 (October 1997). For the text of the 'Leninist-Stalinist platform', see *Glasnost*, 15 May 1998.
27 See the comments of Moscow leader Aleksandr Kuvaev at the CPRF's Fourth Congress (from www.nns.ru/chronicle/sdkprf.html).
28 *IV sezd Kommunisticheskoi partii Rossiiskoi Federatsii 19–20 aprelya 1997 goda (Materialy i dokumenty)*, (Moscow, ITRK RSPP, 1997), p. 9.
29 *KPRF mezhdu umerennostyu i radikalizmom*, p. 2.
30 See C. Freeland, *Financial Times*, 30 April 1998, p. 2; and R. Sakwa, 'Left or right? The CPRF and the problem of democratic consolidation in Russia', *Journal of Communist Studies and Transition Politics*, 14: 1&2 (1998), 136.
31 N. Robinson, 'Classifying Russia's party system: the problem of "relevance" in a time of uncertainty', *Journal of Communist Studies and Transition Politics*, 14:1&2 (1998), 168, 170.
32 J. Linz and A. Stepan, *Problems of Democratic Transition and Consolidation* (Baltimore, MD, Johns Hopkins University Press, 1996), p. 141.
33 Author's interviews with deputy head of CPRF CC department for international affairs, A. Filippov, on 6 December 1997, and with CPRF CC secretary for Connections with Foreign Parties and Movements, N. Bindyukov, on 18 December 1997.
34 A SMD system would have forced each party to organise better locally and exposed them to the pressures of the regional elite. See *Vek*, 5, 30 January–5 February 1998.
35 For more detail than is possible here, see L. March, 'Communism in transition? The Communist Party of the Russian Federation in the Post-Soviet era' (PhD thesis, University of Birmingham, 1999).
36 This is the upper estimate. See A. Frolov, *SR*, 28 April 1998; and *K*, 25 April 1998.
37 See *NG-Stsenarii*, 6:20 (June 1998). Among those who broke ranks were some of the party's most influential figures – such as Maslyukov, Voronin, Seleznev, Goryacheva, Podberezkin and Semago.
38 *Hero of the Day* programme (NTV) on 13 February 1998. On Ilyukhin's challenge see *NG*, 3 October 1997. On an attempt to explain Seleznev's actions to the party see V. Trushkov, *PR*, 21–28 October 1998.
39 *Sedmoe oktyabrya i izmeneniya v levom lagere* (Moscow, Tsentr politicheskykh tekhnologii, 1998)
40 For example compare Ilyukhin *SWB* SU/3259 B/8 (22 June 1998); S. Goryacheva, *NG*, 6 May 1998; Podberezkin, *Moscow News*, 19–25 February 1998.
41 For defections such as those of Vladimir Semago, ex-party whip Oleg Shenkarev and others see *MN*, 17–24 August 1997; *Moscow News*, 19–25 February 1998. For the decline in Duma discipline see A. Frolov, *SR*, 28 April 1998.
42 Twelve of these were delegated to Popular Power and five to the Agrarians. The quote is from CPRF CC Presidium member, A. Frolov (*SR*, 28 April 1998).
43 Following the attempt, the long-standing dissident Avaliani was finally removed from the CC, and other dissidents were silenced (*NG*, 25 June 1998).
44 *Informatsionnyi byulleten*, 15 July–1 August 1998, accessed from web site at:

www.kprf.ru. However, Maslyukov told reporters that half the communist faction in the Duma supported his decision, and it is not impossible that he had Zyuganov's tacit approval. Other party members denounced the move, for example Yurii Belov, head of the Leningrad oblast party committee – see *MN*, 26 July–2 August 1998.

45 *OG*, 3–9 September 1998.
46 *Iz*, 20 November 1998.
47 The government also contained Agrarian Gennadii Kulik as deputy prime minister, and Gennadii Khodyrev (a CPRF member) as minister for anti-monopoly policy. A CPRF ally, Vadim Gustov (governor of Leningrad *oblast*) was also a first deputy prime minister.
48 *Na levom fronte bez peremen* (Moscow, Tsentr politicheskykh tekhnologii, 1998).
49 The charges were: conclusion of the Belovezha accords, shelling the White House in 1993, unleashing the war in Chechnya, collapse of the Russian armed forces and genocide against the people of Russia.
50 *Parliamentskaya gazeta*, 8 June 2000.
51 Although the CPRF leadership blamed the defeat on the other fractions, many rank-and-file communists were truly upset by the failure of impeachment (*Vremya MN*, 17 May 1999).
52 *Dumskii krizis: uroki i posledstviya* (Moscow, Tsentr politicheskykh tekhnologii, 2000).
53 For Putin's view see N. Gevorkyan, N. Timakova and A. Kolesnikov, *Ot pervogo litsa: razgavory s Vladimirom Putinym* (Moscow, Vagrius, 2000). See also A. Kravets, *NG*, 28 January 2000.
54 *MT*, February 12, 2000.
55 Committee chairs direct working groups and consultants to work on legislation and control the committee budgets (*RFE/RL Russian Political Weekly*, 1:20, 26 March 2001).
56 *S*, 21 January 2000.
57 L. Shevtsova, *Literaturnaya gazeta*, 24–30 May 2000.
58 This includes the Edinstvo fraction (approximately eighty votes), the pro-government 'People's deputy' (sixty votes), FAR (sixty), Russia's regions (forty) and URF (thirty) – *S*, 4 April 2000.
59 Boris Nemtsov of URF and Vladimir Lukin of Yabloko were confirmed as deputy speakers with most communists voting against (see *Vremya MN*, 17 February 2000).
60 *NG*, 24 June 2000.
61 For a scathing view of the communists' stance, see Boris Kagarlitsky, *MT*, 23 December 2000.
62 *K*, 21 February 2001.
63 G. Pavlovskii, web site at: www.strana.ru, 21 February 2001.
64 *NG*, 14 December 2000.
65 *Novyi etap v istorii KPRF* (Moscow, Tsentr politicheskykh tekhnologii, 2000).
66 On Rossiya, see for example *Vremya MN*, 15 June 2000, 27 June 2000.
67 *Trud*, 27 June 2000; *P*, 16 November 2000.
68 *P*, 11 May 2000, 15 June 2000.
69 Author's interview with aide to one of the party's top leaders (name withheld), September 2000.
70 Author's interview with rank-and-file member of Moscow city party organisation, Vladimir Sukhadeev, 21 September 2000.

71 Author's interview with CPRF CC secretary for ideological work, Aleksandr Kravets, 22 September 2000; *S*, 15 July 2000.

72 See *SWB* SU/3837 B/2 (11 May 2000); *Pravda* (special issue on Seventh Congress of CPRF), December 2000; *P*, 7 December 2000.

73 *NG*, 5 December 2000.

74 *NG*, 26 September 2000

75 Semigin's membership of the board of the Russian Union of Industrialists and Entrepreneurs was seen as particularly beneficial in this regard.

76 Author's interview with Bindyukov on 20 September 2000.

77 *OG*, December 7–13, 2000.

78 *Politicheskii otchet Tsentralnogo Komiteta KPRF VII sedzu i ocherednye zadachi partii*, from web site at: www.kprf.ru.

79 He apparently stated that about twenty regional committees (that is, 23 per cent) had raised the issue. If true, this assertion was removed from the CPRF's accounts (*Russia Today*, 3 December 2000).

80 He was chair of the Duma committee for federal affairs.

81 According to the secretary of Leningrad obkom Oleg Karyakin (web site at: www.vesti.ru, 3 December 2000.)

82 Phrase from *OG*, 7–13 December 2000. The official reason given for Kravet's removal was that he could not combine his role as Omsk *obkom* (regional committee of CPRF) leader with a leadership post, which was nonsensical as Dagestan first secretary , and fraction leader Sergei Reshulskii was promoted to the Presidium at this Congress. Kravet's far more critical approach to Putin, as well as possible leadership ambitions, was more likely the reason for his removal. See *K*, 2 December 2000. As much was suggested in the author's own interview with a parliamentary aide to a CPRF leader in September 2000.

83 K. Dawisha, 'Democratization and political participation: research concepts and methodologies', in K. Dawisha and B. Parrott (eds), *Democratic Changes and Authoritarian Reactions in Russia, Ukraine, Belarus and Moldova* (Cambridge, Cambridge University Press, 1997), p. 43.

84 Viktor Peshkov, *NG*, 13 January 1999.

85 M. McFaul and N. Petrov, 'Russian electoral politics after transition: regional and national assessments', *Post-Soviet Geography and Economics*, 38:9 (1997), 507.

86 Sakwa, 'Left or right?', 149.

87 Lukyanov apparently abolished the subcommittees of the legislative committee and took personal control, while holding up 'democratic' initiatives and forwarding only those which furthered the strategic aims of the party (*Iz*, 7 February 1996).

88 For example, T. F. Remington, 'From soviets to parliamentarism', in S. White, A. Pravda and Z. Gitelman (eds), *Developments in Russian Politics 4* (Basingstoke, Macmillan, 1997), pp. 77–80; *MT*, 11 June 1997.

89 L. J. Cook and M. A. Orenstein, 'The return of the left and its impact on the welfare state in Russia, Poland and Hungary', in L. J. Cook, M. A. Orenstein and M. Rueschemeyer, *Left Parties and Social Policy in Postcommunist Europe* (Boulder, CO, Westview, 1999), pp. 65–9.

90 E. Huskey, *Presidential Power in Russia* (Armonk, NY, M. E. Sharpe, 1999), p. 180.

91 Urban and Gelman, 'The development of political parties', 199.

92 Extra-parliamentary work in the localities was increasingly left in the hands of parliamentary aides (*Trudovaya Rossiya*, 18, 1997, 2).

93 S. P. Huntington, *Political Order in Changing Societies* (New Haven, CT, Yale University Press), 1968, pp. 408, 412.

94 A. Mahr and J. Nagle, 'Resurrection of the successor parties and democratization in East-Central Europe', *Communist and Post-Communist Studies*, 28:4 (1995), 405–7.

95 *Ibid.*, 407.

96 Solovei, 'Kommunisticheskaya', p. 266.

97 Sakwa, 'Left or right?', 154; J. Barth Urban and V. Solovei, *Russia's Communists at the Crossroads* (Boulder, CO, Westview, 1997), p. 191.

98 *Johnson's Russia List*, 4136, 28 February 2000.

99 McFaul and Petrov, 'Russian electoral politics', 507.

100 J. Hughes, 'Transition models and democratisation in Russia', in M. Bowker and C. Ross (eds), *Russia after the Cold War* (London, Longman, 2000), p. 28.

101 R. Sakwa, 'The regime system in Russia', *Contemporary Politics*, 3:1 (1997), 8–9.

102 L. Shevtsova, in *Johnson's Russia List*, 4556, 4 October 2000. The most sustained treatment of this theme is I. Klyamkin and L. Shevtsova, *This Omnipotent and Impotent Government: The Evolution of the Political System in Post-Communist Russia* (Moscow, Carnegie Moscow Center, 1999).

103 G. Diligenskii, 'Putin i rossiiskaya demokratiya (razmyshleniya po rezultatam oprosov 2000g.) from web site at: www.fom.ru, 18 January 2001.

104 N. Petrov, 'The year 2000 presidential elections: the end of public politics', *Briefing of the Moscow Carnegie Center*, 3 (March 2000) (from web site at: http://pubs.carnegie.ru/english).

105 Huskey, *Presidential Power in Russia*, p. 213.

106 A tendency noted by L. Shevtsova, 'Russia's post-communist politics: revolution or continuity?', in G. W. Lapidus, *The New Russia: Troubled Transformation* (Boulder, CO, Westview, 1995), pp. 30–1.

107 E. T. Bacon, 'Is there any opposition in Russia? Analysis of the influences on and prospects for political opposition in Russia', paper presented to CREES annual conference, Cumberland Lodge, Windsor, 16–18 June 2000, p. 5.

108 Diligenskii, 'Putin'.

Conclusion

That the CPRF continues to polarise opinion says much both about its continued importance in contemporary Russian politics, and perpetual uncertainty over its role and ideological position. To the communists the party remained 'the most numerous, united and active political force in Russia'.[1] Less partisan observers concurred that the CPRF's 'conscious ideology building paralleled by exceptional organisational skills' brought it great success and promised lasting rejuvenation.[2] Yet many would concur with Baburin that the CPRF was 'an eternally dying organisation, a Frankenstein' without prospects and sustained only by inertia.[3]

So how successful was the CPRF, and on what was such 'success' based? Did this promise rejuvenation or decline? Ten years into the 'post-communist' epoch the CPRF remained Russia's best-organised, most popular (with 21.9 million votes for Zyuganov in March 2000) and most durable political party, with its political weight acknowledged by Putin. Yet the party remained poorly integrated within the political system. Moreover, although it was clearly not an unreformed hardline party trading solely on its residual legacy, nostalgia and inertia, and to this degree was a child of post-communism, its residual ideological and organisational legacy did explain much of its success, and seemed in turn to drastically limit the extent of that success. This said much about the limits of the residual Leninism which infused the party's internal life, as well as the poor opportunities for organised party influence in the Russian political system.

We noted in the introduction that unqualified use of terms like 'transition' and 'democratisation' tended to underplay the vitality of historical legacy and entrenched remnants from the old regime, including less quantifiable elements like political culture and ideology which cannot be neatly fitted into such parsimonious schema.

During post-communism, the past 'persists in the values and beliefs of politicians and citizens socialised to accept the norms of the preceding regime'.[4] Although historical legacy should not be seen as a determining factor, it provides the context within which such political change occurs. 'Transition' should be seen as an evolving matrix of historical legacy, political culture, the decisions of actors in a period of relative institutional and normative uncertainty, and the path-dependent effects of the institutions these actors themselves create.

This is still more apparent when we look at the evolution of successor parties like the CPRF. Ishiyama's approach still appears the best entry into understanding the successor party trajectory – as an interaction of previous regime type, the founding process of a party during transition and the political environment a new party faces, although with the experience of the CPRF in mind we would give greater weight to the internal organisational and ideological dynamic within parties as a contributory factor to their development.

Previous regime type appears all-important. 'Patrimonial communism' as a catch-all phrase encompassing countries as diverse as Russia and Bulgaria may risk simplification, but it does highlight some important elements: to recap, the lack of prior history of democracy, the prevalence of a hierarchical elite–society relationship with closed social networks based on patronage and clientelism paramount, and greater regime entrenchment (since it was based on co-optation as well as coercion). Forces developing from the Soviet elite possessed advantageous access to informal networks and elite resources compared with non-elite forces, while such advantages were likely to subvert more formal forms of party organisation and programmatic identity. For successor parties the effect of this was twofold: first, parties had further to travel to evolve into programmatic parties committed to open and democratic competition (and hence in a social democratic dimension) and, second, less need to – there was mileage to be made from a 'red-brown' national communist appeal to those who had benefited from the regime's intensive insider networks.

Much of this does seem to fit Russia, with its hierarchical structure and effective suppression of more humanist forms of socialism, reiterated periodically under Lenin, Stalin and Brezhnev. Although, as Sakwa says, this does not explain how Gorbachev could head a democratic socialist current that had been maturing in the party for decades, it does explain the obstacles his reform faced in mobilising a passive civil society from above and through an entrenched conservative party apparatus.[5] It explains why, long after Gorbachev, Putin still saw the authorities' attachment to 'bribes and backhanders' as a serious threat to society and to the state.[6] Similarly, the hierarchical dominance of leaders over led evident in patrimonial communism is shown not just in the CPRF's inner life, but by claims that the Russian political class had 'adopted self-censorship' in response to the oppressive political climate under Putin.[7] As we have seen, the emergence of successor parties is in large part due to the ex-communist elite's ability to retain and remake alliances with various financial and labour groups. Even in Poland the DLA was grounded less in classical social democratic political philosophy than in a 'vanguard socialism', an elite-led non-ideological technocratism reliant on patronage connections.[8] As Hughes has said, 'leadership style and character are deeply rooted in political culture'.[9] Compared with such East-Central European elites the Russian communist and ex-communist elites appeared stamped by a post-Stalinist 'moral ethos' of clandestine bureaucratic manoeuvring, pragmatism bordering on opportunism, and divorce of public rhetoric and private practice reminiscent of Soviet 'double morality', whereby individuals played lip-service to approved values while completely disregarding them in action.[10]

None of this predetermined the evolution of the CPRF, but it arguably made some outcomes more likely. In a country with an indigenous communist tradition of long duration, superpower status and a post-Stalin miscegenation of Marxism and national bolshevism, statist-patriotic communism of the Zyuganov sort always had a strong social constituency. Certainly it is instructive to compare the Ukraine, where deep ethno-linguistic and geographical schisms between anti-communists (predominantly ethnic Ukrainians in the west) and anti-nationalists (Ukrainians of mixed ethnicity or Russian origin in the south and east) meant that 'nationalism and communism occupy polar extremes'.[11] Similarly, another neo-communist party, the CPBM adopted a conservative communism drawing upon Czech nationalism, while falling short of national chauvinism.[12] Many supposedly 'unreformed' communist parties have developed national specificities and should not be treated as identical.

Transition literature's focus on the importance of the decisions of political actors during periods of rapid political and institutional change is well-placed and these played a great role in the evolution of the CPRF. Gorbachev's failure to split the CPSU has been mentioned, leaving the founding of the RCP in the hands of the hardline wing of the party, mobilised in fundamentalist protest against Gorbachev's reform communism, the diktat of the party *nomenklatura*, and what Sakwa felicitously calls 'proto-nationalist juxtaposition of "Russia" against the . . . All-Union centre'.[13] While no pro-regime party emerged, economic and state collapse discredited the social democratic elements of Gorbachev's reform programme, and socialist values *in toto* became a long-term public taboo. In turn, the RCP's founding ethos proved impervious to social democratic change.

The CPRF's founding moment in 1993 had further implications. The ban on the party ended the internal crisis within the RCP, and allowed the consolidation of its leading group, while at the same time the centrifugal trends of 1991–93 increased the *nomenklatura*-activist dichotomy within the party and permanently devolved central control, while orientating the activity of the moderates within the party towards the state (in the Supreme Soviet and Constitutional Court). There was a clear contingency about this process, and there is room to speculate on how it might have occurred differently. This is not to indulge groundlessly in counterfactual speculation, but just to note that the 'the character of the opposition is tied to the character of the government'.[14] Thus the emergence of an irreconcilable communist opposition evolved as much out of the opportunities and constraints of the Russia political system as the internal dynamics of the party itself, and it is possible that different personal and institutional choices made by Russian leaders might have impacted on the CPRF differently.

Certainly the possibility exists that decisions made by the Yeltsin regime encouraged the outcome of a hardline communist party as the main opposition force. Yeltsin's failure to convoke elections in late 1991 is mentioned so often that it is almost a cliché, but this decision had significant effects. There is enough evidence in the communist moderates' behaviour (particularly the demoralisation leaders such as Zyuganov underwent during 1991–93) to suggest that greater incentives to reform the party might have had different results. A possible election defeat in 1991 could have forced the party to reform its policies, or its nascent proto-groups (the SPW etc.) to emerge as independent electoral forces and challenge its hegemony. The sequencing of the ban itself could have had various effects. Not banning the communists might have allowed them to drift on in internal faction-fighting, as indeed was the case in the CPBM until 1993. Banning the communists permanently and then holding elections (as in Romania) might have spelt the end of the communist party as an organised force, although in all cases the party's former members would doubtless have continued to play a role in post-communist politics.

Significant also was the failure to institutionalise the democratic gains of the early 1990s. The failure to institutionalise a party system has been mentioned. Had a presidential or pro-reform party been created this could have given the communists greater organised competition from the outset, particularly in 1995, when liberal and centrist parties' divisions magnified the CPRF's success, and when it has been alleged that Yeltsin's team deliberately weakened any anti-communist challengers to the presidency.[15] As it was, the communists confronted few organised party challengers until the creation of Edinstvo, and the degree of soul-searching this prompted was notable. Furthermore the failure to provide institutionalised party discipline and transparency among the higher echelons of the state provided the terrain upon which the communists could aspire to infiltrate the values of the elite hierarchy – the attempt might have been harder if the government had been given the collective discipline of party membership. Finally, it is worth considering the different effects of institutional choices: Linz has suggested that presidential systems tend to provoke polarisation between blocs in a winner-takes-all system, dual authority between president and parliament, and the dilution of the party system, whereas parliamentary systems promote relative consensus-building between parties and party cohesion.[16] We have noted that Russia's Duma institutionalises relative party irresponsibility. It is possible that a more balanced and consensual parliamentary system could have forced the CPRF to demonstrate greater responsibility and put more strains on its anti-system opposition, although supporters of presidentialism could argue this would be at the expense of economic reform or permitting the communists back into power.

As it was, the events of 1991–93 further impacted on the development of the communists, with the violent stand-off between president and Supreme Soviet increasing the tendency towards irreconcilable opposition, while Yeltsin's then overtly pro-Western foreign policy provided a stimulus to the further rise of the national-patriotic wing within the CPRF in the person of Zyuganov, itself aided by his considerable organisational and propagandist skills. Zyuganov's national-front strategy flourished in conditions of electoral polarisation, which persisted until 1996 (this in itself might suggest that Yeltsin could profitably have held presidential elections in 1994 as scheduled). As Flikke notes, this hegemonic national front strategy was a residue of the CPSU's stress on national unity above pluralist interests.[17] Hence this was always likely to prove less tenable in more pluralist political conditions, and it is not surprising that after 1996 the CPRF found that it could not formulate an attractive 'all-national idea'.[18]

The persistence of electoral polarisation itself contributed to the lack of a more moderate socialist alternative. This was very significant for the party's further electoral development, for it explains why the Marxist reformers were sidelined in the party's public ideological development – they had no other party competitor to go to. The CPRF then had more electoral manoeuvre to appeal to national-patriots or non-communists, or tack to the left without risking significant defections from its Marxist reformers. However, its ability to manoeuvre was still limited, as its aspirations to unite forces beyond the leftist niche forced it to continually tack between left and centre, and risk pleasing neither. In contrast, the communist parties in the Czech Republic and the Ukraine were unable to capitalise on 'state patriotism' for historical reasons. Confined to a narrower niche, they defined a strongly class-based and far less nationalist position than the CPRF, which monopolised the far left of the political spectrum and ceded the centre ground to more moderate forces such as the Czech Social Democrats and Oleksandr Moroz's Socialist Party of Ukraine (SPU, which expresses a moderate Marxist policy position not dissimilar to the Marxist reformers). Yet the advantage of this niche position was that these parties appeared far more internally unified than the CPRF.

Why could the communists apparently not come to power? The post-1993 political institutions played a role, and as we have said, appeared to be aimed at directly limiting the access of organised electoral institutions to power, particularly communist ones, rather than encouraging political party development, while maintaining the elite and president as arbiters above particularist interest in residual Soviet style. So we have the paradox of what Sakwa calls dual adaptation: the party adapted simultaneously to the formal institutions of power (elections and parliament) and to the 'regime system' – the informal clientelist 'para-democratic' processes by which elite politics operated.[19] In an institutionalised democratic system parties should link the public and elite realm, but in Russia, these two spheres did not always overlap and in fact often conflicted and subverted each other. Election victories in 1995 and 1999 brought the CPRF little in tangible policy benefits, while the 50.1 per cent target of the presidential system remained a distant goal.

Ultimately, the party and regime's elite background subverted the CPRF's opposition and ideological stance, while its 'partyness' prevented it maximising the benefits of its elite links. Certainly, as did many other successor parties, the CPRF inherited political capital which was evident in its relative organisational integrity and entrenched regional support, but compared with countries such as Poland, the majority of these accrued to the non-communist elite. The fact that the party faced few organised parties in the electoral sphere mattered little when the party had to compete with the financial and organisational might of the 'party of power' in presidential elections. The communist elite's *nomenklatura* background allowed them to 'inscribe themselves into the power system', and join the permanent negotiation over the Russian transition.[20] Yet the CPRF hierarchy was at a disadvantage in elite bargaining: its organisation provided negotiating power in regional contests, and in passing laws through the Duma, but party affiliation was seen as a hindrance to effective 'professional' work by ministers who usually remained non-party once in government. The rhetoric of the 'idiotic extremists' with their 'ideological cockroaches' remained a permanent barrier to their full incorporation in the elite.[21]

Simultaneously, the ideological nature of the communist electorate everywhere denied it the ability to manoeuvre. It was the incontrovertible fact that even at the height of post-communist Russia's woes, supporters of the status quo outnumbered those who supported a return to communism, a clear legacy of the party's discrediting in *perestroika*, during the coup and the anti-communist squall that followed. As noted, Russia's socio-economic choices remained broadly left-paternalist, which allowed communists to insist that Russia was inherently a 'left country', but, to their chagrin it seemed that 'Russians want socialism without communists'.[22] Whereas the party was not simply the party of losers, the nostalgic or the alienated, it was not much more than this. Not all of the party's supporters were convinced communists, but this was predominately a pro-Soviet sub-culture, whose values were sharply differentiated from the rest of society, and particularly the younger generation. As Zyuganov admitted, the communists were 'in a fairly spacious niche, but a niche all the same'.[23]

Party structure compounded these features. The CPRF initially appeared to have inherited the worst of both worlds – a militant, impoverished and often doctrinaire membership, and weak central control over that membership. But as the party hierarchy reasserted control, it became clear that party organisation itself contributed to the problem. In channelling a militant internal 'anti-system' party discourse and activist conception of party life, the party appeared to be replacing its internal politics with administration, and so replicating the experience of communist parties like the Italian PCI, using democratic centralism to 'isolate hermetically the Marxist sub-culture' – to contain party debate over the divergence between party programme and practice and to maintain for party members the increasingly illusory image of a revolutionary party.[24] This engendered a vicious circle: the more internal problems, the greater the stress on unity; the greater the stress on unity, the greater the militant pressure on the upper echelons, and the greater the party's ideological rigidity.

Indeed, the party increasingly appeared mired in an internal crisis replicated in West European communist parties elsewhere. This was a simultaneous and multifaceted crisis which was ideological (the declining salience of Marxism-Leninism *in toto*, evidenced by increasingly incompatibility between the party's Stalinist, social democratic and national-patriotic faces, which the party seemed endemically unable to resolve), organisational (the declining and ageing membership, incipient internal fractionalisation and weakened influence over social organisations), strategic (with the party's anti-system stance undercut by its de facto incorporation within the regime) and electoral (with the party entrenched in a niche which was far from activist or even working class). To a degree this was the crisis of all post-Soviet parties, fragmented in ideology and organisation, and having to consolidate in rapidly changing conditions, and with post-Soviet institutions which were mired in a cycle of under-institutionalisation and fragmentation. Compared with them, the CPRF could appear strong, with an inherited organisational and ideological ethos giving a relative stability. Yet its crisis was also worse, because of the gap between anti-system aspirations and rapid incorporation in a 'bourgeois' system, and because this incorporation rarely compensated for the privileged positions which the communists had once held. At the same time, the communists' persistent inability to oppose 'primitive capitalism' made the gap between intent and achievement still starker.

Little in the behaviour of the CPRF contradicted the impression of the concentric closure of Leninist politics, and the apparent inability of Leninist parties to come to power peacefully through pluralist politics. The victory of the Party of Communists of the Republic of Moldova (PCRM) in the parliamentary elections of 25 February 2001 with 50 per cent of the vote was an exception which appeared to prove the rule. First, according to Romanian president Iliescu, this was the choice of the poorest population in Europe, 'at the brink of survival' and beset by legislative-executive deadlock.[25] Second, in such a small country the communists could win with a mere seven hundred and eighty-one thousand votes. Third, and perhaps illustrative of points we have mentioned, the communists came to power through a parliamentary system. Although this in no short measure contributed to the deadlock, it appeared to force the communists into a more constructive position dependent on coalition partners, and to compromise with the president.[26] Finally, although the communist programme was distinctly Marxist-Leninist there was a far clearer Eurocommunist, humanist and internationalist face than expressed by the CPRF.[27] Although this was the first CIS country to re-elect communists, the PCRM's commitment to a government of professional, non-ideological technocrats indicated this was far from a return to communism.

Might the CPRF had been more successful had it taken such a moderate leftist position? This was forcefully argued by the left, who claimed that state patriotism limited the party's ability to exploit class discontent and engage with civil society, and discredited socialist ideas as a whole. This argument has much merit, but it implies that a strategy embedded in the organised working class would have been more successful, which was not certain, when the working class was decimated and the trade unions docile. Certainly the Czech and Ukrainian communist parties, though grounded in working-class constituencies, remained still more marginal than the CPRF. The 'communist' essence of these parties provoked the anti-ideological allergy prevalent in post-Soviet societies, while even democratic Marxist ideologies have so far suffered the same fate. Indeed as we have seen the most successful successor parties combined a clear minimally ideological *cross-class* appeal. It was precisely the ideological nature of the CPRF which denied it this option, and in such circumstances its eclectic blurring of communism, national-patriotism and social democracy was perhaps the only way the party could maximise its ability to manoeuvre without losing part of its electorate.

However, the party remained too communist to capitalise effectively on the national-patriotic vote and the arguments against a coherent centre-left position weakened after 1996.

There was some evidence to support Putin's view that the communist leader 'are prepared to change . . . But they can't do it right now – they're afraid that their constituency will feel betrayed'.[28] The argument for incremental and cautious change was strong, as the communists were caught between an inflexible and maximalist electorate, a manipulative political elite and a political system which impeded coherent opposition. Despite such constraints, they could claim considerable successes: they rebounded from a ban to become the premier opposition force and the pre-eminent political party in the country, despite many challenges to their electorate. The experience of reformed successor parties such as the Polish DLA and the HSP suggested that an exit from communism would be followed by marginalisation and electoral defeat prior to reorientation, but with such voter volatility and regime pressure in Russia there was no certainty of renewal. In such circumstances, political unity and the consolidated communist vote (see below) was a valuable commodity and to lose this would be 'political suicide'.[29] The communist strategy evolving after the Seventh Congress appeared to aim to inject significant new blood into the party and the NPUR, while clamping down on party discontent and reinforcing Zyuganov as the only leader capable of preserving party unity and the balance of interests within the party. Thus the dominance of a pragmatic wing could be gradually consolidated. But such an approach ignored the question of whether the institutions, heritage and even name of the party were the very problem, and prevented it articulating a coherent unifying vision. Ultimately the question of whether it was possible to reform a revolutionary tradition was not confronted: experience suggests there are just two paths from Leninism, retrenchment or transcendence. With the statist-patriotic banner in the hands of Putin, the alternative option of a democratic socialism was one that the party as a whole, irrespective of the private wishes of some leaders, seemed both unwilling and unable to adopt. Despite the risks, a party split might be the only way to resolve its ideological and strategic problems and confront the challenges facing it.

What then were the prospects of the CPRF being 'able to solve the riddle of the 21st century?'[30] The stability of the core communist electorate should not be underestimated, with 53 per cent of

Zyuganov's supporters (approximately 11 million people or 15 per cent of the popular vote) still claiming to be communist in 2000.[31] Despite the likely attrition of the pro-Soviet sub-culture over time, its sub-cultural essence could potentially guarantee the party a significant national and regional weight for a considerable time if, and *because* the party did not change its programmatic positions, thus partially substantiating the leaders' caution. However, in Russia, electoral weight did not translate directly to political influence, and in this regard the party faced increasing problems.

Putin was a more threatening opponent than Yeltsin ever was: his all-embracing statist-patriotic liberalism contained a push-pull dynamic, challenging them to 'work together' and put pragmatism before philosophy, while promising to continue an economic policy (particularly in its emphasis on privatisation and lower tariff barriers) inimical to most of the party's supporters. This opened up the prospect of a more nuanced, flexible and multi-polar opposition than hitherto, and the communists' future prospects would be heavily influenced by both how they responded to this challenge, and the effectiveness of Putin's project as a whole. After the Seventh Congress the CPRF had sought to balance selective support for Putin's 'patriotic' policies with renewed social-class slogans opposing the socio-economic policies of the government. This policy was understandable since it offered to consolidate the party internally, and relied on the likelihood of renewed socio-economic downturn caused by the falling world oil price. Yet, even more left-wing national bolshevism continued to play on the crowded patriotic field, while leaving the valid democratic critique of Putin's authoritarian proclivities to the URF and Yabloko. If Putin's Western-orientated patriotism ultimately succeeded in initiating a Russian recovery, it might marginalise the communists' more inward-looking platform, while it was fully possible that the democratic critique, freed from the taint of Yeltsinism, would benefit from its failure. Certainly, communist success depended heavily on overcoming its inability to exploit socio-economic distress and risked leaving the initiative to more dynamic forces.

Overall, continued rapprochement with the political elite was a double-edged sword offering huge losses without making concomitant gains. Improved access to regional leaders, finance and media resources could compensate for the party's internal crisis tendencies. For instance the proposed law 'On political parties' submitted to the Duma in December 2000 appeared to unduly benefit the CPRF.

Aiming to further the ideal of a two- or three-party system, it stipulated a strict criteria for legal party registration for new parties, providing barriers which some thought only the CPRF and Edinstvo
could surmount.[32] But the stipulation that the president leave a party
while in office showed parties being created administratively without
being given institutional incentive, and threatened grass-roots initiative, while the anti-system orientation of the CPRF's supporters and
ideology prevented its easy incorporation in a systemic party system,
and risked further alienating it from its constituency.

An instructive parallel was the experience of the French
Communist Party, whose participation in the Socialist Mitterand
government from 1981 to 1984 during a period of strict financial aus-
terity allowed the party to be tainted before its protest electorate, presaging the rapid usurpation of the communist vote by the more flexible
and electable Socialists, and Le Pen's far-right National Front, and the
communists' endemic decline and marginalisation in French politics.
Were Putin, like Mitterand, to use the communists as 'a ladder which
he would subsequently kick away', such a fate might await the
CPRF.[33] Rossiya was evidence of the danger. Its chances of immediately supplanting the CPRF as the main party of the left seemed small.
This was less a social democratic party than another bureaucratic
structure created around an ambitious politician (Seleznev) seeking
national popularity, and its foundation only served to demonstrate
the CPRF's continuing cohesion.[34] But were the party able to unite
with other future challengers for the left-centrist niche, its role might
be to consign the CPRF to the far-left spectrum as did the SPU
(Socialist Party of Ukraine) in the Ukraine. Meanwhile the danger of
the CPRF 'missing the moment . . . [to] change internally' was demonstrated by the party's near outflanking by Edinstvo, and the feeling
of many younger radical left trends who saw the CPRF as a 'large
decaying corpse lying in their way'.[35]

Ultimately, the CPRF should be seen not just as an opponent of
Russian reform, but as a product of that reform. The existence of a
large and influential residually Leninist party within the Russian
polity reflected a polity in many ways still afflicted by the 'Soviet syndrome'. The existence of a post-Leninist state weakly integrated with
an alienated civil society was the milieu which sustained the CPRF,
for it remained an almost unique 'social cosmos', providing values,
culture and orientation to its supporters, while able to capitalise on
traditional methods of administrative control to maintain their

loyalty. Similarly, that Russian politics remained a 'bureaucratic pol-
yarchy' where the struggle for power belonged more to a semi-
clandestine world of interdependent bureaucratic, clan and business
structures than open electoral competition was congenial to the communists.[36] The communists' integration in the elite provided it with
social stability, while partially compensating for the CPRF's weaknesses in the public arena, which would arguably have become much
more glaring had they faced organised party competitors and open
political discourse from the outset. This elite-dominated transformation remained problematic, because it imbued politics with a tentative
short-term stability, while the co-optation of political parties weakened the very linkages that might institutionalise the elite's responsibility before society. So the evolution of the CPRF into a modern
democratic left party, able to integrate its policies into a reformist
trend within the political system, balance the political spectrum and
ensure regular rotation of power depended much on the ability of
leaders like Putin and Zyuganov to overcome the administrative
methods in which they were adept. Tuleev thought that 'political-
cultural traditions and mentality . . . the devotion to authoritarian
methods and underestimation of democratic procedures' foreclosed
such an outcome.[37] Such an evaluation did scant justice to many of the
CPRF's individual members, but while the party remained committed to a tradition 'intrinsically . . . impelled towards the destruction of
free politics', it alone bore the burden of proof.[38]

Notes

1 *Ocherednye zadachi KPRF: Tezisy dlya obsuzhdeniya v partiinikh organizatsiyakh k VII sezdu partii*, from www.kprf.ru/statia4.htm.

2 G. Flikke, 'Patriotic left-centrism: the zigzags of the Communist Party of the Russian Federation', *Europe-Asia Studies*, 51:2, 1999, 293.

3 *K*, 14 March 2001.

4 R. Rose, W. Mishler, C. Haerpfner, *Democracy and Its Alternatives: Understanding Post Communist Societies* (Cambridge, Polity Press, 1991), p. 44.

5 R. Sakwa, 'The CPRF: the powerlessness of the powerful', in A. Bozóki and J. Ishiyama (eds), *A Decade of Transformation: Communist Successor Parties in Central and Eastern Europe* (Armonk, NY, M. E. Sharpe, forthcoming).

6 Putin's annual address to the Federal Assembly, *Johnson's Russia List*, 5185, 4 April 2001.

7 L. Shevtsova, *Literaturnaya gazeta*, 24–30 May 2000.

8 J. D. Nagle and A. Mahr, *Democracy and Democratization* (London, Sage, 2000), p. 181.

9 J. Hughes, 'Transition models and democratisation in Russia', in M. Bowker and C. Ross (eds), *Russia after the Cold War* (London, Longman, 2000), p. 19.

10   F. J. Fleron, Jr, 'Post-Soviet political culture in Russia: an assessment of recent
     empirical investigations', *Europe-Asia Studies*, 48:2 (1996), 238.
11   J. Barth Urban, 'The communist parties of Russia and Ukraine on the eve of
     the 1999 elections: similarities, contrasts, and interactions', *Demokratizatsiya*,
     7:1 (1999), 122.
12   S. Hanley, 'From "subcultural party" to neo-communist force? The
     Communist Party of Bohemia and Moravia 1990–2000', *Journal of Communist
     Studies and Transition Politics* (forthcoming).
13   Sakwa, 'The CPRF: the powerlessness of the powerful', p. 1.
14   J. Blondel, 'Political opposition in the contemporary world', *Government and
     Opposition*, 32:4 (1997), 463.
15   See the comments of Georgii Satarov in M. McFaul, 'Russia's 1996 presiden-
     tial elections', *Post-Soviet Affairs*, 12:4 (1996). 325.
16   J. Linz and A. Valenzuela, *The Failure of Presidential Democracy: Comparative
     Perspectives* (Baltimore, MD, Johns Hopkins University Press, 1994).
17   Flikke, 'Patriotic left-centrism', 294.
18   M. Andreev, *P*, 25 May 2000.
19   Sakwa, 'The CPRF: the powerlessness of the powerful', p. 1.
20   *NG*, 25 March 1997.
21   The first quote is from A. Korzhakov, *Boris Eltsin: ot rassveta do zakata* (Moscow,
     Izdatelstvo 'Interbuk', 1997), p. 368; the second from N. Gevorkyan, N.
     Timakova and A. Kolesnikov, *Ot pervogo litsa: razgavory s Vladimirom Putinym*
     (Moscow, Vagrius, 2000).
22   The first quote is from the author's interview with CPRF CC secretary for
     Connections with Foreign Parties and movements, Nikolai Bindyukov, on 20
     September 2000; the second quote is from a survey in *AiF* which in 1997 noted
     that 60 per cent of the population preferred life under socialism, but 52 per
     cent did not want to see communists in power (*RIA Novosti Daily Review*, 1
     November 1997).
23   *Politicheskii otchet Tsentralnogo Komiteta KPRF VII sezdu i ocherednye zadachi
     partii*, from web site at: www.kprf.ru.
24   M. J. Bull, 'Whatever happened to Italian communism?', *West European
     Politics*, 14:4 (1991), 103–4.
25   *RFE/RL Newsline*, 28 February 2001.
26   P. Goble, 'Analysis from Washington – when communists win elections', from
     web site at: www.rferl.org/nca/features/1998/04.
27   See the PCRM programme on web site at: www.ournet.md/~pcrm/ustav/
     prog.html.
28   Gevorkyan, Timakova and Kolesnikov, *Ot pervogo litsa*.
29   Author's interview with CPRF CC secretary for ideological work, Aleksandr
     Kravets, on 22 September 2000.
30   *Politicheskii otchet*.
31   *New Russia Barometer*, XI 14–18 April 2000 from web site at: www.
     russiavotes.org.
32   These barriers involved a minimum of ten thousand members and a hundred
     regional branches in forty-five subjects of the federation. See *MT*, 20
     December 2000.
33   W. Thompson, *The Communist Movement since 1945* (Oxford, Blackwell, 1998),
     p. 173.
34   Although the bloc's CPRF supporters proved to be less than hoped, it got

backing from regional Agrarian Party organisations, marginal left-wing grou-
puscules such as the Ural-based *Mir, Trud, Mai*, and the Party of Worker's Self-
Management, started to created its own fractions in regional parliaments and
competed directly with the CPRF in Volgograd and Bryansk. It claimed
(without basis) organisations in eighty-eight regions and six hundred thousand members (*OG*, 18 January 2001; *NG*, 11 January 2001).

35 Gevorkyan, Timakova and Kolesnikov, *Ot pervogo litsa*; B. Kagarlitskii, *OG*,
    March 8–14, 2001.
36 G. Diligenskii, 'Putin i rossiiskaya demokratiya (razmyshleniya po rezulta-
    tam oprosov 2000g.)' from web site at: www.fom.ru, 18 January 2001.
37 A. Tuleev, *NG*, 12 July 2000.
38 R. Tiersky, *Ordinary Stalinism: Democratic Centralism and the Question of
    Communist Political Development* (London, Allen and Unwin, 1985) p. 56.

Bibliography

Newspapers and electronic publications

Argumenty i fakty (AiF)
Bumbarash 2017
Delovie Lyudy
Delovoi Mir
Den
Duel
Duma
The Economist
EWI Russian Regional Report
Financial Times
Glasnost
Golos kommunista
Harvard Election Watch
Informatsionnyi byulleten (KPRF)
Itogi
Izm
Izvestiya (Iz)
Jamestown Foundation Monitor
Jamestown Foundation Prism
Johnson's Russia List
Kapital
Kommersant (K)
Kommersant vlast (KV)
Komsomolskaya pravda
Limonka
Literaturnaya gazeta
Megapolis-ekspress
Molniya
Moscow News
Moscow Times (MT)
Moscow Tribune
Moskovskaya Pravda
Moskovskie novosti (MN)
Moskovskii komsomolets

Mysl
Ne dai Bog
Nezavisimaya gazeta (NG)
Nezavisimaya gazeta-Stsenarii (NG Stsenarii)
Novaya gazeta
Novoe vremya
Observer
Obshchaya gazeta (OG)
OMRI Daily Digest
OMRI Russian Presidential Election Survey
OMRI Russian Regional Report
OMRI Special Report
Parliamentskaya gazeta
Patriot
Pravda (P)
Pravda 5 (P-5)
Pravda Moskvy
Pravda Rossii (PR)
RFE/RL Newsline
RFE/RL Russian Election Report
RFE/RL Russian Political Weekly
RIA Novosti Daily Review
Rossiiskie vesti
Russia
Russia Review
Russia Today
Segodnya (S)
Sovetskaya kultura
Sovetskaya Rossiya (SR)
Summary of World Broadcasts (SWB)
The Times
Trud
Trudovaya Rossiya
Uchitelskaya gazeta
Vechernyaya Moskva
Vek
Vernost Leninu
Vremya MN
Za SSSR
Zavtra

Web sites

After September 1999 all newspapers cited are web versions (when available).

http://ksgnotes1.harvard.edu/BCSIA/SDI.nsf/www/Home (Harvard Strengthening Democratic Institutions Project)
http://pubs.carnegie.ru/english/elections/president2000 (*Carnegie Bulletin*)
http://rksm.da.ru (Russian Communist Union of Youth)

http://scenario.ng (*NG-Stsenarii*)
http://www.fas.harvard.edu/%7Eponars/ (Harvard program on New Approaches to Russian Security)
www.carnegie.ru/www.ceip.org (Carnegie Endowment for International Peace)
www.duma.gov.ru (Russian State Duma)
www.economist.com (*The Economist*)
www.fci.ru (Central Electoral Commission of the Russian Federation)
www.fom.ru (Public Opinion Foundation)
www.gull.ptt.ru/Asm (Movement in Support of the Army)
www.intellectualcapital.com (Information 'e-zine')
www.international.se
www.kprf.ru/www.cprf.ru (CPRF official pages)
www.moscowtimes.ru (*Moscow Times*)
www.nasledie.ru (Spiritual Heritage)
www.nns.ru (National News Service)
www.ournet.md/~pcrm/ (Party of Communists of the Republic of Moldova)
www.panorama.ru (Panorama)
www.pnp.ru (*Parliamentskaya gazeta*)
www.rferl.org (Radio Liberty/Radio Free Europe)
www.ria-novosti.com (*RIA Novosti Daily Review*)
www.russiatoday.com (*Russia Today*)
www.russiavotes.org (Russia Votes)
www.seleznev.com (Seleznev's web site)
www.sr.park.ru (*Sovetskaya Rossiya*)
www.strana.ru
www.tol.cz (*Transitions Online*)
www.vesti.ru
www.zavtra.ru (*Zavtra*)
www.zyuganov.ru (Zyuganov's web site)

Books and articles

Ágh, A., 'Partial consolidation of the East-Central European parties: the case of the Hungarian Socialist Party', *Party Politics*, 1:4 (1995), 491–514.
Agursky, M., *The Third Rome: National Bolshevism in the USSR* (Boulder, CO, Westview, 1987).
Amalrik, A., 'Ideologies in Soviet society', *Survey*, 2 (1976), 1–11.
Anti-Semitism, Xenophobia and Religious Persecution in Russian's Regions 1998–9 (Washington, DC, Union of Councils for Soviet Jews, 1999).
Aron, L., *Yeltsin: A Revolutionary Life* (London, HarperCollins, 2000).
Ashwin, S., *Russian Workers: The Anatomy of Patience* (Manchester, Manchester University Press, 1999).
Bacon, E. T., 'The Russian presidential election of 1996: electoral systems, multi-partism and the depth of democratisation', paper presented to CREES annual conference, 21–23 June 1996.
Bacon, E. T., 'The Church and politics in Russia: a case study of the 1996 presidential election', *Religion, State and Society*, 5:3 (1997), 253–65.
Bacon, E. T., 'Is there any opposition in Russia? Analysis of the influences on and

prospects for political opposition in Russia', paper presented to CREES annual conference, Cumberland Lodge, Windsor, 16–18 June 2000.

Barylski, R., *The Soldier in Russian Politics 1985–1996* (New Brunswick, Transaction, 1998).

Belin, L., 'Are the communists poised for victory?', *Transition* (1 December 1995), 25–8.

Belin, L., 'The two faces of the Agrarian Party', *Transition* (1 December 1995), 29–31, 69.

Belin, L., 'Zyuganov tries to broaden an already powerful left-wing coalition', *Transition* (31 May 1996), 12–15.

Belin, L. and Orttung, R. W., 'Parties proliferate on eve of elections', *Transition* (22 September 1995), 42–50, 67.

Bellis, P. and Gleisner, J., 'After perestroika: a neo-conservative manifesto', *Russia and the World*, 19 (1991), 1–7.

Belov, Yu, *Russkaya sudba* (Moscow, Soratnik, 1995).

Belov, Yu, *Ne tuzhi, Rossiya* (Moscow, 'Znanie', 1997).

Bernstein, E., *Evolutionary Socialism* (New York, Schocken, 1967).

Bindyukov, N., 'O konseptsii natsionalnoi politiki KPRF v sovremennakh usloviyakh', *Dialog*, 6 (1997), 40–7.

Bindyukov, N. and Lopata, P., 'Put vybran, neobkhodimo uspeshno ego prioiti', *Dialog*, 10 (1997), 41–8.

Blondel, J., Political opposition in the contemporary world', *Government and Opposition*, 32:4 (1997), 463–86.

Bondarev, V., *Kto est kto-politicheskaya elita Rossii v portretakh* (Moscow, NTS Russika, 1995).

Bottomore, T., *A Dictionary of Marxist Thought*, 2nd edn (Oxford, Blackwell, 1991).

Bova, R., 'Political dynamics of the post-communist transition: a comparative perspective', in F. Fleron and E. Hoffman (eds), *Post-Communist Studies and Political Science* (Boulder, CO, Westview, 1993).

Bowker, M. and Ross, C. (eds), *Russia after the Cold War* (London, Longman, 2000).

Bozóki, A., 'The ideology of modernization and the policy of materialism: the day after for the socialists', *Journal of Communist Studies and Transition Politics*, 13:3 (1997), 56–102.

Bremmer, I. and Taras, R., *New States, New Politics* (Cambridge, Cambridge University Press, 1997).

Brown, A., *The Gorbachev Factor* (Oxford, Oxford University Press, 1996).

Brudny, Y. M., 'In pursuit of the Russian presidency: why and how Yeltsin won the 1996 presidential election', *Communist and Post-Communist Studies*, 30:3 (1997), 255–75.

Brudny, Y. M., *Reinventing Russia: Russian Nationalism and the Soviet State 1953–1991* (Cambridge, MA, Harvard University Press, 1998).

Brym, R. J., 'Voters quietly reveal greater communist leanings', *Transition* (8 September 1995), 32–5.

Bull, M. J., 'The West European communist movement: past, present and future', in M. J. Bull and P. Heywood (eds), *West European Communist Parties after the Revolutions of 1989* (Basingstoke, Macmillan, 1994), pp. 203–22.

Bull, M. J., 'Whatever happened to Italian communism?', *West European Politics*, 14:4 (1991), 96–120.

Bull, M. J. and Heywood, P. (eds), *West European Communist Parties after the Revolutions of 1989* (Basingstoke, Macmillan, 1994).

Bibliography

Bunce, V., 'Should transitologists be grounded?', *Slavic Review*, 54:1 (1995), 111–27.
Burbach, R., Nunez, O. and Kagarlitsky, B., *Globalization and Its Discontents: The Rise of Postmodern Socialisms* (London, Pluto Press, 1997).
Buzgalin, A., *Budushchee kommunizma* (Moscow, 'Olma-press', 1996).
Byzov, L., 'What about the voters?', in M. McFaul, N. Petrov, A Ryabov and E. Reisch (eds), *Primer on Russia's 1999 Duma Elections* (Washington, DC, Carnegie Endowment, 1999).
Byzov, L., 'Parliamentskye vybory kak etap v formirovanie konsensusnogo obshchestva', in M. McFaul, N. Petrov and A. Ryabov (eds), *Rossiya v izbiratelnom tsikle 1999–2000 godov* (Moscow, Moscow Carnegie Center, 2000).
Byzov, L., 'Presidentskaya kampaniya – 2000 i novyi electoralnyi zapros', in M. McFaul, N. Petrov and A. Ryabov (eds), *Rossiya v izbiratelnom tsikle 1999–2000 godov* (Moscow, Moscow Carnegie Center, 2000).
Chernyakovsky, S., 'The Communist Party of the Russian Federation', in M. McFaul, N. Petrov, A Ryabov and E. Reisch (eds), *Primer on Russia's 1999 Duma Elections* (Washington, DC, Carnegie Endowment, 1999)
Chernyakovskii, S., 'Kommunisticheskie obedineniya', in M. McFaul, N. Petrov and A. Ryabov (eds), *Rossiya nakanune dumskikh vyborov 1999 goda* (Moscow, Moscow Carnegie Center, 1999).
Chernyakovskii, S., 'Kampaniya G. Zyuganova', in M. McFaul, N. Petrov and A. Ryabov (eds), *Rossiya v izbiratelnom tsikle 1999–2000 godov* (Moscow, Moscow Carnegie Center, 2000).
Chernyakovskii, S., 'Kommunisticheskoe dvizhenie' in M. McFaul, N. Petrov and A. Ryabov (eds), *Rossiya na dumskikh i prezidentskikh vyborakh* (Moscow, Moscow Carnegie Center, 2000).
Clark, B., *An Empire's New Clothes: The End of Russia's Liberal Dream* (London, Vintage, 1995).
Clarke, S., *Labour Relations in Transition: Wages, Employment and Industrial Conflict in Russia* (Cheltenham, Edward Elgar, 1996).
Cohen, S. F., 'Introduction: Ligachev and the tragedy of Russian conservatism', in E. Ligachev, *Inside Gorbachev's Kremlin: The Memoirs of Yegor Ligachev* (Boulder, CO, Westview, 1996), pp. vii–xxxvi.
Cohen, S. F., 'Russian studies without Russia', *Post-Soviet Affairs*, 15:1 (1999), 37–55.
Colton, T. J., 'Economics and voting in Russia', *Post-Soviet Affairs*, 12:4 (1996), 289–314.
Colton, T. J. and McFaul, M., 'Reinventing Russia's party of power: "Unity" and the 1999 Duma election', *Post-Soviet Affairs*, 16:3 (2000), 201–24.
Cook, L. J., *Labor and Liberalization: Trade Unions in the New Russia* (New York, Twentieth Century Fund Press, 1997).
Cook, L. J. and Orenstein, M. A., 'The return of the left and its impact on the welfare state in Russia, Poland and Hungary', in L. J. Cook, M. A. Orenstein and M. Rueschemeyer, *Left Parties and Social Policy in Postcommunist Europe* (Boulder, CO, Westview, 1999).
Cook, L. J., Orenstein, M. A. and Rueschemeyer, M., *Left Parties and Social Policy in Postcommunist Europe* (Boulder, CO, Westview, 1999).
Cox, M. (ed.), *Rethinking the Soviet Collapse* (London, Pinter, 1998).
Dahl, R. A., *Preface to Democratic Theory* (Chicago, University of Chicago Press, 1956).
Davies, R. W., *Soviet History in the Yeltsin Era* (Basingstoke, Macmillan, 1997).
Dawisha, K., 'Democratization and political participation: research concepts and

methodologies', in K. Dawisha and B. Parrott (eds), *Democratic Changes and Authoritarian Reactions in Russia, Ukraine, Belarus and Moldova* (Cambridge, Cambridge University Press, 1997).

Dawisha, K. and Parrott, B. (eds), *Democratic Changes and Authoritarian Reactions in Russia, Ukraine, Belarus and Moldova* (Cambridge, Cambridge University Press, 1997).

Devlin, J., *Slavophiles and Commissars* (Basingstoke, Macmillan, 1999).

Donald, J. and Hall, S., *Politics and Ideology* (Milton Keynes, Open University Press, 1986).

Dumskii krizis: uroki i posledstviya (Moscow, Tsentr politicheskykh tekhnologii, 2000).

Duncan, P., *Russian Messianism: Third Rome, Revolution Communism and After* (London, Routledge, 2000).

Dunlop, J., 'Russia in search of an identity', in I. Bremmer and R. Taras (eds), *New States, New Politics* (Cambridge, Cambridge University Press, 1997).

Duverger, M., *Political Parties: Their Organization and Activity in the Modern State* (London, Methuen, 1964).

Eatwell, R. and Wright, A. (eds), *Contemporary Political Ideologies* (London, Pinter, 1993).

Ermakov, Ia., Shavshukova, T. and Yakunechkin, V., 'The communist movement in Russia during the period of prohibition: From the CPSU to the Communist Party of the Russian Federation', *Russian Politics and Law*, 2:4 (1994), 39–59.

Evans, G. and Whitefield, S., 'Identifying the bases of party competition in Eastern Europe', *British Journal of Political Science*, 23:4 (1993), 521–48.

Femia, J. F., 'Marxism and communism', in R. Eatwell and A. Wright (eds), *Contemporary Political Ideologies* (London, Pinter, 1993).

Fish, M. S., *Democracy from Scratch: Opposition and Regime in the New Russian Revolution* (Princeton, NJ, Princeton University Press, 1994).

Fish, M. S., 'The advent of multipartism in Russia, 1993–5', *Post-Soviet Affairs*, 11:4 (1995), 340–83.

Fish, M. S., 'The predicament of Russian liberalism: evidence from the December 1995 parliamentary elections', *Europe-Asia Studies*, 49:2 (1997), 191–220.

Fleron, F. J., Jr, 'Post-Soviet political culture in Russia: an assessment of recent empirical investigations', *Europe-Asia Studies*, 48:2 (1996), 225–60.

Fleron, F. J., Jr, and Hoffman, E. (eds), *Post-Communist Studies and Political Science* (Boulder, CO, Westview, 1993).

Fleron, F. J., Jr, Ahl, R. and Lane, F., 'Where now in the study of Russian political parties?', *Journal of Communist Studies and Transition Politics*, 14:1&2 (1998), 224–52.

Flikke, G., 'Patriotic left-centrism: the zigzags of the Communist Party of the Russian Federation', *Europe-Asia Studies*, 51:2 (1999), 275–98.

Freeden, M., *Ideologies and Political Theory: A Conceptual Approach* (Oxford, Clarendon Press, 1996).

Freeland, C., *Sale of the Century: The Inside Story of the Second Russian Revolution* (London, Little, Brown and Co., 2000).

Fukuyama, F., *The End of History and the Last Man* (New York, Free Press, 1992).

Gabidullin, R., 'O klassovom podkhode i gosudarstvennom patriotizm', *Dialog*, 10 (1997), 10–14.

Garifullina, N., *Tot, kto ne predal. Oleg Shenin: stranitsy zhizni i borby* (Moscow, Vneshtorgoizdat, 1995).

Gelman, V. and Golosov, G. V., 'Regional party system formation in Russia: the deviant case of Sverdlovsk oblast', *Journal of Communist Studies and Transition Politics*, 14:1&2 (1998), 31–53.

General Lev Rokhlin i perspectivy Rossiiskoi oppozitsii (Moscow, Tsentr politicheskykh tekhnologii, 1997).

Gevorkyan, N., Timakova, N. and Kolesnikov, A., *Ot pervogo litsa: razgavory s Vladimirom Putinym* (Moscow, Vagrius, 2000).

Giddens, A., *Runaway World* (London, Profile, 1999).

Gill, G., *The Rules of the Communist Party of the Soviet Union* (Basingstoke, Macmillan, 1988).

Gill, G., *The Collapse of a Single-Party System: The Disintegration of the Communist Party of the Soviet Union* (Cambridge, Cambridge University Press, 1994).

Gill, G. 'Democratic consolidation in Russia?, *Acta Politica*, 32:3 (1997), 281–301.

Gill, G. and Markwick, R., *Russia's Stillborn Democracy? From Gorbachev to Yeltsin* (Oxford, Oxford University Press, 2000).

Gleisner, J., 'The agitation and propaganda work of the Communist Party of the Soviet Union' (PhD thesis, University of Birmingham, 1978).

Golosov, G., 'Who survives? Party origins, organizational development, and electoral performance in post-communist Russia', *Political Studies*, 46 (1998), 529–39.

Golosov, G., 'From Adygeya to Yaroslavl: factors of party development in the regions of Russia, 1995–1998', *Europe-Asia Studies*, 51:8 (1999), 1333–66.

Golosov, G., 'Gubernatory i partiinaya politika', *Pro et Contra*, 5:1 (2000).

Gregor, A. J., 'Fascism and the new Russian nationalism', *Communist and Post-Communist Studies*, 31:1 (1998), 1–15.

Gustafson, T., *Capitalism Russian-Style* (Cambridge, Cambridge University Press, 1999).

Hanley, S. 'From "subcultural party" to neo-communist force? The Communist Party of Bohemia and Moravia 1990–2000', *Journal of Communist Studies and Transition Politics* (forthcoming).

Hanson, S. E., *Ideology, Uncertainty, and the Rise of Anti-System Parties in Post Communist Russia* (Glasgow, University of Strathclyde Centre for the Study of Public Policy, Studies in Public Policy 289, 1997).

Harding, N., *Leninism* (Basingstoke, Macmillan, 1996).

Harris, J., *Adrift in Turbulent Seas: The Political and Ideological Struggles of Ivan Kuz'mich Polozkov* (Pittsburgh, University of Pittsburgh Press, 1993).

Hass, S., Orttung, R. W. and Soukup, O., 'A demographic who's who of the candidates from the 12 leading parties', *Transition* (1 December 1995), 11–13.

Heywood, A., *Political Ideologies: An Introduction* (Basingstoke, Macmillan, 1992).

Hill, R. J. and Frank, P., *The Soviet Communist Party*, 3rd edn (London, Allen and Unwin, 1986).

Hoare, Q. and Nowell-Smith, G. (trans and eds), *Selections from the Prison Notebooks of Antonio Gramsci* (London, Lawrence and Wishart, 1986).

Holmes, L., *Politics in the Communist World* (Oxford, Clarendon Press, 1986).

Hughes, J., 'Transition models and democratisation in Russia', in M. Bowker and C. Ross (eds), *Russia after the Cold War* (London, Longman, 2000).

Huntington, S., *Political Order in Changing Societies* (New Haven, CT, Yale University Press, 1968).

Huntington, S., *The Third Wave: Democratization in the Late Twentieth Century* (Norman, OK, University of Oklahoma Press, 1991).

Huskey, E., *Presidential Power in Russia* (Armonk, NY, M. E. Sharpe, 1999).

Ilyukhin, V., *Na trone porazit porok* (Moscow, 'Federatsiya', 1997).

Ishiyama, J. T., 'Communist parties in transition: structures, leaders, and processes of democratization in Eastern Europe', *Comparative Politics*, 27:2 (1995), 147–66.

Ishiyama, J. T., 'The sickle or the rose? Previous regime types and the evolution of the ex-communist parties in post-communist politics', *Comparative Political Studies*, 30:3 (1997), 299–330.

IV sezd Kommunisticheskoi partii Rossiiskoi Federatsii 19–20 aprelya 1997 goda (Materialy i dokumenty) (Moscow, ITRK RSPP, 1997).

Kagarlitskii, B., 'Posle vyborov: O prichinakh porazheniya levykh', *Svobodnaya mysl*, 9 (1996), 3–7.

Kagarlitsky, B., 'Social democracy in the East: doomed to be radical', *Labour Focus on Eastern Europe*, 50 (1995), 19–23.

Kagarlitsky, B., 'Five years of the Communist Party of the Russian Federation', *Labour Focus on Eastern Europe*, 59 (1998), 45–52.

Katz, R. S. and Mair, P., *How Parties Organize: Change and Adaptation in Party Organizations in Western Democracies* (London, Sage, 1994).

Kholmskaya, M., 'Kommunisticheskoe dvizhenie Rossii: sovremmenyi etap razvitiya', *Alternativy*, 2:5 (1994), 86–104.

Kitschelt, H., *The Logics of Party Formation* (Ithaca, NY, Cornell University Press, 1989)

Kitschelt, H., *The Transformation of European Social Democracy* (Cambridge, Cambridge University Press, 1994).

Kitschelt, H., Mansfeldova, Z., Markowski, R. and Tóka, G., *Postcommunist Party-Systems: Competition, Representation and Inter-Party Co-operation* (Cambridge, Cambridge University Press, 1999).

Klotsvog, F., 'Sotsializm – osobaya obshchestvenno-ekonomicheskaya formatsiya', *Dialog*, 1 (1997), 53–60.

Klyamkin, I. and Shevtsova, L., *This Omnipotent and Impotent Government: The Evolution of the Political System in Post-Communist Russia* (Moscow, Carnegie Moscow Center, 1999).

Kommunisticheskaya oppozitsiya: ugroza sleva? (Moscow, Tsentr politicheskykh tekhnologii, 1998).

Korzhakov, A., *Boris Eltsin: ot rassveta do zakata* (Moscow, Izdatelstvo 'Interbuk', 1997).

Kosolapov, R., *Idei razuma i serdtsa* (Moscow, 1996).

Kosolapov, R., 'Kakuyu model obshchestva mogut predlozhit kommunisty?', *Dialog*, 1 (1997), 46–9.

Koval, B. I., *Partii i politicheskie bloki v Rossii*, vypusk pervyi (Moscow, Nipek, 1993).

KPRF mezhdu umerennostyu i radikalizmom (Moscow, Tsentr politicheskykh tekhnologii, 1997).

KPSS vne zakona?! Konstitutsionnyi sud v Moskve (Moscow, Baikalskaya akademiya, 1992).

Kto est chto: politicheskaya Rossiya 1995–6 (Moscow, Ministerstvo ekonomiki RF, 1996).

Kurashvili, B., *Kuda idet Rossiya: otsenka Sovetskoi istorii* (Moscow, 'Prometei', 1993).

Kurashvili, B., *Kuda idet Rossiya: otsenka Sovetskoi istorii* (Moscow, Slovo, 1994).

Kurashvili, B., *Novyi sotsializm: k vozrozhdeniyu posle katastrophy* (Moscow, 'Bylina', 1997).

Kurashvili, B., 'Cherez formatsionny krizis k novomu sotsializmu', *Dialog*, 1 (1997), 61–5.

Lapidus, G. W. (ed.), *The New Russia: Troubled Transformation* (Boulder, CO, Westview, 1995).

Larsen, P. F. and Mandel, D., 'The Left in Russia', in R. Miliband and L. Panitch (eds), *The Socialist Register 1994: Between Globalism and Nationalism* (London, Merlin Press, 1994).

Lazar, M., 'Communism in Western Europe in the 1980s', *Journal of Communist Studies*, 4:3 (1988), 243–57.

Lenin, V., *Selected Works 2* (Moscow, Progress, 1970).

Lentini, P. (ed.), *Elections and Political Order in Russia: The Implications of the 1993 Elections to the Federal Assembly* (London, Central European University Press, 1995).

Lester, J., *Modern Tsars and Princes: The Struggle for Hegemony in Russia* (London, Verso, 1995).

Lester, J., 'Overdosing on nationalism: Gennadii Zyuganov and the Communist Party of the Russian Federation', *New Left Review*, 221 (1997), 34–53.

Lewis, P. G., *Political Parties in Post-Communist Eastern Europe* (London, Routledge, 2000).

Ligachev, E., *Inside Gorbachev's Kremlin: The Memoirs of Yegor Ligachev* (Boulder, CO, Westview, 1996).

Linz, J. and Stepan, A., *Problems of Democratic Transition and Consolidation* (Baltimore, MD, Johns Hopkins University Press, 1996).

Linz, J. and Valenzuela, A., *The Failure of Presidential Democracy: Comparative Perspectives* (Baltimore, MD, Johns Hopkins University Press, 1994).

Lloyd, J., *Rebirth of a Nation: An Anatomy of Russia* (London, Michael Joseph, 1997).

Lomax, B., 'Impediments to democratization in post-communist East-Central Europe', in G. Wightman (ed.), *Party Formation in East-Central Europe: Post-Communist Politics in Czechoslovakia, Hungary, Poland and Bulgaria* (Aldershot, Edward Elgar, 1995), pp. 179–201.

Lopata, P., 'Na puti ideinogo obnovleniya', *Dialog*, 2 (1997), 17–23.

Löwenhardt J., *The Reincarnation of Russia: Struggling with the Legacy of Communism, 1990–1994* (Harlow, Longman, 1995).

Mahr, A. and Nagle, J. D., 'Resurrection of the successor parties and democratization in East-Central Europe', *Communist and Post-Communist Studies*, 28:4 (1995), 393–409.

Makarkin, A., *KPRF i ee soyuzniki posle vyborov* (Moscow, Tsentr politicheskykh tekhnologii, 1996).

Makarkin, A., *Kommunisticheskaya partiya Rossiiskoi Federatsii* (Moscow, Tsentr politicheskykh tekhnologii, 1996).

March, L., 'Communism in transition? The Communist Party of the Russian Federation in the post-Soviet era' (PhD thesis, University of Birmingham 1999).

March, L., 'For victory? The crises and dilemmas of the Communist Party of the Russian Federation', *Europe-Asia Studies*, 53:2 (2001), 263–90.

Markowski, R., 'Political parties and ideological spaces in East-Central Europe', *Communist and Post-Communist Studies*, 30: 3 (September 1997), 221–54.

Materialy IX plenuma tsentralnogo ispolnitelnogo komiteta KPRF (Moscow, 1994).

Materialy Vserossiiskoi konferentsii Kommunisticheskoi partii Rossiiskoi Federatsii (Moscow, 1994).

Matsuzato, K., *The Split of the CPSU and the Configuration of Ex-Communist Factions in the Russian Oblasts: Cheliabinsk, Samara, Ul'ianovsk, Tambov and Tver (1990–95)*, Occasional Papers on Changes in the Slavic-Eurasian World 12 (Sapporo, Slavic Research Center, Hokkaido University 1996).

McAllister, I. and White, S., 'Democracy, political parties and party formation in postcommunist Russia', *Party Politics*, 1:1 (1995), 49–72.

McDaniel, T., *The Agony of the Russian Idea* (Princeton, NJ, Princeton University Press, 1996).

McFaul, M., *Post-Communist Politics: Democratic Prospects in Russia and Eastern Europe* (Washington, DC, Center for Strategic and International Studies, 1993).

McFaul, M., *Russia between Elections: What the December 1995 Results Really Mean* (Moscow, Carnegie Moscow Center, 1996).

McFaul, M., 'Russia's 1996 presidential elections', *Post-Soviet Affairs*, 12:4 (1996), 318–50.

McFaul, M. and Petrov, N., 'Russian electoral politics after transition: regional and national assessments', *Post-Soviet Geography and Economics*, 38:9 (1997), 507–49.

McFaul, M., Petrov, N., Ryabov, A. (eds), *Rossiya nakanune dumskikh vyborov 1999 goda* (Moscow, Moscow Carnegie Center, 1999).

McFaul, M., Petrov, N., Ryabov, A. (eds), *Carnegie Bulletin 3: Itogam vyborov* (Moscow, Carnegie Moscow Center, 2000).

McFaul, M., Petrov, N., Ryabov, A. (eds), *Rossiya na dumskikh i prezidentskikh vyborakh* (Moscow, Moscow Carnegie Center, 2000).

McFaul, M., Petrov N., Ryabov, A. (eds), *Rossiya v izbiratelnom tsikle 1999–2000 godov* (Moscow, Moscow Carnegie Center, 2000).

McFaul, M. Petrov, N., Ryabov, A., Reisch E. (eds), *Carnegie Bulletin 2: Parliamentary Elections in Russia* (Moscow, Moscow Carnegie Center, 1999).

McFaul, M. Petrov, N., Ryabov, A., Reisch, E. (eds), *Carnegie Bulletin 4: Itogi vyborov* (Moscow, Moscow Carnegie Center, 1999).

McFaul, M. Petrov, N., Ryabov, A., Reisch, E. (eds), *Primer on Russia's 1999 Duma Elections* (Washington, DC, Carnegie Endowment, 1999).

McInnes, N., *The Communist Parties of Western Europe* (London, Oxford University Press, 1975).

Mercer, C., 'Fascist ideology', in J. Donald and S. Hall, *Politics and Ideology* (Milton Keynes, Open University Press, 1986).

Middlemas, K., *Power and the Party: Changing Faces of Communism in Western Europe* (London, Deutsch, 1980).

Miliband, R. and Panitch, L., *The Socialist Register 1994: Between Globalism and Nationalism* (London, Merlin Press, 1994).

Millard, F., 'The 1995 Polish presidential election', *Journal of Communist Studies and Transition Politics*, 12:1 (1996), 101–9.

Molchanov, M. A., 'Russian neo-communism: autocracy, orthodoxy, nationality', *Harriman Review*, 9:3 (1996), 69–79.

Moser, R. G., 'The electoral effects of presidentialism in post-Soviet Russia', *Journal of Communist Studies and Transition Politics*, 14:1&2 (1998), 54–65.

Moser, R. G., 'The impact of parliamentary electoral systems in Russia', *Post-Soviet Affairs*, 13:3 (1997), 284–302.

Myagkov, M., Ordeshook, P. and Sobyanin, A., 'The Russian electorate, 1991–1996', *Post-Soviet Affairs*, 13:2 (1997), 134–66.

Na levom fronte bez peremen (Moscow, Tsentr politicheskykh tekhnologii, 1998).

Nagle, J. D. and Mahr, A., *Democracy and Democratization* (London, Sage, 1999).

Novyi etap v istorii KPRF (Moscow, Tsentr politicheskykh tekhnologii, 2000).

O' Donnell, G. and Schmitter, P. C., *Transitions from Authoritarian Rule: Tentative Conclusions about Uncertain Democracies* (London, Johns Hopkins University Press, 1986).

O'Gorman, F., *British Conservatism: Conservative Thought from Burke to Thatcher* (London, Longman, 1986).

Oates, S., 'Vying for votes on a crowded campaign trail', *Transition* (23 February 1996), 26–9.

Oates, S., 'Party platforms: towards a definition of the Russian political spectrum', *Journal of Communist Studies and Transition Politics*, 14:1&2 (1998), 76–97.

Ocherednye zadachi KPRF (Moscow, 2000)

Offe, C., 'Capitalism by democratic design? Democratic theory and the triple transition in East Central Europe', *Social Research*, 58:4 (1991), 865–92.

Oleshchuk, V., Pavlenko, V, *Politicheskaya Rossiya: partii, bloki, lidery. God 1997* (Moscow, 'Ves Mir', 1997).

Olsen, J., 'Germany's PDS and varieties of "Post-Communist" socialism', *Problems of Post-Communism*, 45:6 (1998), 42–52.

Oppozitsiya ego velichestvu: IV sezd KPRF (Moscow, Tsentr politicheskykh tekhnologii, 1997).

Orenstein, M., 'A genealogy of communist successor parties in East-Central Europe and the determinants of their success', *East European Politics and Societies*, 12:3 (1998), 472–99.

Orttung, R. W., 'The Russian right and the dilemmas of party organisation', *Soviet Studies*, 44:3 (1992), 445–78.

Orttung, R. W., 'Duma elections bolster leftist opposition', *Transition* (23 February 1996), 6–11.

Orttung, R. W., 'Duma votes reflect north-south divide', *Transition* (23 February 1996), 12–14.

Osadchii, I., 'Vybory v Rossii: vozmozhnosti i perspektivy levykh sil', *Dialog*, 9 (1995), 38–51.

Osadchii, I., 'Pravda o nepravde', *Dialog*, 3 (1996), 63–9.

Osadchii,I., 'Gody borba i trevoga', *Dialog*, 12 (1996), 50–9.

Otto, R. C., 'Gennadii Zyuganov: the reluctant candidate', *Problems of Post-Communism*, 46:5 (1999) 37–47.

Padgett, S. and Paterson, W. E., *A History of Social Democracy in Postwar Europe* (London, Longman, 1991).

Panebianco, A., *Political Parties: Organisation and Power* (Cambridge, Cambridge University Press, 1988).

Parrott, B., 'Perspectives on postcommunist democratization', in K. Dawisha and B. Parrott (eds), *Democratic Changes and Authoritarian Reactions in Russia, Ukraine, Belarus and Moldova* (Cambridge, Cambridge University Press, 1997).

Peshkov, V. (ed.), *Kommunisty: pravo na vlast* (Moscow, Inform-znanie, 1998).

Petrov, N., 'The year 2000 presidential elections: the end of public politics', *Carnegie Briefing 3* (2000).

Petrov, N. 'Broken pendulum, recentralization under Putin', *PONARS Memo*, 159 (2000).

Podberezkin, A. (gen. ed.), *Chto takoe "Dukhovnoe nasledie", i pochemu ono podderzhivaet na prezidenskikh vyborakh G. A. Zyuganova* (Moscow, Obozrevatel, 1996).

Podberezkin, A., 'Na puti k natsionalnoi idee' *Dialog*, 1 (1995), 63–7.

Podberezkin, A., *Russkii put* (Moscow, RAU-Universitet, 1999).

Polan, A., *Lenin and the End of Politics* (London, Methuen, 1984).

Programma Kommunisticheskoi partii Rossiiskoi Federatsii, prinyata III sezdom KPRF, 22 yanvarya 1995 goda (Moscow, Informpechat, 1995).

Razumov, E., *Krushenie i nadezhdy: politicheskie zametki* (Moscow, Politekh-4, 1996).

Rees, E. A. (ed.), *The Soviet Communist Party in Disarray* (London, Macmillan, 1992).

Remington, T. F., 'Regime transition in communist systems: the Soviet case', in F. Fleron and E. Hoffman (eds), *Post-Communist Studies and Political Science* (Boulder, CO, Westview, 1993).

Remington, T. F., 'Democratization and the new political order in Russia', in K. Dawisha and B. Parrott (eds), *Democratic Changes and Authoritarian Reactions in Russia, Ukraine, Belarus and Moldova* (Cambridge, Cambridge University Press, 1997).

Remington, T. F., 'From soviets to parliamentarism', in S. White, A. Pravda and Z. Gitelman (eds), *Developments in Russian Politics 4* (Basingstoke, Macmillan, 1997).

Remington, T. F., 'Political conflict and institutional design: paths of party development in Russia', *Journal of Communist Studies and Transition Politics*, 14:1&2 (1998), 201–23.

Remington, T. F., *Politics in Russia* (London, Longman, 1999).

Remnick, D., 'Gorbachev's last hurrah', *The New Yorker* (11 March 1996), 68–83.

Remnick, D., 'Hammer, sickle and book', *The New York Review of Books* (23 May 1996), 45–51.

Remnick, D., 'The war for the Kremlin', *The New Yorker* (22 July 1996), 40–57.

'Resolutsiya IV sezda KPRF ob otnoshenii k pravyashchemu v Rossi politicheskomu rezhimu', *IV sezd Kommunisticheskoi partii Rossiiskoi Federatsii 19–20 aprelya 1997 goda (Materialy i dokumenty)* (Moscow, ITRK RSPP, 1997).

Robinson, N., *Ideology and the Collapse of the Soviet System: A Critical History of Soviet Ideological Discourse* (Aldershot, Edward Elgar, 1995).

Robinson, N., 'What was Soviet ideology? A comment on Joseph Schull and an alternative', *Political Studies*, XLIII (1995), 325–32.

Robinson, N., 'Classifying Russia's party system: the problem of "relevance" in a time of uncertainty', *Journal of Communist Studies and Transition Politics*, 14:1&2 (1998), 159–77.

Rogachevskii, A., 'The murder of General Rokhlin', *Europe-Asia Studies*, 52:1 (2000), 95–110.

Rose, R., *Ex-Communists in Post-Communist Societies* (Glasgow, University of Strathclyde Centre for the Study of Public Policy, Studies in Public Policy 253, 1995).

Rose, R. and Tikhomirov, E., 'Russia's forced-choice presidential election', *Post-Soviet Affairs*, 12:4 (1996), 351–79.

Rose, R., Mishler W. and Haerpfner, C., *Democracy and Its Alternatives: Understanding Post Communist Societies* (Cambridge, Polity Press, 1991).

Rose, R., Tikhomirov, E. and Mishler, W., 'Understanding multi-party choice: the 1995 Duma election', *Europe-Asia Studies*, 49:5 (1997), 799–823.

Rossiya-95: Nakanune vyborov (Moscow, 'Akademia', 1995).

'RUSO', *Dialog*, 12 (1996), 61–86.

'RUSO-Rekommendatsii konferentsii "Rezultati i uroki vyborov v gosdume. Strategiya i taktika levykh sil v predstoyashchikh prezidentskykh vyborakh"', *Izm*, 2:10 (1996), 42–4.

Rutland, P., 'Russia's broken wheel of ideologies', *Transitions*, 4:1 (1997), 47–55.

Rutland, P., 'Putin's path to power', *Post-Soviet Affairs*, 16:4 (2000), 313–54.

Sakwa, R., *Gorbachev and his Reforms 1985–1990* (Englewood Cliffs, NJ, Philip Allan, 1991).

Sakwa, R., *Russian Politics and Society* (London, Routledge, 1993).

Sakwa, R., 'The Russian elections of December 1993', *Europe-Asia Studies*, 47:2 (1995), 195–227.

Sakwa, R., *Russian Politics and Society*, 2nd edn (London, Routledge, 1996).

Sakwa, R., *The Communist Party of the Russian Federation and the Electoral Process* (Glasgow, University of Strathclyde Centre for the Study of Public Policy, Studies in Public Policy 265, 1996).

Sakwa, R., 'The regime system in Russia', *Contemporary politics*, 3:1 (1997), 7–25.

Sakwa, R., *Soviet Politics in Perspective* (London, Routledge, 1998).

Sakwa, R., 'Left or right? The CPRF and the problem of democratic consolidation in Russia', *Journal of Communist Studies and Transition Politics*, 14:1&2 (1998), 128–58.

Sakwa, R. 'The crisis of the Russian state', paper presented at the CREES annual conference, 18–20 June 1999.

Sakwa, R., 'Russia's permanent (uninterrupted) elections of 1999–2000', *Journal of Communist Studies and Transition Politics*, 16:3 (2000), 85–112.

Sakwa, R., 'The CPRF: the powerlessness of the powerful', in A. Bozóki and J. Ishiyama (eds), *A Decade of Transformation: Communist Successor Parties in Central and Eastern Europe* (Armonk, NY, M. E. Sharpe, forthcoming).

Sandle, M., 'Gorbachev's ideological platform: a case study of ideology in the USSR' (PhD thesis, University of Birmingham, 1993).

Sartori, G., *Political Parties and Party Systems: A Framework for Analysis* (Cambridge, Cambridge University Press, 1976).

Schmitter, P. with Lynn Karl, T., 'The conceptual travels of transitologists and consolidologists: how far East should they attempt to go?', *Slavic Review*, 53:1 (1994), 173–85.

Schull, J., 'What is ideology? Theoretical problems and lessons from Soviet-type societies', *Political Studies*, XL (1992), 728–41.

Scruton, R., *The Meaning of Conservatism* (Basingstoke, Macmillan, 1990).

Sedmoe oktyabrya i izmeneniya v levom lagere (Moscow, Tsentr politicheskykh tekhnologii, 1998)

Seleznev, G., *Vsya vlast zakonu* (Moscow, Gosudarstvennaya Duma, 1997).

Shabanov, A., Sokolov, K. and Sivkov, K., *Dukhovnaya borba* (Moscow, Izdatelstvo Moskovskogo universiteta, 1997).

Shendrik, A., 'Obraz sotsializma v trudakh klassikov Marksizma-Leninizma i ego znachenie dlya vyrabotki strategii levykh partii v sovremennoi Rossii, *Dialog*, 1 (1997), 41–5.

Shenfield, S., 'Making sense of Prokhanov', *Detente*, 9/10 (1987), 28–9.

Shevtsova, L., 'Russia's post-communist politics: revolution or continuity?', in G. W. Lapidus, *The New Russia: Troubled Transformation* (Boulder, CO, Westview, 1995).

Shevtsova, L. (ed.), *Politicheskaya Rossiya* (Moscow, Moscow Carnegie Center, 1998).

Shlapentokh, V., *Soviet Ideologies in the Period of Glasnost: Responses to Brezhnev's Stagnation* (New York and London, Praeger, 1988).

Shore, C., *Italian Communism: The Escape from Leninism* (London, Pluto Press, 1990).

Slater, W., 'Imagining Russia: the ideology of Russia's national patriotic opposition, 1985–1995' (PhD thesis, University of Cambridge, 1998).

Slater, W., 'Russia's imagined history: visions of the Soviet past and the new 'Russian Idea', *Journal of Communist Studies and Transition Politics*, 14:4 (1998), 69–86.

Slavin, B., 'Otkaz ot marksizma pogubit kompartiyu-otkrytoe pismo Zyuganovu G. A.', *Mysl*, 10 (1994).

Slavin, B., *Posle sotsializma . . .* (Moscow, 'Flinta', 1996).

Slavin, B., 'Za kakoi sotsializma my boremsya?', *Dialog*, 1 (1997), 50–2.

Slider, D. 'Regional and local politics', in S. White. A. Pravda and Z. Gitelman (eds), *Developments in Russian Politics 4* (Basingstoke, Macmillan, 1997).

Smolar, A., 'Kwasniewski's legitimacy deficit', *Transition* (22 March 1996), 17–21.

Solnick, S., 'Gubernatorial elections in Russia 1996–7', *Post-Soviet Affairs*, 14:1 (1998), 48–80.

Solovei, V., 'Kommunisticheskaya i natsionalisticheskaya oppozitsiya v kontekste postkommunisticheskoi transformatsii Rossii', in L. Shevtsova (ed.), *Politicheskaya Rossiya* (Moscow, Moscow Carnegie Center, 1998).

Sovremennyi Rossiiskaya idea i gosudarstvo (Moscow, Obozrevatel, 1995).

Stoner-Weiss, K. 'The limited reach of Russia's party system: under-institutionalization in the provinces', *PONARS Memo*, 122 (2000).

Suvanto, P., *Conservatism from the French Revolution to the 1990s* (Basingstoke, Macmillan, 1997).

Szabo, M., 'Nation-state, nationalism and the prospects for democratisation in East-Central Europe', *Communist and Post-Communist Studies*, 27:4 (1994), 377–99.

Teague, E., 'North-south divide: Yeltsin and Russia's provincial leaders', *RFE/RL Research Report* (26 November 1993), 7–22.

Teague, E. and Tolz, V., 'CPSU R.I.P', *Report on the USSR* (22 November 1991), 1–8.

'The Russian left debates its future', *Labour Focus on Eastern Europe*, 50 (1995), 43.

Thompson, W., *The Communist Movement since 1945* (Oxford, Blackwell, 1998).

Thorson, C., 'Has the Communist Party been legally suspended?', *Report on the USSR* (4 October 1991), 4–8.

Thorson, C., 'The fate of the Communist Party in Russia', *RFE/RL Research Report* (18 September 1992), 1–6.

Tiersky, R., *Ordinary Stalinism: Democratic Centralism and the Question of Communist Political Development* (London, Allen and Unwin, 1985).

Tolz, V., 'Russia's parliamentary elections: what happened and why', *RFE/RL Research Report* (14 January 1994), 1–8.

Tolz, V., 'The civic accord: contributing to Russia's stability?', *RFE/RL Research Report* (13 May 1994), 1–5.

Tolz, V. and Busygina, I., 'Regional governors and the Kremlin: the ongoing battle for power', *Communist and Post-Communist Studies*, 30:4 (1997), 401–26.

Townsend, J., *The Politics of Marxism: The Critical Debates* (London, Leicester University Press, 1996).

Trushkov, V., Russkaya ideya v rossiiskom politicheskom prostranstve', *Dialog*, 5 (1997), 12–15.

Urban, J. B., 'The communist parties of Russia and Ukraine on the eve of the 1999 elections: similarities, contrasts, and interactions', *Demokratizatsiya*, 7:1 (1999), 111–34.

Urban, J. B. and Solovei, V., *Russia's Communists at the Crossroads* (Boulder, CO, Westview, 1997).

Urban, J. B. and Solovei, V., 'Kommunisticheskoe dvizhenie v postsovetskoi Rossii', *Svobodnaya mysl*, 3 (1997), 14–28.

Urban, M., *The Rebirth of Politics in Russia* (Cambridge, Cambridge University Press, 1997).

Urban, M. and Gelman, V., 'The development of political parties in Russia', in K. Dawisha and B. Parrott (eds), *Democratic Changes and Authoritarian Reactions in Russia, Ukraine, Belarus and Moldova* (Cambridge, Cambridge University Press, 1997).

Verkhovskii, A. (ed.), *Levye v Rossii: ot umerennykh do ekstremistov* (Moscow, Panorama, 1997).

Von Beyme, K., *Political Parties in Western Democracies* (Aldershot, Gower, 1985).

Vujacic V., 'Gennadiy Zyuganov and the "third road"', *Post-Soviet Affairs*, 12:2 (1996), 118–54.

Walicki, A., *A History of Russian Thought: From the Enlightenment to Marxism* (Oxford, Clarendon Press, 1980).

Walker, R., 'Marxism-Leninism as discourse: the politics of the empty signifier and the double bind', *British Journal of Political Science*, 19 (1989) 161–89.

Waller, M., *Democratic Centralism* (Manchester, Manchester University Press, 1981).

Waller, M., 'Adaptation of the former communist parties of East-Central Europe: a case of social-democratization?', *Party Politics*, 1:4 (1995), 473–90.

Welsh, H. A., 'Political transition processes in Central and Eastern Europe', *Comparative Politics*, 26:4 (1994), 379–94.

White, S., 'Background to the XXVIII Congress', in E. A. Rees (ed.), *The Soviet Communist Party in Disarray* (London, Macmillan, 1992).

White, S., 'Rethinking the transition: 1991 and beyond', in M. Cox (ed.), *Rethinking the Soviet Collapse* (London, Pinter, 1998).

White, S., *Russia's New Politics* (Cambridge, Cambridge University Press, 2000).

White, S. and Kryshtanovskaya, O., 'From Soviet nomenklatura to Russian elite', *Europe-Asia Studies*, 48:5 (1996), 711–34.

White, S. and McAllister, I., 'The CPSU and its members: between communism and postcommunism', *British Journal of Political Science*, 26:1 (1996), 105–22.

White, S., Pravda, A. and Gitelman, Z. (eds), *Developments in Russian Politics 4* (Basingstoke, Macmillan, 1997).

White, S., Rose, R. and McAllister, I., *How Russia Votes* (Chatham, NJ, Chatham House, 1997).

White, S., Wyman, M. and Oates, S., 'Parties and voters in the 1995 Russian Duma election', *Europe-Asia Studies*, 49:5 (1997), 767–98.

Whitefield, S. and Evans, G., 'Support for democracy and political opposition in Russia, 1993–1995', *Post-Soviet Affairs*, 12:3 (1996), 218–42.

Wightman, G. (ed.), *Party Formation in East-Central Europe: Post-Communist Politics in Czechoslovakia, Hungary, Poland and Bulgaria* (Aldershot, Edward Elgar, 1995).

Williams, R., 'Towards many socialisms', *Socialist Review*, 16:1 (1986), 62.

Wilson, A., 'The Ukrainian left: in transition to social democracy or still in thrall to the USSR?', *Europe-Asia Studies*, 49:7 (1997), 1293–316.

Wishnevsky, J. and Teague, E., '"Democratic Platform" created in CPSU', *Report on the USSR* (2 February 1990), 7–9.

Wright, A., 'Social democracy and democratic socialism', in R. Eatwell and A. Wright (eds), *Contemporary Political Ideologies* (London, Pinter, 1993).

Bibliography 287

287

Wyman, M., 'Developments in Russian voting behaviour: 1993 and 1995 compared', *Journal of Communist Studies and Transition Politics*, 12:3 (1996), 277–92.

Wyman, M., 'Elections and voting behaviour', in S. White, A. Pravda and Z. Gitelman (eds), *Developments in Russian Politics 4* (Basingstoke, Macmillan, 1997), pp. 104–28.

Wyman, M., 'Political culture and public opinion', in M. Bowker and C. Ross (eds), *Russia after the Cold War* (London, Longman, 2000).

Yanov, A., *Posle Eltsina: 'Veimarskaya' Rossiya* (Moscow, KRUK, 1995).

Yanov, A., *The Puzzles of "Patriotic Communism": Gennadi Zyuganov, the Russian Milosevic* (Boston, MA, University of Boston, ISCIP Publication Series 12, June 1996).

Yeltsin, B., *Midnight Diaries* (London, Weidenfeld and Nicolson, 2000).

Ziblatt, D. F., 'The adaptation of ex-communist parties to post-communist East Central Europe: a comparative study of the East German and Hungarian ex-communist parties', *Communist and Post-Communist Studies*, 31:2 (1998), 119–37.

Zubek, V., 'The reassertion of the left in post-communist Poland', *Europe-Asia Studies*, 46:5 (1994), 801–37.

Zubek, V., 'The phoenix out of the ashes: the rise to power of Poland's post-communist SdRP', *Communist and Post-Communist Studies*, 28:3 (1995), 275–306.

Zyuganov, G., *Drama vlasti* (Moscow, Paleya, 1993).

Zyuganov, G., *Derzhava* (Moscow, Informpechat, 1994).

Zyuganov, G., *Rossiya i sovremennyi mir* (Moscow, Obozrevatel, 1995).

Zyuganov, G., *Veryu v Rossiyu* (Voronezh, 'Voronezh', 1995).

Zyuganov, G., *Za gorizontom* (Orel, Veskie vody, 1995).

Zyuganov, G., *Rossiya-rodina moya: ideologiya gosudarstvennogo patriotizma* (Moscow, Informpechat, 1996).

Zyuganov, G., *Znat i deistvovat: otvety na voprosy* (Moscow, 'Paleya', 1996).

Zyuganov, G., *My Russia: The Political Autobiography of Gennady Zyuganov* (Armonk, NY, M. E. Sharpe, 1997).

Zyuganov, G., *Uroki zhizni* (Moscow, 1997).

Index

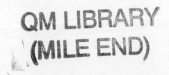